THE OAKWOOD LIBRARY OF RAILWAY HISTORY   OL140

The Isle of Wight Railways
from 1923 onwards

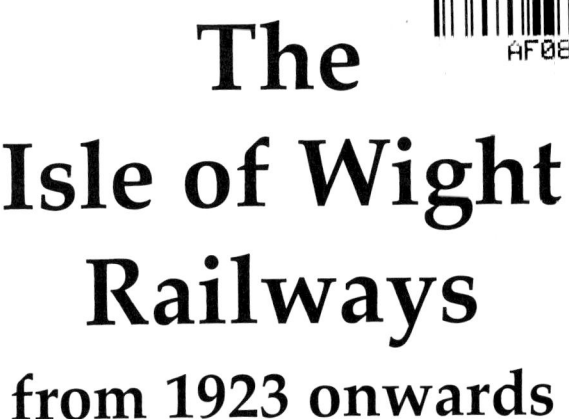

by
R.J. Maycock & R. Silsbury

THE OAKWOOD PRESS

© Oakwood Press & R.J. Maycock & R. Silsbury 2006
Reprinted 2019 with addendum updating the book.

British Library Cataloguing in Publication Data
A Record for this book is available from the British Library

ISBN 978 0 85361 740 2

Typeset by Oakwood Graphics.
Repro by PKmediaworks, Cranborne, Dorset.
Printed by Blissetts, Shield Drive, West Cross Ind Pk, Brentford, TW8 9EX

All rights reserved. No part of this book may be reproduced or transmitted in any form or by any means, electronic or mechanical, including photocopying, recording or by any information storage and retrieval system, without permission from the Publisher in writing.

I have long cherished the hope that this reprieved Isle of Wight line between Ryde and Shanklin might be preserved by some kind of Emmett railway: a haven of steam in a diesel world. I felt that there were sufficient mad railway enthusiasts in this country who, given the right kind of publicity, would flock to see and ride on such a contraption that British Railways Board would gain from increased revenues not only on the island but on their shipping services from Portsmouth as well.

A civil servant in the Ministry of Transport, 25th November, 1965

Published by
The Oakwood Press, 54-58 Mill Square, Catrine, KA5 6RD.
01290 551122   www.stenlake.co.uk

Contents

	Abbreviations	4
	Foreword and Acknowledgements	5
	Introduction	7
Chapter One	The Southern Railway	9
Chapter Two	Ryde to Ventnor and the Bembridge Branch	19
Chapter Three	The Isle of Wight Central's Lines	37
Chapter Four	Newport to Freshwater	65
Chapter Five	Developments at Ryde	73
Chapter Six	Traffic and Timetables 1923 to 1939	89
Chapter Seven	Hopes, War and Recovery	105
Chapter Eight	Omnibuses, Ferries and Aircraft in SR days	118
Chapter Nine	Nationalisation and the First Closures	129
Chapter Ten	Traffic and Timetables after Nationalisation	143
Chapter Eleven	The Second Round of Closures	159
Chapter Twelve	Southern Vectis, Vectrail and Others	171
Chapter Thirteen	Steam Locomotives	177
Chapter Fourteen	Passenger and Goods Rolling Stock	203
Chapter Fifteen	'Modernisation'	219
Chapter Sixteen	The Ryde to Shanklin Line	231
Chapter Seventeen	Rolling Stock after 1966	249
Chapter Eighteen	Railway Preservation in the Isle of Wight	261
Appendix One	Isle of Wight Chief Officers from 1923 to 1966	269
Appendix Two	Relevant Acts of Parliament	269
Appendix Three	Signal Diagrams	271
Appendix Four	Dates of Opening and Closure of Stations	276
Appendix Five	Summary of Steam Locomotives	277
Appendix Six	Summary of Passenger and Goods Stock	279
Appendix Seven	Summary of Stock after 1966	281
Appendix Eight	The SR Floating Crane	284
Appendix Nine	Isle of Wight Vessels Operated by the SR and its successors	286
	Bibliography	287
	Addendum	288
	Index	296

Abbreviations

The following abbreviations have been used in this book:

BHIR	Brading Harbour Improvement & Railway
BR	British Railways (Southern Region)
CNR	Cowes & Newport Railway
FYN	Freshwater, Yarmouth & Newport Railway
GCR	Great Central Railway
IW	Isle of Wight
IWC	Isle of Wight Central Railway
IWNJ	Isle of Wight (Newport Junction) Railway
IWR	Isle of Wight Railway
IWSR	Isle of Wight Steam Railway
LBSCR	London, Brighton & South Coast Railway
LCDR	London, Chatham & Dover Railway
LSWR	London & South Western Railway
LT	London Transport
MR	Midland Railway
NGStL	Newport, Godshill & St Lawrence Railway
REC	Railway Executive Committee
RNR	Ryde & Newport Railway
RPC	Ryde Pier Company
SECR	South Eastern & Chatham Railways
SER	South Eastern Railway
SR	Southern Railway
SVOC	Southern Vectis Omnibus Company
TUCC	Transport Users' Consultative Committee

Although many of the plans and drawings are to scale they are for illustrative purposes and should not be relied upon as accurate in all respects. No attempt has been made to update imperial measurements or pre-decimal currency. Several drawings are reproduced with permission of Railtrack Plc (now Network Rail) and remain their copyright. The illustrations and drawings have been selected for their historical interest and a few may not be to the standard we would wish.

Porter 3765 proudly poses on one of the second series of Lister tractors, T3, at Ryde Pier Head. *R.A. Silsbury Collection*

Foreword and Acknowledgements

This book has been written in such a way that it could be read in conjunction with one or more of our previous publications, all published by The Oakwood Press:

The Isle of Wight Railway
The Isle of Wight Central Railway
The Freshwater, Yarmouth & Newport Railway
The Piers, Tramways and Railways at Ryde

Extensive use has been made of Southern Railway (SR) and British Railways (BR) records, working timetables, press cuttings and official Government documents. As on previous occasions we have been greatly assisted by members of the Isle of Wight's steam railway, both by their writings in magazines or in the use of material for the book. In particular, we must thank Tim Cooper, John Mackett, Alan Blackburn, Mark and Roy Brinton and archivists at Havenstreet, the National Archives, Kew and the National Railway Museum, York.

Dates of Opening and Closure of Railways and Tramways for Passenger Traffic in the Isle of Wight

Railway/Tramway	Owning Company	Distance miles	Date opened	Date closed
Cowes to Newport	CNR	4 ¼	16th June, 1862	21st February, 1966
Ryde St Johns Road to Shanklin	IWR	7 ¼	23rd August, 1864	
Ryde Pier Gates to Pier Head *	RPC	½	29th August, 1864	27th January, 1969
Shanklin to Ventnor	IWR	4	10th September, 1866	18th April, 1966
Ryde Pier Gates to the Castle *	RPC	¼	28th January, 1870	5th April, 1880
The Castle to St Johns Road *	RPC	½	7th August, 1871	5th April, 1880
Sandown to Shide	IWNJ	8 ¼	1st February, 1875	6th February, 1956
Shide to Pan Lane (Newport)	IWNJ	½	6th October, 1875	6th February, 1956
Ryde St Johns Road to Newport	RNR	7 ¾	20th December, 1875	21st February, 1966
Pan Lane to Newport	IWNJ	½	1st June, 1879	6th February, 1956
Ryde St Johns Road to Ryde Esplanade	LSWR & LBSCR	¾	5th April, 1880	
Ryde Esplanade to Ryde Pier Head	LSWR & LBSCR	½	12th July, 1880	
Brading to Bembridge	BHIR	2 ¾	27th May, 1882	21st September, 1953
Newport to Freshwater	FYN	12	20th July, 1889	21st September, 1953
Merstone to St Lawrence	NGStL	5 ½	20th July, 1897	15th September, 1952
St Lawrence to Ventnor Town	NGStL	1 ¼	1st June, 1900	15th September, 1952

Ventnor Town was renamed Ventnor West on 1st June, 1923. Ryde Pier Head to Shanklin closed 31st December, 1966 for electrification. Reopened 20th March, 1967.

Total railway mileage			*Total tramway mileage	
IWR	14		Pier tramway	½
IWC	28		Pier Gates to St Johns Road	¾
FYN	12		Total	1 ¼
LSWR/LBSCR Joint	1 ¼			
Total	55 ¼			

The IWSR has reopened for seasonal traffic:

	Distance	Date reopened
Havenstreet to Wootton	1 ½	24th January, 1971
Havenstreet to Smallbrook Junction	3 ¼	20th July, 1991

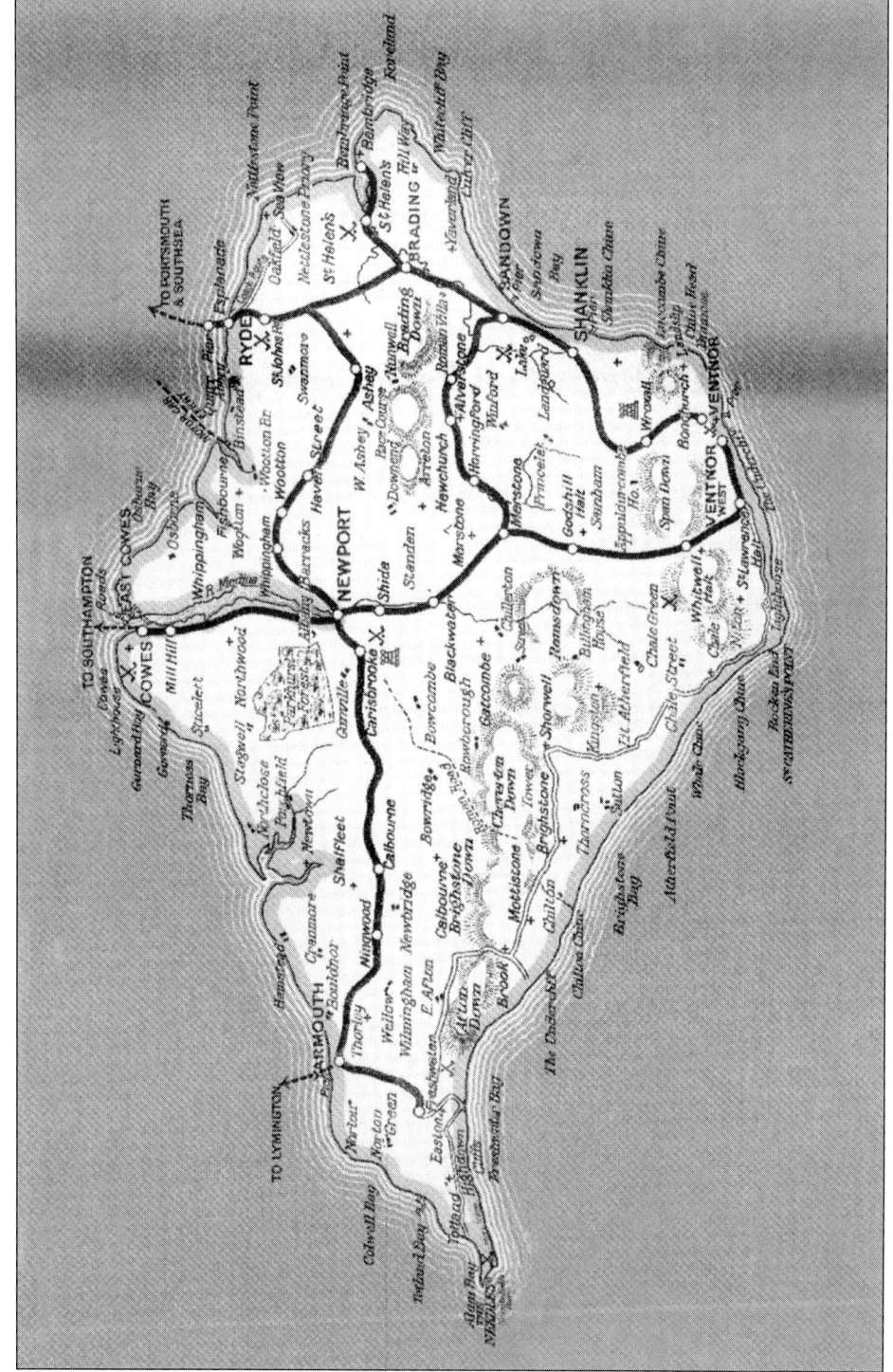

Introduction

This is the fifth and final book in our series of histories of the Isle of Wight railways.

In the first book, *The Isle of Wight Railway*, we saw how attempts to create an Island-wide network of railways fell by the wayside. Instead, an unprepossessing proposal for a railway along the eastern seaboard gained the approval of Parliament. The resulting company had considerable difficulties in getting its railway opened from Ryde to Ventnor in 1866 and barely avoided bankruptcy in the process. Salvation came in the development of holiday resorts along its line and by the turn of the century it was the most prosperous of the Island's railways. The Isle of Wight Railway (IWR) bought the branch line to Bembridge, opened in 1882, and the adjoining harbour from the liquidators of the Brading Harbour company in 1898. Passenger traffic to the Island was growing but the IWR lacked the capital to invest in its future and some of its assets were distinctly old fashioned by 1923.

The Isle of Wight Central Railway was an amalgamation of three bankrupt companies, the Cowes & Newport Railway (CNR) opened in 1862, the Ryde & Newport Railway (RNR) in 1875 and the Isle of Wight (Newport Junction) Railway (IWNJR) from Sandown to Newport between 1875 and 1879. Optimism evaporated as quickly as the company's capital and during the 1890s it was engulfed in a catalogue of mishaps and criticism. A new century marked the beginning of a slow recovery but it was not until after a change of management in 1911 that the railway approached the efficiency of the IWR. The Newport, Godshill & St Lawrence Railway (NGStL), opened to Ventnor in 1900 and absorbed by the Isle of Wight Central Railway (IWC) in 1913, was an expensive side show.

The Freshwater, Yarmouth & Newport Railway opened in 1889 was a typical country railway that slipped into bankruptcy when income failed to match the enormous capital outlay. Operated by the Isle of Wight Central Railway, relations between the two companies were never good and in 1913 the Freshwater, Yarmouth & Newport Railway (FYN) took over the running of its railway after purchasing its own locomotives and stock. The railway was owned latterly by financiers who saw the railway as an asset when a Solent tunnel was built.

The Piers, Tramways and Railways at Ryde recounted the complicated interplay between the pioneering Ryde Pier Company (RPC) and others who challenged its monopoly. The pier company opened its pier in 1814, completed a separate pier carrying a horse tramway between the pier gates and pier head in 1864 and extensions across the town to the railway terminus in 1871. The cost of the tramway and its extensions reduced the company's profitability, a situation not helped by the opening of a railway between St Johns Road and Pier Head by the London & South Western (LSWR) and London, Brighton & South Coast (LBSCR) railways in 1880. The pier company received a toll as compensation for the loss of its tramway extensions but retained the pier tramway. The company embarked on an ill-fated encounter with steam power before adopting electric traction. The pier and tramway took on a neglected air during World War I and it was with some relief that the Southern Railway purchased the company in 1924.

This book, *The Isle of Wight Railways from 1923 onwards*, begins with the formation of the Southern Railway and the acquisition of 55¼ miles of railway,

The water crane awaits its removal following severing of the southern junction with the Newport-Sandown line at Sandown in 1957. 'O2' class 0-4-4T No. 17 *Seaview* departs for Shanklin with a Ventnor line train. *A.E. Bennett*

a pier at Ryde and two of the three main ferry routes between the mainland and Island. The company transformed a disparate group of lines into a self-contained integrated network with greatly improved stations, locomotives and rolling stock. Wartime shortages and neglect were only partly overcome before Nationalisation in 1948 and the start of a lengthy period of decline. Most of the Island railway network closed between 1952 and 1966 and the Ryde Pier tramway followed in 1969.

In 1967 the remaining 8½ mile railway from Ryde to Shanklin reopened after electrification operated with second-hand London Transport (LT) tube stock. The line has survived to see its rolling stock renewed in 1989 and the granting of a franchise in 1996. Railway preservation began in a small way in 1966, but has steadily developed to become an operating steam railway from Wootton to Havenstreet and Smallbrook Junction worked by a historic collection of locomotives and carriages.

Unit No. 032 in blue/grey livery heads a down working at Ryde St Johns Road on 15th August, 1987. *R.A. Silsbury*

Chapter One

The Southern Railway

Right from the birth of railways politicians sought ways of controlling their activities. Parliament passed numerous Acts that dictated how companies should be constituted and managed, placed on them obligations as regards safety and regulated charges for the carriage of passengers and goods. In the early years of the 20th century more Acts forced companies to improve working conditions for railway staff. It was no coincidence that the increasing burden of legislation added to operating costs and reduced profitability; the effect on the Isle of Wight Railway was an excellent example of this.

At the beginning of World War I most of Britain's railways came under Government control. Management was delegated to a Railway Executive Committee (REC) of managers from the principal companies but day to day operation remained in the hands of each company. The REC existed primarily to facilitate the movement of troops and war material but it demonstrated that the creation of larger companies could lead to significant economies. That was an opportunity for those who felt that the railways should be run for the benefit of the nation, but they were not in the majority and attempts to nationalise Britain's railways in 1919 were thrown out. An amended Grouping scheme became law on 19th August, 1921.

The 1921 Railways Act laid down a framework for the amalgamation of 120 of Britain's railways into four privately-owned regional companies. The Southern group included the London & South Western, London, Brighton & South Coast and South Eastern & Chatham (SECR) railways (the London, Chatham & Dover Railway (LCDR) and South Eastern Railway (SER) were still separate companies). These constituent companies had to negotiate both a settlement for shareholders and an allocation of seats on the Board of the new company. Old rivalries guaranteed that this would be a difficult process and it was not until December 1922 that shareholders accepted terms for the creation of the Southern Railway Company on 1st January, 1923.

Control of the SR was vested in a Board of 21 Directors elected by shareholders of the constituent companies, eight from the LSWR, five from the LBSCR, five from the SER and three from the LCDR. None were Directors of the Isle of Wight companies apart from Sir Charles Owens, a LSWR Director, who also sat on the Board of the IWR. Sir Hugh Drummond, the LSWR Chairman, was elected Chairman. The headquarters were at Waterloo station, London.

It took six months to create an organizational structure for the SR and during that time continued to operate as three separate railways. On 7th June, 1923 the Board approved appointments to the principal managerial posts including Sir Herbert Walker, the LSWR General Manager, as General Manager of the whole undertaking. His career has been charted elsewhere* but it is pertinent to note that he had an excellent track record and was an inspired choice for one of the most difficult jobs in railway management. Routine matters were delegated to

* *Sir Herbert Walker's Southern Railway* by C.F. Clapper, Ian Allan, 1973.

a network of committees chaired by the department heads or their deputies. For the record they included:

- Edwin C. Cox, operating superintendent; operating and stations,
- A. D. Jones, locomotive running superintendent; locomotives and running sheds,
- Alfred W. Szlumper, Chief Engineer; maintenance of bridges, permanent way and stations
- Richard E.L. Maunsell, chief mechanical engineer; locomotive and rolling stock construction and maintenance
- Gilbert S. Szlumper, docks and marine manager; including Southampton docks and the ferries.

Railways had developed within the Isle of Wight in a piecemeal fashion and although some consolidation had taken place it was still served by a complex tangle of companies:

- The Isle of Wight Railway from Ryde St Johns Road to Ventnor and Brading to Bembridge.
- The Isle of Wight Central Railway radiating from Newport to Cowes, Ryde, Sandown and Ventnor Town.
- The Freshwater, Yarmouth & Newport Railway from Newport to Yarmouth and Freshwater.
- The London & South Western and London, Brighton & South Coast railway companies jointly owned the railway between Ryde Pier Head and Ryde St Johns Road over which IWR and IWC trains operated, and the Portsmouth to Ryde ferries. The LSWR also owned the Lymington to Yarmouth ferry service.
- The Ryde Pier Company owned the promenade pier and electric tramway at Ryde.
- Ferry services between Southampton and Cowes were run by the Southampton, Isle of Wight and South of England Royal Mail Steam Packet Company (later known as Red Funnel steamers). The company did not become part of the SR.

This fragmentation greatly frustrated Islanders who wanted an integrated network and the loss of control over their railways seemed a small price to pay. The *Isle of Wight County Press* also looked forward to 'a much-needed boom in the development of the Island as a visitors' and health resort'.

To simplify the process of amalgamation, constituent companies were encouraged to purchase subsidiary undertakings of which the Southern group had 14 including the Isle of Wight companies. Sir Herbert Walker, LSWR General Manager, visited the Island in October 1921 and sent written offers for their purchase to the IWR, IWC and FYN in March 1922. Face to face negotiations resulted in some concessions acceptable to the IWR and IWC and the date of absorption with the LSWR was set for midnight 31st December, 1922, an event overshadowed by the formation of the SR on 1st January, 1923. No agreement could be reached with the FYN so a three man tribunal, who oversaw amalgamations and arbitrated in disputes, imposed a settlement on 11th August and the FYN was taken over by the SR at midnight on Sunday/Monday 26th/27th August. The assets of the RPC were purchased with effect from 1st January, 1924 but that was not a direct consequence of the 1921 Act. Payment was by the issue of shares and debentures paying interest at rates comparable to those that shareholders had become accustomed to receiving. At a stroke the Island railways were freed from servicing their capital, a burden that passed onto the broad shoulders of the SR.

Despite these acquisitions, in financial terms, the Isle of Wight was a small cog in the SR's wheel. This is best demonstrated by comparing income and expenditure for the IWR, IWC and FYN with that for all the Southern's companies in 1922:

	Gross income £	Expenditure £
IWR	74,512	53,995
IWC	82,412	65,550
FYN	14,282	9,810
SR group	25,481,042	20,025,806

For operational purposes the IWR and IWC became part of the former LSWR system, described in early SR correspondence as the South Western Section. Just to confuse matters, the Isle of Wight District included the Isle of Wight Railway and Isle of Wight Central sections. These titles were short lived and within 12 months they were in the Isle of Wight Section of the London (West) Division based at Waterloo.

Management of most Isle of Wight matters was delegated to two men. The first acting district superintendent was George R. Newcombe; based in the IWC offices at Newport, he dealt with operational and commercial matters. Appointed IWC manager following the death of Russell Willmott in 1920, Mr Newcombe was previously Willmott's assistant successively on the Great Central Railway, Stratford-upon-Avon & Midland Junction Railway and the IWC. He soon gained promotion and was replaced at the end of 1923 by Charles N. Anderson, one of a number of junior managers given experience in running the Island railways. Charles A. de Pury took over from Mr Anderson at the end of 1925.

Horace D. Tahourdin, IWR Engineer and Locomotive Superintendent, had a dual role as engineering assistant for the Isle of Wight and acting district locomotive & carriage and wagon superintendent initially based at Newport. Mr Tahourdin's difficulties in serving several masters were mentioned during an inspection of the Island railways in August 1923 when it was decided that he would report,

> ... to Mr Maunsell or Mr Warner in regard matters connected with the maintenance of Locomotives, Carriages or Wagons, to the District Engineer at Brighton on matters connected with the maintenance of Permanent Way, Stations, Buildings, etc. and with Mr A. D. Jones on matters connected with the running of locomotives.

Within a short time Mr Tahourdin's health broke down. John C. Urie, son of the LSWR chief mechanical engineer, took over management of the locomotive sheds and workshops and early in 1926 Mr Tahourdin bowed out.

In December 1922 a 'commission' of LSWR managers visited the Island to look at organisational and staffing matters. The commission identified savings of 58 staff (14 per cent) amounting to £10,755 (17½ per cent) and expected further economies after the absorption of the FYN. Henry Day, IWR Manager and

Station Masters in 1922 and 1935

	1922	1935	Managed by
Ryde Pier Head and Esplanade	G.H. French	H.E. Millichap	
Ryde St Johns Road	C.H. Lee		Ryde Pier Head
Brading	W. Wheway	H.J. Attril	
Sandown	A. Wheway	A. Wheway	
Shanklin	C.H. Colenutt	C.H. Colenutt	
Wroxall			Shanklin
Ventnor	P. Jenkin	P. Hawkins	
St Helens	T.G. Weeks	C.D. Willcocks	
Bembridge	W. Daish		Brading
Ashey	W. Swetmen		Wootton
Haven Street	G.H. Spinks		Wootton
Wootton	F.G. Dew	F.G. Dew	
Whippingham	G.H. Edwards		Wootton
Newport	H. Young	A. Holdaway	
Medina Wharf	J. Ranger (wharfinger)	T.H. May	
Mill Hill	P. Hawkins		Cowes
Cowes	H.L. Hill	H.L. Hill	
Alverstone	W.A. Young		Sandown
Newchurch	W. Whittington		Sandown
Horringford	H.J. Attril		Sandown
Merstone	F.T. Newland		Sandown
Blackwater	W.A. Barnard		Newport
Shide	G.H. Hayward		Newport
Godshill	F. Stay		Ventnor
Whitwell	J.W. Cooper		Ventnor
St Lawrence	P.H. Corrick		Ventnor
Ventnor West	C.H. Dennett		Ventnor
Newport FYN	Mr Bennett		
Carisbrooke	Mr Priestley		Newport
Watchingwell	Mrs Prouten		Newport
Calbourne & Shalfleet	Mr Henley		Newport
Ningwood	E. Rolfe		Yarmouth
Yarmouth	Mr Hodges	A.W. Young	
Freshwater	S. Urry	S. Russell	

In 1922 the station master at Ventnor also had responsibility for Wroxall.

In 1935 the station masters at St Helens and Yarmouth also had responsibility for St Helens Quay and Yarmouth Pier.

Secretary, and William J. Sawkins, IWC Secretary, with their clerical staff remained at work until the end of February 1923 to prepare the accounts for 1922. Mr Day then retired and Mr Sawkins moved to the Accountant's Department in London. The clerical staff suffered the brunt of the redundancies and long service was no guarantee that they would have a job with the new company.* Some senior IWC staff, including the permanent way inspector and traffic inspector, kept their jobs but were given responsibility for both lines on the same rates of pay! More economies followed an amalgamation of the workshops and stores at Ryde and Newport, but they were partly offset by a need for additional footplate crews and guards. The Island companies had persisted in retaining station masters at the smaller stations even though they were paid little more than porters. Senior men were gradually moved to the larger stations and replaced with junior staff (in 1931 the retirement of one station master triggered a chain of transfers that reduced the wages bill by £100 a year). Temporary staff at busier stations were laid off at the end of the summer season and had to fend for themselves in an Island heavily dependent on the tourist for employment. They all had to get used to new rules, timetables, train rosters and operating practices.

During the period of Government control, the trade unions increased their influence by becoming involved in negotiations to standardise wages and conditions. By 1923 Britain had slipped into recession and when a slump in prices was followed by pay cuts the unions called a national railway strike between 20th and 29th January, 1924. Similar pay cuts in other industries led to the General Strike which lasted from 3rd to 12th May, 1926, although railwaymen did not return to work until a day later. The railwaymen gained a concession that pay cuts would be staged but more reductions in 1928 were not restored for 10 years.

Taking an idea that originated on the IWC, the SR Directors contributed to competitions for the best kept stations, lengths of permanent way and for prize-winning vegetables and flowers at the railwaymen's annual show. For the best kept station competition, stations were grouped according to their size and competed annually for one of three specially made teak benches each carrying the SR coat of arms. In 1938-1939 the winners were: group 1 - Newport, group 2 - Shide, group 3 - Blackwater. The last surviving seat is at Havenstreet.

Sir Herbert Walker made frequent visits to parts of the company's system accompanied by some of his department heads and occasionally by Directors. The trips were excellent opportunities to discuss problems and gave an insight into the thinking of management at the time. The first inspection of the Isle of Wight railways under SR auspices took place on 30th, 31st August and 1st September, 1923 when pre-Grouping practices predominated. The Island lines were not seen as great assets but with prudent investment and careful management could be expected to bring a modest return. Crucial decisions were made that set the scene for improvements taking 10 years to complete. The LSWR had a number of branch lines in the West Country that carried a sizeable summer traffic so it was natural that expenditure would be directed at bringing

* To give the IWC as an example, the assistant manager F.B. Willmott, two chief clerks, eight clerks in the Secretary's department were all declared redundant; most of the men had served the IWC for upwards of 30 years.

the Island railways up to the same standard. The difference was in the existence of a stretch of water separating them from the rest of Britain's railway system! There was no overall programme but each department prepared plans to:

- centralise administrative, commercial, legal and estate matters
- strengthen bridges, relay track and modernise signalling
- carry out station improvements to cater for greater numbers of summer passengers or make economies
- transfer standard locomotives and rolling stock that would be cheaper to maintain
- rebuild piers and quays to reduce repair costs

Early in 1923 most office work was transferred to Waterloo and the IWR offices at Sandown closed. Fresh agreements were made on an Island-wide basis for services such as electricity, gas, telephones, bookstalls, refreshments and advertising (a by-product was the removal of many enamel advertisements that cluttered the stations). The Island companies' tickets, parcel labels and other paperwork were replaced by SR designs when stocks ran out.

By March 1924 the majority of the Island companies' Minute books, legal and estates documents had been sorted and dispatched to London but 12 months later the IWR offices at Sandown had 10 tons of other papers lying in cupboards, on the floor and in basements; they ended up in the local authority's 'crusher'. The absence of all the documents conveying land to the Island companies led to much scratching of heads. To save money the CNR had not prepared written agreements in many cases and there were similar gaps in the FYN paperwork. A great deal of time was spent writing to local solicitors in the hope that their document stores would yield copies of missing conveyances and agreements. The Island companies also had many commitments to pay rent for land they could not afford to purchase. Typical was a £40 annual rent charge to the estate of the late Thomas Chatfield-Clarke for land at Wootton that the SR redeemed for £860; a three guinea ground rent for a cottage at Haven Street was purchased for £312. Not all rent charges were redeemed; a section of trackbed, spoil heap and land of over nine acres near Wootton station, generating a charge of £67 a year, was offered for sale at auction for £1,620 on 13th August, 1927 but attracted no offers.

The Chief Engineer's Department had to strengthen bridges and track so that heavier locomotives could operate throughout the Island. On 1st May, 1924 authority was given to spend £6,500, later increased to £10,274, on a six-year programme of bridge works, much of it on the IWC. A meeting at Waterloo on 17th October, 1929 was told that 66 per cent of the programme had been completed, but the rate of reconstruction slowed to three bridges a year as more needed attention than first thought.

Concurrent with the bridge works was a programme of track renewals mainly using LSWR second-hand bullhead rail in 30 ft or 45 ft lengths on cast-iron chairs and wooden sleepers. Materials were shipped from the permanent way depot at Redbridge on the mainland by barge to St Helens Quay. Sidings were gradually relaid in chaired track using an assortment of old LSWR, IWR and IWC material. Dredgings from Bembridge harbour were used as ballast but encouraged too many weeds and by the 1940s stone was being bought from the quarry at Blackwater. The last flat-bottom rails were laid through Mill Hill tunnel in 1925, although the same pattern was on Newport drawbridge when the line closed. It took time to achieve the desired rate of renewing five miles a year as this extract from a 1927 report showed:

Permanent way renewals				Estimated future progress	
Year	miles	chains	yards	Year	miles
1923	2	33	0	1928	7
1924	3	77	9	1929	7
1925	3	46	20	1930 and onwards not less than 5 a year	
1926	1	79	3		
1927	5	40	0		
Total	17	36	10	(plus 7½ miles on which rails only had been renewed)	

The Island companies had been forced by the Board of Trade to provide adequate signalling during the 1890s, so the priorities lay in modernising the existing equipment and making economies where possible. There was an influx of LSWR lower quadrant signal fittings often mounted on existing posts, but more usually with new lattice posts in a variety of lengths. Tall lattice posts, with co-acting sky arms appeared at stations such as Brading and Ryde St Johns Road where bridges obstructed sight of the up starting signals. Concrete was used where a standard 30 ft-high post was required, Haven Street being particularly favoured when its crossing loop was installed in 1926 (see *Chapter Three*). Haven Street was also one of the first stations to have the arms of its distant signals repainted from red to yellow with a black chevron. SR practice had taken over at Newport and Ryde St Johns Road by 1937 when illuminated repeaters for the up starters were provided halfway along the platform. With the exception of Cowes, where the signalling had been renewed in 1918, there was a distinct absence of ground shunting signals, but point indicators of the Stevens flap design were a common sight. At smaller stations, sidings were fitted with ground frames locked by an Annett's key attached to the train staff and at those without signals white marker lights on concrete posts were erected about half a mile each side of the stopping place. The single line staff instruments were left untouched, although the IWR telephones were removed from the same circuit as the staff instruments and second-hand instruments used to convert the single needle instruments to a telephone circuit.

The Island's stations received a fresh coat of paint and some modest tidying up. New running-in boards of a LSWR concrete design with white raised letters on a green background were widely used. Signs varied in length to suit the size of the station name, with those at junctions such as Brading having larger boards that announced passengers could 'change for St Helens and Bembridge'. Elsewhere, small locally-made wooden boards were hung below the signs carrying additional information. The Ventnor stations gave their height above sea level, Yarmouth 'alight here for slipway for boats to Lymington' and Freshwater 'for Alum Bay and Totland Bay'. There was a common LSWR design of station lamp often mounted on old posts, SR designs of seats (and a former SER seat at Ryde St Johns Road), notice boards and other signs. Concrete fence posts, gradient posts, telegraph poles and, after the SR re-measured the

SOUTHERN RAILWAY
L.&S.W.R. LB.&S.C.R. S.E.&C.R.

CARISBROOKE CASTLE
Open to the public every weekday, 9-30 a.m. till sunset. Admission 6d
Book to Newport or Carisbrooke Stations.

Isle of Wight

OSBORNE HOUSE (EAST COWES)
Home of Her Late Majesty Queen Victoria.
Open to the public every Monday, Wednesday and Friday throughout the season. Admission, Children 3d Adults 6d
Book to Cowes or Mill Hill Stations.

CHEAPER TRAVEL
to and in the
ISLE OF WIGHT.

Considerable reduction has been made in 1st & 3rd class fares (ordinary, tourist, week-end & excursions), to the Isle of Wight, from all parts of Great Britain, also in ordinary fares & cheap day trips between all stations on the Island Railways.

WHIPPINGHAM CHURCH
Designed by the late Prince Consort
with its beautiful Memorial Chapel.
Book to Whippingham Station.

lines from Ryde Pier Head, concrete mileposts made an appearance. The larger stations were complemented by large green metal boards over the entrances proclaiming their 'SOUTHERN RAILWAY' ownership.

The economic situation was not conducive to investment and much remained to be done when Alistair MacLeod, the best known of the Island's managers, transferred to the Isle of Wight in 1928 as assistant to the chief mechanical engineer and locomotive running superintendent. In January 1930 he became the first Assistant for the Isle of Wight when also appointed assistant divisional operating superintendent and assistant divisional commercial manager; this coincided with the merging of the SR operating and commercial departments. Mr MacLeod oversaw the completion of several large projects that had been in prospect since 1923.

When J.E. Bell took over as Assistant for the Isle of Wight from Mr MacLeod in early 1934 he inherited a unified railway system so transformed that it was equal to the best of the railways on the mainland. Mr Bell's period of management has been looked on as a golden age for the Isle of Wight railways. However, following the retirement of Sir Herbert Walker in 1937 there were fewer inspections and a more remote senior management began to take root.

In the next chapters we will look further at the SR inheritance from the Isle of Wight companies and changes instigated by the new company.

R.W. Kidner took this excellent view of Ryde works yard on 25th April, 1937. 'O2' class No. 29 *Alverstone* is receiving some work on its rear bogie.

The first locomotive of class 'O2' to reach the Island is seen being lifted ashore at Ryde Pier Head in May 1923, in LSWR livery and numbered 211. Its companion 206 can just be made out still on the deck of the crane bottom right. *R.A. Silsbury Collection*

To accommodate class 'O2' locomotives the turntable at Ventnor was replaced by points. Looking towards the buffer stop the curved wall at the end of the platform indicates where it stood. *R.A. Silsbury Collection*

Chapter Two

Ryde to Ventnor and the Bembridge Branch

From the Isle of Wight Railway Company the SR inherited an 11¼ mile railway from Ryde St Johns Road to Ventnor with intermediate stations at Brading, Sandown, Shanklin and Wroxall; crossing loops existed at every station except Wroxall. Coal and heavy goods were landed at a quay near St Helens, the only intermediate station on a short branch line from Brading to Bembridge. The company's offices were at Sandown but the locomotive running shed and workshops were at Ryde St Johns Road; a locomotive shed at St Helens had closed in 1921.

The IWR had the good fortune to serve the popular holiday resorts of Ryde, Sandown, Shanklin and Ventnor. In the years 1913 to 1923, the number of passengers using the Portsmouth-Ryde ferries grew by roundly 50 per cent and in 1922 the IWR carried over 1,000,000 third class passengers. This came home forcibly to Sir Herbert Walker and his staff during an inspection of the Island railways at the height of the 1923 summer season, when they noted that 'The traffic has quite outgrown the accommodation'.

Ready for the arrival of two LSWR locomotives in May 1923, a cattle creep near Brading was rebuilt and a turntable removed from the far end of the platforms at Ventnor (photographs suggest it was large enough only for the IWR locomotives); it is not known precisely when replacement points were installed because it was not mentioned in early SR documents. The permanent way was already laid in chaired track and it was only necessary to check clearances along the railway. Two aspect colour light signals were installed just inside Ventnor tunnel in place of a awkwardly sited gantry; this probably coincided with repair work in the tunnel. On the trains themselves second class seating was abolished, season ticket holders being given the option of changing to first or third class.

The gradients on the single line beyond Shanklin meant that down trains were taking at least 14 minutes to travel from Shanklin to Ventnor. To improve time keeping Mr Newcombe recommended the provision of a crossing loop at Wroxall. The idea was by no means new as a loop had been envisaged when the line was built in the 1860s and discussed by the IWR Board in 1902. Drawings produced by Mr Newcombe for a loop and second platform were probably dusted-off copies prepared for the IWR as there were changes when work began in May 1924 at a cost of £2,700. Instead of a separate signal box, the SR installed a lever frame in the booking office. By employing porter-signalmen who combined their signalling duties with the issue of tickets, the crossing loop could be used throughout the year instead of solely during the summer months as originally envisaged. The crossing loop came into use on 8th July, 1924 but it was two years before Major Hall carried out an inspection on behalf of the Ministry of Transport:

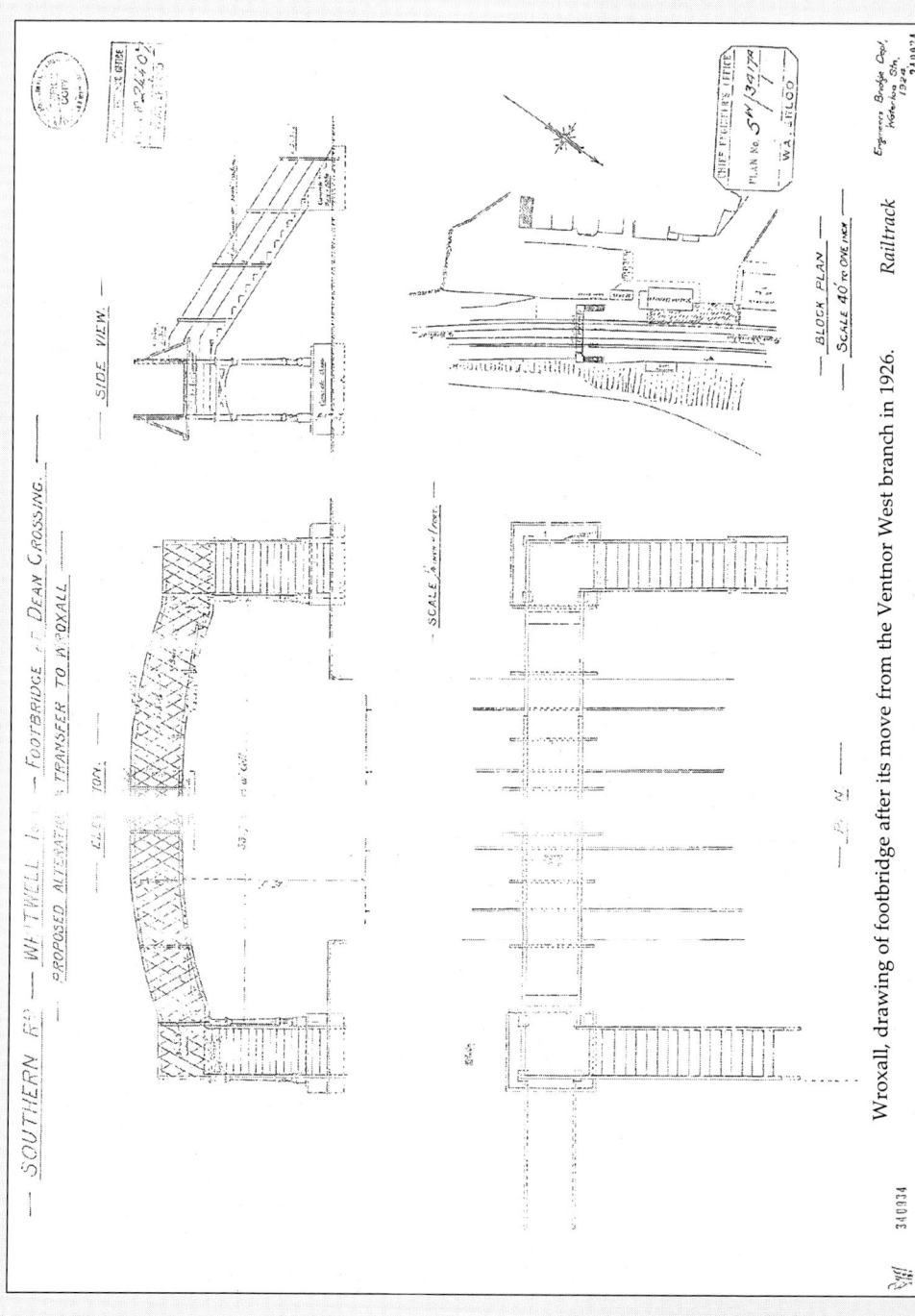

Wroxall, drawing of footbridge after its move from the Ventnor West branch in 1926. Railtrack

A new passing loop and down platform has been constructed at this station, the lever frame and staff instruments being placed in the Booking Office on the up platform. The new down platform, which has a brick walling and gravel surface, is equipped with Name Board and gas lighting and a small waiting shed has been erected.

The station was equipped with lower quadrant, lattice post pattern signals carrying the characteristic LCDR finial, apparently removed during electrification works near Cannon Street. The starting signals were interlocked with the single line instruments. To avoid employing a ticket collector, passengers crossed the line by a foot crossing rather than the road overbridge. The implications for safety were not mentioned by Major Hall, but someone noticed as on 7th August, 1926 a cast-iron footbridge at Dean Crossing on the Ventnor West line was dismantled and moved to Wroxall.

In October 1924 the SR Board authorized alterations at Sandown costing £825. The Board followed this up in January 1925 with a further £625 for Shanklin after the original plan had been rejected because the space in the booking and parcels office was too small; the work was carried out during the next winter. At both stations the buildings were too close to the track, despite the removal of a bay window to the station master's office, so part of the ground floor was demolished and ugly steel beams inserted to support the first floor - they are still there.

When the refreshment room at Ventnor was let to the LSWR contractors Spiers & Pond in March 1923, they offered to operate at Sandown (the well known establishment at Wroxall was part of a hotel and never in railway ownership). Plans were drawn up for converting the IWR offices back to refreshment rooms but Spiers & Pond withdrew their offer and no tenant could be found. Part of the building was then let as an ice cream factory for several years. One resident clearly remembers the free ice cream handed out at the end of the summer season!

At Ventnor £5,400 was spent at the end of 1926 on alterations that, as with those at Sandown and Shanklin, included improved toilets and a larger parcels office. The drawing showed stairs to a subway between the platforms, but it was never built because the island platform was too narrow for regular use.

It seems to have been Mr Tahourdin who suggested that a funicular connecting the station and town might be a good investment, even though the local authority and IWR had both previously rejected the idea on cost grounds. The SR Engineer was given the task of updating plans and estimating the likely cost; powers for the funicular were obtained in SR's 1925 Act and the company purchased several properties along the intended route. By then a motor bus had begun operating between the town and station so the SR Board decided on 24th November, 1927 to abandon the project; a decision to sell the surplus properties was made in May 1930, six months before the Parliamentary powers expired.

Wroxall station figured in an incident on the evening of 2nd August, 1924 when a locomotive failure on a Ventnor train so confused the porter-signalman that he failed to retrieve the train staff from the driver. The Ventnor signalman could not withdraw a train staff for the next up train so the man at Wroxall assumed the instruments had failed and instituted pilot working. The error was discovered after assistance arrived from Ryde but the signalman wrongly

Above: The crossing loop at Wroxall c.1926/7 after the footbridge has been added. Ventnor line trains were formed of IWR, ex-Metropolitan, rigid 8-wheelers with a LSWR 4-wheel guard's van at the Ryde end.
IWSR Collection

Right: The island platform at Ventnor was too narrow to permit either a subway or footbridge to be built and access was provided by a 'ships type' gangway; two widths were available and here the narrow version is in use.
J. Mackett

allowed the train to proceed under the pilotman's ticket and returned the train staff to the instrument; he received a severe reprimand and was taken off signalling duties. On 31st December a down train ploughed into a flock of 400 sheep on an occupation crossing near Apse Manor Farm, north of Wroxall, and on 20th January, 1925 a train passed the Wroxall down home signal at danger before entering the crossing loop at the same time as an up train was arriving in the other platform.

At Shanklin on 5th February, 1925, the porter-signalman carelessly showed a green light towards the driver of the afternoon goods from Ventnor, who then drove his train into the down loop at the same time as a passenger train was arriving from Sandown; fortunately the trains stopped before they met. The signalman was demoted to porter whilst the station master and district inspector were reminded that the down loop was not to be entered from the south by up goods trains, something that had been allowed in IWR days. At Brading on 9th May some carriage underframes were derailed whilst *en route* from St Helens, where they had been stripped of the bodies, to Newport for scrapping. It took all night to clear the line despite the assistance of the Ryde breakdown gang and a steam crane from St Helens. It seems that a porter who was acting as guard failed to notice that a lump of coal had stopped the points closing.

Permission to double the track between Sandown and Shanklin was given by the SR Board on 9th October, 1924 and the compulsory purchase powers were included in the 1925 Act. However, a study of traffic flows prompted a decision that the 'first instalment' of the widening should be between Brading and Sandown. Consequently, the SR 1926 Act authorized:

> A widening (1 mile 5 furlongs 8.5 chains in length) of the Isle of Wight Railway on the north east side thereof commencing in the Urban District of Sandown at the North Eastern end of Sandown station and terminating in the parish of Brading at the South Western end of Brading station.

During the course of this work, which was carried out by the company's staff, the Engineers had to cope with chalk, every hue of clay - red, yellow, brown, blue 'slipper' and black sand, sandstone, shale, ballast and even a vein of lignite in the 1¾ mile length. Small wonder the cutting north of Sandown has caused problems. The second track was ready for use on 23rd June, 1927 having cost £28,000. Lt Col Mount carried out an inspection on behalf of the Ministry of Transport and, on 5th December, 1927, wrote:

> An additional running line has been laid on the west side of the existing single line to form a new up road between these stations, a distance of 1m 5 furs. 7.3 chns.
> The formation has been widened to 30 ft., the deepest cutting (near Sandown) in clay being 34 ft. and the highest bank 15 ft. Maximum gradient is 1 in 62.63 and the sharpest curve has a radius of 30 chns. The central interval between the tracks is 11 ft. 2 ins. except under the existing arched overbridge near Brading where rail level has been lowered 6 ins. and the interval reduced to 10 ft. 8 ins. permitting a clearance of 1 ft. 4½ ins. between guards' lookouts of the widest stock used on the line. The span of the bridge is 24 ft. 8 ins. and the corresponding side clearance 2 ft. 4 ins.

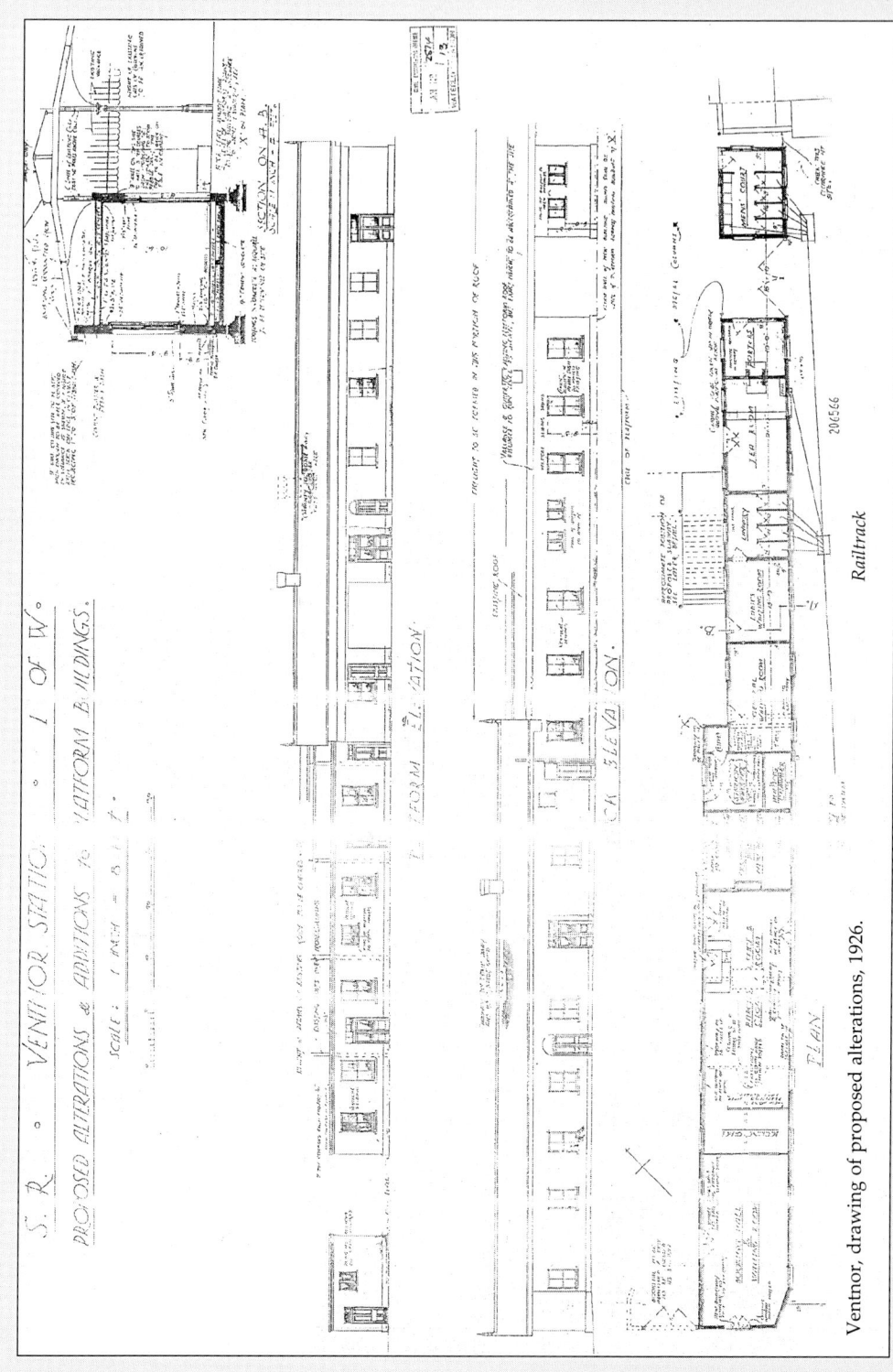

Ventnor, drawing of proposed alterations, 1926. *Railtrack*

The line has been laid with second-hand B.H. [bull head] material, the rails being 85 lb. per yard, 30 ft. long secured in 46 lb. chairs with new oak keys, the chairs being fixed to second-hand sleepers (12 per rail) by wrought iron spikes and oak trenails. The ballast comprised flint, sandstone and pit gravel of which there appeared to be a sufficient quantity. Drainage of the formation also appeared to be satisfactory, attention having been particularly paid to the deep cutting near Sandown where 6 ins. side drains in rubble have been provided. The track was to gauge and generally in good order, the only remark which I have to make being that some respiking and renewal of the second-hand trenails is still required, work in this respect being in hand.

There are six occupation level crossings on the section, one private and one public footpath. In addition to the overbridge already mentioned there is a public foot-overbridge, comprising a lattice girder span of 40 ft. situated in the cutting at Sandown. The existing span was raised to provide a headway of 15 ft. The existing abutments of natural sandstone being utilised.

There are four widened underbridges of the following spans:- 7 ft. 6 ins. steel troughing, cattle creep; 20 ft. 0 ins. segmental reinforced concrete arch over the Sandown River; and plate girders over the Sandown public road, headway 14 ft. 6 ins.

In respect of the last mentioned bridge the inside girder has a span of 34 ft. 8 ins. and the outside girder 50 ft. 6½ ins. the track being carried by longitudinal timbers or cross-girders resting upon the bottom flanges. The abutments and wing walls are of concrete. Under test with an 0-4-4 type engine, the heaviest on the Island, weighing 45 tons, the maximum deflection of the main girders measured respectively ⅛ inch and ½ inch bare.

There is also a widened culvert at 0m. 74 chns. having one span of 15 ft. 0 ins. in extension of the existing two spans of 15 ft. 2 ins.

At Brading and Sandown stations the existing single line facing connections have been suitably altered to accommodate double line working, the frames have been relocked and the electric staff instruments replaced by three-position block instruments. The necessary alterations to the running signals have been effected, new shunt signals have been added and the distant signals provided with yellow arms and lights.

At Brading a down advanced starter has been added some 550 yards from the box, and a track circuit has been installed in rear of it which when occupied locks the down starter. At Sandown an up advanced signal has also been provided.

Preparations were made for an extension of double track to Shanklin but the SR Board evidently decided that the costs would not be worthwhile; the Parliamentary powers expired on 1st October, 1930. The Brading-Sandown section figured in two mishaps, one just before and one after the doubling of the line. On 28th February, 1927 services were suspended for the day after part of an embankment gave way, passengers being conveyed by 'motor cars'. On 31st October locomotive No. 27 passed the Brading down advanced starter signal at danger and proceeded to Sandown; there, the home signal had been left at clear so it ran into the station about 100 yards behind the preceding down train. The driver was suspended and the Sandown signalman was told to reset his signals somewhat quicker in future!

After 10 years of SR management and almost continuously growing passenger numbers, additional accommodation was needed at Sandown, Shanklin and Ventnor. In 1933 the sidings at Ventnor were rearranged to accommodate a set of bogie carriages that had recently been introduced on the line. There had been delays in unloading luggage at Ryde at peak times so a campaign was mounted to encourage the sending of passengers luggage in advance (PLA). This was so successful that during the winter of 1934-1935 canopies were erected over the dock road platforms at Sandown and Shanklin to provide more covered space.

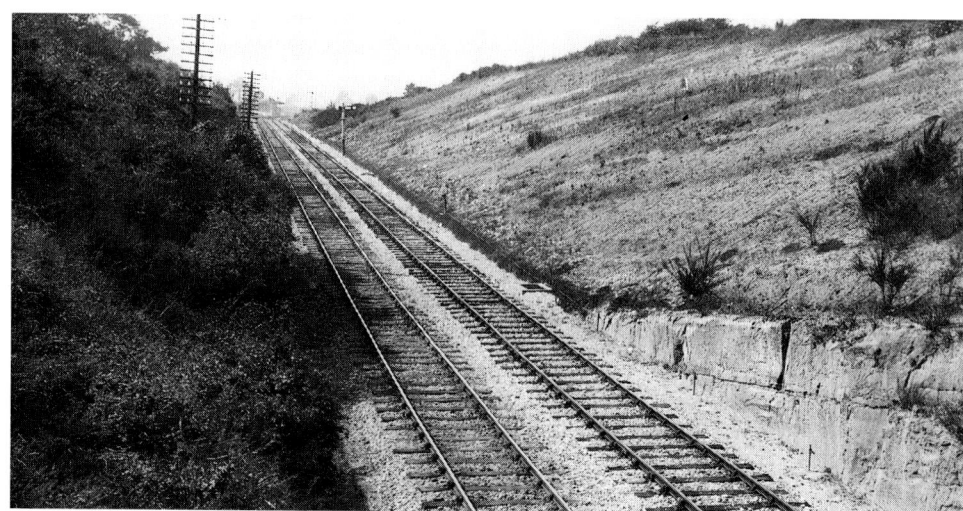

The newly-doubled line between Brading and Sandown viewed from Foxes Bridge with Sandown visible in the distance. Note the angle of the sandstone strata, also the up advanced starting signal. *R.A. Silsbury Collection*

The 1933 rearrangement of sidings at Ventnor saw two double slips replace pairs of back-to-back points, a space-saving but complicated solution to a problem. This classic view from the downs shows the slips as well as the local merchants' coal stacking grounds in the post-war period. The goods shed is disused, the yard crane has gone and the loading gauge stands forlornly over No. 1 siding. *IWSR Collection*

In 1936 plans approved by the 'Modernisation Committee' to spend £2,595 at Sandown were sent back for reconsideration with a hefty list of changes. Work finally began at Sandown in late 1938 when the Ventnor line platforms were raised and lengthened at the south end. The IWR office building was demolished, new toilets built and the booking hall rearranged. Concrete running-in boards carried the station name on enamel panels in the latest style. A request for a station at Lake was again refused, although it is ironic that the suggested site was where BR built a halt in the 1980s.

Recommendations to spend £3,585 at Shanklin were rejected as it was felt that nothing short of a complete reconstruction of the buildings would solve its overcrowding problems. The station was put on a list awaiting rebuilding but was never destined to become one of the company's 'Odeon style' show stations. During work in 1938 a fireplace was removed from the booking office and additional doors installed to the platform, where more circulation space was created by the removal of W.H. Smith's bookstall. A bookstall was built in part of the ladies waiting room, the remainder becoming a general waiting room and a smaller ladies room. With new furniture the station was better able to cope with the summer crowds whilst retaining a degree of comfort for winter travellers.

Ventnor station was repainted and given improved lighting, new furniture and more covered space for luggage. The island platform was only used at certain times of the day but, as a safety measure, a bell code was introduced so that the signalman could tell staff in which platform the next train would arrive. There was also a hand bell, called the five minute bell, that was rung to warn intending passengers of the departure of the train and a sedan type chair for carrying invalids; both probably dated from IWR days.

Passengers luggage in advance traffic, especially to Sandown and Shanklin, was handled in the open until provision of canopies at these two stations. This is Shanklin c.1932.
IWSR Collection/A.B. Macleod

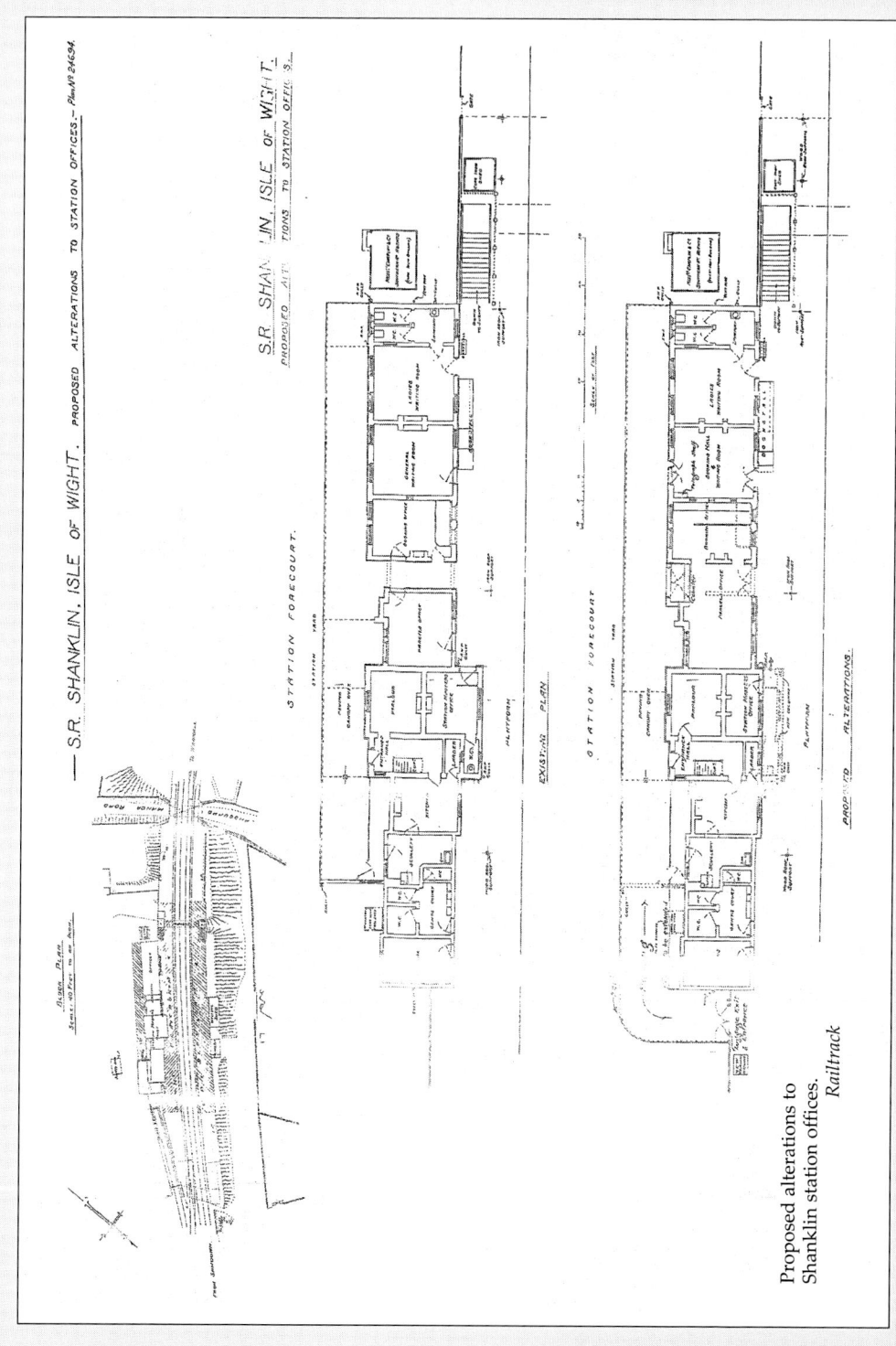

Proposed alterations to Shanklin station offices.
Railtrack

There were a number of accidents during the 1930s. At Wroxall in July 1931 a gauge glass burst on the locomotive of an up train. The train overran onto the single line to Shanklin but after the signalman allowed it to reverse the carriages spread-eagled on the points; fortunately an approaching down train was stopped short of the derailment. On 11th July, 1932 the down goods left Shanklin carrying the wrong train staff; the error was compounded by the Shanklin station master who told the signalman to replace the Shanklin-Wroxall staff in the instruments so that the goods locomotive could return with the Sandown staff rather than taking it by road as was the rule. The driver and Shanklin signalman were suspended and the 'District Superintendent has taken up the matter severely' with the station master who had claimed that trains would have otherwise been delayed and, anyway, everyone knew the circumstances. Since he was an old IWR man, one wonders how often this expedient had been adopted in the past.

Barely a week after the 1934 peak service began, on 21st July a porter was killed at Sandown. Standing in the down platform was a train that terminated at the station, the locomotive had run round but was waiting until the passing of a non-stop train from Shanklin before shunting onto the single line south of the station and drawing into the up platform. The porter was pulling a luggage trolley across the foot crossing north of the platforms when he was struck by the fast train as it passed through the station.

Early on 13th September, 1935 another mishap from IWR days was repeated. A ballast train of 27 wagons and two brake vans halted at the Wroxall down home signal to divide the train so that the locomotive could run round. A porter, who was the acting guard, said he applied the brakes on the rear brake van, signalled the driver to back up to slacken the couplings and then undid the couplings between the 14th and 15th wagon. The rear of the train ran away through Shanklin, Sandown and Brading stations! The Brading signalman allowed the wagons to continue towards Ryde knowing that they would come to a stand on the adverse gradient before reaching Smallbrook. Upon rolling back to Brading they were secured and sent forward with the fish and parcels train to be reunited with the rest of the ballast train at Sandown.

On 3rd July, 1937 the Shanklin signalman was relieved of his duties after he accepted a down train when the previous one was still standing in the station. The same fate awaited the Ventnor signalman on 5th July, when the driver of a down train leaving Ventnor tunnel just managed to stop his train 15 yards short of an up train standing in the same platform to which he had been signalled!

Private sidings existed to the gas works at Shanklin, a quarry at Apse and a bacon factory at Wroxall. There were regular coal deliveries to the siding at Shanklin, but Apse was little used. SR rules warned that special permission had to be obtained as Apse siding was on a 1 in 70 gradient falling towards Shanklin; it could not bear the weight of a locomotive nor be shunted after dark, during fog or falling snow. By 1935 the siding at Wroxall was in a bad state of repair but Flux & Co., the factory's occupant, was unwilling to pay more than a nominal sum so it was removed shortly afterwards. The firm also had a water supply piped from the tunnel at Ventnor, as SR records noted that the rent was increased in 1923 when the pipes were renewed.

The incident at Ventnor on 5th July, 1937, when a down train was signalled into platform 1, already occupied by another passenger train.
J. Mackett Collection

Shanklin gas works lay well below the level of the railway and was served by a trailing siding off the up loop. A simple shelter was provided to protect the labourers manually shovelling coal out of wagons into a chute to the coal pens.
R.A. Silsbury Collection

RYDE TO VENTNOR AND THE BEMBRIDGE BRANCH

Wroxall from the north showing the various sidings. Flux's bacon factory siding is on the left and apparently disused, the public siding is opposite on the up side. The down home signal on its tall post is just visible against the edge of the factory building, between the telegraph poles. This view dates from the early 1930s. *IWSR Collection/A.B. Macleod*

The Brading-Bembridge Branch

Management of the Bembridge branch included the quays at St Helens and the whole of Brading Harbour. St Helens handled a considerable amount of coal, timber, cement and building materials in IWR days; the peak year had been 1913 when up to 20 vessels at a time were berthed at the three quays. Chaplin & Co. operated barges which called at the north and west quays to land goods, parcels and containers, a traffic that the SR tried to encourage by the introduction of its own containers. The south quay handled mainly coal for the local merchants. The SR introduced a monthly cargo service from Southampton carrying railway stores; the service was sub-contracted to James Dredging, Towage and Transport Co., a firm that did much of the local dredging work.

In August 1923 Mr Tahourdin was authorized to rebuild the west quay so that its 10 ton crane could deal with containers and other heavy goods. There was a reluctance to incur further expenditure until plans for Medina Wharf had been settled but in 1926 permission was given to rebuild the north and south quays, measuring approximately 800 ft in total. Taking three years to complete, the work was contracted to A. Jackaman of Slough. Reinforced concrete 16 in. by 18 in. diameter piles were connected by pre-cast reinforced concrete slabs, the whole anchored by old rails to a concrete beam running about 55 ft behind the quay wall; new jarrah timber fenders and elm rubbing pieces completed the contract. The quay surface and track was reinstated by the SR Engineer's staff.

Brading Harbour was an asset that the IWR had assiduously developed. There was a hefty income in rents from occupants of houseboats and businesses bordering the harbour but with it came responsibility for dredging and other maintenance. Work started on rebuilding in concrete the wooden railway and road bridges over the river Yar at St Helens; the first half of the road bridge

The newly-rebuilt North Quay at St Helens, showing the two covered unloading sheds and with a selection of mainly LBSCR covered wagons.
R.A. Silsbury Collection

came into use on 23rd October, 1924 raising the weight limit to five tons and tolls for motor vehicles to 'Small motors 6d, Large motors 1/- and Char-a-bancs 1/6'; this was designed to discourage a competing omnibus service. In 1925 a replacement for a dredger inherited from the IWR was purchased for £1,270, plus £619 for fitting it out and repairing an 1879 Grafton steam crane transferred from the old vessel; *Ballaster* was sold in 1959 to Newport Corporation for dredging the River Medina and has only recently been retired.

One of several derailments on the indifferent track occurred at Brading on 4th November, 1924 in such an awkward spot on a 5½ chain curve that it was late the next day before recovery was completed; a check rail was fitted. On 18th May, 1929, locomotive No. 13 *Ryde* was on Bembridge turntable when, owing to a faulty hand brake, the trailing wheels were derailed; an identical incident occurred on 9th September. The driver drove his locomotive off the turntable on 18th August, 1930 after he misheard a call from his fireman and the same happened on 16th November when the driver of No. 3 *Carisbrooke* heard a passer-by shout 'right' and thought it was his fireman. On 19th July, 1931 the driver drove his locomotive into the stop blocks at Brading for which he received a day's suspension from duty.

Despite the line being worked by 'one engine in steam', each station had a signal box and full complement of signals. In 1929 all the signals were removed apart from only those approaching Brading and the level crossing at Brading Quay. St Helens signal box was replaced by a three-lever ground frame but to save money the box at Bembridge was left in place, worked when required by the train guard. During an inspection in May 1930, permission to rearrange the sidings at St Helens was refused because the work would have cost £5,500; instead one siding was lengthened and a crossover provided when the track on the branch was renewed shortly afterwards.

The stations were little changed from IWR days, apart from a repaint in SR livery; neither St Helens nor Bembridge gained the LSWR pattern running-in boards that appeared elsewhere. Bembridge got a telephone in 1936 only after Bembridge School complained that it needed to contact the station to make travel arrangements for its pupils and staff.

The small size of the turntable at Bembridge (16 ft 6 in.) restricted the types of locomotive that could operate on the branch. The matter was mentioned during the 1923 inspection, but the cost of substituting points, extending the platform and moving the coal siding outweighed any potential gain. Ten years later the Island companies' locomotives had been replaced by LBSCR class 'A1x' 0-6-0Ts, two of which were kept at Ryde solely for the branch, one in service and a second in steam for emergencies. During an inspection in May 1935 it was pointed out that a larger turntable would allow one class 'O2' locomotive to cover for a failure on both the main line and branch. In November the traffic managers authorized the provision of a 25 ft diameter turntable costing £1,003. During its installation in April 1936 class 'A1x' locomotives Nos. 13 *Carisbrooke* and 10 *Cowes* took turns with LCDR set No. 484 to maintain the passenger service, the only known occasion when the branch was push-pull worked. When 'O2' No. 19 *Osborne* was used to test the turntable it had to travel to and from Bembridge coupled to the branch train and locomotive; in May the 'O2s' took over the branch duty.

Amongst the railway assets in Bembridge Harbour was this wharf with its boat sheds and complete with a length of standard gauge track and two hand cranes which could be used to lift boats in and out of the water. One of the cranes is now on display in the IWSR car park at Havenstreet.
IWSR Collection/A.B. Macleod

Bembridge turntable being reconstructed on 11th April, 1936. Prominent is the ex-IWR 10 ton crane. Just visible behind the crane match wagon is the end of LCDR push-pull set 484, in use whilst run-round facilities were unavailable. Note the '1877' date built into the brickwork on the end of the station building.
IWSR Collection

RYDE TO VENTNOR AND THE BEMBRIDGE BRANCH

Goods traffic gradually fell away. In May 1933 Mr H.E. Faithfull, the tenant of Carpenters siding, had his rent reduced because it handled only 250 tons in 1932; relaying the siding was deferred. After Medina Wharf became the main point of entry for coal, the coal screens at St Helens fell into disuse and in 1936 were removed to the mainland. A brief resurgence in traffic at Brading Quay ended after the Brading Cement Company ceased trading and in May 1937 a £16 7s. 4d. bill for stone and lime carried between Brading and St Helens Quay was written off as a bad debt.

The arrangements for handling general goods, parcels, containers, etc. changed after the four railway companies purchased Pickfords in 1933. On 23rd September, 1937, Messrs Crouchers, a subsidiary who operated a freight ferry service from the mainland, began carrying the Chaplin traffic to Thetis Wharf, Cowes for delivery by motor lorry. Thetis Wharf had been enlarged for the purpose and was formally reopened in October by Sir Herbert Walker in one of his last acts as SR General Manager. The SR received £1,100 a year in compensation for the loss of traffic but Pickfords claimed they made no profit from the railway work and ended the payments 10 years later. During an inspection in September 1936 the managers discussed the amount of Isle of Wight traffic that was being carried by road between London and Portsmouth or Southampton, but attempts to get it transferred to rail did nothing to help the Island railways. On the Bembridge branch only a small amount of goods traffic remained. Railway stores were landed at the south quay, there was coal to St Helens gasworks and tar from the mainland was transported by tank wagon to all parts of the Island.

Bembridge Harbour still had to be maintained. In April 1936 the Engineer reported that Fraser & White of Portsmouth had offered to dredge for shingle, they being paid for material that could not be sold. This was not as advantageous to the SR as it appeared because a report in December 1937 disclosed that the SR received 2d. a ton on 677 tons of saleable material, but had to pay 2s. 6d. a ton for the 1,906 tons that were 'unprofitable'. To make matters worse, the SR discovered that a Mr Ball was taking large quantities of shingle from the foreshore in front of his property and that was denuding the foreshore in front of the SR's sea wall. Fraser & White agreed to take over Mr Ball's business and pay an annual rent of £225 for the right to dredge ballast and exploit Duver beach for pleasure purposes, the SR being left with a £6,000 bill for paying off Mr Ball and erecting groynes!

Pan Lane crossing between Newport and Shide was unique in that the signals protecting it were the only double arm types on the Island. The distants were Newport down and Shide up; photograph taken in post-war days when upper quadrant arms had replaced the earlier LSWR lower quadrant types.
J. Mackett

Chapter Three

The Isle of Wight Central's Lines

The Isle of Wight Central Railway operated a network of single track lines radiating from the Island's capital at Newport to Cowes, Ryde, Sandown and Ventnor. The Cowes-Newport line had an intermediate station at Mill Hill and halts at Medina Wharf and Cement Mills. At Medina Wharf there was a wooden jetty used for landing coal and other goods traffic. Cement Mills siding was the destination for private-owner wagons carrying chalk from a quarry at Shide. The line to Ryde had stations at Whippingham, Wootton, Haven Street and Ashey; crossing loops were at Whippingham and Ashey. The railway to Sandown had stations at Shide, Blackwater, Merstone, Horringford, Newchurch and Alverstone; the only crossing loop was at Merstone, the junction of the branch to Ventnor Town with intermediate stations at Godshill, Whitwell (where there was a crossing loop) and St Lawrence. The company's headquarters, locomotive running shed and workshops were at Newport. The IWC lacked the holiday traffic on the IWR but handled a sizeable amount of coal and other goods. The poor roads across the centre of the Island brought some traffic onto the railway.

The bridges and track were regarded with suspicion by the SR and restrictions were imposed on the use of certain locomotives including the Central's 4-4-0T No. 6 which was banned from the IWC altogether! In June 1924 the *Southern Railway Magazine* reported that 19 bridges on the Newport-Sandown line, many of which had been built in timber, were being strengthened using reinforced concrete or steel. Work on the bridges and track was sufficiently complete to permit class 'O2' locomotives to run between Newport and Sandown on 22nd September, 1924 and from Ryde to Newport and Cowes on 12th July, 1925. Twelve months later Cement Mills viaduct had been strengthened but a 10 mph speed restriction was not lifted until 1927.

Probably the oldest signal was on the Newport-Sandown line at Pan Lane level crossing where a single post carried stop arms for both directions. They were replaced by home signals guarding the level crossing on separate posts also carrying the Shide up and the Newport South down distant arms (the only such signals in the Island). The new installation came into use on 19th August, 1924. Pan Lane was one of seven level crossings across public roads on the Newport-Sandown line that had to be staffed whenever trains were running. The large number of level crossings contrasted with the Ryde-Cowes line which had just one manned crossing at Smithards Lane near Mill Hill.

The SR inherited a number of special operating practices from the IWC. The drawbridges at Newport still had to be opened for shipping several times a day and Newport gas works needed supplies of coal unloaded overnight from wagons standing on the running line. The signal boxes on the Ryde-Newport line, which closed overnight, had to be reopened to allow the morning mail train to pass, the points and signals being worked by the train's guard. Goods trains could be propelled from Medina Wharf to Cowes even when Cowes signal box was closed.

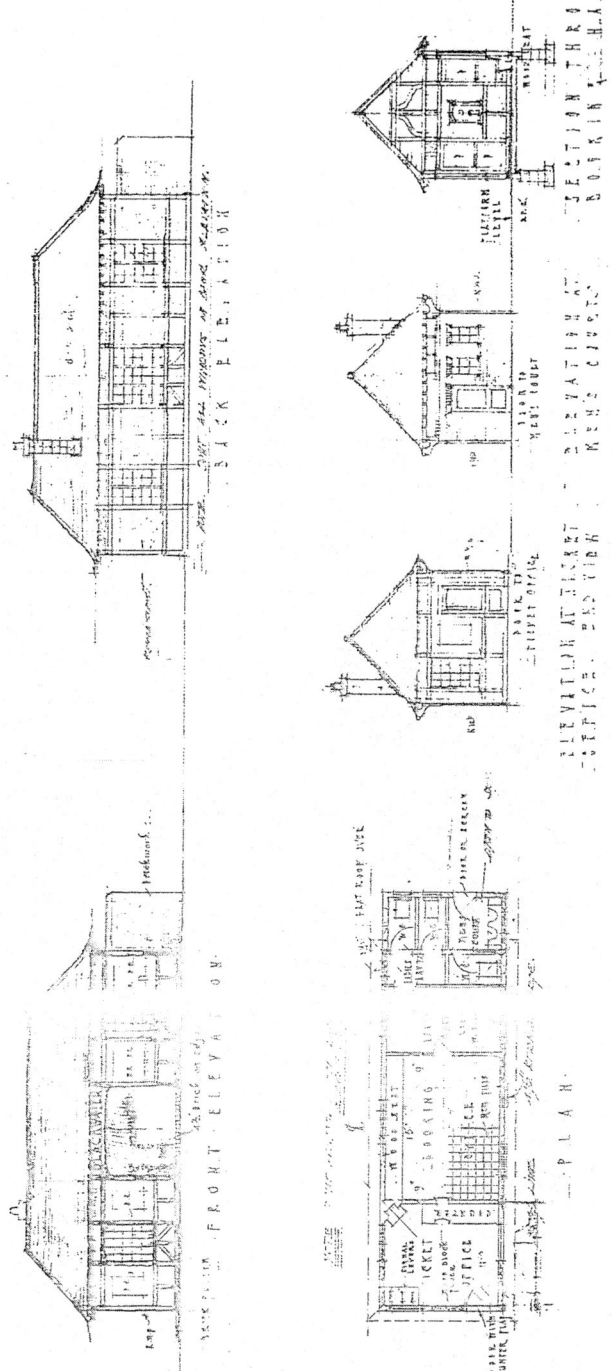

Drawing of proposed station never built at Blackwater.

Railtrack

THE ISLE OF WIGHT CENTRAL'S LINES

The SR did not want to spend much money on the IWC stations except at Newport and Medina Wharf. However, passenger facilities were so poor that it was soon decided to rebuild Blackwater, Newchurch, Haven Street and Alverstone at the rate of one a year. The chief operating superintendent considered whether cattle guards could be provided at Blackwater, the crossing keeper dispensed with and the station downgraded to a halt. This was impracticable but within 12 months Horringford lost its station master and the house was let out. Horringford was typical of the savings introduced at the smaller stations. The resident station master would be withdrawn, the house let out and the station staffed by two porters working opposite shifts. They issued and collected tickets, handled parcels, luggage, etc., opened and closed the crossing gates, kept the station clean and tidy and acted as agents for parcels and goods traffic. In 1925 alone the siding at Horringford dealt with 68 trucks of cattle and 18 other goods wagons; small wonder that that SR decided to buy from Mr Pittis the land on which the siding stood. A proposal to introduce push-pull trains between Newport and Sandown was not pursued so the SR was unable to replace station staff with lower paid crossing keepers. The daily traffic in milk churns to the creamery at Newport grew to such an extent that carriages with large luggage compartments were eventually allocated to the line.

One occupation crossing on the Cowes-Newport line was the scene of several mishaps. On 21st July, 1924 an afternoon Cowes to Ryde passenger train collided at Cement Mills with a lorry loaded with cement; the accident was attributed to a want of care on the part of the lorry driver. A derailment at the same spot on 8th September, 1925 took nearly four hours to put right and a collision on 16th September injured a horse and smashed a cart; the carter, who was deaf, had been following another cart and failed to keep a proper lookout.

To increase capacity on the Ryde-Ventnor line, the Ryde-Newport service was altered in 1925 so that trains crossed at Ashey instead of between Ryde Pier Head and St Johns Road. A few months later the Directors authorized the expenditure of £4,300 on a crossing loop at Haven Street 'to facilitate the working of the summer traffic between Ryde and Newport, and thus improve the train connections between Cowes and Ryde'. Work began in early 1926 on a new island platform a few yards west of the road bridge. A single-storey brick station building was erected on the north side of the line containing a signal box and booking office from which the porter-signalman issued tickets through a hatch to passengers in the adjoining waiting room; the remainder was given over to a ladies room and toilets. The entrance to the waiting room was originally open to the elements but a door and windows were later added along with a porch to the staff doorway at the eastern end. The SR would not pay for the installation of a gas or electricity supply so the station continued to be lit by oil. Major Hall visited the station on behalf of the Ministry of Transport on 5th August, 1926 and wrote:

> At this station a new passing loop on the single line, to take the place of that at Ashey, has been constructed and a new block post and staff station established. At this station there is a single island platform, access to which is provided by means of a sleeper crossing over the up loop line.

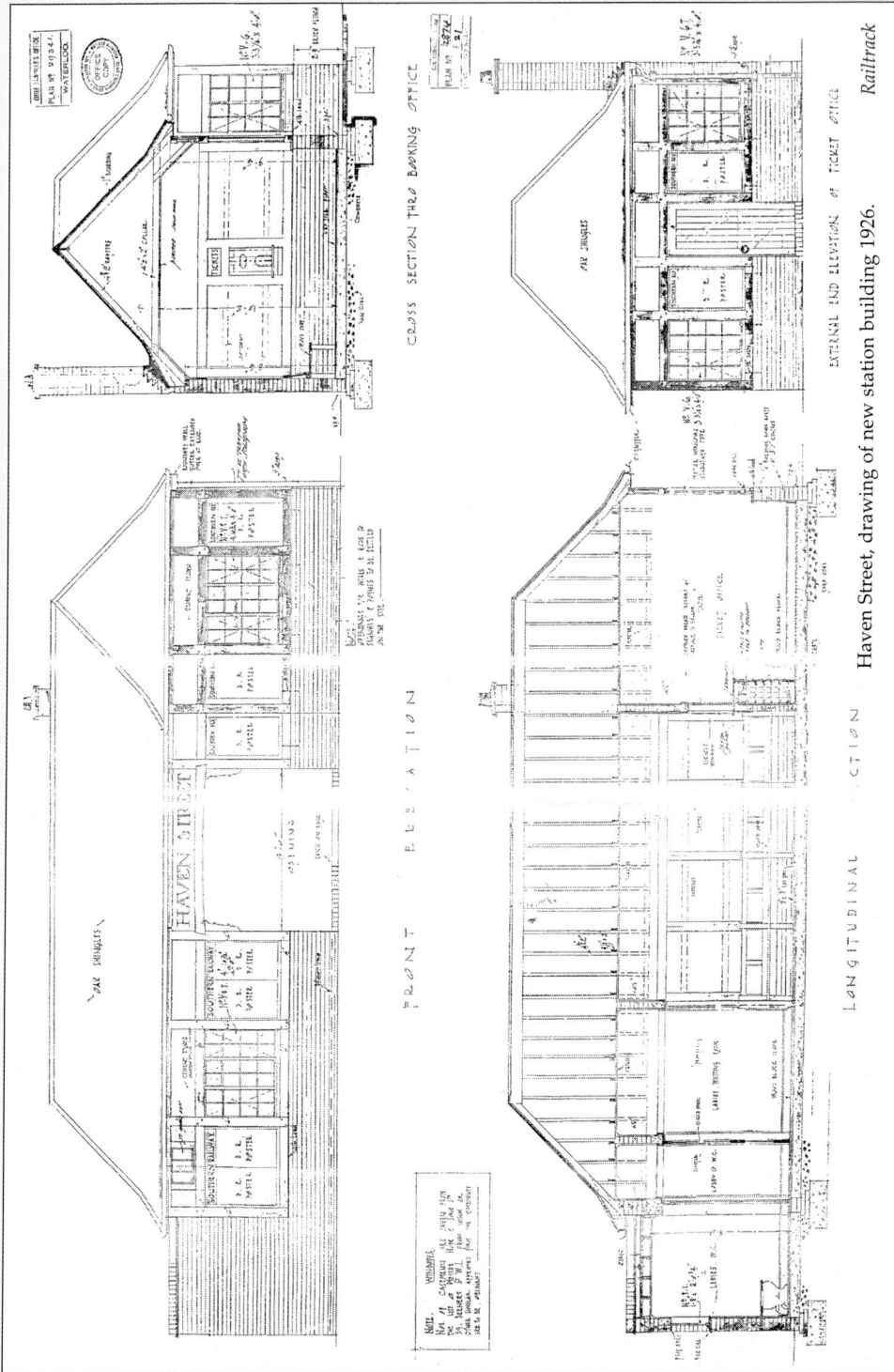

Haven Street, drawing of new station building 1926. *Railtrack*

THE ISLE OF WIGHT CENTRAL'S LINES

The newly-built station buildings at Haven Street; note that the waiting room is open-fronted and that no porch has been provided to protect the signal box door. The original station was off to the right of the picture.
R.A. Silsbury Collection

The wooden buildings provided at Newchurch on the Sandown line in 1934 were little better than those they replaced. The signal box was relocated into the booking office with an oriel window and remained a block post until the line closed. This pre-war view shows that the siding does not look regularly used. The station house was an unlikely casualty of a World War II bombing raid.
IWSR Collection

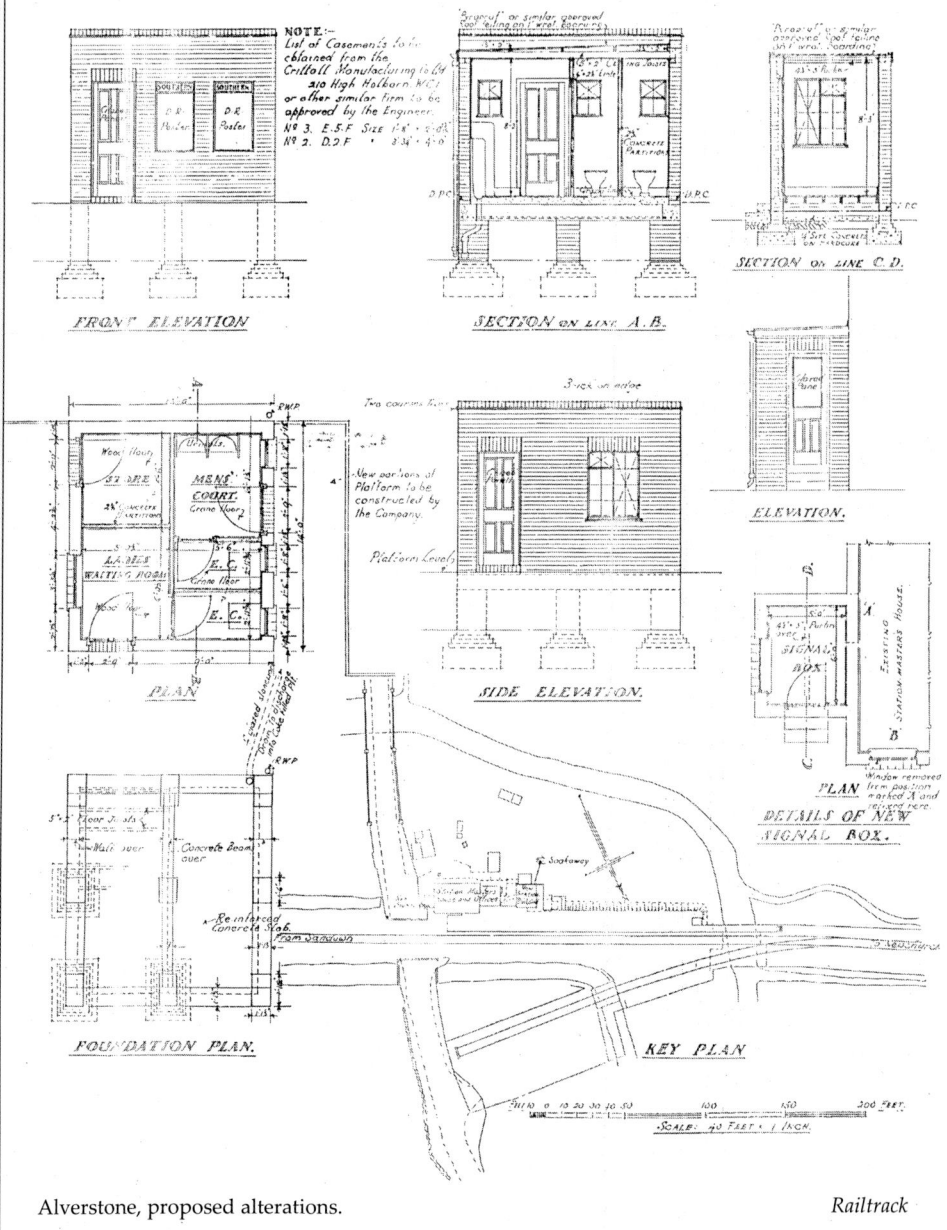

Alverstone, proposed alterations. Railtrack

Left: The aftermath of the collision at Cement Mills crossing on 21st July, 1924. Ex-IWR No. 15 *Ventnor* has acquired a liberal coating of cement dust as well as a garland of tarpaulins whilst the remains of the lorry have been pushed onto the viaduct. Fortunately the locomotive was not derailed, otherwise the outcome could have been much more serious.
R.A. Silsbury Collection

Below: The siding at Horringford. In IWCR days a connection led from the far end into Pittis' gravel pit and all the land on which it stood was owned by Mr Pittis. Although traffic had been quite substantial, this post-war view shows that traffic had dwindled to almost nothing. Note the concrete post with LSWR fittings of the up home signal.
R.A. Silsbury Collection

The new station buildings are in course of erection comprising, Waiting Rooms and Lavatories, with the signal lever frame, which contains 16 levers of which 3 are spare, fixed in the Ticket and Booking Office.
The island platform has concrete walling with a gravel surface and is equipped with Name Board and platform lamps.
Ashey is to be discontinued altogether as a staff station. The down loop will be fitted with trap points at the east end, and the normal lie of the siding points at the west end will be altered away from the main line.

Haven Street crossing loop came into use on 18th July, 1926 when the single line sections became Smallbrook Junction (summer) or Ryde St Johns Road (winter)-Haven Street, Haven Street-Whippingham and Whippingham-Newport. The hourly summer service crossed at Haven Street but Whippingham remained available so that trains could be held back when the Newport drawbridges opened or as a crossing point for an additional through train or goods working. Whippingham station was situated a hefty distance from the village, but a request to rename it to Belmont was refused as the SR already had a station of that name. To permit the running of longer trains the platform at Wootton was extended to approximately 330 ft. At Ashey the loop was taken out of use so that the station could become unstaffed and the house let out. The track was left in place until December 1927 when it was written:

The siding leading from Ashey Station on to the Race Course ... is no longer required, and it is recommended that it be dispensed with as between the Grand Stand and the boundary gate, as well as the siding at the back of the down platform, the up platform road to be made use of for both up and down trains, and the existing down platform road converted to a siding. This will involve the termination of the agreement dated the 28th February, 1920, between the old Isle of Wight Central Railway and the owners of the race course.

Horse racing at Ashey ended in 1930 after a fire burned down the grandstand. By then the track through the station had been relaid and the racecourse siding removed.
The Newport-Sandown line was a continuing source of difficulty for maintenance staff. The line frequently flooded during the winter months despite the cutting of deeper ditches and more ballasting. This followed a derailment on 27th October, 1923 near Blackwater down distant signal owing to the sodden state of a peat embankment. On 24th April, 1924 a locomotive with 14 wagons of coal and a brake van approached Blackwater with an extra working to Ventnor, but passed the signals at danger and smashed through the crossing gates. The station master claimed he did not hear the warning bell that signalled the train's departure from Shide but it was commented that he had not been 'so alert as he should have been'. One of the few fatal accidents took place on 2nd August at Alverstone when an acetylene lamp exploded killing a signal linesman. On the evening of 13th April, 1927 a train to Cowes left Sandown without the train staff; the driver discovered his error after three-quarters of a mile whereupon the Sandown station master, who was travelling in the train, instructed the driver to set back to the home signal where it was met by the signalman with the staff. The signalman said he forgot to issue the train staff because he had up and down trains on the main line whilst communicating with Merstone about a light engine.

Haven Street was destined to be the only one of the small stations to receive a new building. Drawings for a booking office at Blackwater costing £1,765 and toilets for Alverstone at £765 were rejected in September 1927 as the traffic was insufficient to justify the expense. When work was put in hand at the end of the decade Blackwater and Newchurch had to make do with wooden buildings more akin to garden sheds than railway stations; nevertheless they lasted until the line closed in 1956. The station houses were let to railway staff and the signal boxes replaced by lever frames in the booking offices. The increasing number of through trains prompted the preparation of a drawing in 1934 for a footbridge to the island platform at Merstone but it was never built.

Several drawings were prepared of proposed alterations at Newport. Had the SR decided to concentrate locomotive and rolling stock maintenance at Newport there would have been a new carriage workshop south of the IWC locomotive shop and a 210 ft paint and trimming shop alongside the up loop platform; neither was built. During their inspection of the station in 1923 the managers decided to alter the junction with the Freshwater line, enlarge the IWC goods yard and abolish the FYN station and goods yard. Twelve months later it was decided to convert the workshop into a four-road carriage cleaning shed and rearrange sidings at the west end of the building. Another year elapsed before a fresh plan was produced, but then it was decided to alter the station buildings and enlarge the locomotive running shed (after the extensions for the rail motors were demolished). The project then fell foul of a Directors' inspection in 1926 when the £30,000 estimate was considered too high and the luckless Engineer had to delete the running shed extension and rearrangement of sidings on the up side of the station.

South of Newport station, because of concerns about the downhill gradient from Whippingham and the risk of runaway trains, trains halted at the home signals (which were fixed at danger) before being admitted to the station by calling-on arms. In April 1926 the home signals were brought into use and the calling-on arms abolished. A complete renewal of the signalling had to wait until after 20th October, 1926 when the SR Board authorized alterations at the station costing £25,000; work began in the Autumn of 1927 and lasted until the summer of 1930. The loop line in front of the North signal box was upgraded to a third running line to give access to the bay platform and IWC goods yard, which was given more cart road accommodation and a cattle dock with truck washing facilities. The FYN carriage siding behind the signal box was extended to form a run-round loop and access to the Freshwater yard, the latter losing the FYN locomotive, rail car sheds, etc. in exchange for three sidings holding 58 wagons. Freshwater passenger trains could still be propelled in and out of the station provided the speed did not exceed five mph, the train did not exceed nine vehicles and had a brake van and guard at the leading end. Ministry of Transport inspections had become somewhat tardy and it was 1933 before Col A.C. Trench visited Newport.

> The running track of the Freshwater branch and its connections to the Station and the Cowes line have been rearranged and altered in alignment and are now generally in accordance with the plans submitted. The permanent way consists of mainly 87 lb. serviceable material.

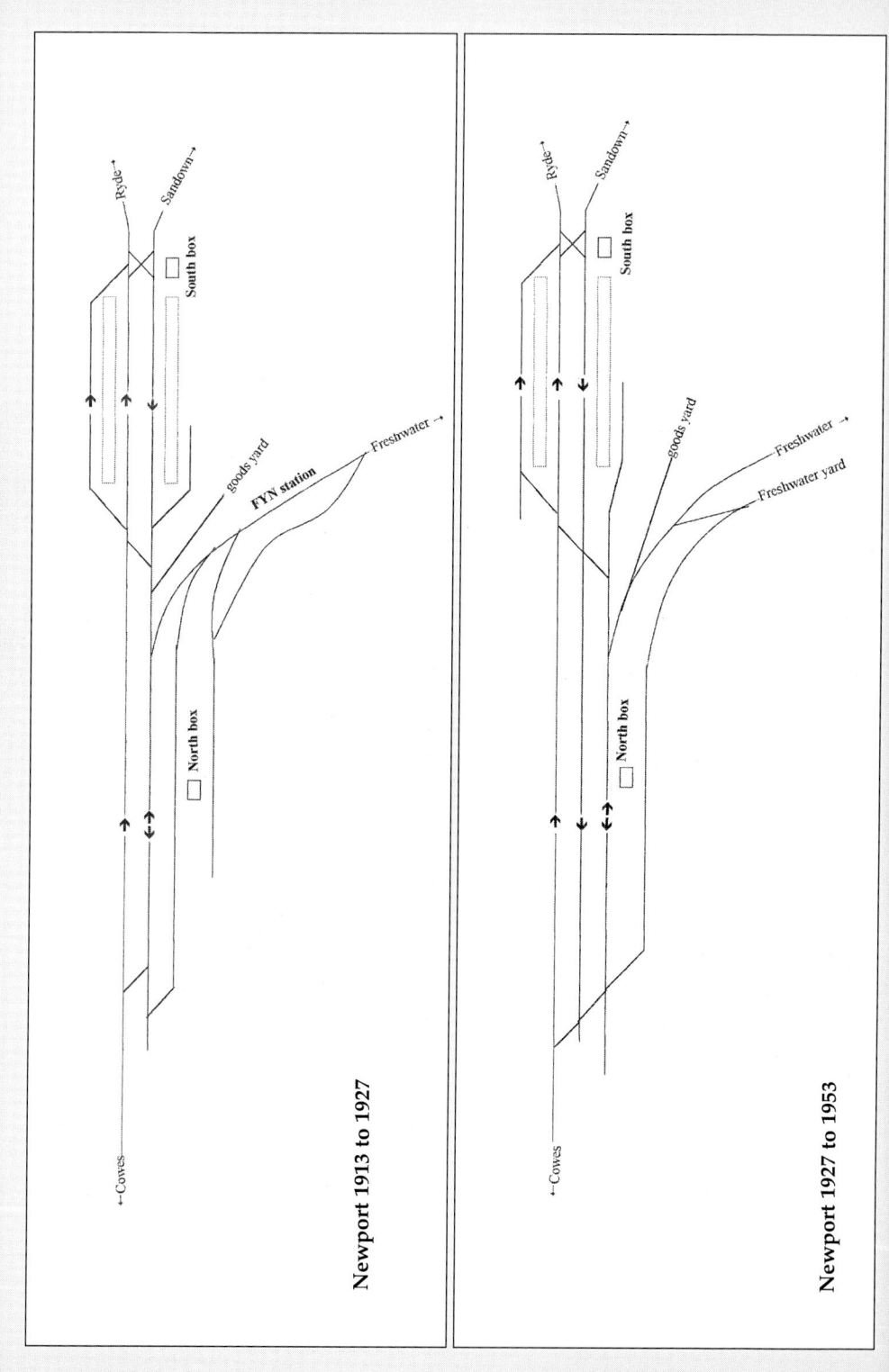

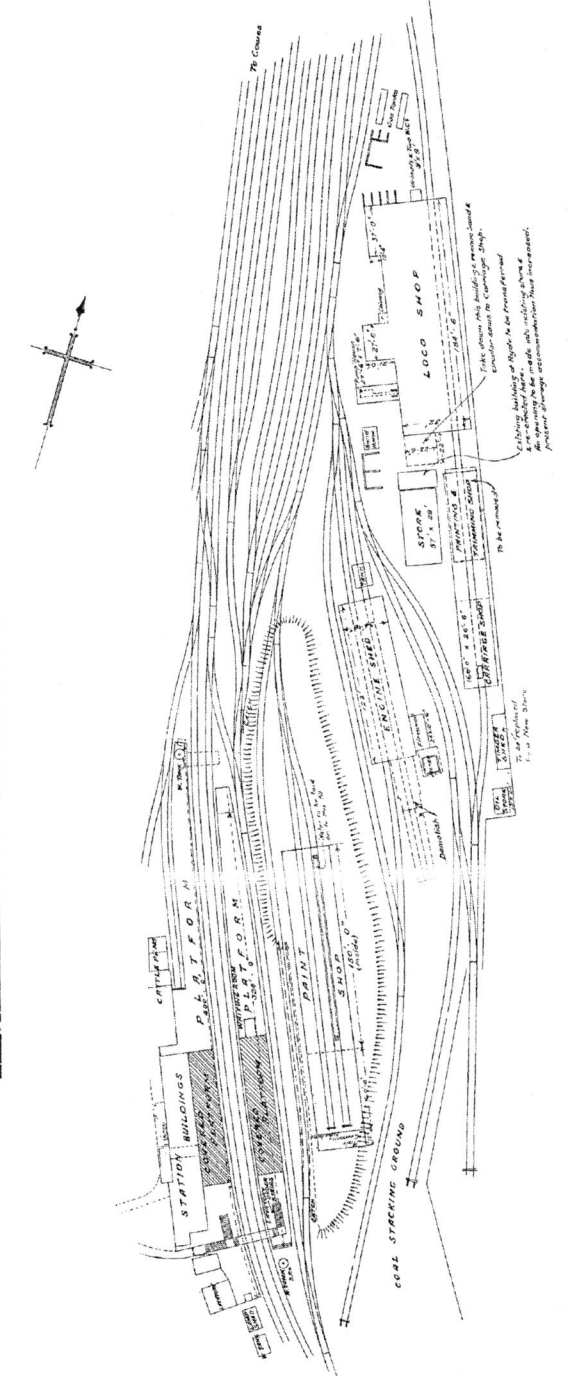

Proposed alterations at Newport (not implemented). *Railtrack*

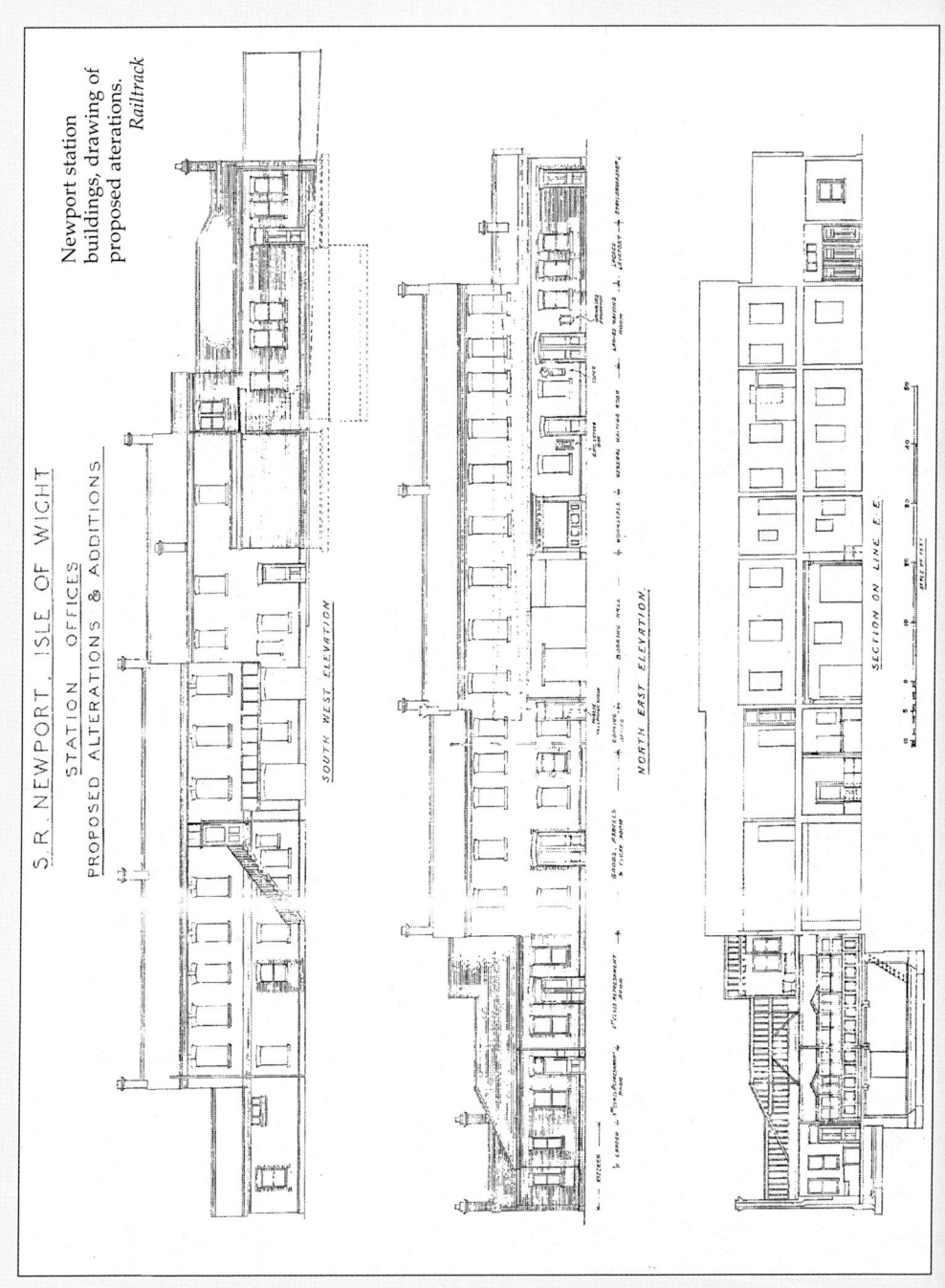

Newport station buildings, drawing of proposed alterations. *Railtrack*

THE ISLE OF WIGHT CENTRAL'S LINES

The new connections between the Freshwater branch and the Cowes line. The arriving Freshwater train, six LCDR 4-wheelers hauled by 'A1X' No. 8 *Freshwater*, is signalled into the 'Dead End' by the ground signal to enable the length of the train to clear the branch points.
R.A. Silsbury Collection

The new gantry next to the North signal box signalled both the Freshwater and main lines. Because of limited space, the post was at one side and heavily guyed for stability.
R.A. Silsbury Collection

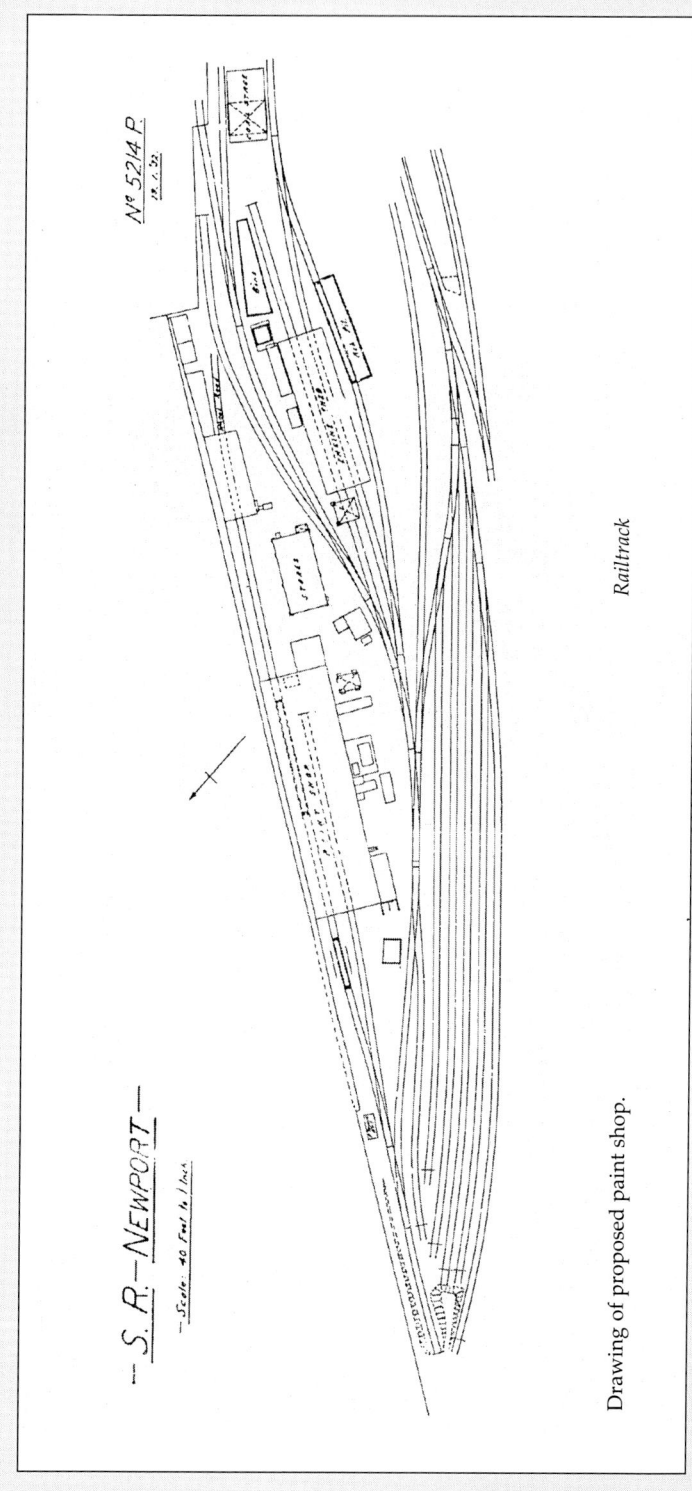

Drawing of proposed paint shop.

THE ISLE OF WIGHT CENTRAL'S LINES

Looking north from the end of the up platform at Newport. New down starting and up home signal gantries and the remodelled entry to the up sidings with an unusual arrangements of catch points are depicted. 'O2' class No. 29 *Alverstone* arrives with a Cowes-Sandown train of LCDR 4-wheelers, whilst another 'O2' stands in the Freshwater bay. Note the amount of mail bags on the platform.
IWSR Collection/S.W. Baker

A general view of Newport from the up sidings, showing the rebuilt down platform, new balloon water tower, down starting gantry and the carriage cleaning siding on the left.
R.A. Silsbury Collection

At the south end of Newport a new up starting gantry, with an assortment of dolls and finials, was unusually placed some distance laterally from the platform roads but afforded good sighting from arriving trains. South signal box is visible on the far left.

IWSR Collection/J.W. Sparrowe

A locomotive coal stacking bank was created by A.B. Macleod utilising old wagon underframes at the south end of the up yards. *IWSR Collection/A.B. Macleod*

THE ISLE OF WIGHT CENTRAL'S LINES

In addition to this the down platform has been extended and the bay road realigned to provide an increased length of platform face.

The usual working of the Freshwater branch trains is that after stopping on the branch line a short distance north of the signal box, the engine runs round its train by way of the shunting neck and then draws the train into the main or bay platform of the station. In the opposite direction the train is frequently propelled up to the signal box, prior to departure in the ordinary way along the Freshwater line.

In the station area, the down and bay platforms were extended and raised to standard height. The ground floor of the station building was virtually rebuilt with a larger parcels office and a single-storey extension at the south end with first and third class refreshment rooms replacing a flight of steps from the footbridge to a separate exit. The disused workshop was converted into a carriage paint shop; it could accommodate five bogie carriages and latterly gave employment to three painters. The locomotive shed was repaired and clad in corrugated asbestos sheeting, there was a new locomotive pit, ash dump and a coal stage made from wagon underframes covered with old sleepers. A locomotive hoist and concrete coal stage were provided at the south end of the yard in 1939.

Medina Wharf figured in the notes of inspections but it was years before there was anything tangible to report. In 1923 it was thought that the wharf might become the main point of entry for goods traffic to the Island. The cost proved prohibitive so in September 1924 it was decided to use the wharf only for 'coal and other rough traffic' with the remainder being landed at St Helens. However, capacity at Medina Wharf was restricted as the three 30 cwt steam travelling cranes could only deal on average with three 3,000 ton colliers a week and the wooden jetty needed repairs costing upwards of £40,000. Instead of merely repairing the jetty, it was proposed to replace it with a concrete wharf along the river bank. This suggestion had originated in a conversation with Mr Gilbert, former Chairman of the IWR and a Director of coal merchants Fraser & White Ltd, who owned the adjoining land. The SR included powers to compulsorily purchase the necessary land in its 1927 Bill, but Newport Corporation objected to the development on the grounds that its quay in Newport would lose business; the Corporation was bought off with an increase in the compensation it had received since 1878 from £40 to £100 a year. In an agreement with Fraser & White dated 7th April, 1927, the coal firm was given use of the wharf but had to use rail transport if only to Newport; the sole road access was a rough track.

On 27th October, 1927 the SR Board authorized the expenditure of £84,000 on Medina Wharf and Charles Brand & Son gained a contract worth £33,104 3s. 9d. for a quay wall fronting the river bank. Construction did not go to plan as in January 1930 it was reported that the wall had begun to move; it cost £15,200 to strengthen but £4,500 was saved by shortening the proposed quay at its north end by 106 ft. According to the *Isle of Wight County Press* the first collier to use the new facilities in April 1931 was *The Marchioness* of Glasgow. Meanwhile, the existing jetty continued to deal with traffic and even the arrival of locomotives and rolling stock by floating crane until it was demolished in February 1932. Since Medina Wharf was purely for goods traffic the Ministry of Transport never carried out a formal inspection of the new facilities.

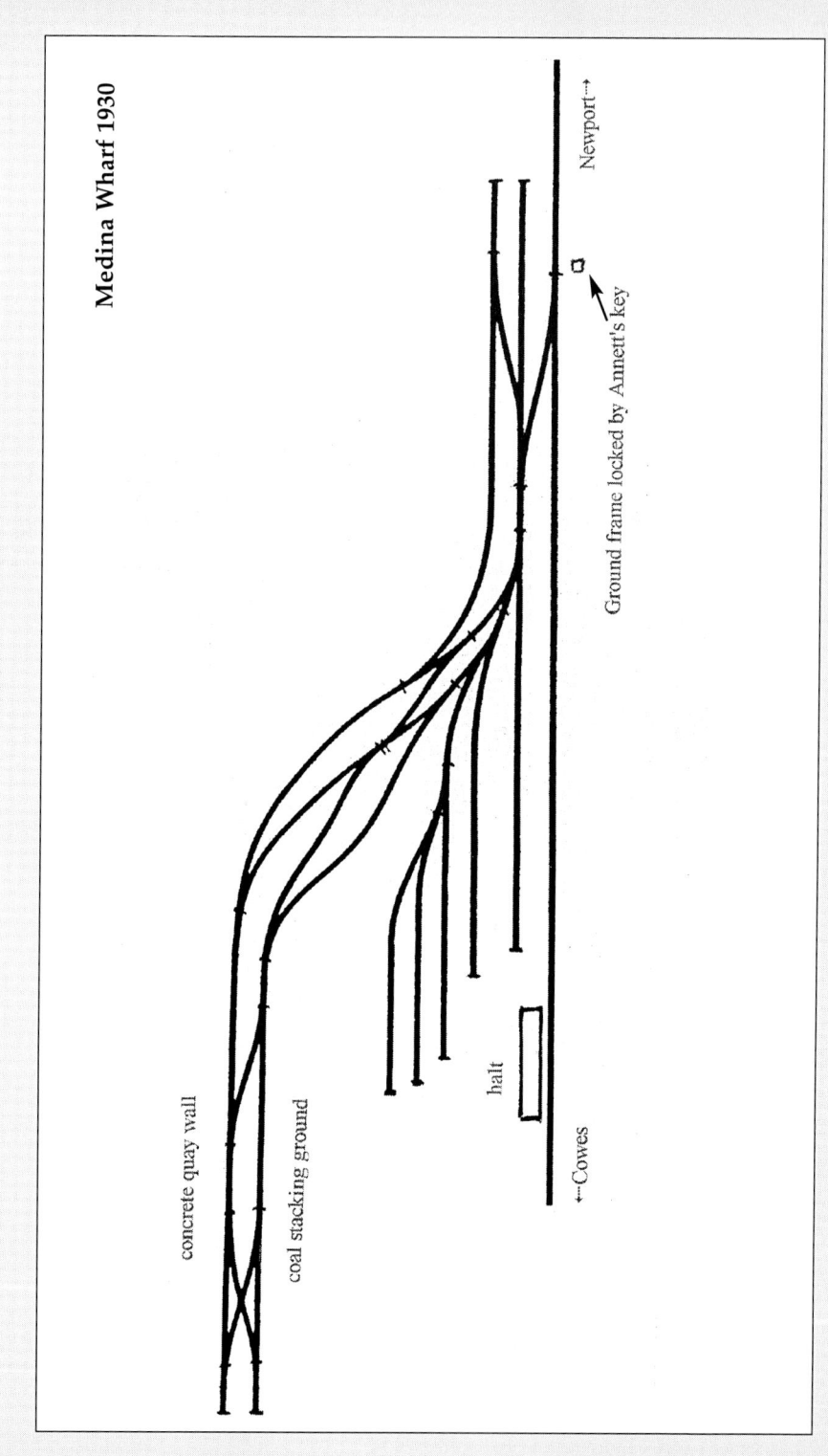

The southern approach to Newport from the Sandown line viaduct showing one of those hidden corners seen only by railway passengers. New home signals and the 'Speed 5 miles per hour' are visible as well as the station in the left distance above Sharp's timber stores and wharf. Note also the buildings and chimneys of the gas works with associated gas holder.
R.A. Silsbury Collection

The new Medina Wharf under construction in 1930 with one of the coal transporters and associated hopper in place. On the ramshackle old wharf three steam cranes and a water tank can be seen. *R.A. Silsbury Collection*

Above: The completed new Medina Wharf c.1933 with the two coal transporters which revolutionised coal handling, although a cloud of dust still pervaded during unloading operations. The coal could either be unloaded into railway wagons utilising the large hoppers, or stacked at the back of the wharf until required.
IWSR Collection/A.B. Macleod

Right: Advert of Fraser & White, coal merchants.

CODES:— 4th EDITION A,B,C, 5 LETTER & BENTLEYS   ESTABLISHED 1846   Phone:— Portsmouth Trunks 3379, Local 2128   Telegrams:— FRASER, PORTSMOUTH

FRASER & WHITE L^{TD} F.I.C.S.

STEAMSHIP, TUG, BARGE & LIGHTER OWNERS

COAL MERCHANTS & FACTORS, SHIPBROKERS,
STEVEDORES, WAREHOUSEMEN & HAULAGE CONTRACTORS

PROMPT & EXPEDITIOUS HANDLING OF CARGOES & CUSTOMS BUSINESS

Agents for the P. & O. AND ALL THE PRINCIPAL STEAMSHIP LINES

This Silo at Portsmouth is constructed of ferro-concrete on the Kahncrete principle and has a capacity of 12,000 tons. The discharging plant was supplied by Messrs Sir William Arrol & Co. Ltd. of Glasgow and is designed to handle over 300 tons per hour. The transporters, as can be seen, are of the travelling type, and two vessels can be dealt with simultaneously.

OFFICES, WHARVES & DEPOTS AT —
PORTSMOUTH, COWES I.W., GOSPORT, FAREHAM, LYMINGTON Etc.

HEAD OFFICE:—
23 East Street, Town Quay, PORTSMOUTH, ENG.
LLOYDS AGENT, PORTSMOUTH (H. D. GILBERT)
COWES I.W. Office–Fountain Yard. Phone:- 177 Cowes, Telegrams:- Fraser, Cowes

BUNKER COAL & FRESH WATER SUPPLIED AT SHORTEST NOTICE

STEAM TUGS ALWAYS AVAILABLE

The wharf was a far cry from the privations of the wooden jetty with a 738 ft concrete quay wall dredged to give a depth of 10 ft at low tide and 22 ft at high tide, a 500 ft-long coal stacking ground, sidings for 110 wagons, mess rooms, lavatories, electricity and water supplies. Stothert & Pitt supplied four electrically powered capstans and two 3½ ton coal transporters costing £5,512 each on their own broad-gauge tracks. The transporters were not without their problems and after one collapsed during a gale on 4th November, 1931 it had to be reconstructed at a cost of £3,307 0s. 4d.; more damage in 1936 created some welcome overtime when day and night working was instituted until repairs were carried out.

Neither Cowes nor Mill Hill stations changed significantly under SR management, the former having been extensively altered by the IWC in 1918. Cowes was the site of a derailment on 7th December, 1931 of a locomotive and passenger luggage van. A permanent way ganger found some rails were ¾ in. wide to gauge and began to adjust the chairs between the arrival of a train at 9.10 and its departure at 9.45 am. Unfortunately he failed to warn the driver or signalman. He then discovered that a sleeper needed renewal and despite having two men to help him three chairs were not in position and three others were unspiked when the train departed; he was suspended from duty for one week.

Of all the private sidings in the Isle of Wight those at Shide and Cement Mills were the most lucrative. The chalk siding at Shide was extended at its south end crossing the existing goods siding on the level; it was ready for use by the end of July 1927. An engineer's wagon derailed on the flat bottom rails on 19th April, 1928 followed by similar incidents on 3rd and 9th October, 1929; soon afterwards the permanent way was relaid. Col Trench inspected the station in 1933 when he wrote:

> The connections to two existing sidings have been altered as indicated on the plans and two signals have been relocated to suit this permanent way alteration.
> The material of the connections is 87 lb. second-hand, and they are equipped with Blacks economical facing point locks and are suitably trapped.
> The line in question is single with electric tablet control. Shide Station signal box contains 9 levers, of which the two distants are out of use, their arms being fixed in the on position, the altered locking is correct.
> The sidings at the Newport end is for supplies of chalk to Cement Works located on the other side of Newport. It is used about four times daily up to about ten trucks at a time. The normal movements are a train of empties from the Newport direction being put into the siding and the full trucks being withdrawn, after which the latter are propelled through Newport Station to the Cement Works. This method of working has been in force for many years without difficulty and in view of local traffic conditions does not appear to be objectionable.

The siding at Cement Mills was not relaid with heavier rails so the chalk trains were left in the hands of the smaller class 'A1x' locomotives. In a fresh contract concluded with the cement company in 1929, the SR was paid a nominal rent of £1 a year and for haulage at the rate of 10d. per ton with a minimum of 8 tons per truck; any chalk supplied to the Engineer was charged at 1s. a ton. The contract with the cement mill called for regular trains from Shide to Cement Mills hauling 6,000 wagon loads carrying 50,000 tons a year. Of the other private sidings, that to Ashey quarry had long since fallen into disuse, the gasworks at Haven Street

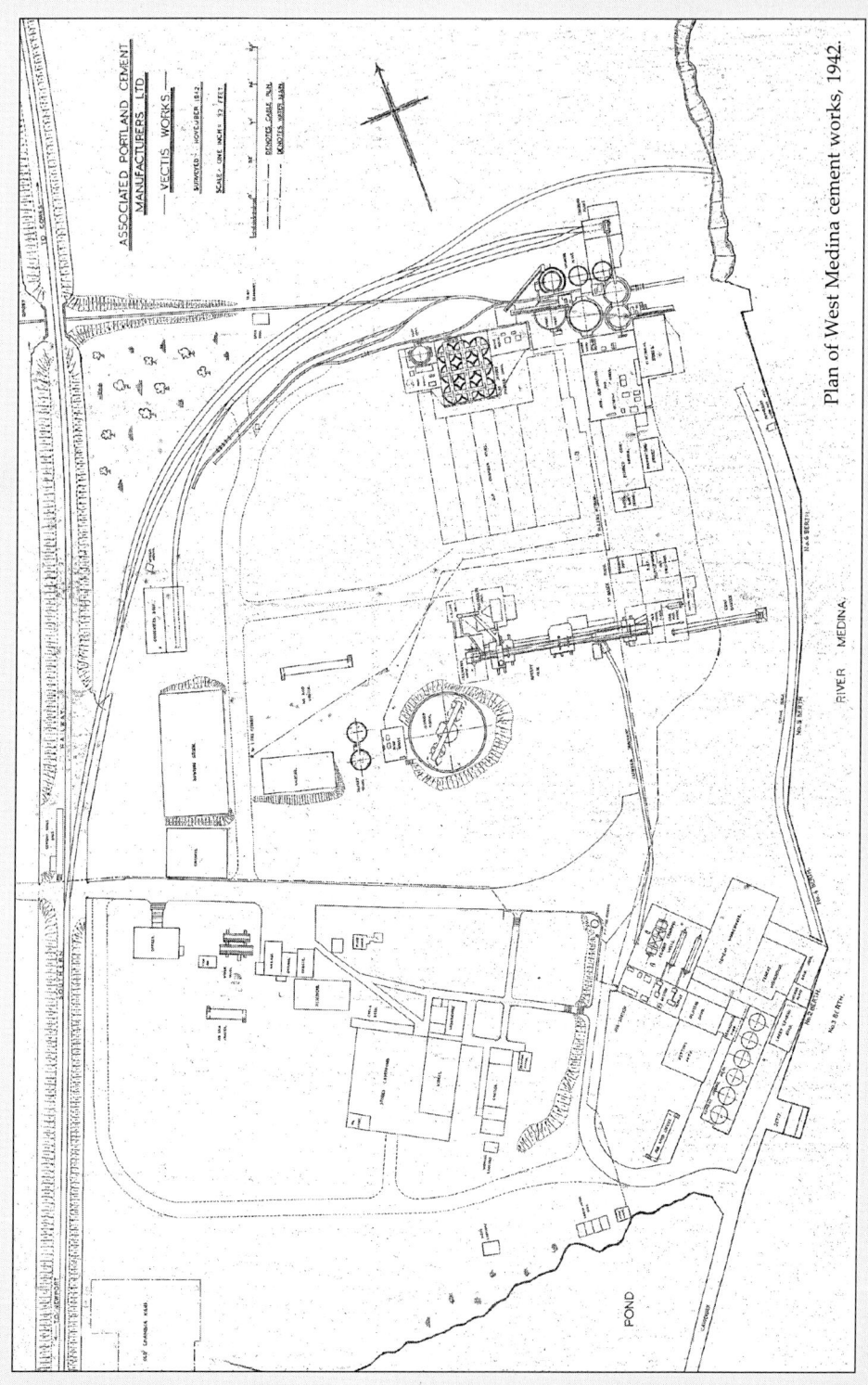

Plan of West Medina cement works, 1942.

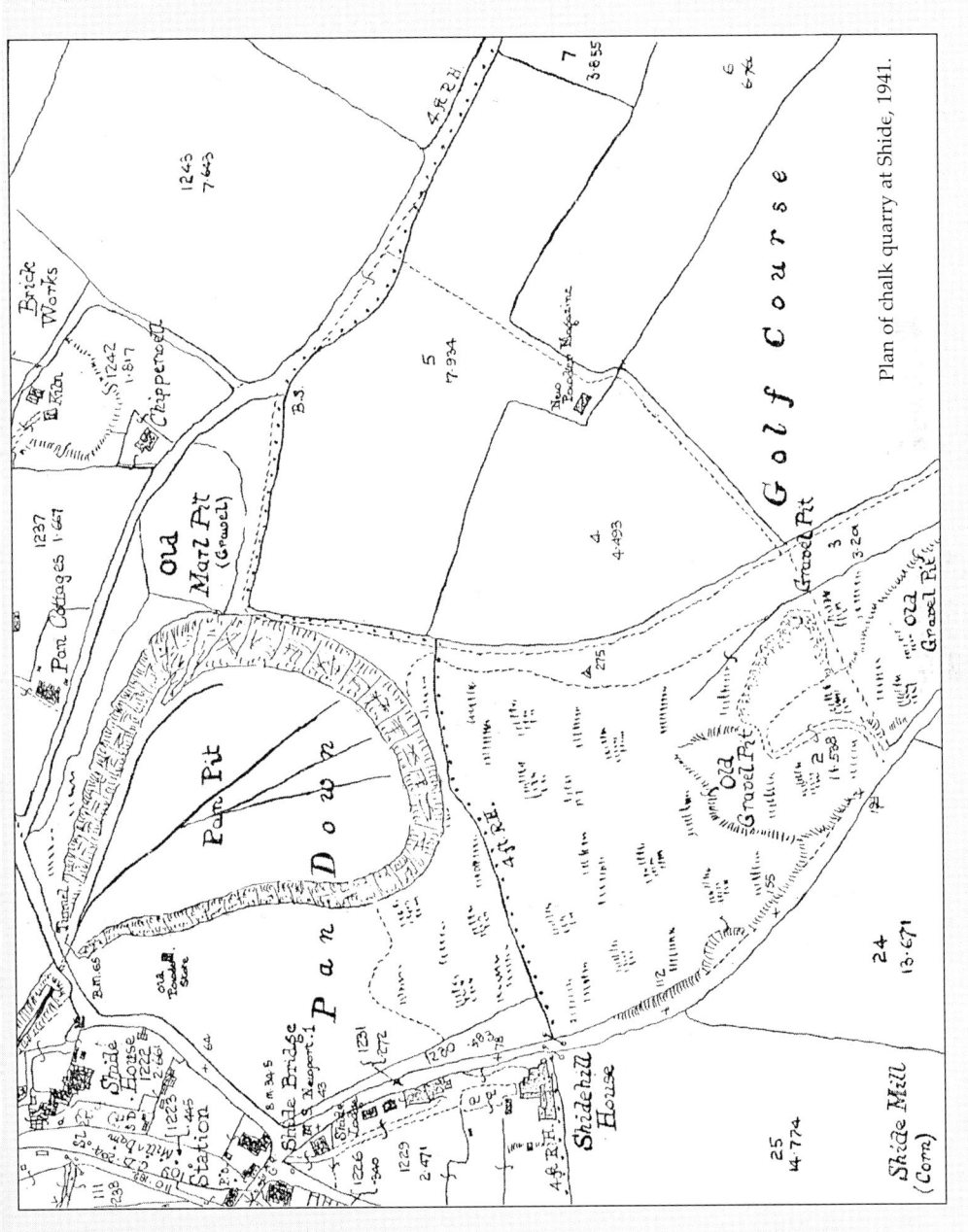

Plan of chalk quarry at Shide, 1941.

> **Propelling on Running Lines** (*Rule 179*).—The propelling of Goods Trains on Running Lines is authorised between the following points only :—
>
> | | Maximum Load of Wagons |
> |---|---|
> | Medina Wharf and Cowes | 15 |
> | Shide and Cement Mills | 20 |
> | Brading and St. Helens | 30 |
> | St. Helens and Bembridge | 15 |
> | Yarmouth and Freshwater | 10 |
> | Newport and Gunville Siding | 8 |
> | Gas Company's Siding (Ryde St. John's Road) and Ryde St. John's Road Station | 15 |
>
> In every case a Brake Van (in which the Guard must ride) must be the leading Vehicle.

Propelling on running lines, extract from SR Appendix to Working Timetable 1930.

Shide crossing arrangements, extract from SR Appendix to Working Timetable 1930.

> **Shide.—Crossing Arrangements.**—Passenger Trains running in opposite directions must not be allowed to cross each other at this Station.
>
> A Goods Train, Ballast Train or Light Engine, may, however, be shunted for a Passenger Train to pass, but permission must not be given to Newport South or Merstone, as the case may be, for a Tablet to be drawn for the Passenger Train until the Goods Train, Ballast Train or Light Engine, has been shunted clear of the Running Line.
>
> The Station Master or person in charge will be held personally responsible for seeing that the Goods Train, Ballast Train or Light Engine, as the case may be, has been shunted clear of the Running Line before the Tablet is restored to the Instrument.

The north end of Shide showing the interlaced points serving the sidings. Photographed postwar, the wagons are standing on the chalk siding, whilst that leading behind the platform was used for loading ballast. *R.A. Silsbury Collection*

This view of Shide Pit was taken from above the short tunnel leading to the exchange siding. A rake of empty wagons await loading whilst a steam excavator can be seen at work in the distance.
IWSR Collection/A.B. Macleod

R.W. Kidner captured the Cement Mills chalk train as it passes through Newport on 26th March, 1937. The green locomotive contrasting with the yellow painted wagons bearing a Blue Circle emblem must have been quite a sight.
R.W. Kidner

Although the loop was removed at Whitwell during the 1930/31 relaying, the old down platform and its waiting shelter remained and survive to this day. Looking from the north, the little used siding can be seen; the end dock terminated by the wooden shed.

R.A. Silsbury Collection

Newly relaid bullhead track and Whitwell down distant signal viewed from above the north portal of High Hat tunnel, 1930.

R.A. Silsbury Collection

THE ISLE OF WIGHT CENTRAL'S LINES   63

had closed, leaving a siding that handled local coal traffic, and there were sidings at Pan Mill and to the electricity works at Newport. Although always a public siding, that at Blackwater mainly handled ballast from a quarry on the opposite side of the Newport-Sandown road.

The Merstone-Ventnor Branch

The Merstone-Ventnor railway had been well-built with substantial earthworks, bridges and steel flat bottom rails. However, traffic never reached expectations and it was hardly surprising that the SR would regard the branch as ripe for rationalisation. As a first step, the terminus at Ventnor was renamed Ventnor West on 1st June, 1923 to avoid confusion with the IWR station. During an inspection in August 1923 it was decided to introduce a push-pull train on which the guard would issue and collect tickets. A proposal to spend £165 on an additional bedroom at St Lawrence station was abandoned, the station master was moved elsewhere and the house let to a member of staff.

Push-pull working apparently began in 1924 after the arrival of suitable rolling stock. At Ventnor West, changes were made to the locking in the signal box so that it could be switched out; a 'king' lever locked the points and signals allowing a train to run in and out of the main platform. This made it possible to open the box only when a more intensive service was needed, e.g. during Ventnor Carnival. Whitwell was available as a crossing point but its sole use in 1923 was to cross a passenger train with the daily goods working that ran when required; no trains were timetabled to cross at the station after 1924. The signal box was fitted with its own 'king' lever to release tokens for the Ventnor-Whitwell and Whitwell-Merstone sections or a long staff covering the whole branch; this arrangement was later repeated at Ningwood on the Freshwater line. In 1927 St Lawrence and Godshill stations were reduced to unstaffed halts; Whitwell remained staffed during the summer months until 1st July, 1941 when the goods yard closed.

Whitwell was the scene of a fire on 3rd July, 1926 when a spark from the 8.28 am train from Ventnor West set light to a packing case containing lamps; the packing case and lamps were destroyed, the window frame of the porters room was burnt and the platform roof scorched. On 10th November, 1926 two wagons derailed on the points to a siding at St Lawrence; the sleepers were in poor condition and had allowed the rails to shift under the weight of the locomotive.

On 4th February, 1930 the 7.51 am train to Ventnor ran into earth that had fallen on the line just beyond High Hat tunnel; the eight passengers had to walk along the line to St Lawrence Halt. On 12th August the train ran from Merstone to Whitwell without the staff after the signalman forgot to hand it to the driver; the return trip missed its connection at Merstone and had to continue as a special working to Newport. The signalman was suspended from duty for one day and the driver for four. On 21st November heavy rainfall and overflowing ditches flooded the railway at Dean crossing between Whitwell and St Lawrence, resulting in 'slight delays' because the crossing keeper could not reach the ground frame and had to handsignal trains across the crossing. On the following evening a large branch fell across the track near Ventnor West and was struck by a train; the line was later blocked by a tree trunk at the same spot and passengers for Ventnor West had to travel to Ventnor via Sandown.

The flat bottom rails, dating from the opening of the line between 1897 and 1900 sufficed until the track was relaid in standard second-hand bullhead material during the winter of 1930-1931. At Whitwell the signalling, signal box, down loop and a dock road in the goods yard were all removed; the working of points to the sidings had already been transferred to a ground frame. The siding at St Lawrence was removed on 30th September, 1930 whilst a siding to a quarry near Ventnor that existed in IWC days had already gone. The track layout at Ventnor was unchanged apart from the removal of a crossover to the sidings west of the signal box. The restrictions on the use of locomotive power were eased but since none of the class 'O2' 0-4-4Ts were push-pull fitted the 'A1x' 0-6-0Ts continued to monopolise branch services.

Such changes as occurred during the 1930s were aimed at staff savings. From 5th March, 1934 the branch train operated without a guard, his duties passing to the driver and a travelling porter. When a push-pull fitted locomotive was not used, a guard had to be provided to work the Ventnor West signal box as the locomotive had to round its train. The branch was at its busiest on Ventnor Carnival day when special through trains were run.

There was still some goods traffic on the line. There was a daily goods working that ran when required, but between 1935 and 1937 the SR replaced it with a mixed train for which purpose a goods guard worked the early turn. In addition to a small amount of coal to local merchants, coal for Ventnor gasworks was conveyed by rail to Ventnor West and then carted through the town. During the summer there were special workings of sugar beet for onward transit to the mainland; at Godshill on 2nd December, 1938 a sugar beet managed to wedge open a stock rail derailing two wagons!

At Ventnor West the 1930 alterations lasted until closure in 1952. This c.1948 view shows both the Platform 2 home and starting signals pulled off. The yard crane lacks a wire hoist and the yard appears little used apart from the storage of carriages, including a newly refurbished SECR saloon composite. *R.A. Silsbury Collection*

Chapter Four

Newport to Freshwater

The Freshwater, Yarmouth & Newport Railway served West Wight and was the poor relation of the Island railway companies. Its meandering 12 mile railway began at a junction with the IWC just north of the Newport station with an awkward connection facing Cowes. The company had its own station at Newport and at Carisbrooke, Watchingwell, Calbourne, Ningwood, Yarmouth and Freshwater; Watchingwell was a private station for the exclusive use of visitors to the nearby residence of the Simeon family. There were crossing loops at Carisbrooke, Ningwood and Yarmouth, although only that at Ningwood was still in use. The company's offices were at Newport in a corrugated iron building near the entrance to the goods yard at the foot of Hunnyhill. There were sheds for locomotives, the rail motor and carriages at both Newport and Freshwater.

The FYN served a small resident population and had been in the hands of receivers since taking over the operation of its railway from the IWC in 1913. The poor state of the roads in West Wight helped to bolster passenger and goods traffic, particularly livestock to the market at Newport and to Yarmouth for shipment to the mainland. After the SR introduced vehicle ferries between Portsmouth and Fishbourne it became more economic to carry livestock by lorry and the railway lost the traffic. The railway from Newport to Freshwater was difficult to operate as it followed the contours of the land with numerous sharp curves and changes of gradient. There were viaducts near Newport and Calbourne that needed strengthening and the permanent way still contained steel flat bottom rails that had been laid for the opening of the railway in the 1880s.

The line's deficiencies were all too obvious to Sir Herbert Walker and his staff during their inspection in August 1923. It was unlikely to make much of a profit and consequently the General Manager 'considered that with push & pull trains, many of the station master positions could be abolished' by downgrading stations to unstaffed halts, tickets being issued by the guard. However, it was later established that seasonal fluctuations in the level of traffic made this impractical.

Orders were given for the immediate closure of the FYN station at Newport and Mr Newcombe was instructed to arrange for coal merchants using the FYN goods yard to be accommodated in the IWC station. According to the *Isle of Wight County Press*, Newport FYN station had already closed to passengers at the start of the summer timetable on 9th July, 1923 but remained open for other traffic until 1st September.

There were a number of dubious working practices that needed to be eradicated. C.N. Anderson had the single line staffs for the Newport-Carisbrooke and Carisbrooke-Ningwood sections welded together so the drivers no longer had to carry two staffs between Newport and Ningwood. He also locked away a special key used to operate the points to the Newport FYN goods yard when the train staff was elsewhere. The practice of propelling goods trains from Yarmouth to Freshwater and Newport to Gunville siding when required was written into the Rule Book.

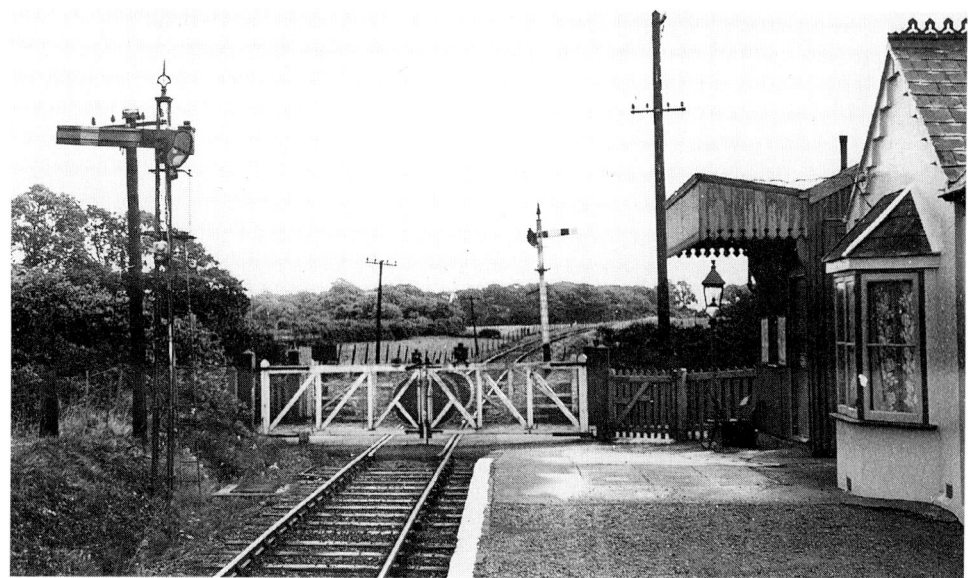

The new arrangements at Calbourne saw LSWR pattern home signals installed to protect the level crossing and the former booking office from Newport FYN resited at the up end of the platform. This view is looking towards Newport. *R.A. Silsbury Collection*

The alterations at Freshwater in 1926 left the water tank in splendid isolation. Although the running line and loop have been relaid with bullhead rail, the sidings remain old flat-bottomed rail. In 1927 'A1X' class No. 11 arrives with a train of LBSCR Billinton 4-wheelers strengthened with an IWC/GER third, passing the starkly-new rebuilt platform and LSWR starting signal.

IWSR Collection

The stations were early targets for a fresh coat of paint and other improvements, 'all spick and span' as the *Southern Railway Magazine* described them. Work began at Yarmouth, Ningwood and Calbourne in May 1924 and reached Watchingwell and Carisbrooke in June. The FYN signal box at Newport was taken out of use on 23rd July, 1924 and control of the siding points transferred to ground frames. The remains of the station were swept away during alterations at Newport in 1929. The company's old office became Newport Railwaymen's Institute with a billiard table, a card room and 'as we have all caught the wireless craze ... a listening set'.

Permission was given in September 1924 for the removal of crossing loops, signal boxes and signals at Carisbrooke and Yarmouth, the work being carried out that winter. Calbourne ceased to be a block post in July 1925 when it was downgraded to a halt from the start of the summer timetable. In September the gate keeper gained the exclusive use of his sitting room after the station acquired the ticket office from the FYN station at Newport. The signal box was replaced by ground frames, one working the siding and the other on the platform for the signals protecting the level crossing and the gate lock; the starting signals were removed and the arms of distant signals fixed at caution. Trains called at Watchingwell when signalled to do so by the station attendant, who would operate a two-lever ground frame on the platform to set at danger one of two home signals sharing the same post; the SR installed distant signals worked in the same manner. Carisbrooke was downgraded to a halt in 1927 saving £170 a year in staff costs and allowing the building to be let out. Other stations did not share Carisbrooke's fate because they were adjacent to level crossings across public roads and had to be continuously manned.

In one of many such incidents, on 28th September, 1924 the gates at Petticoat Lane level crossing were demolished by a locomotive, ballast wagon and brake van returning from Freshwater earlier than expected; the crew escaped censure as the weather was misty and the rails greasy. On 23rd October, 1924 the mail and goods train killed a cow between Calbourne and Ningwood, for which the farmer promptly claimed £27 compensation. At lunch time on 17th February, 1926 the locomotive hauling a Newport-bound passenger train broke its rear axle between Freshwater and Yarmouth; normal service was resumed during the evening. On 19th October, 1926 the leading wheels of the locomotive on an afternoon Newport-Freshwater train derailed near Watchingwell station. The train was thought to have been exceeding the line's 30 mph speed limit, made worse by the locomotive's fixed wheelbase and the light permanent way. The LBSCR 0-6-0Ts were briefly banned from working the line, a temporary 25 mph speed limit was slapped on the Newport-Ningwood section and seven or eight minutes added to journey times.

The station at Freshwater was inspected in September 1925 when plans for alterations were approved. Work began during the following winter on the demolition and removal of the locomotive shed, carriage shed, coal stage and their sidings leaving just the water tower. There were improvements to the booking and parcels office, the concourse was enlarged and since the platform was sinking it was rebuilt and fenced with standard SR concrete fencing panels; apart from a short length near the concourse the width was reduced to 12 feet.

Freshwater

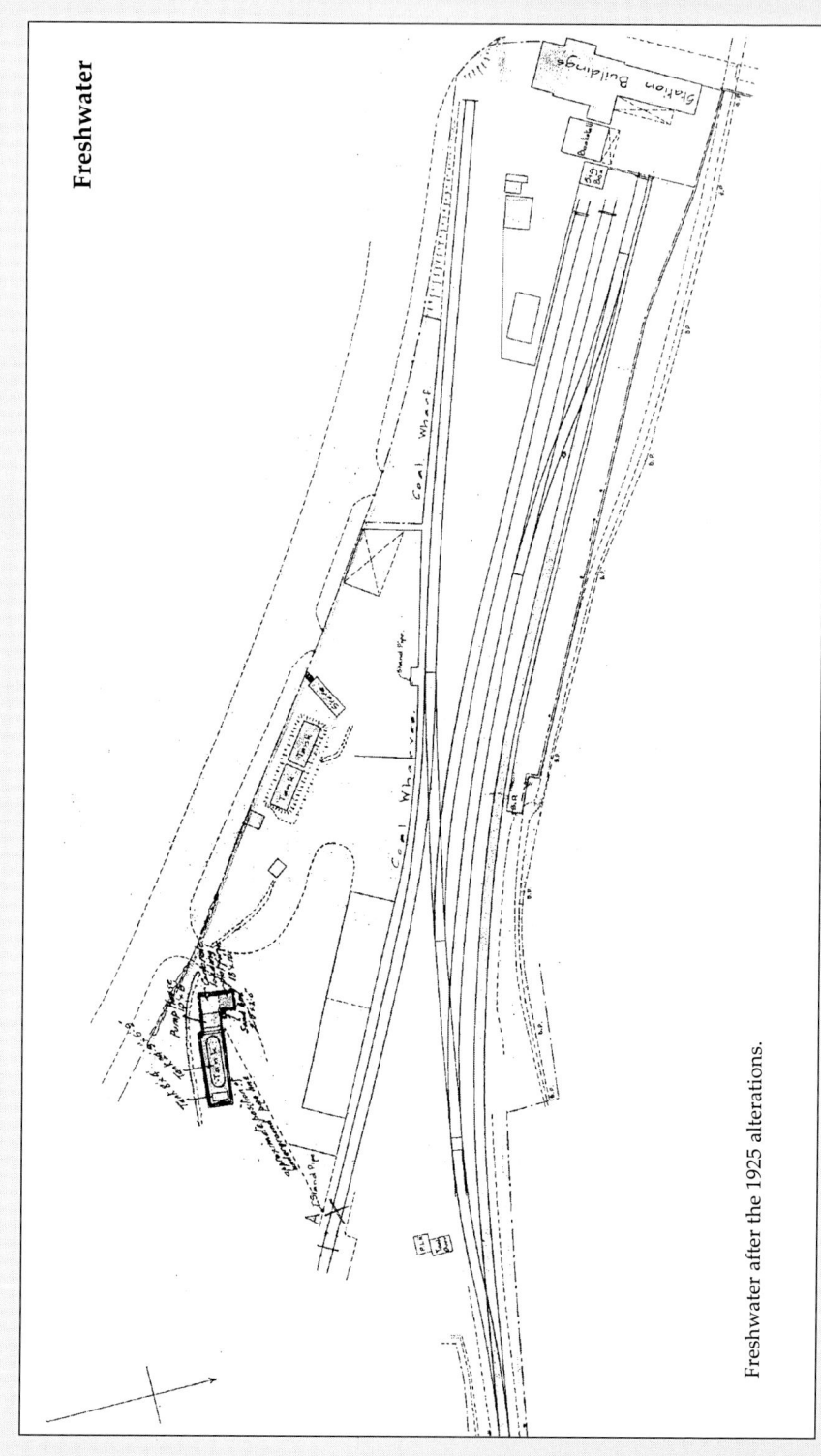

Freshwater after the 1925 alterations.

The dilapidated signal box was replaced by the box from Newport FYN station in a more convenient place behind the buffer stops; it came into use on 18th May, 1927. The site for the new signal box had been occupied by W.H. Smith's bookstall so they were given the option of having the existing hut moved or paying for a new bookstall. Lt Col Mount wrote on 5th December, 1927:

> To effect economy in working a new signal box with 8 working levers and 2 spare has been installed near the offices of this terminal station. Certain alterations have been made in respect of the siding connections, the facing points in the main line have been relaid with second-hand 84 lb. material, a new box provided, and the crossover near the buffer stops has been relaid and shifted and a new shunt signal provided to control movements over it.
> The home signal and other shunting signals have also been shifted, the distant signal being fixed in the warning position and provided with a yellow arm and light.

Similar economies were implemented at Ningwood where the crossing loop was used only during the summer. In the signal box a 'king' lever locked the Freshwater-Ningwood and Ningwood-Newport single line instruments and released a special long staff; the points were set for the down line and the appropriate signals left in the clear position. This changeover could only take place when there was a down train standing at the station. So few passengers used the station that it was not worth closing the signal box and moving the lever frame to the booking office.

Ningwood regularly appeared in the reports of misdemeanours to the traffic officers. A train ran from Newport to Ningwood without the train staff on 23rd August, 1930, and in the opposite direction on 13th June, 1931 when the porter-signalman was distracted by the need to load a perambulator onto the train. On 27th July, 1933 the driver of a Newport-bound train was again given the wrong train staff.

Parts of the FYN station at Newport lingered on for years after its closure in 1923. It lost the ticket office to Calbourne, the signal box to Freshwater and a grounded GCR van body replaced an older body at Yarmouth. Parts of the platform were removed when the track was relaid in the Autumn of 1928 but the remainder, including the waiting shelter, lasted only until the site was cleared a few months later.

Relaying the track took years to complete and as late as March 1929 the section between Newport and Ningwood was still unable to take the weight of the heaviest locomotives. The LBSCR class 'A1' and 'A1x' 0-6-0Ts were hardly masters of their work as one correspondent wrote:

> The almost exhausted beat of the engine as it breasted the Watchingwell bank, and the sudden burst of speed in descending towards Carisbrooke, with the ancient castle coming into view on the right, had a fascination not found elsewhere.

Restrictions on the motive power were finally removed by the Engineer towards the end of 1931 but running times were not reduced. The viaducts at Newport and Calbourne had been strengthened with additional steel struts but Calbourne still had a 15 mph speed limit when the line closed.

The introduction of cheap rover tickets increased the number of day trippers travelling to West Wight. The first through trains from Ryde, Sandown,

In front of the station buildings is the signal box transferred from Newport FYN in 1927. The platform is constructed from SR standard concrete sections, whilst the carriage is the saloon portion of the former IWC railmotor, probably laying over between use on 'The Tourist'.

IWSR Collection

The narrow, 1936 extension to the platform at Freshwater was constructed to accommodate six bogie carriages used on 'The Tourist' through train.

R.A. Silsbury Collection

The prominent speed restriction board guarding Calbourne viaduct, with Calbourne's fixed distant signal behind. Although taken in 1950, this scene was unchanged from the 1920s.
R.A. Silsbury Collection

Shanklin and Ventnor appeared in the summer 1933 timetable and became so popular that in May 1934 plans were prepared for an extension of the platforms and crossing loop at Ningwood. The matter was raised during an inspection in October 1935, when it agreed to lengthen the loop from 260 ft to 400 ft, but since the trains would not be stopping it was decided not to lengthen the platforms. At Freshwater the platform was lengthened and the starting signal relocated at a cost of £442, but to save money the platform extension was only 6 ft wide; they were ready for use on 2nd June, 1936. Additional toilets were built as there were lengthy queues at the 'Ladies' after the arrival of a train!

Perhaps the most serious accident to occur on the line took place in January 1939. The *Isle of Wight County Press* carried the headline 'Island Railway Services Stopped' after heavy rain on Wednesday 25th January flooded the Newport-Sandown line. However, most of the article was given over to an accident the next morning. During the night the embankment near bridge No. 10 at Great Park Farm, Watchingwell slipped and so undermined the track that the mail train was derailed at 5.00 am at about 40 mph. There were no passengers nor serious injuries amongst the crew. The mails were rescued and carried across the fields to Post Office vans sent from Freshwater. Breakdown crews from Newport and Ryde rerailed the locomotive and a van but two carriages, a second van and two wagons were cut up on the spot. The track was reinstated but it was not until 1946 that a new drain and two catch pits were put in after an easement had been obtained from a nearby landowner.

The SR inherited three private sidings along the line. Dowtys siding ceased to be listed in working timetables in 1929 when the connection was taken out during track relaying. Wellow siding was disused by January 1938, when the owners were paid £60 in compensation for its removal; the siding had been put in at FYN expense in part payment for land on which the railway ran. Gunville siding remained *in situ* until after the line closed but is unlikely to have seen any traffic after the brickworks closed during the 1940s. Gunville siding could be worked by a train propelled from Newport with a brake van in the lead. Another siding at Watchingwell served Swainston estate but was removed in 1944. It was quite common during SR days to pay nominal sums to landowners for permission to remove occupation crossings and several were taken out along the line.

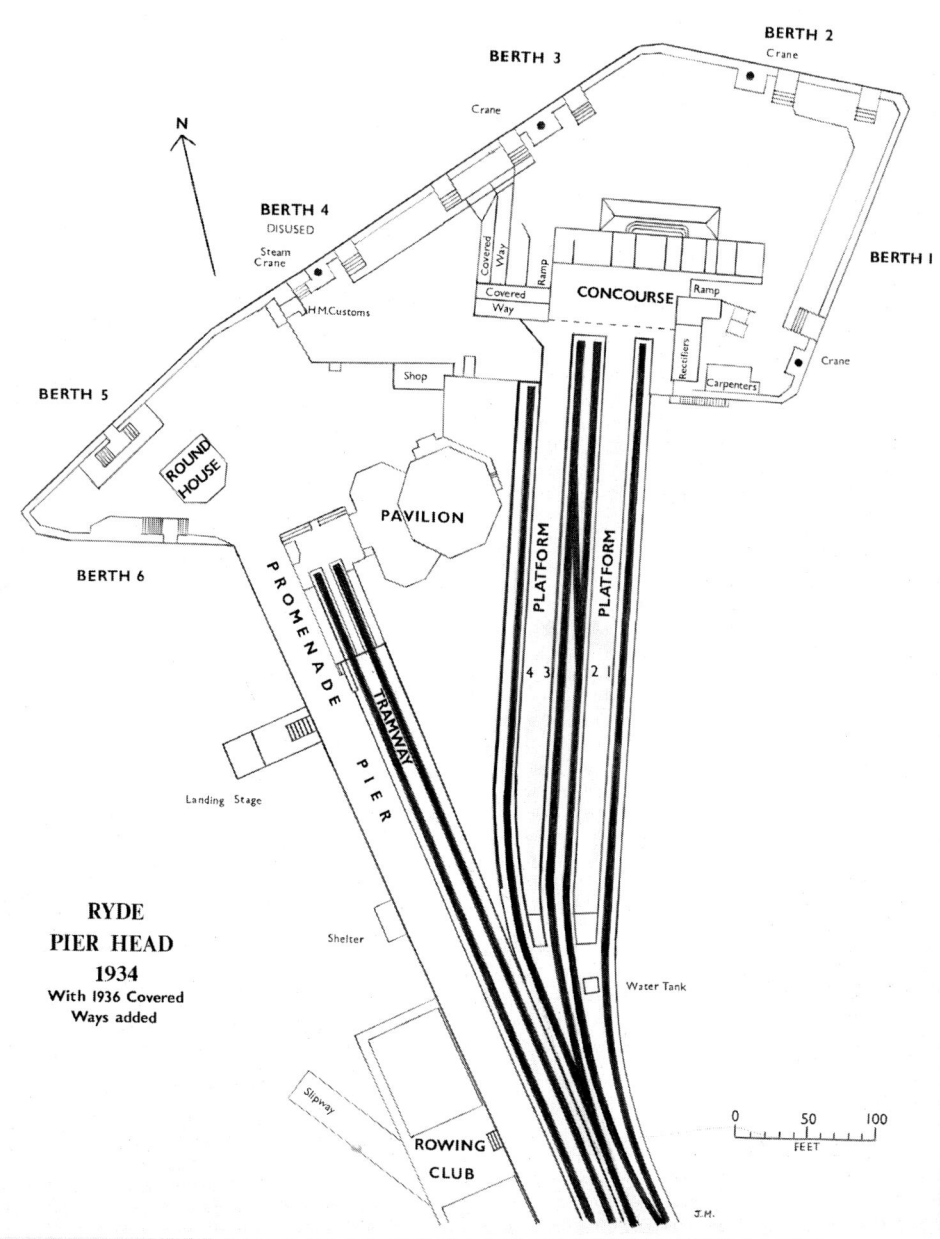

Chapter Five

Developments at Ryde

At Ryde ownership of the ferries, pier, tramway and railways was somewhat complicated. The Ryde Pier Company owned the promenade pier and the electric tramway. The Portsmouth-Ryde ferries, railway pier and ¾ mile railway through the town were owned jointly by the LSWR and LBSCR. The mainland companies staffed the railway stations at Ryde Pier Head and Ryde Esplanade but possessed no locomotives or rolling stock in the Island, the IWR and IWC having running powers over the mainland companies' line. The track through St Johns Road station and to the parting of the Ventnor and Cowes lines near Smallbrook Farm was owned by the IWR.

The Promenade Pier and Tramway

Since the assets of the Ryde Pier Company were not acquired until 1924, improvements to the promenade pier and tramway had to wait until after an inspection of the Island railways in September that year. Maintenance had been neglected during the Great War and there was much to be done. The Engineer reported that the pier head was in poor condition and recommended that it be reconstructed in ferro-concrete. Estimates were obtained and a contract was awarded to the contractors who were carrying out similar work on the railway part of the pier head; the whole project took until the early 1930s to complete. The SR had little interest in the promenade pier and pavilion and rented them to the local authority from 1st August, 1927 for £2,000 a year; the SR retained responsibility for maintenance and the tramway.

The tramway's two tracks were worked independently each by a motor car and trailer operating in a push-pull manner. The permanent way was laid in steel flat bottom rails spiked to the structure, as was a continuous steel conductor rail laid beside the track. By SR days there was a single crossover near the pier gates but it could not be traversed by cars under power so was of limited value; it was finally removed in 1948.

Electricity was fed to the conductor rails from gas-powered generators, an arrangement dating from the 1880s when the town lacked a reliable supply. The tramway's electrical equipment dated from the 1880s and was so obsolete that it could be kept going only with much ingenuity. The SR investigated alternative methods of supply but found that the local electricity company could not guarantee the amount of electricity needed at busy times. Consequently, it was decided to abandon electric traction. In November 1927 two newly-delivered petrol-motored tramcars began working with the existing trailers; the trailers were replaced during the 1930s. Only one class of passenger was carried. The mundane task of transporting thousands of people along the pier continued year after year until the tramway closed in 1969.

Ryde St Johns Road to Smallbrook Junction
1880 to 1926

(diagram showing St Johns Road North box, St Johns Road South box, Ryde Esplanade, Brading, Ashey)

Single track operation St Johns Road South to Brading and Ashey
Double track operation Ryde Pier Head to St Johns Road North

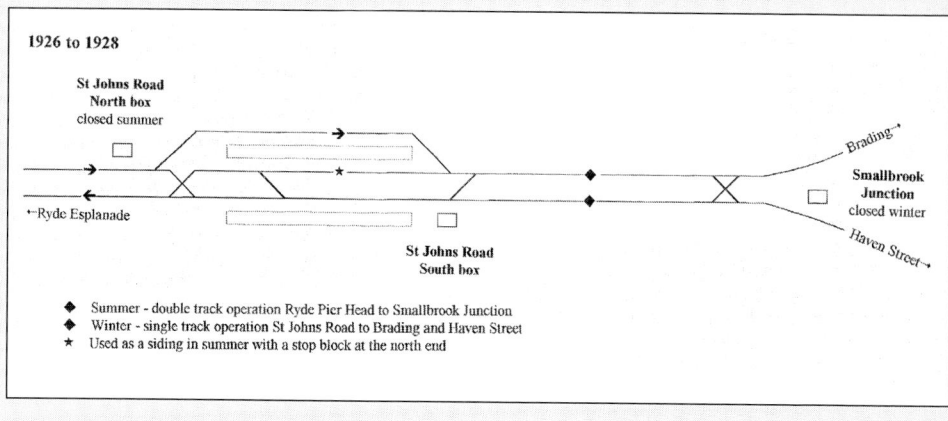

1926 to 1928

- Summer - double track operation Ryde Pier Head to Smallbrook Junction
- Winter - single track operation St Johns Road to Brading and Haven Street
- ★ Used as a siding in summer with a stop block at the north end

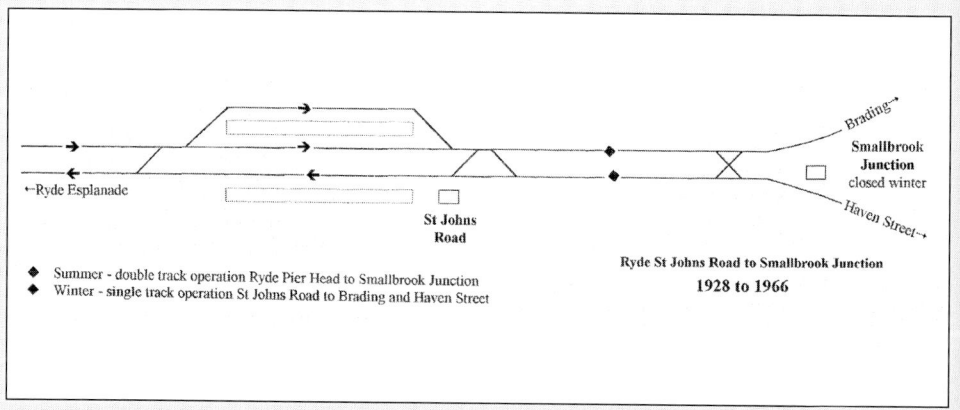

- Summer - double track operation Ryde Pier Head to Smallbrook Junction
- Winter - single track operation St Johns Road to Brading and Haven Street

Ryde St Johns Road to Smallbrook Junction
1928 to 1966

The Railway through Ryde

The timber decking of the railway pier had been renewed in ferro-concrete in 1906 but not the pier head, station and landing stages. Their condition had deteriorated during World War I so the LSWR and LBSCR sought tenders in 1922 for a reconstruction of their pier head in ferro-concrete. A decision was not made until 1st March, 1923 when a contract was let by the SR Board to A. Jackaman & Son of Slough. Work began shortly afterwards.

Half the concrete decking at the pier head came into use on 18th June, 1925 leaving 143 piles and 3,800 yards of superstructure to be replaced; they were completed in time for the 1926 summer season. At the end of that summer the station buildings were replaced by a steel framed building in brick faced with roughcast. Three of the four steam cranes were removed for service elsewhere and replaced by electrically driven cranes supplied by Chatteris Engineering Co.; they saved £166 a year in running costs. The water supply for locomotives was also improved at a cost of £838. By September 1927 only the erection of a glazed roof over the concourse and a weather screen on the west side remained to be completed.

Whilst the work at pier head was under way, a number of incidents appeared in the official reports. During an easterly gale on 3rd April, 1924 a barge dragged its anchor before colliding with, and becoming wedged under, the railway pier, 'Serious delays to traffic resulted'. On 17th October, 1926 a sneak thief broke into the buffet but was disturbed after consuming half a pint of whisky and left the contents of the till on the counter! On 26th September, 1926 a train spread the permanent way whilst entering platform 2, derailing the locomotive and a brake van; turnover locomotives had to be employed until the next day. On 30th October the signalman accidentally moved the points under a train shunting into platform 2. The resulting derailment put platforms 2 and 3 out of use for four hours during which Ventnor trains used platform 1 and Newport trains terminated at St Johns Road. A gale on 20th November, coupled with an abnormally high tide, led to the suspension of services for several hours after the sea began washing over the pier decking.

At Ryde Esplanade, the signal box had closed on 19th July, 1922 when control of the signals there was transferred to the Pier Head box. Train capacity was unaffected as the signalman could accept a train from St Johns Road and hold it at Esplanade if other conflicting movements were taking place; similarly a train might be sent forward to Esplanade before St Johns Road was ready to accept it. This took no account of human error as on 11th August, 1926 a train passed the Esplanade starter at danger and continued to St Johns Road, fortunately without mishap. Flooding of the railway tunnel under the Esplanade and neighbouring streets took place during stormy weather on 31st October and 1st November, 1924. There was also a fatal accident in the tunnel on 26th June, 1927 when an assistant linesman travelling in a passenger luggage compartment fell against a door that gave way.

Alterations to the passenger and staff accommodation at Esplanade station were authorized during an inspection in September 1927 and formally approved by the Traffic Committee on 29th March, 1928. The pier company's

Smallbrook Junction taken from a down Ventnor train in the early 1930s showing its rural nature.
IWSR Collection

Smallbrook Junction signal box stands surrounded by peaceful woodland that each summer resounded to the constant noise of trains passing every few minutes. On Whit Monday 7th June, 1954, the signalman takes the token from the fireman of an 'O2' hauling a scratch three-coach train of mixed LBSCR and SECR carriages as it leaves the single line to Havenstreet, Newport and Cowes.
Pamlin Prints

timber buildings, including the tramway machine room, were replaced by a brick building containing ladies and gentlemen's toilets. New ticket, enquiry and parcels offices were erected at the opposite end of the station. The work was complete by May 1930.

The road overbridge at Ryde St Johns Road marked the boundary between the mainland and Isle of Wight companies and the end of double track working. IWC trains passed onto a single line through the original platform whilst IWR trains used both sides of an island platform. The joint companies owned and staffed a signal box that controlled points and signals at the north end, but most of the station was worked from an IWR box situated at the south end of the main platform. A primitive corrugated iron locomotive running shed holding six locomotives was hemmed in by a goods yard on the west side of the station; the IWR workshops were on the east side.

During the 1923 inspection there was discussion as to the best means of merging the IWR and IWC locomotive, carriage, wagon and permanent way shops at Newport and Ryde. Eastleigh works' drawing office prepared drawings showing alternative arrangements of buildings and internal layouts based on a concentration of work wholly at Newport or partly at Newport and Ryde. Both options were rejected and the SR Board authorized the expenditure of a modest £936 at Ryde so that the workshop at Newport could be closed. The General Manager expected to see some progress by the next inspection in September 1924 but the chief mechanical engineer (CME) explained that no decision had yet been made whether to retain the down loop line. He was told to dispense with it and get on with the work!

There was no space for a new locomotive running shed within the confines of Ryde works so a plan was prepared for a shed on land north of the road overbridge; it assumed that the North signal box and down loop road would be removed. Evidently the chief operating superintendent had not been consulted about the changes and during the September 1925 inspection voiced his concerns. The loop was kept, but the need to prepare and discuss more plans delayed the redevelopment of the station.

Meanwhile, the CME completed his reorganization of Ryde works. The easterly of the two locomotive workshops was an erecting shop with blacksmith's forges and other heavy equipment. The brick-built turnery or machine shop, which contained a wheel lathe, was rearranged to accommodate additional machines transferred from Newport; a new 4 ton crane was supplied and erected by Herbert Morris Ltd at a cost of £145. The sheer legs outside the machine shop were demolished and replaced by a 25 ton lifting hoist from Bournemouth; owing to its position, locomotives requiring a lift had to enter works bunker first. Originally hand worked, the hoist was fitted with an electric motor after Nationalisation. The wooden and corrugated iron carriage and wagon shops were left largely unaltered but a windmill, used to pump water from the nearby stream, was demolished, along with a chimney from a boiler that had powered the machinery in IWR days.

In March 1926 the SR Board authorized the expenditure of £3,500 on a crossover, signals and signal box almost a mile south of St Johns Road station where the Ventnor and Cowes lines diverged. Built on a concrete base between

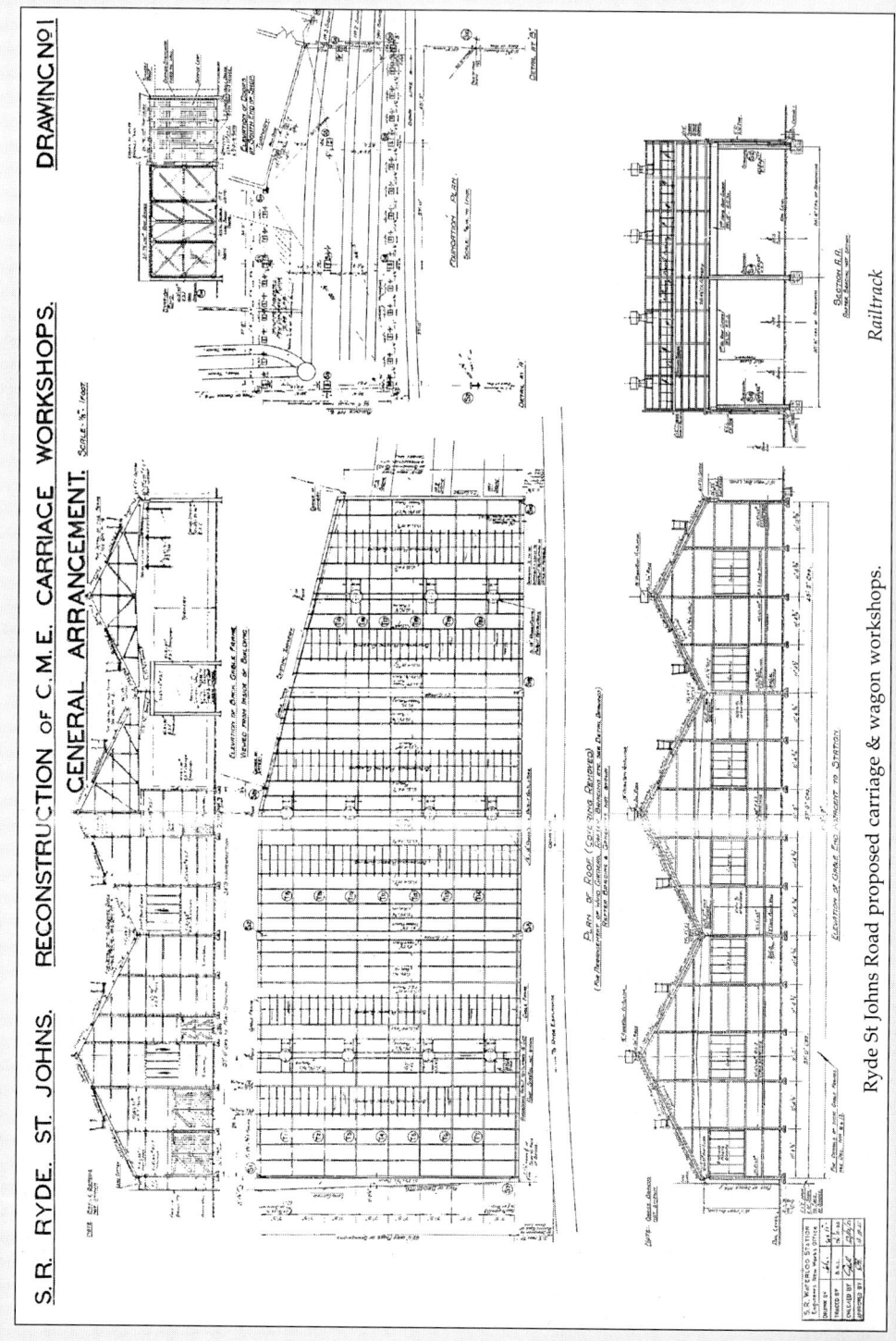

Ryde St Johns Road proposed carriage & wagon workshops.

Railtrack

DEVELOPMENTS AT RYDE

Above: A pre-World War II view of the workshops at Ryde with one of the LBSCR 'A1x' class 0-6-0Ts standing in front of the sheer legs, whilst in front stand a LSWR road van, LBSCR machinery wagon No. 60579 and a LCDR four-wheel third class carriage.
IWSR Collection

Left: The 25 ton hoist transferred from Bournemouth was erected over No. 4 road and was hand operated. The carriage and wagon workshop, behind, with its old doors would be rebuilt in 1938.
R.A. Silsbury Collection

Proposed internal alterations to Ryde St Johns Road station. *Railtrack*

the diverging lines, the box looked little larger than a garden shed with a wooden balcony across the north end so that the signalman could exchange single line tokens with train crews. Construction was delayed by the General Strike and the box lacked a roof when brought into use at the start of the summer timetable on 18th July; being remote from a station it never had electric light or mains drainage. On 10th August Major Hall reported to the Board of Trade:

> A new signal box has been erected at Smallbrook Junction with a scissors crossing between the two single lines. Single line working now terminates at this junction and ordinary double line working takes the place of the parallel single lines between this point and Ryde St Johns. In effect, therefore, the scissors crossing referred to forms a pair of double line junctions between the Ryde double line and the Newport and Ventnor single lines.
> The new junction box contains 20 levers of which 5 are spare, and the interlocking is correct.
> The junctions have been laid with second-hand Brighton Section 95 lbs. material and facing point bars 33 ft. long have been provided on all four sets of points.
> Up outer home signals have been provided on each of the single lines and also a down outer home signal on the double line. A train waiting treadle has been laid in rear of the last named. These signalling arrangements therefore provide free acceptance for trains in any of the three directions.
> During winter months it is the intention not to man the Smallbrook Junction box, and during this period all four sets of points will be bolted, clipped and secured in the normal positions. The working at Ryde St Johns during this winter period will revert to the previous used. At present during the summer period certain connections at the North end of Ryde St Johns Station have been secured in the normal position and the Ryde St Johns North box closed. It is the Company's intention, I understand, shortly to reconstruct St Johns Station and this reconstruction is expected to be completed next summer.
> The arms of all signals which are not used at Ryde St Johns when Smallbrook Junction is open have been removed and, similarly, it is the Company's intention to remove the arms of all signals at Smallbrook during the period when this is closed.
> The Newport and Ventnor single lines are both worked on the electric staff system, the staff instruments being at Smallbrook Junction box when this is in use during the summer and at Ryde St Johns when Smallbrook box is closed during the winter months.

Double track working through St Johns Road station became permanent following the closure of the North signal box on 4th December, 1928. Col Trench made an inspection of St Johns Road for the Board of Trade four years later when he wrote:

> The old North signal box has been closed and control is centred on a new South box which contains 29 working and 11 spare levers. There are also two existing and one new ground frames of 2 levers each, controlled by Annett's keys on suitable interlocked release levers in the signal box.
> The working at this station is unusual in that during the winter season the two tracks in the south direction to Smallbrook Junction, are used as single lines leading to the Newport and Ventnor lines respectively, while in the summer these two tracks are operated as an ordinary double track road, the lines in the station and to the north thereof to Ryde Pier being always worked as double track.

Rebuilding work in progress at Ryde St Johns Road in November 1928. The 'new' signal box is in position with the old IWR south box behind and the up platform has received concrete facing and capping stones, although much of the old order still remains.
R.A. Silsbury Collection/H.C. Casserley

The completed rebuilding with platforms featuring standard SR concrete products, the 'new' signal box and down starting gantry in summer mode. Note that the signal box steps were at the south end when first commissioned. The new locomotive shed and the upper arm of the co-acting up starting signal is also just visible above the platform canopy. *R.A. Silsbury Collection*

When the lines to Smallbrook are in use as double track the arms are removed from signals Nos. 4, 32 and 35 and the fixed distant of No. 2, and facing crossover No. 13 is disconnected. When used as two single tracks the two lines have large and small electric staff systems, while 3-position block is provided for double track working.

The platforms at St Johns Road were raised to standard height and rebuilt in concrete surfaced with asphalt backed by concrete fencing panels and a concrete running-in board. The island platform was widened to accommodate a water crane and introducing a curve in the running lines south of the station. The station buildings were rebuilt internally to enlarge the booking hall and parcels office. A few yards north of the IWR signal box a concrete base was laid down for a replacement box from Waterloo East (SECR) containing a 40-lever Stevens lever frame. Originally the stairs were at the southern end but, after the signalmen complained in October 1935 about the dangers of having to walk in front of the box, £22 was spent on moving them to the north end. The IWR box was completely removed but the brick base of the North box survived demolition of the upper works and was re-roofed for use as a store. The existing signals were replaced by a LSWR lower quadrant design on lattice posts; they included a large bracket signal on the down platform and a tall co-acting up starting signal just north of the road overbridge.

St Johns Road goods yard was rearranged with two long sidings, one of which served a small wooden store shed which sufficed for perishable goods. A third siding was provided for carriage stock and a fourth served as a reception road and headshunt to a locomotive running shed. Situated on land west of the station yard south of the road bridge, the shed was virtually identical to that proposed for the north end of the station apart from minor changes to fit the site. Built in concrete with redundant LBSCR overhead electric girders and asbestos roofing, it could hold eight locomotives on two tracks with inspection pits, washout points, a sand furnace and staff mess rooms; in front of the building were water cranes and ash pits. Separate sidings served a coal stage and a home for the breakdown van. The facilities were completed in May 1930 ready for the summer season. There was no space for carriage cleaning, a siding being provided for that purpose at Newport, and during busy times locomotive coal wagons were often parked in the siding at Ashey.

Apart from minor derailments during shunting, Ryde St Johns Road was relatively free of accidents until 1st October, 1926 when van No. 995, at the rear of a Ventnor-bound train, left the rails when the train braked on a sharp curve that was 1 in. over gauge. On 30th August, 1927 a derailment necessitated single-line running to Smallbrook for much of the morning and earned reprimands for no less than eight employees owing to the unsafe manner in which they dealt with the accident.

During an inspection of Ryde Pier Head in September 1927 the Chief Engineer pointed out that the railway platforms and roofing were dilapidated and needed renewal. The chief operating superintendent 'strongly urged' that the opportunity be taken to provide a fourth platform and on 19th December, 1929 the Traffic Committee sanctioned a staged reconstruction of the running lines and platforms at an estimated cost of £38,500. The decision to add a fourth platform was not considered final until an inspection in November 1930:

Locomotive shed at Ryde St Johns Road completed in 1930.

Railtrack

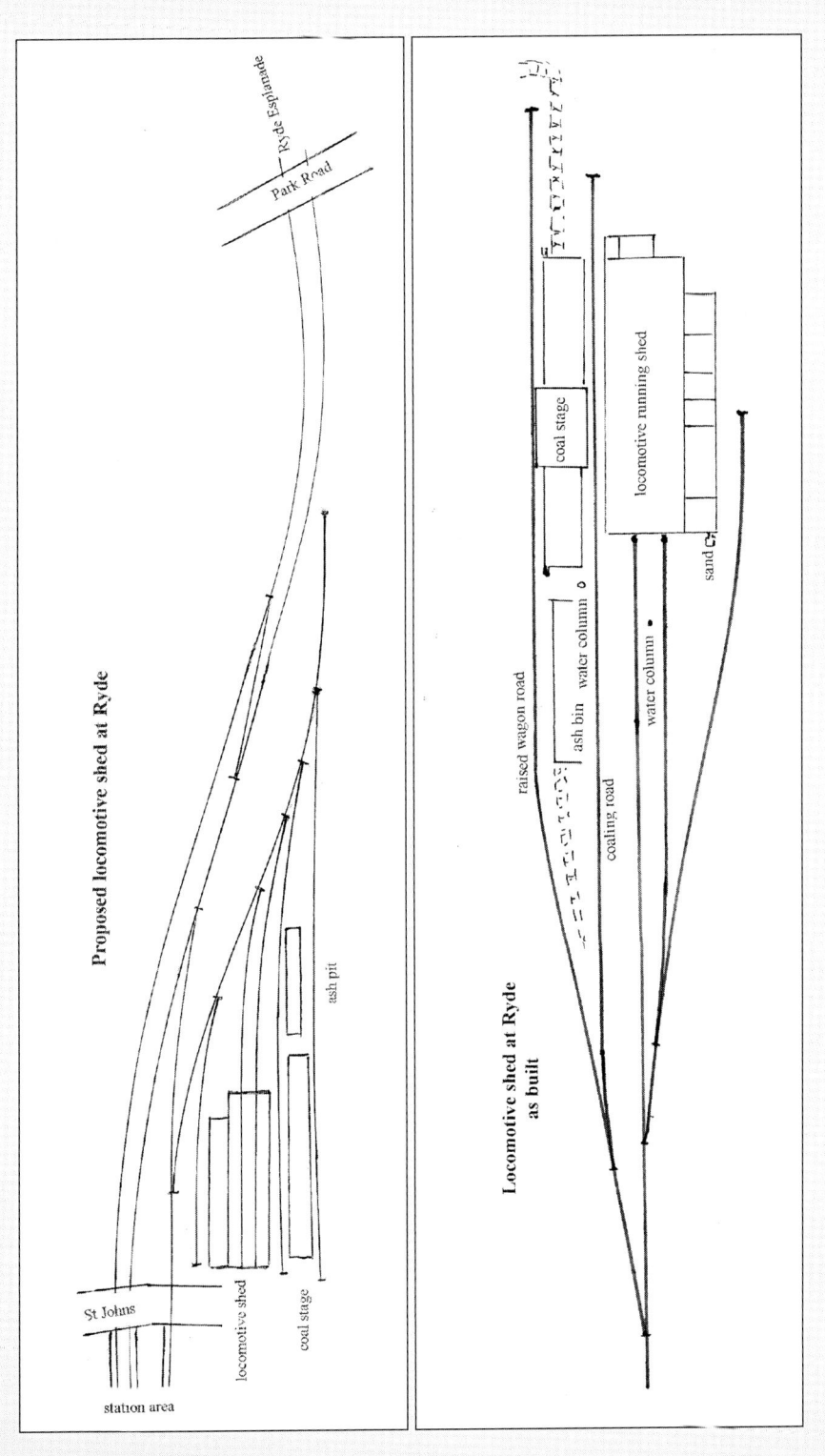

'O2' class No. 29 indulges in a little shunting below the new down starting gantry, the four arms in place denoting that winter working was in force, the two lines south from St Johns being used as separate single lines. *R.A. Silsbury Collection/A.B. Macleod*

The new locomotive shed at Ryde St Johns under construction, showing how the old LBSCR electrification girders were incorporated into the structure. *IWSR Collection/A.B. Macleod*

DEVELOPMENTS AT RYDE

The new Ryde St Johns locomotive shed soon after completion in 1930, with the coal stage to the left.
R.A. Silsbury Collection

The Traffic Manager confirmed his previously expressed opinion that, whilst the three platform roads afford sufficient accommodation for dealing with the present traffic, the Saturday service in the Summer taxes them to their fullest capacity, leaving no margin for further development. He considered that, if the traffic continues to grow as it has during the last few years it will become necessary in a year or two to increase the track capacity between Sandown and Shanklin, so as to run a still more frequent service as between Ryde and Shanklin, but this could not be done without the provision of a fourth platform line at the Pier Head. He therefore recommended that in view of this the opportunity should be taken whilst the under structure is being rebuilt to make provision for the fourth road, and that this road, together with a screen on the west side, should be constructed ... The General Manager decided that this should be done.

A month later, a contract was let to A. Jackaman & Son at a cost of £42,606 18s. 4d. for renewal of the platforms in concrete surfaced in asphalt, new canopies and an additional platform road on the western side of platform 1. The *Isle of Wight County Press* reported on 21st February, 1931 that work had begun, but progress was slow as it had to be suspended during the summer season. The fourth platform came into use on 1st July, 1933 following a renumbering of the platforms in reverse order. After the Directors got rather wet during an inspection in October 1935, they promptly authorized a further £1,930 on a covered way between the main landing stage and station! Suggested improvements to luggage handling at Pier Head included a proposed electric luggage trolley that could be purchased for £500 and, with maintenance charges of £101 a year, would save the wages of one porter amounting to £119 12s. 0d. a year. Instead, a Lister motor-powered tractor was delivered in 1928 and a second in 1930. Nos. T1 and T2 were replaced by T3 and T4 in 1934 and by T5 and T6 in 1940. There were 100 7-8 cwt cages each carrying about a ton of luggage that travelled backwards and forwards in the holds of the ferries. An encounter with a porter driving a tractor and 'train' of luggage cages was quite an experience!

Ryde Pier head after the provision of a fourth platform. 'O2' class No. 21 awaits departure from platform 1 on the right, whilst sets of LCDR bogies stand in platforms 2 and 4.
IWSR Collection

During an inspection at St Johns Road in November 1930 the Chief Engineer warned that the wooden buildings forming the locomotive and carriage workshops were 'in a very unsatisfactory condition'. This time the General Manager was not sympathetic and the matter was not mentioned again until December 1934, when the Chief Engineer produced plans showing how the roof beams from Kingston station could be utilised in a replacement building. On 26th June, 1935 approval was given to spend £3,991 on a new steel-framed workshop with a minimum 16 ft headroom over two tracks 157 ft in length and one 146 ft. The arches under the road overbridge were used as a trimmers' shop for repair of carriage seats or stores. The corrugated iron wagon shop in the yard overhauled carriage bogies. The facilities came into full use during 1938.

The only private siding on the joint railway was to the local gasworks north of St Johns Road station. Its operation was controlled by an Annett's key that, when withdrawn from the lever frame, locked signals to prevent the dispatch of another train along the up road; empty trains would be propelled back along the up line from the gasworks to the station.

One of the first two Lister tractors on Ryde Pier Head towing one of the luggage cages loaded with milk churns. Further cages standing under the electric crane at Berth 2 can be seen on the left.
IWSR Collection

Chapter Six

Traffic and Timetables 1923 to 1939

When the SR took charge of the Island railway system in 1923 it was faced with two opposing trends. The local population was deserting the railways for the omnibus but the availability of paid holidays encouraged more people to visit the Isle of Wight.

The Island companies had offered a number of cheap tickets to encourage rail travel. Holiday 'runabout' tickets issued by the IWC and IWR, for travel on weekdays after 11.00 am and all day Sundays, were continued by the SR and extended to include the Freshwater line from 29th September, 1923. There was also a range of daily combined rail and ferry tickets to Portsmouth, Southsea and Southampton. From 1st May, 1928, a seven-day 'All-Island' railway ticket was being advertised in the local press at 10s. 6d. first class or 7s. 6d. third class. In 1929 a rover ticket was introduced that gave unlimited use of the Island railways and the ferries between Ryde and Southsea; 12 months later the *Isle of Wight County Press* was carrying adverts for cheap day return tickets on weekday trains after 8.00 am and all day on Sundays.

Ryde had become the preferred point of entry for railway passengers to the Island. Cowes was no challenge, especially after relations deteriorated between the SR and the Southampton ferry company. Passengers landing at Yarmouth usually found it more convenient to use road transport. Helped by some astute marketing by the publicity department, traffic on the Portsmouth-Ryde route continued to grow.

Passengers carried Portsmouth-Ryde

Year	Total	Year	Total
1913	845,885	1928	2,013,870
1918	740,918	1933	1,996,920
1923	1,304,958	1938	2,441,421

Traffic was especially heavy at certain times of the year. On the Thursday before Easter 1924, nearly 3,000 passengers arrived at Ryde Pier Head from the mainland between 6 pm and 9pm and on Easter Monday a further 16,000 passed through the station. This was surpassed at Whitsun when by Monday numbers exceeded 19,000.

Just how the numbers varied between summer and winter is shown in the following statistics for Sandown.

Month of	February 1927	August 1927
Number of passenger tickets issued	5,279	28,884
Number of tickets collected	9,265	62,460
Cash income	£513	£2,997

The SR continued to make contributions to the annual regattas at Cowes, Sandown, Bembridge and Ryde. This was not, of course, purely altruistic because

Timekeeping of passenger trains

Numbers of trains	run	on time		1-5 mins late		5-10 mins late		11-20 mins late		over 20 mins late		Average
		No.	% of total	No.	% of total	No.	% of total	No.	% of total	No.	% of total	mins.
October 1925, Weekdays	3,922	2,260	57.62	1,340	34.17	245	6.25	73	1.88	4	.10	1.52
October 1926, Weekdays	3,558	2,107	59.33	1,220	34.29	180	5.06	43	1.21	8	.22	1.51
July 1927, Weekdays	4,069	1,816	44.63	1,543	37.70	533	13.10	164	4.03	22	0.54	2.72
July 1927, Sundays	413	183	44.31	137	33.18	42	10.17	38	9.20	13	3.14	3.77
July 1928, Weekdays	4,855	2,346	48.32	1,641	33.80	543	11.18	296	6.10	29	0.60	2.79
July 1928, Sundays	450	168	37.34	127	28.22	99	22.00	50	11.11	6	1.33	4.47
August 1927, Weekdays	4,717	1,618	34.30	1,852	39.26	825	17.49	351	7.44	71	1.51	3.91
August 1927, Sundays	342	142	41.52	95	27.78	61	17.83	35	10.23	9	2.63	4.27
August 1928, Weekdays	4,384	1,197	27.30	1,482	33.80	922	21.03	655	14.95	128	2.92	5.54
August 1928, Sundays	421	124	29.46	100	23.75	90	21.38	82	19.48	25	5.93	6.93
December 1931, Weekdays	2,772	1,634	58.95	877	31.64	214	7.72	41	1.48	6	0.21	1.71
December 1931, Sundays	342	243	71.06	80	23.39	13	3.80	5	1.46	11	0.29	1.17
June 1931, Weekdays	4,008	2,319	57.86	1,190	29.70	373	9.30	121	3.02	5	0.12	1.94
June 1931, Sundays	378	215	56.88	119	31.49	36	9.52	8	2.11	-	-	1.83
June 1932, Weekdays	4,607	3,589	77.90	897	19.47	108	2.34	13	0.29	-	-	0.68
June 1932, Sundays	1,208	1,012	79.82	187	14.73	43	3.39	25	1.97	1	0.07	1.00

The poor timekeeping on occasions can be explained by the extensive works that were taking place during the first ten years of SR ownership.

the railways gained extra business from these events and put on additional trains. For the Royal Naval Review at Spithead on 26th July, 1924 large numbers of passengers were carried on the ferries and trains. The Saturday following the August Bank Holiday saw the Ryde-Ventnor line carry about 20,000 passengers, thousands visited Ventnor on its Carnival Day on 27th August and the railways carried over 6,000 into Newport for its carnival in September. The *Southern Railway Magazine* reported that 'King Carnival' was greeted at Newport by a red carpet, the locomotive hauling the 'Royal' train being adorned with flags and a crown.

A spate of incidents affected train services in 1926. On 21st April a Ventnor-Ryde train hit some metal near Smallbrook placed by two lads aged 12 and 10 who were caught and sentenced to three strokes of the birch. On 27th October a Ventnor train near Shanklin ran over stones placed by some small boys. Later that day locomotive No. 29 *Alverstone* hauling a Cowes-Sandown train jumped the rails at Jeals Lane crossing between Alverstone and Sandown after stones had been placed on the line; fortunately no passengers were injured but the locomotive suffered damage to its front end and 380 ft of track was ripped up.

The first Island-wide working timetable under SR auspices began on 9th July, 1923 and betrayed its pre-Grouping origins by having separate pages for the SR's two ferry routes, the LSWR/LBSCR joint railway at Ryde, IWR and IWC services; an additional page for Freshwater line services appeared in the October timetable. In later issues the format was simplified to reflect the disappearance of old company boundaries but it was many years before a fully integrated service was in operation. The Island passenger service was rearranged on a regular time interval basis giving better connections at Ryde and, to a lesser extent, at Cowes and Yarmouth. Mainland train times were adjusted to improve connections with the ferries.

Ryde-Ventnor and the Bembridge Branch

During 1923 the hourly Ryde-Ventnor service was supplemented on summer Saturdays by short workings to Shanklin during the afternoon and early evening; hourly services operated between Brading and Bembridge. On Sundays the first down train left Ryde for Ventnor at 11.25 am and then maintained a two-hourly frequency until the evening; the last trip from Ventnor arrived at St Johns Road at 9.40 pm. Services reverted to hourly from the start of the winter timetable on 1st October whilst Sundays were two-hourly, a pattern that was repeated each year until 1966. Extra trains ran at busy times or in the early and late parts of the season.

On 14th July, 1924 the summer timetable commenced with a service of two trains an hour crossing at Sandown and the new loop at Wroxall. The same service operated in 1925, except on summer Saturdays when the timings differed. The practice of running a combined mail and daily goods train from Ryde Pier Head to Ventnor continued under SR management, but from July 1924 a second goods train was worked by the Bembridge branch engine to Brading before taking up its duties on the branch. The up goods working from Ventnor ran in the evening because of the demands of the passenger service. In 1925 a daily Newport-Ventnor goods train was introduced.

The Ventnor line continued to use ex-IWR carriages for the first few years after Grouping. A down service headed by 'O2' class No. 22 passes Sandown down distant signal with a mixed bag comprising two IWR saloon composites, a North London Railway third, three Metropolitans and two IWR vans in 1924/25. Interestingly the locomotive is not carrying any headcode lamps.
R.A. Silsbury Collection

By 1928 Ventnor services were mostly formed of LCDR 4-wheelers. 'O2' class No. 19 heads two close-coupled sets sandwiching two loose thirds along Ryde Pier.   *R.A. Silsbury Collection*

TRAFFIC AND TIMETABLES 1923 TO 1939

Extract from weekday working timetable (up trains) beginning 10th July, 1927.

Around 1930 the Bembridge branch has a two-set of LCDR 4-wheelers strengthened with a loose third with a LBSCR van added for luggage, here seen at Bem bridge in the charge of 'A1X' class No. 9 *Fishbourne*.
R.A. Silsbury Collection

After 1934 the two refurbished IWC Lancaster bogies were the allocated Bembridge branch set, strengthened with a LCDR bogie third when required. 'O2' class No. 28 *Ashey* is unusual power, probably running in after repair at Ryde works.
R.A. Silsbury Collection

No trains ran at the start of the General Strike on 3rd May, 1926 but within days volunteers were running four return trips on the Ryde-Ventnor line connecting at Brading with a train making five trips to Bembridge and four to Brading. Supplies of continental coal were bought from local merchants such as Fraser & White, Jolliffe Bros of Ryde and Dunlop & Co. at prices between 75s. and 90s. a ton (the following year Stephenson Clarke was delivering British coal to Medina Wharf at 27s. 10d. and 28s. 10d. a ton!).

The summer 1926 half-hourly Saturday service started at 8 am even though the advertised ferry service remained hourly until 10 am; in subsequent years they were properly co-ordinated. The hourly Sunday service was supplemented by additional trains when required. From 10th July, 1927 the early morning mail and goods train from Ryde to Ventnor ran in two sections on Thursdays when the mail train carried passengers and collected parcels vans at Brading from Chaplin & Co.'s depot at St Helens. Twelve months later a daily fish and parcels train was introduced.

Beginning on 8th July, 1929 the two train per hour peak service was supplemented on Saturdays by a handful of short workings to Shanklin, the first tangible benefits of the doubling of the Brading-Sandown section and other improvements at Ryde.

From 4th May, 1930 there were more workings for early season visitors but they often ran only if traffic justified. A timetable for Saturdays between 6th June and 4th July had one down train per hour until about 11.00 am increasing to three per hour between noon and 7.00 pm. On Saturdays beginning 12th July there were more workings in the morning and a three per hour frequency beginning at 11.00 am easing back to two after 4.00 pm; all trains ran through to Ventnor. On other weekdays there were two per hour, a third during lunch times and afternoons with paths for extra trains at other times.

The 1931 timetable was similar to 1930 but the Saturday timetable beginning on 6th June had two trains per hour in the morning and three in afternoons and evenings; a handful of Ventnor-Ryde trains ran non stop between Brading and Ryde Pier Head. The 4 am mail train no longer carried goods because the Bembridge branch locomotive hauled goods as far as Sandown; traffic south of Sandown was worked by the Newport-Ventnor goods.

The availability of a fourth platform at Ryde Pier Head permitted an increase in the peak service. Beginning on 1st July, 1933 the Saturday service increased to four trains per hour; one Ventnor train ran non stop to Sandown (Shanklin in subsequent years), a second stopped at all stations to Ventnor, the third to Ventnor was non stop to Sandown and the fourth served all stations to Sandown where it terminated; a similar pattern operated in the up direction. Monday to Friday services were more relaxed with two trains per hour and an extra train at busy times.

An early summer timetable began on 2nd June, 1934 with up to three trains per hour. The 1933 peak service was repeated on Saturdays in July, August and September. In 1935 the daily fish and parcels train was joined by trains

---

Up Ryde-Ventnor Section Trains, Busy Days.—In order to obtain uniform loading, Passengers waiting for Up Trains at Shanklin, Sandown and Brading, must be directed to the rear end of the Train.

Up Ryde to Ventnor section trains, busy days. Extract from SR Appendix to Working Timetable 1930.

SATURDAYS ONLY.

The timings shown on this page will apply from 3rd June to 9th September inclusive.

RYDE—VENTNOR, BRADING—BEMBRIDGE.

DOWN TRAINS. SATURDAYS ONLY.	Distance from Ryde Pier Head	Distance from Brading	Pass. and Mail.		Freight.		Pass.		Fish and Parcels.		6.0 a.m. Freight Newport.		Fish and Parcels Train.		Pass.		Parcels.		Parcels. E	
			arr.	dep.	arr.	dep.	arr.	dep.	arr.	dep.	arr.	dep.	arr.	dep.	arr.	dep.	arr.	dep.	arr.	dep.
	m c.	m. c.	a.m.	a.m.	a.m.	a.m.	a.m.	a.m.	a.m.	a.m.	a.m.	a.m.	a.m.	a.m.	a.m.	a.m.	a.m.	a.m.	a.m.	a.m.
Ryde Pier Head	— —	— —	...	4 0	...	...	...	6 52	...	...	...	...	...	7 25	...	7 50	...	8 12	...	8 12
„ Esplanade	— 32	— —	4 2	4 4	...	...	6 54	6 58	...	...	...	...	7 27	7 32	7 52	7 55	8 14	8 21	8 14	8 21
„ St. John's Road	1 19	— —	4 7	4 8	...	4 30	7 1	7 2	...	...	...	...	7	35	7 58	8 0	8 24	8 25	8 24	8E29
Smallbrook Jct.	2 10	— —	4	10½	4	33	7	4½	...	...	...	...	7	37½	8	2½	8	27½	8	31½
Brading	4 55	— —	4 16	4 19	4 39	4 50	7 10	7 12	...	...	...	...	7 43	7 46	8 8	8 11	8 33	8 37	8 37	8 41
Brading	— —	— —	...	...	...	5 30	...	...	...	7 25	...	...	...	...	...	8 23	Commencing 1st July.		Until 24th June only.	
St. Helens	— —	1 51	...	...	5 36	...	...	...	7 31	7 41	...	...	...	...	8 29	8 29½				
Bembridge	— —	2 61	...	...	...	...	...	...	7 45	...	...	...	...	...	8 33	...				
Sandown	6 41	— —	4 23	4 28	4 55	...	7 16	7 18	...	...	6 30	7 4	7 50	7 56	8 15	8 17	8 41	8 45	8 45	8 49
Shanklin	8 28	— —	4 33	4 38	...	...	7 23	7 26	...	...	7 10	7●50	8 1	8X 9	8 22	8 24	8 50	...	8E54	9† 1
Wroxall	11 3	— —	4 46	4 47	...	...	7 34	7 35	...	...	7 59	8x 2	8 17	8 20	8 32	8 33	...	...	...	...
Ventnor	12 44	— —	4 52	...	...	...	7 40	...	...	...	8 8	...	8 25	...	8 38	...	...	...	9†13	...

DOWN TRAINS. SATURDAYS ONLY.	Empty.		Pass.		Empty.		Pass.		Pass.		Empty.		Engine and Empty.		Empty.		Pass.		Pass. (Commencing 1st July.)	
	arr.	dep.	arr.	dep.	arr.	dep.	arr.	dep.	arr.	dep.	arr.	dep.	arr.	dep.	arr.	dep.	arr.	dep.	arr.	dep.
	a.m.	a.m.	a.m.	a.m.	a.m.	a.m.	a.m.	a.m.	a.m.	a.m.	a.m.	a.m.	a.m.	a.m.	a.m.	a.m.	a.m.	a.m.	a.m.	a.m.
Ryde Pier Head	...	...	...	8 45	...	...	...	9 20	...	9 52	...	...	...	10‖ 5	...	...	...	10 25	...	10 45
„ Esplanade	...	...	8 47	8 49	...	...	9 22	9 24	9 54	9 56	...	...	...	...	...	...	10 27	10 30	10 47	10 49
„ St. John's Road	...	8†44	8 52	8 53	...	...	9 27	9 28	9 59	10 0	...	10†14	10‖10	10†20	...	10†20	10 33	10 36	10 52	10 55
Smallbrook Jct.	8	46½	8	55½	...	...	9	30½	10	2½	10	16½	10	22½	10	22½	10	38½	10	57½
Brading	8	52	9 1	9 2	...	9†26	9 36	9 38	10 8	10 9	10	22	10	28	10	28	10 44	10 46	11 3	11 4
Brading	Commencing 1st July.		...	9 18	Commencing 1st July.		...	...	...	10 10	Commencing 1st July.		Until 24th June only.		Commencing 1st July.		...	10 46	...	11 15
St. Helens			9 24	924½			...	...	10 16	1016½							10 52	1052½	11 21	1121½
Bembridge			9 28	...			...	...	10 20	...							10 56	...	11 25	...
Sandown	8	56	9 6	9 9	9	30	9 42	9 45	10 13	10 16	...	...	10	32	10†32	...	10 50	10 53	11 8	11 10
Shanklin	9	1	9 14	9 17	9 35	9X36	9 50	9X53	10 21	10X23	10 32	10X40	10 37	10X41	...	...	10 58	11X 0	11 15	11X19
Wroxall	...	...	9 25	9X27	9 44	9X47	10 1	10X 2	10 31	10X32	10 48	10X51	10 49	10X51	...	...	11X 8	11F 9	11 27	11X29
Ventnor	9†13	...	9 32	...	9†52	...	10 7	...	10 37	...	10†56	...	10†56	...	...	...	11F14	...	11 34	...

DOWN TRAINS. SATURDAYS ONLY.	Pass. (Until 24th June only.)		Pass.		Pass.		Pass.		Pass. B		Pass.		Pass.		Pass.		Pass. B		Pass.	
	arr.	dep.	arr.	dep.	arr.	dep.	arr.	dep.	arr.	dep.	arr.	dep.	arr.	dep.	arr.	dep.	arr.	dep.	arr.	dep.
	a.m.	a.m.	a.m.	a.m.	a.m.	a.m.	a.m.	a.m.	a.m.	a.m.	p.m.	p.m.	p.m.	p.m.	p.m.	p.m.	p.m.	p.m.	p.m.	p.m.
Ryde Pier Head	...	10 55	...	11 15	...	11 23	...	11 50	...	11 53	...	12 15	...	12 23	...	12 50	...	12 53	...	1 12
„ Esplanade	10 57	11 0	...	...	11 25	11 28	...	...	11 55	11 57	...	...	12 25	12 28	...	...	12 55	12 57	...	...
„ St. John's Road	11 3	11 4	...	...	11 31	11 32	...	...	12 0	12 1	...	...	12 31	12 32	...	...	1 0	1 1	...	...
Smallbrook Jct.	11	6½	11	22	11	34½	11	57½	12	3½	12	22	12	34½	12	57½	1	3½	1	20
Brading	11 12	11 14	11	27	11 40	11 43	12	3	12 9	12 11	12	27	12 40	12 43	1	3	1 9	1 11	1	26
Brading	...	11 15	Commencing 1st July.		...	11 45	Commencing 1st July.		...	12 15	Commencing 1st July.		...	12 45	Commencing 1st July.		...	...	Commencing 1st July.	
St. Helens	11 21	1121½			11 51	1151½			12 21	1221½			12 51	1251½			...	...		
Bembridge	11 25	...			11 55	...			12 25	...			12 55	...			...	...		
Sandown	11 18	11 21	11 31	11 33	11 47	11 50	12 7	12 10	12 15	12B19	12 31	12 33	12 47	12 50	1 7	1 10	1 15	1B19	1 30	1 33
Shanklin	11 26	11X29	11 38	11X41	11 55	11X59	12 15	12X19	12 24	12X29	12 38	12X41	12 55	12X59	1 15	1X19	1 24	1X20	1 38	1X41
Wroxall	11 37	11 38	11 49	11X50	12X 7	12A10	12 27	12X20	12 37	12 38	12 49	12X50	1X 7	1A10	1 27	1X20	1 37	1 38	1 49	1X50
Ventnor	11 43	...	11 55	...	12A15	...	12.34	...	12B43	...	12 55	...	1A15	...	1 34	...	1B43	...	1 55	...

DOWN TRAINS. SATURDAYS ONLY.	Pass.				Pass.		Pass. B		Pass.		Pass.				Pass.		Pass. B		Pass.	
	arr.	dep.			arr.	dep.	arr.	dep.	arr.	dep.	arr.	dep.			arr.	dep.	arr.	dep.	arr.	dep.
	p.m.	p.m.			p.m.	p.m.	p.m.	p.m.	p.m.	p.m.	p.m.	p.m.			p.m.	p.m.	p.m.	p.m.	p.m.	p.m.
Ryde Pier Head	...	1 23	...	...	...	1 50	...	1 53	...	2 15	...	2 23	...	...	...	2 50	...	2 53	...	3 15
„ Esplanade	1 25	1 28	...	...	...	...	1 55	1 57	...	...	2 25	2 28	...	...	...	...	2 55	2 57	...	...
„ St. John's Road	1 31	1 32	...	...	...	...	2 0	2 1	...	...	2 31	2 32	...	...	...	...	3 0	3 1	...	...
Smallbrook Jct.	1	34½	...	...	1	57½	2	3½	2	22	2	34½	...	...	2	57½	3	3½	3	22
Brading	1 40	1 43	...	...	2	3	2 9	2 11	2	27	2 40	2 43	...	...	3	3	3 9	3 11	3	27
Brading	...	1 45	...	...	Commencing 1st July.		...	2 15	Commencing 1st July.		...	2 45	...	...	Commencing 1st July.		...	3 15	Commencing 1st July.	
St. Helens	1 51	1 51½	...	...			2 21	2 21½			2 51	2 51½	...	...			3 21	3 21½		
Bembridge	1 55	...	...	...			2 25	...			2 55	...	...	...			3 25	...		
Sandown	1 47	1 50	...	...	2 7	2 10	2 15	2B19	2 31	2 33	2 47	2 50	...	...	3 7	3 10	3 15	3B19	3 31	3 33
Shanklin	1 55	1X59	...	...	2 15	2X19	2 24	2X29	2 38	2X41	2 55	2X59	...	...	3 15	3X19	3 24	3X20	3 38	3X41
Wroxall	2X 7	2A10	...	...	2 27	2X29	2 37	2 38	2 49	2X50	3X 7	3A10	...	...	3 27	3X29	3 37	3 38	3 49	3X50
Ventnor	2A15	...	...	...	2 34	...	2B43	...	2 55	...	3A15	...	...	...	3 34	...	3B43	...	3 55	...

DOWN TRAINS. SATURDAYS ONLY.	Pass.		Pass.				Pass. B		Pass.		Pass.		Pass.				Pass. B		Pass.	
	arr.	dep.	arr.	dep.			arr.	dep.	arr.	dep.	arr.	dep.	arr.	dep.			arr.	dep.	arr.	dep.
	p.m.	p.m.	p.m.	p.m.			p.m.	p.m.	p.m.	p.m.	p.m.	p.m.	p.m.	p.m.			p.m.	p.m.	p.m.	p.m.
Ryde Pier Head	...	3 23	...	3 50	...	...	...	3 53	...	4 15	...	4 23	...	4 50	...	...	...	4 53	...	5 15
„ Esplanade	3 25	3 28	...	...	...	...	3 55	3 57	...	...	4 25	4 28	...	...	...	...	4 55	4 57	...	...
„ St. John's Road	3 31	3 32	...	...	...	...	4 0	4 1	...	...	4 31	4 32	...	...	...	...	5 0	5 1	...	...
Smallbrook Jct.	3	34½	3	57½	...	...	4	3½	4	22	4	34½	4	57½	...	...	5	3½	5	22
Brading	3 40	3 43	4	3	...	...	4 9	4 11	4	27	4 40	4 43	5	3	...	...	5 9	5 11	5	27
Brading	...	3 45	Commencing 1st July.		...	...	...	4 15	Commencing 1st July.		...	4 45	Commencing 1st July.		...	...	...	5 15	Commencing 1st July.	
St. Helens	3 51	3 51½			...	...	4 21	4 21½			4 51	4 51½			...	...	5 21	5 21½		
Bembridge	3 55	...			...	...	4 25	...			4 55	...			...	...	5 25	...		
Sandown	3 47	3 50	4 7	4 10	...	...	4 15	4B19	4 31	4 33	4 47	4 50	5 7	5 10	...	...	5 15	5B19	5 31	5 33
Shanklin	3 55	3X59	4 15	4X19	...	...	4 24	4X29	4 38	4X41	4 55	4X59	5 15	5X19	...	...	5 24	5X29	5 38	5X41
Wroxhall	4X 7	4A10	4 27	4X29	...	...	4 37	4 38	4 49	4X50	5X 7	5A10	5 27	5X29	...	...	5 37	5 38	5 49	5X50
Ventnor	4A15	...	4 34	...	...	...	4B43	...	4 55	...	5A15	...	5 34	...	...	...	5B43	...	5 55	...

A—2 mins. earlier, Wroxall to Ventnor, until 24th June inclusive. B—Terminates at Sandown, commencing 1st July. E—Attach empty train at Ryde St. John's Road and detach parcels vans at Shanklin. F—1 min. later, commencing 1st July.

Extract from Saturday Working Timetable (down trains) beginning 3rd June, 1933.

specifically for carrying Passengers Luggage in Advance; two return journeys between Ryde and Ventnor ran each Friday and their were paths for two additional workings on Thursdays. The same timetable operated each year until the outbreak of war in 1939. So intense was the service on summer Saturdays that the Smallbrook-Brading section was occupied by trains for a minimum of 40 minutes in every hour making it the most intensively worked length of single line railway in the country.

The IWC and FYN lines

An hourly Saturday service was operated during the summer of 1923 between Newport-Sandown and Ryde-Newport; most Ryde trains continued to Cowes but only during the middle of the day did Sandown trains run to Cowes and at other times passengers had a half-hour wait for a connection at Newport. Several early morning trains were run to Cowes carrying shipyard workers. On Saturday evenings there were extra trains from Sandown to Newport. Between Merstone and the newly renamed Ventnor West station there were eight trains each way and an additional working on Saturdays; every other train worked through to Newport whilst those that terminated at Merstone connected with the Newport-Sandown trains. On Sundays the Sandown and Ryde lines had a roughly 1½ hourly service but there were no trains to Ventnor West. Each line had a daily goods train and there were the chalk trains between Shide and Cement Mills. The FYN did not become part of the SR until August 1923 but during that summer operated eight trains from Newport to Freshwater and nine in the reverse direction with an extra working on Saturday evenings; there were five return trips on Sundays.

From 1st October, 1923 the Ryde-Newport and Sandown-Newport trains were two-hourly but most continued to Cowes. There were four return workings between Newport and Ventnor West. Sunday services were two hourly except for the Ventnor West branch which had none. The Freshwater line summer service was continued except for one weekday afternoon return working which was reduced to Saturdays only; on Sundays there were four trains each way. These frequencies were repeated in subsequent winters.

From July 1924 the hourly Ryde-Newport trains crossed at Newport and continued to Cowes shortly after the arrival of one from Sandown; separate Newport to Cowes workings gave that section a half-hourly service during much of the day. The Merstone-Ventnor West service was recast to provide 10 trains a day connecting with Sandown line trains at Merstone; the branch had an extra working on Saturday evenings but none on Sundays. The SR did its best to exploit the Freshwater line and increased the service to approximately hourly, the best ever, giving it nine return workings and five on Sundays. An afternoon goods train was introduced from Newport to Ventnor in place of one to Sandown in the morning that ran when required; it soon disappeared from the timetable.

In 1925 some Newport-Cowes workings were replaced by through Sandown or Ryde trains and a few crossed the old company boundary at Sandown when extended to Shanklin. The daily goods train on the Ventnor West branch ran when required.

The new order on IWC lines is well illustrated in this view of ex-IWR No. 13 *Ryde* in SR livery leaving Sandown with a Newport train formed of an IWC/Great Eastern Railway third and one of the LSWR bogie 3-sets.
R.A. Silsbury Collection

LCDR 4-wheelers came to dominate former IWC line services, typified by this view of 'O2' class No. 29 *Alverstone* on a Ryde-bound train near Newport in 1933. A close-coupled 4-set plus loose third is headed by two LSWR vans. Close inspection reveals the destination boards on the sides of both brake thirds whilst the composite appears to be steel-sheeted.
R.A. Silsbury Collection/H.C. Casserley

TRAFFIC AND TIMETABLES 1923 TO 1939

Extract from weekday Working Timetable (down trains) beginning 10th July, 1927.

In 1924 two sets of LCDR push-pull carriages were transferred and spent much of their life on the Ventnor West branch, singly in the winter and together in the summer. 'A1x' class No. 13 *Carisbrooke* takes water at Ventnor West in August 1936 sandwiched between the two sets. Note the gangway offset to the left on composite No. 6368, that on 6369 being offset to the right to enable the two sets to be coupled together if necessary. *IWSR Collection*

Newport had four 3-carriage sets of LBSCR bogies in the late 1930s, which could be strengthened by the addition of a third in the summer. Such a formation is seen behind 'O2' class No. 28 *Ashey* on duty 14 heading a down train into Yarmouth. *IWSR Collection/S.W. Baker*

During much of the General Strike in May 1926, the Ryde-Newport line had five return trips, three of which worked through to Cowes as did the three journeys between Sandown and Newport; the Freshwater line had three return trains and only the Ventnor West branch lacked a service. That summer, the timing of Ryde-Newport trains was adjusted to use the newly opened crossing loop at Haven Street. On the Ventnor West branch the Saturday afternoon service was increased to hourly during the summer; it was the only year when such a frequency operated as the custom simply wasn't there. There were more Sunday trains between Ventnor or Shanklin and Newport or Cowes but they were not always advertised between Sandown and Shanklin to limit their use to Newport line passengers.

Until 1927 the mail and goods train to Newport and Cowes departed from Ryde St Johns Road; that year it left Ryde Pier Head at 4.05 am as a mail and passenger train on Thursdays. The daily mail and goods train also started from Pier Head from July 1931 but only carried mail from July 1933 when the Ryde-Newport line was finally given its own daily goods train. On occasions the mail train might have passenger accommodation although it was not a public service.

In 1933 Cowes was finally given a regular service of two trains an hour to Newport with alternate trains continuing to Ryde or Sandown. In 1934 the Ventnor West branch had a service of two through trains to Newport and Freshwater on Sundays. In 1935 there were so many through trains on the Ryde-Newport line that the Saturday service was increased to a half-hourly, although usually only one train an hour served the intermediate stations.

Through trains

The operation of through passenger trains between the former IWR and IWC lines was first tested in 1930 when there was a return trip each morning from Newport to Shanklin and a second from Cowes to Ventnor. They were followed in 1932 by a Shanklin-Freshwater train (on Saturdays it ran from Sandown) calling at Sandown, Merstone, Newport, Carisbrooke and Yarmouth. Carrying boards lettered 'East-West Through Train' in gold on a red background, it was very popular with holiday makers and often ran full to capacity.

		Monday to Friday am	Saturday am			Monday to Friday pm	Saturday pm
Shanklin	dep.	10.06	-	Freshwater	dep.	6.10	6.10
Sandown	dep.	10.12	10.12	Sandown	arr.	7.17	7.17
Freshwater	arr.	11.13	11.13	Shanklin	arr.	7.24	-

The additional trains had to pick their way through an increasingly crowded timetable. So tight were timings that any delay would react through the single line sections to affect the whole Island network. To illustrate this, on a summer Saturday in 1932 the 2.25 pm Ryde Pier Head-Ventnor train crossed five trains from Ventnor in the course of its journey: the 1.45 pm at Ryde Esplanade, the 2.05 pm near Smallbrook Junction, the 2.25 pm between Brading and Sandown,

SATURDAYS ONLY

The timings shown on this page will apply from 9th July to 24th September inclusive.

DOWN TRAINS.	Empty.		Pass.		Pass.		Pass.				Pass.		Pass.		Empty.		Pass.	
	arr. a.m.	dep. a.m.	arr. a.m.	dep. a.m.	arr. a.m.	dep. a.m.	arr. a.m.	dep. a.m.	a.m.	a.m.	arr. a.m.	dep. a.m.	arr. a.m.	dep. a.m.	arr. a.m.	dep. a.m.	arr. a.m.	dep. a.m.
Portsmouth Hbr. ⎫ Southsea ⎬ Boat (Clarence Pr.) ⎭	...	...	8 20	...	...	...	...	...	8 50	9 0	...	...	...	...	...	...	...	...
Ryde Pier	...	...	8 50	...	...	...	...	...	9 20	9 25	...	...	...	...	...	...	...	...
Ryde Pier Head	...	...	...	9 11	...	9 15	...	...	...	...	...	9 30	...	...	...	...	9 48	9 48
„ Esplanade	...	...	...	...	9 17	9 19	...	...	...	...	...	...	...	...	...	...	9 50	9 53
„ St. John's Rd.	...	9†2	...	...	9 22	9 23	...	...	...	...	...	...	...	...	...	...	9 56	9 57
Smallbrook Jct.	9 5	...	...	9 18	9 26	...	...	...	...	...	9 30½	...	...	...	...	...	10 0	...
Brading	...	...	9 23	9 25	...	...	...	...	...	...	9 41	...	...	...	9†50	10 5	10 8
Brading															9 44			
St. Helens															9 49			
Bembridge															9 52			
Sandown	9†15	...	9 29	9 32	...	...	...	...	...	...	9 45	9 49	...	...	9†54	...	10 12	10 21
Shanklin	...	...	...	9 37	9X40	...	...	...	...	...	9 54	9X58	...	...	...	...	10 26	10X31
Wroxall	...	...	...	9 48	9X51	...	...	...	...	...	10 6	10X 7	...	...	...	...	10 39	10X42
Ventnor	...	...	...	9 56	...	...	...	...	...	...	10 12	...	...	...	...	...	10 47	...
Ashey						9 30												
Haven Street						9 34												
Wootton						9 38												
Whippingham						9 41	9X42											
Ventnor West								9 40				Pass.						
St. Lawrence Halt								9 44										
Whitwell								9 50				arr. a.m.	dep. a.m.					
Godshill Halt								9 57										
Sandown													9 49					
Alverstone													9 53					
Newchurch													9 56					
Horringford													9 59					
Merstone	...	...	...	...	...	...	10 1½	...	...	...	10 3	10 3½	...	...	...	...	...	...
Blackwater													10 8					
Shide													10 12					
Pan Lane Siding																		
Newport	...	...	...	...	9 47	9 50	...	...	...	...	10 15	...	...	...	...	...	...	...
Cement Mills					To Freshwater.													
Medina Wharf																		
Gas Works Siding																		
Mill Hill																		
Cowes																		

DOWN TRAINS.	Pass.		Pass.		Pass.		Pass.		Pass.		Pass.			Pass		Pass.	
	a.m.		arr. a.m.	dep. a.m.	arr. a.m.	dep. a.m.	arr. a.m.	dep. a.m.	arr. a.m.	dep. a.m.	arr. a.m.	dep. a.m.	a.m.	arr. a.m.	dep. a.m.	arr. a.m.	dep. a.m.
Portsmouth Hbr. ⎫ Southsea ⎬ Boat (Clarence Pr.) ⎭	9 15		...	...	9 35	...	...	...	...	...	...	...	10 15	10 15	...	...	...
Ryde Pier	9 45		...	...	10 5	...	...	...	...	...	...	...	10 40	10 45	...	...	...
Ryde Pier Head	...		9 58	...	...	10 7	...	10 15	...	10 28	...	10 33	...	10 43	...	10 58	...	11 7
„ Esplanade	...		10 0	10 2	...	...	10 17	10 20	10 30	10 32	10 35	10 37	10 45	10 48	...	11 0	11 2	...
„ St. John's Rd.	...		10 5	10 6	...	...	10 23	10 26	10 35	10 36	10 40	10 41	10 51	10 54	...	11 5	11 6	...
Smallbrook Jct.	...		10 9	...	...	10 14	...	10 29	...	10 39	...	10 44	10 57	...	...	11 9	...	11 13½
Brading	...		...	...	10 19	10 22	10 34	10 36	...	...	10 49	10 52	11 2	11 4	...	...	11 18½
Brading						10 23								11 6				
St. Helens						10 28								11 11				
Bembridge						10 31								11 14				
Sandown	...		...	...	...	10 26	10 40	10 43	...	...	10 56	11 1	11 8	...	...	...	11 26	11X31
Shanklin	...		...	...	...	...	10 48	10X51	...	...	11 6	11X11	...	...	...	...	11 39	11X42
Wroxall	...		...	...	...	...	10 59	11X 2	...	...	11 19	11X22	...	...	...	...	11 47	...
Ventnor	...		...	...	...	...	11 7	...	...	...	11 27	...	Pass.		...	...	...	...
Ashey	...		...	10 13	...	...	...	...	10 43	10 44	...	...			...	11 13	...	...
Haven Street	...		10X17	10 18	...	...	...	...	10 49	10X50	...	...	arr. a.m.	dep. a.m.	...	11 17	11X18	...
Wootton					10.0 a.m. Pass.											11 22		
Whippingham																11 25		
Ventnor West					Ventnor.								10 58				Pass.	
St. Lawrence Halt					arr. dep. a.m. a.m.								11 24				arr. a.m.	dep. a.m.
Whitwell													11 8					
Godshill Halt													11 14					
Sandown	...		...	...	10 19	10 21	...	...	...	...	...	...	...	...	...	...	11 8	
Alverstone																	11 12	
Newchurch																	11 15	
Horringford																	11 18	
Merstone	...		...	...	X 10 31½	...	...	...	...	...	11 19½	...	...	...	...	11X22	11 23½
Blackwater																	11 28	
Shide																	11 32	
Pan Lane Siding																		
Newport	...		10 28	10 31	10 41	10 46	...	...	11 0	11 3	...	...	...	...	11 30	...	11 35	11 39
Cement Mills					To Freshwater.													
Medina Wharf																		
Gas Works Siding																		
Mill Hill	...		...	10 40													11 48	
Cowes	...		10 42	...	...	...	...	...	11 12	...	...	...	...	...	11 50	...	...

Extract from Saturday Working Timetable (down trains) beginning 9th July, 1938.

the 2.45 pm at Shanklin and at Wroxall the 3.05 pm Ventnor departure; it was timed to arrive at Ventnor at 3.16. Had the train been late near Smallbrook it would have crossed the 2.08 pm from Cowes. A delayed Cowes train might upset the Newport-Sandown-Cowes service and, as the Sandown line trains crossed at Merstone, connections with the Ventnor West train. The only self-contained services were to Bembridge and Freshwater, the latter worked at peak time by two trains that crossed at Ningwood.

In 1933 the Shanklin to Freshwater train was renamed 'The Tourist' and ran each weekday (Saturdays included) from Ventnor to Freshwater and back; the number of stops was reduced to Shanklin, Sandown, Newport and Yarmouth.

| Ventnor | dep. | 9.55 am | Freshwater | dep. | 5.20 pm |
| Freshwater | arr. | 11.12 | Ventnor | arr. | 6.46 |

The introduction of 'The Tourist' and other through trains between Ryde Pier Head and Freshwater completed the transformation of the Freshwater line from a mere branch to a fully integrated part of the Island's network.

Whilst the Island railway services had been greatly improved, there was more to do on the mainland. On 4th July, 1937 electric services began between Waterloo and Portsmouth with one fast and two stopping trains to Portsmouth every hour during the week with extra trains on Saturdays, virtually double the previous service. Linked with the introduction of a new steamer *Ryde*, the SR gained some useful publicity which resulted in an increase in passengers and their luggage to and from the Island:

Reputed to be the inaugural return run of the 'East-West through train'. 'E1' class No. 3 *Ryde* departs from the Newport loop at Sandown towards Shanklin, the train being a LCDR bogie 4-set, strengthened by two LCDR 4-wheel thirds. The Ventnor-Newport and return leg of this train was always a rostered 'E1' turn. *IWSR Collection*

Passengers	Portsmouth to Ryde			Ryde to Portsmouth		
	Mon.-Fri.	Sat.	Sun.	Mon.-Fri.	Sat.	Sun.
August 1936	141,447	110,296	56,426	157,363	105,785	58,698
August 1937	158,610	83,283	59,406	176,458	95,758	63,755

Passengers luggage on the Ryde-Ventnor line

	Ryde		Sandown		Shanklin		Ventnor	
	dispatched	received	dispatched	received	dispatched	received	dispatched	received
August 1936	3,048	2,660	6,085	4,881	8,432	6,680	3,214	2,630
August 1937	3,465	2,632	5,960	6,252	8,200	6,790	3,334	2,710

Despite the greater complexity of the Island timetable, reports on timekeeping prepared for the traffic officers show a steady improvement but this was at the expense of lengthier travelling times. This might have been acceptable on the Ryde-Ventnor line with its heavy traffic, but journeys over the Newport-Ryde and Freshwater lines were leisurely, to say the least.

	Average Journey Times in minutes	1888	1915	1923	1937
IWR	Ryde Pier Head to Ventnor	45	45	44	44-50
	Brading to Bembridge	10	10		
		1894	1919	1923	1937
IWC	Cowes to Newport	15	10	15	11-15
	Newport to Sandown	30	26	25	26-31
	Newport to Ryde	30	30	30	46-55
	Merstone to Ventnor		20	20	20-22
			1919	1924	1937
FYN	Newport (IWC) to Freshwater		42	35	40-45

By the late 1930s, bogie stock was being used exclusively. 'O2' class No. 17 *Seaview* heads a down Ventnor working south of Shanklin, formed of a scratch set of five LBSCR carriages and a bogie LSWR van. Most regular sets were a mixture of LBSCR and LCDR vehicles. *R.A. Silsbury Collection*

Chapter Seven

Hopes, War and Recovery

Railway travellers who have watched the many improvements introduced on the Island railways since grouping was effected some 10 years ago cannot fail to recognise the advantage which the Island as gained as the result of unified control by the Southern Railway.

So read an article in the *Isle of Wight County Press* in August 1932 to mark the first 10 years of SR ownership. There was much to be proud of. New vessels brought increasing numbers of visitors to an Island whose railways had been transformed by some judicious expenditure.

Islanders, particularly hoteliers who had been hit by the economic depression that afflicted Britain, hoped that the SR would continue its investment in the Isle of Wight. Their concerns were put to Charles de Pury, who had risen to assistant divisional superintendent, at a meeting of the Sandown Hotel and Boarding House Association in November 1935. He reminded delegates that railways were essential to the development of the Island, but the SR was a commercial undertaking that had to justify capital expenditure and see a return on its investment. Whilst the Island railways were profitable at certain times, they barely covered their expenses in the lean months.

Mr de Pury was well aware of discussions concerning the Ryde-Ventnor line as it was already operating at saturation point on summer Saturdays. There was no cheap way of increasing the number or length of the trains and it was difficult to justify the cost of doubling the single line from Smallbrook Junction to Brading and south of Sandown.

The electrification of the Waterloo to Portsmouth line in 1937 exacerbated the difficulties in the Island as 80 per cent of passengers crossing to Ryde came from London. A report to the superintendent of operation in October listed their destinations on the Ventnor line:

Tickets issued and collected June-August 1937	Ryde	Sandown	Shanklin	Ventnor
issued	91,929	58,311	57,779	41,703
increase/decrease on previous year	+ 446	- 3,440	- 1,186	- 919
collected	340,456	154,415	199,010	99,766
increase/decrease	not known	+ 8,933	+ 7,558	+ 6,302
numbers of weekly season tickets issued		32,504		
increase		+ 3,671		

The report suggested that the peak service on the Ryde-Ventnor line could be increased from four trains to six trains per hour, i.e. three to Ventnor, one to Shanklin and two to Sandown. As an alternative to doubling the line as far as Shanklin, it was necessary to provide:

- intermediate signals in the Smallbrook-Brading, Brading-Sandown and Sandown-Shanklin sections to allow trains to follow each other at two minute intervals and ease running round at Sandown and Shanklin,

SOUTHERN RAILWAY

CHEAP RETURN TICKETS

BETWEEN ISLE OF WIGHT STATIONS

Daily by all trains at the following 3rd Class★ fares :—

FROM \ TO	BEMBRIDGE.	BRADING.	COWES (or Mill Hill).	FRESHWATER.	NEWPORT (for Carisbrooke).	PORTSMOUTH HARBOUR.	RYDE (St. John's Rd.)	RYDE (Esplanade).	SANDOWN.	SHANKLIN.	SOUTHAMPTON (via Cowes).	ST. HELENS.	TOTLAND BAY.	VENTNOR.	WROXALL.	YARMOUTH.
	s. d.	s. d.	s. d.	s. d.	s. d.	s. d.	s. d.	s. d.	s. d.	s. d.	s. d.	s. d.	s. d.	s. d.	s. d.	s. d.
BEMBRIDGE ..	—	-/6½	2/5	3/5	1/10	2/8	-/11	1/1	-/11	1/1	4/8	-/4½	3/9	1/7	1/5	3/2
BRADING ..	-/6½	—	2/1	3/1	1/6	2/4	-/6½	-/7½	-/4½	-/7½	4/5	-/4½	3/5	1/2	1/-	2/10
COWES (or Mill Hill)	2/5	2/1	—	2/2	-/7½	3/8	1/10	1/10	1/10	2/1	—	2/3	2/6	2/2	2/2	1/11
NEWPORT ..	1/10	1/6	-/7½	1/7	—	2/11	1/3	1/4	1/4	1/6	A2/10	1/9	1/11	1/7	1/7	1/4
RYDE, Espl. ..	1/1	-/7½	1/10	2/11	1/4	—	—	—	1/-	1/2	4/1	-/9½	3/3	1/9	1/7	2/8
„ St. John's	-/11	-/6½	1/10	2/10	1/3	1/11	—	—	-/11	1/2	4/1	-/9½	3/2	1/8	1/5	2/6
„ Pier ..	1/1	-/8½	1/11	2/11	1/4	1/7	—	—	1/1	1/3	—	-/11	3/3	1/10	1/8	2/8
ST. HELENS ..	-/4½	-/4½	2/3	3/4	1/9	2/8	-/9½	-/9½	-/7½	-/11	4/8	—	3/8	1/5	1/3	3/1
SANDOWN ..	-/11	-/4½	1/10	2/11	1/4	2/8	-/11	1/-	—	-/4½	4/1	-/7½	3/3	1/1	-/9½	2/8
SHANKLIN ..	1/1	-/7½	2/1	3/1	1/6	2/11	1/2	1/2	-/4½	—	4/5	-/11	3/5	-/9½	-/6½	2/10
WROXALL ..	1/5	1/-	2/2	3/3	1/7	3/2	1/5	1/7	-/9½	-/6½	4/5	1/3	3/7	-/4½	—	3/-
VENTNOR ..	1/7	1/2	2/2	3/3	1/7	3/5	1/8	1/9	1/1	-/9½	4/5	1/5	3/7	—	-/4½	3/-
„ West	—	—	2/1	3/1	1/6	—	—	—	—	—	4/5	—	3/5	—	—	2/10
SEAVIEW ..	1/10	1/4½	2/7	3/8	2/1	2/5	—	—	1/9	1/11	—	1/6½	4/-	2/6	2/4	3/5

★ **1st Class Tickets also issued at Fares about 50% above the 3rd class Fares.**

A Issued on Wednesdays, Saturdays and Sundays only.

Handbills giving full particulars including facilities from certain other stations; also Special Arrangements for Pleasure Parties, obtainable at local stations, or of

Divisional Superintendent, Southern Railway, NEWPORT, I.W.

The Cheapest way to see the Island.

A 7-day "All-Island" Season

Covers the 32 Isle of Wight Stations

(See Map, page 362).

Price, **11/-** 1st Class; **8/-** 3rd Class.

(Children under 14 half-price.)

TRAVEL WHERE YOU LIKE—
WHEN YOU LIKE—
AS OFTEN AS YOU LIKE.

These Tickets are issued from April 1st to October 31st, and are obtainable on demand, any day, at any S.R. Isle of Wight Station.

NOTE:—7-Day Season Tickets as above, and including Southern Railway Steamboats between Ryde, Southsea Pier Heads (Clarence & South Parade) and Portsmouth, 19/- 1st Class; 15/9 3rd Class rail and 1st Class boat, excluding Pier Tolls.

Advert for cheap return tickets 1939.

HOPES, WAR AND RECOVERY

- a bay platform at Shanklin and longer Newport line platform at Sandown so that seven coach sets could reverse clear of the main line,
- a catch point with sand drag on the down line at Smallbrook Junction, water columns in various locations and an additional carriage siding at Ryde St Johns Road,
- two more locomotives and a seven coach train.

Sample timetables were prepared for a more intensive service but a decision was deferred for 12 months. In the meantime, two sets of carriages were lengthened to seven carriages and employed on the short workings from Ryde to Sandown and Shanklin; they could not be used on all trains because of the steep gradients beyond Shanklin and short platforms at Ventnor. The use of seven-carriage trains ended for ever with the onset of war.

More cases of overcrowding were identified and the matter was raised again at the end of 1938. Drawings were prepared for catch points at Smallbrook and an additional siding at Ryde St Johns Road, but the project ground to a halt when it became obvious there would be a war.

On 3rd September, 1939 Britain declared war on Germany and within a week the Island emptied of visitors. On Monday 11th September an emergency timetable was introduced reducing the Ryde-Ventnor line to a mere branch line, with just six return trips a day connecting with the same number of Portsmouth ferries. The absence of visitors was partly offset by an increase in traffic to Cowes, where naval shipbuilding and aircraft production grew to cope with wartime demand. Since over half the 8,000 workers lived outside the town, a relatively generous service operated between Cowes and Newport with some trains continuing to Ryde, Sandown and Shanklin, Ventnor West and Freshwater. Petrol rationing forced the local population to use the railways and on market days trains were packed. The goods trains operated normally.

Preparations for war had been evident since the previous winter when eight pylons were erected on St Boniface Down to serve a radar station. To comply with blackout regulations attempts were made to shade and reduce lighting at stations; even the lamps in signals were said to be too bright! Hazards caused by the blackout took longer to emerge and it was months before white paint was applied to the platform edges and the posts of lamps etc. to make them more visible. The large station name boards had to be removed after it was claimed that they could be seen from the air; glass in vulnerable places such as the platform coverings at Cowes was removed or covered up with netting. A number of air raid shelters were built, including a brick shelter at Cowes beside platform 2 which survived the end of war by many years, at Ventnor in the coal caves and in arches under the road overbridge at Ryde St Johns Road. Every station was equipped with a stretcher and a tall cupboard to keep it in. Much effort was spent in digging foundations for barriers across the tracks to stop tanks driving along the railway.

War brought about a re-imposition of Government control and the recreation of a Railway Executive Committee. The SR departmental committees ceased to meet and were replaced by brief General Manager's meetings. Of the Island's railway staff, J.E. Bell left for war work and never returned; he later became Ashford works manager. Mr Bell's replacement was George Gardener who, apart from a spell absent on war service, remained Assistant for the Isle of Wight until

The white bands painted around structures to aid visibility during the wartime blackout lasted long after the end of hostilities, as seen here at Ventnor in 1950. This also shows to advantage a precast concrete running-in board with local embellishment regarding altitude!

R.A. Silsbury Collection

The aftermath of the collision of 7th April, 1940. 'O2' class No. 16 *Ventnor* suffered front end damage, particularly to the smokebox and was repaired but LBSCR brake third 4167 was less fortunate and was broken up. *IWSR Collection*

steam working ended in 1966. Many staff joined the forces despite the railways being a reserved occupation and women were recruited as ticket collectors, guards and station painters. Rationing brought its own problems as railway workers were entitled to additional food; there was much correspondence over the years about such essentials as cheese, thermos flasks, and as late as 1952 tea, sugar and milk; allotments sprang up on every suitable site.

One accident caused by the blackout took place on 7th April, 1940 when the driver of locomotive No. 16 *Ventnor* approaching Ryde St Johns Road mistook the signals and his train collided with empty carriages in the down loop; damage to the locomotive could be repaired but a brake carriage had to be broken up.

Plans for a more frequent ferry and train service during the summer of 1940 were abandoned after the fall of France. The Government issued an order on 9th July, 1940 prohibiting travel to and from the Isle of Wight and much of the south coast for holiday and pleasure purposes. The threat of invasion resulted in the cutting through of piers (Ryde excluded!) and beaches were barricaded with old rails and obstructions to make landing difficult. Evacuation of the whole Island was briefly considered by various Government departments. Islanders had to look elsewhere for their few pleasures; Alverstone station became popular for outings to the nearby mill, boats on the river and a tea garden. Operation of the mail boat and trains were put back by two hours; they did not revert to pre-war timings until 1947. Numerous unadvertised trains were run for the military, carrying soldiers travelling to and from the Island to bolster its defences or under training. There was a continuing demand for the necessities of life, much of which was supplied locally. Increased agricultural production included tomatoes after the enemy captured the Channel Islands. A repeat of the 1939 emergency timetable, prepared but not introduced, warned that the service might have to be suspended completely; an invasion was a real fear.

If the summer of 1940 was notable for a lack of visitors, it also marked the beginning of air attacks. The first to affect the railways occurred on 12th August when an attack was mounted on the radar station at Ventnor. Bombs fell near Three Arch bridge between Shanklin and Wroxall, damaged the track and closed the line beyond Shanklin for 10 days whilst two unexploded bombs were removed. On the 16th, Ventnor station was closed because of unexploded bombs on the downs above, on the 22nd a bomb exploded above Ventnor tunnel and on the 28th Ventnor West station was damaged by bombs dropped at random by aircraft returning from raids. Bombs damaged Ningwood on 9th September, Petticoat Lane crossing house on the 10th and Sandown on 17th October. Bombs fell near St Helens on 15th and 22nd November, near Whippingham on the 16th and off Ryde Pier on the 22nd. More seriously, at 6.45 pm on 5th December a bomb landed on the track north of Ryde St Johns Road and derailed the locomotive of the 6.35 pm Ryde Pier Head to Ventnor train blocking both lines. All this activity was minor when compared with the bombing at Southampton and Portsmouth.

On 11th March, 1941 an unexploded shell was found north of St Johns Road station. Whitwell and Bembridge stations suffered broken windows on 19th January and 11th April respectively. On 24th May the locomotive and two

Local railwaymen were trained in air raid precaution techniques and exercised regularly. Here a team practice behind the locomotive shed at Ryde St Johns, watched by an assessor.
IWSR Collection

Sugar beet loaded into LBSCR open wagons stand on the back road at Newport awaiting movement to Medina Wharf, viewed from Newport North signal box. *IWSR Collection*

Bomb damage at Three Arch bridge in August 1940.   *IWSR Collection*

Railway staff and service personnel pose with an unexploded bomb near Whippingham in November 1940.   *IWSR Collection*

SOUTHERN RAILWAY.

LONDON (WEST) OPERATING AND COMMERCIAL DIVISIONS.

TELEPHONE:
NEWPORT 33.

Acting
Office of Assistant for Isle of Wight,

NEWPORT, I. OF W.

REFERENCE.
MY M2/EA/17.
YOUR

C.M.E. WATERLOO.

11th. May, 1942.

DAMAGE BY ENEMY ACTION, 4TH/5TH. MAY.

   I give below particulars regarding enemy action on the night of the 4th/5th. inst. during the operation of "Red" Air Raid warnings between the hours of 10.50pm, 4th., and 12.32pm, 5th., and between 3.35am and 4.40am on the 5th.
   Mr. Dabney, Assistant to the London West Divl. Superintendent, Mr. Frampton (Ministry of Home Security), Mr. Figgin (N.U.R), Mr. Smith, (Acting Wharfinger) and myself, together with a Driver, Fireman and Guard and Transporter Drivers and Coal Gang, were present at Medina Wharf during the night of the 4th. in connection with a lighting test, and this party was present when the first raid took place. Whilst taking cover a high explosive bomb dropped close, and Mr. Dabney received several wounds in his right arm, as a result of which he was later conveyed to the Ryde Hospital and has since been transferred to a hospital at Basingstoke. Two Electricians of the Docks Dept., and Driver W. Baines, Loco.Dept., also sustained minor injuries.
   During the first raid the Switch Cabin was hit by shrapnel, and considerably damaged, and the cabin of the North Transporter was burnt out. This damage has resulted in both Transporter being out of action for the time being, but the Docks Electrical Dept have the repair work in hand, and it is hoped to get the South Transporter working at an early date.
   Covered Goods Van No. 46932 which was at Medina Wharf loaded with equipment for the Docks Electrical Dept. was damaged in the second raid by indendiary bombs with the result that the body was burnt beyond repair.
   Delayed action bombs discovered in the vicinity of the railway necessitated cancellation of the train services between Newport and Cowes from 12.5pm on the 5th. inst. until 1.8pm the next day, passengers being conveyed bus.
   During the raids delayed action bombs were dropped in the station yard at Shide. and in land adjoining the running line between Newport and Shide, and in consequence the services between Newport and Merstone were suspended and substituted by road services. The Bomb Disposal Unit is at present dealing with these bombs.
   At Cowes Station the glass in the roof was smashed, and windows broken.

carriages from the 7.12 pm Newport-Cowes train were derailed during bombing of the Cement Mills.

Although most of the damage was relatively minor, the bombing kept the Engineers busy with repairs in addition to work for the war effort. In 1942 unknown facilities were provided at Carisbrooke for the Ministry of Aircraft Production, whilst increased passenger traffic at Shide justified the raising of the platform to a more practical height of 2 ft. 6 in.

The year 1942 was marked by the start of 'hit and run' raids using small numbers of aircraft but there were also several large raids. On the night of 4th-5th May considerable damage was inflicted at Cowes during a raid on the aircraft works and shipyards. Cowes station and other railway buildings in the area escaped relatively lightly but the electric supply at Medina Wharf was put out of action, a covered goods van burned out and two members of staff injured. Services from Cowes to Newport and Newport to Merstone had to be suspended until unexploded bombs could be disposed of; one bomb in Shide goods yard was not removed until 27th May. An anti-aircraft shell exploded in the goods yard at Newport on 25th May damaging a carriage and track.

By October 1942 the passenger train service had settled down to a two-hourly frequency on most lines supplemented by workmen's trains to and from Cowes in the early morning, at lunch time and early evening. The same service operated in 1943 and 1944, with a handful of extra trains during the summer months timed to connect with evening ferry sailings to Portsmouth Harbour.

On 3rd January, 1943 five bombs were dropped at Shanklin killing several people; the station received blast damage to the platform coverings, signal box and station building. During a second raid on 17th February a nearby church received a direct hit. Another raid at Newport on 7th April caused minor damage to the station. Essential dredging at Medina Wharf and in Fishbourne Channel had to be specially authorized. The Island railways lost a valuable traffic when the cement company decided that it would be cheaper to supply cement from the mainland. The cement mills closed in July 1943 and the quarry at Shide was abandoned.

The year 1944 was a mixed year for the Island. St Helens, Whitwell, Cowes, Bembridge, Godshill, Carisbrooke, Sandown and Ventnor West all suffered some damage at various dates. On 16th May a bomb landed on the track near Newchurch station and left a large crater that promptly filled with water; the blast so wrecked the station house that it had to be demolished. Preparations for the invasion of France included the laying of the *Pluto* fuel pipeline along the railway from Whitefield Woods to Sandown, where a pumping station disguised in an ice cream factory marked the start of an underwater section to France. In preparation for an inspection, the weed-killer wagons were taken on a tour of the system on 13th, 14th and 15th June. Orders were given to remove redundant sidings at Ashey, Horringford, Whitwell and Ventnor West (the last two being tracks to end loading docks) but the exercise was abandoned because of a shortage of labour.

Anticipating the end of the war, the 1945 Ryde-Ventnor service was increased to two trains per hour with a third on Saturdays in July and August if required; Sunday trains were hourly. The Ryde-Cowes and Newport-Sandown lines were

WEEKDAYS.

DOWN TRAINS.				Eng.		Freight. Q		Eng.	10.56 a.m. Cowes.		Eng. & Brake.					10.33 a.m. Freight ex V'nor
	a.m.	arr. a.m.	dep. a.m.	arr. a.m.	dep. a.m.	a.m.	arr. a.m.	dep. a.m.	a.m.	arr. a.m.	dep. a.m.	arr. a.m.	dep. a.m.	a.m.	arr. a.m.	dep. a.m.	arr. a.m.	dep. a.m.
Portsmouth Hbr. Southsea (Clarence Pr.) } Boat	8 20														10 55			
Ryde Pier	8 55														11 30			
Ryde Pier Head		9 27	9 25 9 29	9 37	9 35 9 39	9||40										11 47	11 45 11 49	
„ Esplanade		9 32	9 33	9 42	9 43	9||45										11 52	11 53	
„ St. John's Rd				9 50	9 52		10 37	10 38		10 45						12 0	12 1	
Brading					9 55												12 3	
St. Helens				10 3	10 0						11||18					12 11	12 8	
Bembridge																		
Sandown				9 56	9 58		10 42	10 43	10 50			11 35	11 38			12 5	12 7	
Shanklin				10 3	10 5		10 48	10 49				11 43				12 12	12 14	
Wroxall				10 13	10 14		10 57	10 58								12 22	12 23	
Ventnor				10 19			11 3									12 28		
Ashey				9 39														
Haven Street				9 43			Freight. Q											
Wootton				9 47	arr. a.m.	dep. a.m.	arr. a.m.	dep. a.m.								arr. p.m.	dep. p.m.	
Whippingham				9 50														
Ventnor West							10 0				Eng.							
St. Lawrence Halt																		
Whitwell											arr. a.m.	dep. a.m.						
Godshill Halt																		
Sandown					10 11												11 15	11 40
Alverstone					10 15													
Newchurch					10 18													
Horringford					10 21													
Merstone				10 25	10 25½		10 35				10||50						12 0	
Blackwater					10 30													
Shide					10 34						10 58					a.m. 50 Eng.		
Pan Lane Siding																		
Newport		9 55	9 58	10 37	10 39						11|| 2		11 20	11||45		12 0	12 10	
Cement Mills													11 25					
Medina Wharf																		
Gas Works Siding																		
Mill Hill				10 7	10 48												12 9	
Cowes		10 9		10 50												11||55	12 11	

DOWN TRAINS.			SX 'Q' 12.0 noon Shanklin.		10.33 a.m. Freight. Ventnor.				50	12.58 p.m. Cowes.		50 Engine.					
		arr. a.m.	dep. a.m.	arr. p.m.	dep. p.m.	arr. p.m.	dep. p.m.	p.m.	arr. p.m.	dep. p.m.	p.m.	arr. p.m.	dep. p.m.	p.m.	arr. p.m.	dep. p.m.	arr. p.m.	dep. p.m.
Portsmouth Hbr. Southsea (Clarence Pr.) } Boat											12 55							
Ryde Pier											1 30							
Ryde Pier Head		11 52	11 50 11 54			12 27	12 25 12 29	12 47	12 45 12 49	1||5					1 42	1 40 1 44	1 47	1 45 1 49
„ Esplanade		11 57	11 58			12 32	12 33	12 52	12 53	1||10					1 47	1 48	1 52	1 53
„ St. John's Rd								1 1	1 2								2 1	2 2
Brading								1 15									2 12	
St. Helens								1 17									2 17	
Bembridge						1 23									2 20			
Sandown								1 6	1 8		1 38	1 39				2 6	2 8	
Shanklin								1 15	1 16		1 44					2 13	2||15	
Wroxall								1 24	1 25							2 23	2 24	
Ventnor								1 30								2 29		
Ashey		12 4					12 39								1 54			
Haven Street		12 8				12||43	12 47							1 58	1||59			
Wootton		12 12					12 51								2 3			
Whippingham		12 15					12 54								2 6			
Ventnor West								Freight.										
St. Lawrence Halt																		
Whitwell								arr. p.m.	dep. p.m.									
Godshill Halt																		
Sandown				12 4	12 7	11 50	12 23					1||40						
Alverstone					12 11													
Newchurch					12 14	12 30	12 35											
Horringford					12 17													
Merstone				12 21½	12 43	12 46						1 51						
Blackwater					12 26													
Shide					12 30	12 56			1 37									
Pan Lane Siding																		
Newport		12 20		12 33	12 42	1 1		12 50	1 11	1 42			2|| 0		2 11	2 13		
Cement Mills								1 47										
Medina Wharf																		
Gas Works Siding					12 51										2 22			
Mill Hill								1 20										
Cowes				12 53				1 22							2 24			

Extract from Working Timetable (down trains) beginning 3rd May, 1943.

hourly whilst the Freshwater and Ventnor West lines were two-hourly. Locomotive crews were borrowed from Nine Elms shed, but staff and stock shortages prevented the running of through trains apart from 'The Tourist'. Railway traffic exceeded that carried in 1937, even though the numbers of passengers using the ferries were 25 per cent below 1937 levels.

A programme to repair and repaint bridges, culverts, signal boxes and station buildings began in 1945. Mill Hill tunnel had been repaired during the war but suffered from poor drainage. The permanent way had been relaid using flat bottom rails in 1925, but during 1945 there were two breaks of rail so the tunnel was closed between 2nd and 16th February, 1946 to renew drains, ballast and track, the latter using bull head rails on steel sleepers. Some dredging was carried out at Ryde Pier and in Fishbourne Creek ready for the start of the season. A fitter was killed when he fell from a ladder at Medina Wharf on 23rd February.

The 1946 summer service was a repeat of 1945, except that one of the Saturday Ryde-Ventnor trains non-stopped the Ryde stations. On Sundays the Portsmouth-Ryde ferries operated a half-hourly service if required and additional trains to Ventnor were put on to connect with them; there was also a Sunday train between Shanklin and Freshwater.

The year 1947 began with a period of very severe weather, said to have been the worst in living memory, and Britain ground to a halt amidst severe coal shortages. Instructions were given that the summer service be reduced to save coal and the official timetable advertised a distinctly inferior service. Hourly ferries were met at Ryde by an hourly train on the Ventnor line during the week. A half-hourly ferry service on Saturdays was matched by the same frequency to Ventnor, with extra workings to Sandown and Shanklin at lunch times and in the afternoons. A daily parcels train from Ryde to Ventnor ran if required and a through train from Shanklin to Freshwater was curious by having no return working! To what extent the printed timetable can be relied on is unclear as there were 2,500,000 visitors to the Island that year, for which the ferries ran unadvertised workings connecting with many 'ghost' trains. On a more positive note, a five day (Monday to Friday) Isle of Wight runabout ticket was advertised at 13s. 9d. first class and 10s. third for the summer season; 20,168 tickets were sold bringing in £9,553 18s. 1d. and all 11,394 copies of a special timetable folder had been sold at 2d. apiece. The exercise was so successful that all restrictions on the issue of cheap tickets were removed.

Ryde Corporation gave up its tenancy of Ryde's promenade pier in April 1944, but other tenants had more faith in the future. In 1947, £1,450 was spent on repairs to the tramway station and the down railway platform at Ryde Esplanade. At St Helens, the Duver wall and huts (IWR Metropolitan Railway carriage bodies) were leased to C.J. Coombes for seven years at £150 plus repairs estimated at £350. Elsewhere, the coal merchants Jolliffe Bros were reconstituted as Wood & Jolliffe Co. and numerous leases for offices and coal stores at stations passed to the new firm.

During an inspection of the Island railways in June 1944 permission was given to proceed with several improvements. In preparation for a push-pull train on the Bembridge branch, a drawing was prepared in 1946 for a standpipe

Inspection of the Island's railways by top brass in July 1944. *Above:* at Ryde St Johns Road. *Below:* at Ningwood. *(Both) IWSR Collection*

HOPES, WAR AND RECOVERY

at Brading because the water tower was at the wrong end of the station; the standpipe was never installed because none of the Ryde locomotives were equipped with push-pull fittings. Other work to increase the capacity of the Ryde-Ventnor line was not proceeded with.

Gordon Nicholson, who was acting Assistant for the Isle of Wight, explained* that he proposed to operate lengthy push-pull trains on the Ryde-Ventnor line and wanted to see what a more powerful locomotive would do. After a template carriage was run over the Island system in August 1944, a great deal of preparatory work was done during which clearances were checked, track slewed and obstructions removed or repositioned in numerous places. A LBSCR class 'E4' 0-6-2T locomotive, No. 2510, and a 60 ft-long carriage were prepared for transfer in late 1946 but gales and heavy snow delayed their arrival until 22nd February, 1947. When the carriage was taken on a tour of the Island it was found that there was a wide gap between the carriage foot boards and curved platforms, particularly at Ventnor. The gap needed to be even larger for the locomotive so, by the time it entered service in April, No. 2510 had been banned from working into Ventnor station and on the Bembridge branch where it fouled the retaining wall surrounding the turntable. In May the carriage was returned to the mainland in exchange for three shorter SECR carriages, the precursors of a further 49 sent in 1948 and 1949 as replacements for old stock. The locomotive returned to the mainland in April 1949.

On 1st January, 1948 the Southern Railway became part of a national railway network, thus removing control of the Island railways even further away from their users. The *Isle of Wight County Press* marked the end of 85 years of private ownership in the following terms:

> The Island's proud position as one of the most popular holiday resorts in the country has been maintained in no small way by its railway, and it is to its credit that it has several enviable records in dealing with exceptionally heavy traffic. It is fitting at this time to pay tribute to its proud record of service to the travelling public, and to record the appreciation of the courtesy shown by the officials at all times.

---

* *Rails in the Isle of Wight* by P.C. Allen and A.B. MacLeod, George Allen & Unwin Ltd, 1967.

Chapter Eight

Omnibuses, Ferries and Aircraft in SR Days

Private motor cars, omnibuses and lorries made an appearance on the Island's roads early in the 20th century but horse-drawn transport continued to be the norm. The Great War changed everything. Ex-servicemen, who had learned to drive when in military service, used their gratuities to buy army surplus vehicles and set themselves up in transport businesses. People soon discovered that buses could serve places not reached by railways and fares were cheaper. Equally, lorries were cheap to operate and reduced transhipment costs. The railway companies responded by offering discounted fares but damaging strikes in 1919 and 1921 badly affected their standing as transport undertakings. The Government did the railways no favours by fixing most passenger fares and goods rates that could be readily undercut by competitors who gained a large amount of business hitherto carried by rail.

Omnibuses

In 1921 Dodson Brothers, trading as the Vectis Bus Service, began operating buses in competition with the Island railways and some long-standing operators. The business expanded rapidly, particularly after more railway strikes in January 1924 and May 1926. To the chagrin of railwaymen, the firm gained much public support by operating additional services. A devastating fire at its Newport garage on 2nd October, 1927 destroyed several buses, but was only a temporary setback.

The railway companies appreciated that a decline in railway passengers might be reversed or stemmed if they took an interest in omnibus services. The four regional railway companies placed Bills before Parliament and in 1928 the Southern Railway (Road Transport) Act gave the SR powers to operate buses. The Southern Vectis Omnibus Company Ltd (SVOC) was formed and purchased the Vectis bus business with effect from 1st March, 1929. The Chairman of the company was Gilbert Szlumper and a Director was Charles de Pury; he was soon replaced by Alistair MacLeod. The assets of the Vectis company were paid for in shares that Dodson Brothers later sold to the Tilling and British Automobile Traction group, owners of several regional bus companies. SVOC consolidated its position by purchasing the stage carriage businesses of several small operators to create a comprehensive network of routes.

The SR had some agreements with local operators that it inherited from the Island railway companies. A.H. Creeth & Sons, who operated Clarkson steam buses for many years, carried excursion passengers to Seaview by char-a-banc at the rate of 9*d*. per return journey, whilst Messrs Barton ran motor excursions between Newport and Carisbrooke Castle at the same price. Passengers were charged 2*s*. 3*d*. per adult for the journey from Ventnor to Blackgang Chine by

OMNIBUSES, FERRIES AND AIRCRAFT IN SR DAYS

Mr Sprake and in 1924 the SR was offering combined rail and motor excursions to Totland Bay and Alum Bay. All this contract work was transferred to SVOC in 1930.

Local traffic gradually shifted to buses. The SR responded by running more trains and offering cheap fares after 10 am; the return rail fare was often less than a single bus fare. From June 1931 holders of bus tickets were allowed to use certain railway lines for the return journey; four years later the facility was extended throughout the Island. The principal bus garage was at Newport but there were a number of satellite depots in other towns. In 1937 SVOC was granted a 99 year lease on railway land in Park Road, Ryde for a bus garage at a rent of £15 a year; the previous tenants paid £12 15s. 5d.!

Increasing traffic placed greater demands on the roads and forced local authorities to institute repairs and lay a tarmac surface. The railways gained some traffic from carrying road stone, but the respite was short-lived and by the end of the decade road transport had become a potent competitor to the railways.

Services were cut back following the introduction of petrol rationing and requisition of buses for war work, priority being given to workers travelling to and from Cowes. The end of the war was followed by a lengthy period of recovery, but by the time the company was nationalised in 1948 steady progress had been made in making good shortages.

A Southern Vectis double-deck bus at Ryde Esplanade. *IWSR Collection*

SR Ferries

The SR inherited from the LSWR and LBSCR two of the three ferry routes between the mainland and the Isle of Wight, namely Portsmouth-Ryde and Lymington-Yarmouth. On the Ryde route were five paddle steamers, a tug and towboats. Based at Lymington were two passenger-carrying paddle steamers, tugs and more towboats.

The Island's politicians were dissatisfied with the service to Ryde and in March 1923 a deputation met the SR General Manager, Sir Herbert Walker. Shortly afterwards the SR introduced cheap weekly tickets on the ferries. This wiped out competitors who tried to re-establish cross-Solent ferry services to Seaview and Bembridge; only a small launch service continued to operate from Ryde to Seaview.

Vessels operating between Portsmouth and Ryde called at Clarence Pier, Southsea *en route* except at peak times when Southsea was served by a separate shuttle service. An advertised half-hourly frequency was operated on summer Saturdays, although in practice every available vessel was in service. *Shanklin* was delivered in 1924 as a replacement for a wartime casualty, followed by *Merstone* and *Portsdown* in 1928; they were copies of the existing paddle steamers with a slight increase in carrying capacity. *Southsea* and *Whippingham* (originally to have been named *Sandown*), delivered in 1930, were larger and useful for weekday excursions to Sandown, Shanklin (after a new concrete landing stage was completed for the 1931 season), Ventnor, 'Round the Island', Southampton Docks and in 1932 to Bournemouth; during Navy Week there were sailings to Portsmouth Dockyard. These excursions were liberally advertised in the local press and attracted a considerable traffic that had been carried by the Southampton steamers and other private operators. *Sandown*, launched on 1st May, 1934, was slightly smaller than *Whippingham* and *Southsea* but had better accommodation in poor weather. *Ryde*, launched on 23rd April, 1937, was a sister to *Sandown* and completed the replacement of the pre-Grouping vessels.

Arrangements for transporting vehicles and livestock had not kept up with demand. A tug and towboats operated between slipways at Broad Street, Portsmouth and George Street, Ryde. Each tow boat could carry no more than five cars, only 1,163 were carried in 1923, and traffic was being lost to the SR's rival at Cowes. Ryde's slipway could not be used at low tide and during poor weather the service was frequently suspended or diverted to East Cowes. During an inspection in August 1923 four alternatives were discussed:

- dredging at Ryde so that the slipway could be used at all stages of the tide was prohibitively expensive
- a 5 ton crane could lift cars out of the barges onto Ryde Pier but a 2s. 6d. toll to the pier company and the danger cars posed to pedestrians on the promenade pier would be unacceptable
- Medina Wharf was too far from Portsmouth and unacceptable to car owners
- near Fishbourne was a two acre site adjoining Wootton Creek that could be developed

On 10th March, 1925 construction began at Fishbourne of a slipway and facilities, including waiting rooms for ladies and gentlemen, a telephone and a petrol pump from which motorists could purchase 'No. 1 Perfection motor spirit' (bought by the SR at 1s. 5d. per gallon but sold at the retail price of 1s. 7½d.). There was a house for staff and standing for 15 cows (with tethering accommodation), pens for 100 pigs and six boars. An improved access road to Fishbourne Lane and other additions raised the cost from an estimated £16,000 to £19,230. Difficulties in dredging a suitable channel meant that a planned opening in August 1925 was delayed until 15th March, 1926, initially with two trips a day; the tow boats carried about 4,000 cars that year.

On 27th January, 1927 the SR Board placed an order for a vessel capable of carrying 18 cars for £12,700 (it actually cost £13,254). With its flat deck *Fishbourne* was similar to a barge that had been fitted with an engine and end loading ramps (originally they were hand operated). Apart from a small deckhouse the machinery was below the deck. *Fishbourne* came into service on 23rd July and proved most successful, despite taking almost an hour to make the crossing. The tow boats were kept for emergencies and livestock 'on the hoof' but that traffic soon transferred to lorries. The tow boats became redundant after *Wootton* entered service on 21st June, 1928 and *Hilsea* on 14th June, 1930. A healthy increase in traffic fully justified the SR's investment.

Numbers carried	Portsmouth-Fishbourne			Lymington-Yarmouth	
Year	Cars	Lorries	Passengers	Cars	Passengers
1927	7,002	708	19,795	not known	
1929	12,799	984	36,259	1,778	239,854
1932	15,409	1,019	41,911	1,738	180,099
1935	20,402	1,264	52,290	2,251	205,246
1938	23,219	1,979	60,611	4,217	225,784

The Lymington-Yarmouth route had eight sailings a day during the 1927 season, of which three continued to Totland Bay (a service to Alum Bay ended at the start of World War I and that to Totland Bay soon vanished). A paddle steamer *Freshwater* was delivered in 1927 but the tow boats continued to carry motor cars, cargo and livestock.

The introduction of vehicle ferries between Portsmouth and Fishbourne was not repeated at Lymington and Yarmouth, at least for a time. Frank Aman, who had been a FYN Director, made an agreement with the SR in November 1934 to take over the ferry service. He formed the Isle of Wight Ferry Company to purchase vehicle ferries and begin operations by 30th June, 1936; the SR would receive £63,500 for land at Lymington, the existing ferries, tow boats and goodwill. Land was purchased at Fort Victoria west of Yarmouth on the Freshwater peninsula and two vehicle ferries that had operated between Birkenhead and Liverpool were reserved by the company. In July 1935 the ferry company gave formal notice that it would be applying to Parliament for powers to introduce a service between Keyhaven and Fort Victoria in place of the Lymington-Yarmouth route. The Isle of Wight County Council and local councils at Yarmouth, Lymington, Totland and Cowes all lodged objections. Mr Aman was unable to raise the necessary capital and the scheme was abandoned.

Excursions from Portsmouth or Ryde 1924-1939

Year	Event	Numbers carried
1924	Royal Naval review	5,809
1925	Cowes regatta	4,918
	'Great Attack on Southsea Castle'	2,665
1926	Ryde Sports Club to Southampton	612
1927	Ryde Sports Club to Southampton	612
1928	Cowes regatta and fireworks	9,618
	Cruises in the Solent	189
1929	Southampton docks cruises (June)	1,153
	Southampton dock excursions (July)	85
	Other special excursions	5,842
	Cowes regatta and fireworks	6,030

Numbers carried

	March	April	May	June	July	August	September	October
1930		3,140	8,841	12,011	15,092	42,858	24,932	
1931		1,158	2,653	11,159	30,258	57,198	28,301	
1932			2,892	11,169	24,857	75,957	22,300	
1933		549	3,013	7,740	35,259	61,799	23,638	
1934			2,360	9,650	33,255	56,077	23,374	
1935			4,427	7,404	45,094	60,036	11,929	
1936	3,031	22,213	7,902	9,458	24,227	54,647	15,246	1,639
1937			695	6,707	28,998	51,848	15,199	375
1938	329	392	572	5,798	20,589	39,513	16,053	
1939			1,458	3,620				

In 1936 the SR had obtained Parliamentary powers to purchase additional land and on 17th February, 1937 the Docks and Marine Committee authorized the expenditure of £27,000 on a vehicle ferry and £13,000 on improving the slipways at Lymington and Yarmouth. It was hoped that the £1,500 annual loss on working the route could be reduced by laying up *Freshwater* in winter and withdrawing the tow boats. The dangers in the existing arrangements came to the fore on 16th July, 1937 when a tow boat (No. 4) being towed by *Solent* collided with a collier *Obsidian* moored off Yarmouth Pier and sank with its load of two motor cars and containing five occupants, an empty lorry with its driver and some cargo. The humans were taken aboard an accompanying motor boat but the tow boat and its contents were lost.

On 22nd September, 1937 a contract was signed with William Denny & Bros. of Dumbarton for the construction of a vessel similar to the Portsmouth-Fishbourne trio, but with more passenger accommodation. The SR subsequently decided to adopt the Voith Schneider propulsion system to improve manoeuvrability in the shallow waters of the Lymington river which increased the price to £29,800. *Lymington* was launched on 1st April, 1938 but broke down soon after entering service and, when difficulty was experienced in obtaining spare parts from Germany, the tow boats came back into use.

Following the outbreak of war, ferry services were reduced to winter frequencies, the Portsmouth-Ryde route being worked by two vessels with a third in reserve. The threat of air raids in Portsmouth, Gosport and Southampton prompted the evacuation of 126,914 school children, teachers and helpers. In all 23,800 were to be taken by ferry from Clarence Pier, Southsea to Ryde and by train to different parts of the Island. However, when the evacuation was carried out on 1st and 2nd September, 1939 only 4,040 travelled to the Island on the first day and 1,070 on the second. The expected air raids failed to materialise so many soon drifted back to their homes. The exercise had to be repeated on 27th and 28th June, 1940 but this time plans to send 4,500 to the Isle of Wight were abandoned. During the next month there were more evacuations from towns all along the south coast and restrictions were placed on travel to the Island.

The War Office requisitioned *Sandown, Ryde* and *Southsea* for conversion to mine sweepers. *Southsea* struck a mine on 16th February, 1940 when mine sweeping off the Tyne and, although beached, was declared a total loss. All vessels that could be spared were involved in the evacuation from Dunkirk* and towards the end of 1940 *Freshwater* was taken for use as a port guard ship. Twelve months later *Whippingham* was requisitioned when at Southampton undergoing an overhaul but, before it could enter war service, was extensively damaged when the starboard paddle box received a direct hit during an air raid.

Portsmouth suffered badly from bombing and Clarence Pier was an early casualty. The SR did its best to maintain a regular service between Portsmouth and Ryde but the vessels were frequent targets. The greatest misfortune occurred on the night of Saturday 20th September, 1941 when *Portsdown* was working the 4.00 am mail service to Ryde; a mine exploded, breaking the vessel in half and killing eight crew, 12 service personnel and three civilian passengers. One of the crew later told the *County Press:*

* Their exploits are recounted in *Isle of Wight Here We Come* by H.J. Compton, Oakwood Press, 1997.

SOUTHERN RAILWAY

ATTRACTIVE EXCURSIONS TO LONDON
EVERY SUNDAY (until Sept. 24)

Depart			from	Fare	Depart			from	Fare
a.m.	a.m.	a.m.			a.m.	a.m.	a.m.		
7.30	—	—	Freshwater	11/3	8. 8	9.26	9.56	Cowes	10/5
7.35	—	—	Yarmouth	11 2	8.10	9.27	9.57	Mill Hill	
8.42	9.42	10.42	Ventnor	10 2	8.23	9.38	10.38	Newport	9/8
8.47	9.47	10.47	Wroxall	9 11	9.15	10.15	11.15	Ryde St. J. Rd.	8 8
8.54	9.54	10.54	Shanklin	9 8	9.20	10.20	11.20	,, Espl'd'e	8/4
9. 1	10. 1	11. 1	Sandown	9 5	9.35	10.35	11.35	,, Pier H'd.	
9. 7	10. 7	11. 7	Brading	9/1					

RETURN SAME DAY FROM WATERLOO 4.50 p.m. or 6.50 p.m.
See Bill 1331

ATTRACTIVE SEA TRIPS
by the FINE NEW STEAMERS "SOUTHSEA" and "WHIPPINGHAM,"
Weather and other circumstances permitting.

EVERY WEDNESDAY until 6th SEPTEMBER
ROUND THE ISLAND

From
Ryde Pier 2.0 p.m.

FARE Including Pier Tolls

Arriving Back
about
6.15 p.m.

THURSDAYS 24th & 31st August and 7th September
TO BOURNEMOUTH

From
Ryde Pier 2.0 p.m.
(Allowing about 1¾ hours ashore).

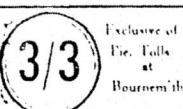
RETURN FARE Exclusive of Pier Tolls at Bournem'th

Return Bournemouth
Pier 5.30 p.m.
Back about 7.30 p.m.

TO SOUTHAMPTON DOCKS
for Inspection of R.M.S. "QUEEN MARY"
TUESDAY 29th AUGUST

Leaving Ryde Pier 12.30 p.m.   Return from Docks 4.15 p.m., due back about 5.15 p.m.

RETURN FARES :	Including Admission to Liner.		Not including Admission to Liner.	
	Adults	Children	Adults	Children
	7 8	6 4	2 8	1 4
	Including Pier Tolls.			

Children 3 and under 14 years half fare except where otherwise shown.

For full particulars of these and other excursions, bookings from surrounding stations, "MONTHLY RETURN" TICKETS, Cheap Day Tickets, etc., see handbills, or write or 'phone your local Stationmaster.

Advert for excursions in *Isle of Wight County Press*, 19th August, 1939.

We left Portsmouth Harbour Pier at 4.00 a.m., and I took up my position as lookout in the bows. After we had cleared the Portsmouth Harbour Channel buoys, I reported this to Captain Chandler on the bridge, and the vessel was then rounded up to go through the swashway to continue our journey to Ryde. About a minute after this, and before the vessel had completed her turn, I heard a scraping noise along the port side of the ship, and then, after what must have been a few seconds, there was a terrific explosion. I was looking out across the port bow, and I was thrown into the sea. When I came to the surface, I grasped a piece of floating wood and swam to the after port side sponson, where I climbed on board and assisted in getting out the lifeboats, both of which were lowered and loaded with passengers.

After *Shanklin* was slightly damaged at Ryde Pier on 11th December, 1941 a vessel had to be hired from Red Funnel. *Solent* was borrowed from the Lymington-Yarmouth route where *Lymington* was left to soldier on with the tow boats and occasional assistance from one of the Portsmouth-Fishbourne vessels. Just before 'D' day, the Portsmouth-Ryde service was suspended and the passenger ferries requisitioned to take troops to their ships; passengers for Ryde had to use the Fishbourne service. One pilot who flew over the armada later recalled that 'The Isle of Wight was surrounded and appeared as if it was being towed out to sea'.

When restrictions on travel to the Island were relaxed temporarily in 1943 passengers sometimes had to be left behind. The restrictions were finally removed in mid-1944 when it was warned that '... some system of regulation of passengers to the Island may be necessary'. In September that became fact when local passengers travelling from Portsmouth had to be restricted to 300 a boat leaving the remaining 500 spaces for passengers travelling from London and elsewhere. A large number were servicemen going on or coming off leave.

Following the end of war, *Ryde* was brought back into use for the beginning of the summer timetable on 7th July, 1945. It was just possible to maintain a two-hourly service with extra sailings at busy periods. The return of *Solent* to Lymington permitted an increase in the service to Yarmouth in the hope that it would relieve pressure at Ryde. *Freshwater* returned in late 1945 but *Whippingham* did not re-enter SR service for another 12 months.

Nos. carried	Portsmouth-Ryde	Portsmouth-Fishbourne			Lymington-Yarmouth	
Year	Passengers	Cars	Lorries	Passengers	Cars	Passengers
1944	1,142,034	2,362	8,318	20,562	2,849	114,439
1945	2,163,917	7,362	4,473	24,819	11,267	261,832
1946	2,642,615	18,177	3,620	49,920	24,381	343,600
1947	2,772,706	19,422	3,700	54,708	32,488	360,618

The SR invested in new vessels to make good wartime losses and cater for growing traffic. For the Portsmouth-Ryde route, William Denny & Bros designed a broad-beamed diesel-powered screw vessel with a shallow draft suitable for all states of the tide. *Southsea* and *Brading* were delivered to Portsmouth in October 1948; they immediately proved their worth during 'The Great Fog' from 27th November to 1st December when the radar-equipped vessels maintained the service with only a handful of delays and cancellations.

One of the Southern Railway-built paddle steamers, *Whippingham*, approaches Ryde pier.
IWSR Collection

MV *Southsea* on passage in Spithead in 1949. IWSR Collection

OMNIBUSES, FERRIES AND AIRCRAFT IN SR DAYS

For the Lymington-Yarmouth ferry route, a second vehicle ferry, *Farringford*, was delivered in March 1948 as a replacement for *Solent* and the towboats. *Farringford* relied on paddle wheels instead of the revolutionary Voith Schneider propulsion system carried by *Lymington*. Given *Lymington's* past problems, the towboats were not immediately disposed of and two were still at Lymington until at least 1950.

From 1st June, 1951 first class accommodation was abolished on the Portsmouth-Ryde ferries. This increased circulation space and speeded up loading and unloading. The third class monthly return fare was increased from 3s. 3d. to 3s. 8d. to make good the loss of revenue. A third diesel vessel, *Shanklin*, came into service on 18th June, replacing the last of the small paddle steamers, leaving the three large coal-fired paddle steamers *Whippingham*, *Sandown* and *Ryde* for cruises and relief work.

Aircraft

Apart from a short-lived flying boat service in 1919, there were no scheduled flights to the Isle of Wight before the late 1920s. However, aircraft did contribute to the SR's income when special trains were run from all over the south of England to see seaplanes compete for the Schneider Trophy. First presented in 1913 by Jacques Schneider, a French aviation patron, the annual competition was made biennial in 1927 and came to the Solent in 1929. Held during the August Bank Holiday, the race followed a triangular route from East Cowes to West Wittering and a point opposite the entrance to Bembridge harbour. The ferries operated excursions and special trains were run within the Island to bring spectators to Ryde Pier or Cowes where stands were erected. The competition was repeated in 1931, but there were only two challengers, and when the Italians withdrew at the last moment the British team was left to fly the course in isolation; this was the last year that the competition was held.

On 27th June, 1932 the Portsmouth, Southsea and Isle of Wight Aviation Company began operating an air passenger service between newly-opened airfields at Portsmouth and Ryde; free road transport to the town centres was included in the (6s. single, 10s. return) fares. The service quickly expanded to include Shanklin and other mainland destinations. On 12th May, 1933 Spartan Airlines commenced operating flights from Cowes and Ryde to London (Heston). The SR had obtained an Act of Parliament giving it powers to operate air services and made an agreement with Spartan for a jointly-run service connecting Cowes, Ryde and London (Croydon), with free transport to Victoria and the Island town centres. It began operating on 1st May, 1934 under the title *Southern Air Services*. Tickets costing 30s. single or 50s. return could be purchased at railway stations for a journey that was advertised as taking just 1½ hours between London and the Isle of Wight; the return ticket was valid for return by rail first class if required. An Air Service clerk was stationed at Cowes station and provided with a telephone so that he could contact the airfield. The mainland terminal was transferred to Gatwick in 1936. On the same day the Portsmouth, Southsea and Isle of Wight Aviation Company introduced a Ryde-

Heston route, but there were plenty of passengers for both airlines and they could barely cope at peak times.

Meanwhile the Southern, Great Western, London Midland & Scottish, London North Eastern railways and Imperial Airways formed Railway Air Services Ltd with each of the five companies holding a 20 per cent share. On 30th July, 1934 it began a service connecting Birmingham, Bristol, Southampton and Cowes; again, tickets could be purchased at railway stations. From 25th May, 1935 flights were diverted to Portsmouth and the Island was served by a connecting flight between Sandown, Cowes and Southampton, operated under charter by Spartan Airlines and advertised as Railway Air Services-Spartan Airlines. A new route from Sandown, Cowes, Southampton, Portsmouth and Shoreham, where the airfield was close to a SR station, gave connections that made it possible to fly to almost every town of any size in Britain.

The number of travellers during the summer season could not compensate for operating losses during the rest of the year, despite the high fares. On 15th February, 1937 the SR Aviation Committee was told that between 23rd May and 3rd October, 1936 two aircraft had made 698 Gatwick-Ryde flights, 528 Ryde-Cowes and 84 direct trips between Gatwick and Cowes carrying 2,964 passengers. SR receipts amounted to £1,531 but its share of the operating costs was £3,664; support for the air service was abandoned and Spartan Airlines, which had become a subsidiary of British Airways, ceased operating.

From 1st July, 1937 the Channel Air Services company began operating a route to the Isle of Wight. In 1938 the Great Western and Southern Railways Airlines company was formed, owned 25 per cent by the two railway companies and 50 per cent by Channel Air Services. The various air services were gradually taken over and a pooling arrangement was made with the Portsmouth, Southsea and Isle of Wight Aviation Company. The services disappeared when war broke out on 3rd September, 1939 and, unlike other forms of local transport, have never been re-established.

In the next chapters we will see how road transport and the ferries came to threaten the existence of the Island railways.

Chapter Nine

Nationalisation and the First Closures

The election of a Labour Government in 1945 brought with it a commitment to nationalise Britain's transport system. When a Bill was presented to Parliament in the Autumn of 1946, Hugh Dalton, Chancellor of the Exchequer, declared that 'this railway system of ours is a very poor bag of physical assets', comments designed to justify the taking of the railways from their shareholders at the cheapest possible cost to the Exchequer. Coming so soon after the end of war, some thought the timing of the Bill was unfortunate especially as state control in other countries had been dismal failures. Nevertheless, the proponents of Nationalisation gained the upper hand and the Bill became law. The 1947 Transport Act created a British Transport Commission to oversee the railways, road transport, docks and inland waterways. The Southern Railway became the Southern Region of the Railway Executive on 1st January, 1948; the title British Railways (BR) was used for publicity purposes but before 1963 had no legal status.

Nationalisation was carried out relatively cheaply because shareholders were given British Transport stock paying 3 per cent per annum. The burden of servicing this debt fell on the railways, as did a portion of the Commission's management costs. Growing staff, coal and material costs meant that it was not long before passenger services were being run 'at a substantial loss'. The Commission was expected to break even financially and integrate the various forms of transport; cross-subsidies were discouraged.

The railways, including the SR, had no established policy of branch line closures, but that had changed well before April 1952 when the Parliamentary Secretary to the Minister of Transport declared: 'We must be realistic and it must be admitted that the closing of ... Branch Lines would have been inevitable, with or without Nationalisation'. The 1947 Act anticipated this by introducing a procedure to withdraw services without the need to obtain an expensive Act of Parliament in every case. In the case of branch lines, a withdrawal of services inevitably resulted in permanent closure.

The Isle of Wight railways were heavily dependent on the holiday trade. That might have passed unnoticed were it not for a letter from F.W. Bright, Secretary of the Isle of Wight Chamber of Commerce, to the Chief Regional Officer of the Southern Region on 23rd November, 1949:

> It is felt that the Isle of Wight is, perhaps, in a peculiar position. The Railway System, except on Saturdays, is lightly loaded even in the peak summer months, the buses on the other hand are fully loaded in the winter months and, in the summer, definitely overcrowded. It is commonplace for overcrowded buses to pass almost empty trains, whilst bus queues, particularly in country districts and between terminal points, are undiminished for long periods.
>
> Despite Cheap-Day tickets, there is still, generally speaking, a higher return fare payable by train than comparable road services, so the travelling public are influenced to use road transport in preference to the railway.

Mr Bright cannot have known what forces he unleashed. The letter was passed to the British Transport Commission which responded:

> The Isle of Wight would appear to be an ideal place in which to experiment with a common commercial service covering both passenger and goods. It should also be possible to achieve equalisation of fares without creating precedents for the mainland: the experimental 1¼d. fare might be tried.

To consider the points made in the letter, a committee was set up of senior officers from Southern Region, Southern Vectis Omnibus Company and Carter Paterson, road transport subsidiaries of the British Transport Commission. Since they had to look solely at the integration of passenger and freight services within the Isle of Wight, the ferries were not represented; this was a pity because they were profitable and the brightest jewels in the crown of the Commission. The committee established that railway fares were charged at a rate of 2½d. a mile and cheap fares 1¼d. Bus fares varied according to the level of competition but approximated to 1¼d. a mile. An increase in bus fares was not recommended because it would place the bus company at a disadvantage. Equally, a reduction in railway fares to the level charged by SVOC 'could only result in a loss of revenue to the Commission'. A detailed census of passenger traffic showed that the railways were essential for the dispersal of passengers arriving by ferry at Ryde at peak times but could not operate competitively elsewhere within the Island. The committee concluded that there was no alternative to line closures.

Meanwhile, another part of the British Transport Commission had been looking at the viability of the Isle of Wight railways. In March 1949 the Railway Executive created a Branch Lines Committee to which each Region put forward suitable candidates for closure. The committee dealt with relatively few branch lines in the south of England but in January 1951 issued a report that 'demonstrated the completely unremunerative nature of *all* the Island railways'. Figures were produced that ignored any contributory income received from passengers who used the mainland railways and ferries to reach the Island:

Income and losses for each line	Income £	Expenditure £	Interest* £	Loss £
Ryde-Ventnor	87,832	112,846	42,462	67,476
Ryde-Cowes	48,061	97,103	20,583	69,625
Newport-Sandown	16,234	36,281	10,072	30,119
Freshwater line	7,860	34,469	10,430	37,039
Bembridge branch	3,531	18,491	4,519	19,479
Ventnor West branch	1,291	14,418	4,865	17,992
other receipts	26,956			-26,765
Total	191,765	313,608	92,931	214,774

Contributory income from	Passengers £	Parcels £	Total £
	638,065	77,445	715,510

* The interest on capital bore no relation to the line's original costs but represented a share of the railways' total interest bill.

The signal is off for the departure of the Benbridge train standing off the picture as 'O2' class No. 19 *Osborne* in malachite green livery pulls into Brading station with a train from Ryde Pier Head. The bracket signal is a recent replacement for a wooden IWR example, 26th June, 1950.
Pamlin Prints

The committee accepted that any attempt to close the whole system would provoke considerable opposition and be difficult to carry through. Even so, several lines were *prima facie* cases for closure. A member of the Railway Executive added: 'I think it is clear that no means are likely to be found, either by making economies, or by securing additional traffic, to place the railways in the Isle of Wight on a self-supporting basis'. The policy of closure was settled.

The Ventnor West branch had long been regarded as a candidate for closure because it did not generate enough income to pay the wages of the 18 staff employed on the line, let alone other costs. In June 1951 BR announced that it proposed to withdraw services on the branch. Ventnor Urban District Council duly lodged objections but the Isle of Wight County Council asked only that an adequate alternative bus service be provided. The South-Eastern area committee of the Transport Users' Consultative Committee (TUCC), a creation of the 1947 Transport Act, met in private on 1st July, 1952 to consider any objections. The committee heard that passenger traffic had been lost to the omnibus and BR could not justify spending £27,000 on renewing the permanent way; over one poor section the 30 mph speed limit had already been reduced to 15 mph. The committee agreed with BR's wish to withdraw services. Although a deputation of members from Ventnor Council went to Waterloo on 29th August, they failed to gain any concessions and services to Ventnor West were withdrawn with effect from Monday 15th September.

The process of closing more lines had already begun. On 4th May, 1951 a Joint Working Party was formed to discuss how the road subsidiaries of the British Transport Commission might take traffic displaced by the closure of all but the Ryde-Ventnor line. There was widespread alarm when its existence became public in August, but members of the Isle of Wight County Council and Chamber of Commerce were assured that their views could be put to the working party. The Islanders submitted a memorandum that later formed the basis of the County Council's opposition to the closures.

The last day at Ventnor West, 13th September, 1952. The morning shift pose with 'O2' class No. 27 *Merstone*, which carried a simple headboard 'BR Farewell to Ventnor West 1900-1952'. *Left to right*, on the locomotive are fireman Bob Burch and driver Monty Harvie, whilst on the ground are porter Alec Widger, station master Mr Harris and porter? *IWSR Collection*

;E1' class No. 2 *Yarmouth* departs Newport with a goods train on 17th September, 1953. The train significantly includes the three LBSCR cattle wagons and a horse box on their final journey to St Helens Quay where they were broken up. Soon the locomotive itself will follow them to oblivion. *Pamlin Prints*

Mr Gardener, Assistant for the Isle of Wight, convinced his fellow members of the working party that the 'price' of closing the Ryde-Cowes line was not worthwhile. The Ryde Pier tramway was working to capacity on summer Saturdays and could not cope with more passengers unless £24,000 was spent on reconstruction to take larger vehicles. At Ryde St Johns Road an unloading ramp costing £1,500 was needed for locomotive coal carried by road from Medina Wharf (ongoing road costs for the Ventnor line's requirement of 5,500 tons were assessed at £2,000 a year). To replace facilities at Newport a siding for carriage cleaning was needed costing £3,000 and accommodation for carriage painting, lighting and stores at £4,300. A building also had to be found to house the Assistant for the Isle of Wight and his staff. It would cost £7,000 alone to lay a road surface along Medina Wharf and if the access road was improved, the owners Fraser & White Ltd might be tempted to compete for the traffic. All this work would cost upwards of £50,000 and delay closure of the Cowes line for three years. In the meantime the Civil Engineer's Department had to spend £5,000 on repairs that would extend the line's life for at least five years. This justified a 'gradual approach of a policy of closing ... and... when the time comes for Ryde-Cowes to be closed it can be done in a more favourable atmosphere...' No such limitations existed on the other lines.

When the conclusions of the working group became public, the uproar generated a flood of letters to local newspapers, the Railway Executive, British Transport Commission and the Ministry of Transport. Typical was one from J. Temple-Smith, Secretary of the Cowes Professional and Business Men's Association, to the Ministry on 1st December, 1952:

> It is the opinion of the Association that the reason why the railways on the Island are running at a loss is because the public have been deliberately driven away from using them owing to the incompetent and inefficient manner in which they have been run ....

The furore came to the attention of the national press, including the *Sunday Times*:

> It is more than doubtful if the Island Railways have ever been a paying proposition, but the private enterprise which ran them under the aegis of the Southern Railway would never have been allowed to close them without an Act of Parliament which no Government would have dared pass. The Companies, like many another business concern, had to take the rough with the smooth, and could not expect to make a profit on every department of their activity.

The Bembridge branch had not originally been a candidate for closure because of the traffic it contributed to the Ryde-Ventnor line and the use of St Helens Quay for landing railway stores. However, the road lobby convinced railway managers they could supply the Island by road and within a short time even locomotive boilers began to arrive at Thetis Wharf, Cowes for onward delivery by lorry. The permanent way had not been relaid since the war so its condition was used to justify the introduction of a revised winter timetable on 2nd February, 1953 lengthening journey times to five minutes from Brading to St Helens and another five to Bembridge. This coincided with a letter from BR to the local authorities announcing the withdrawal of services on 8th June, followed by Newport-Sandown, Newport-Freshwater and stations at Ashey, Wootton and Whippingham on 21st September. The June date (two weeks before the Review of the Fleet) was an attempt to get the TUCC to hold an early hearing into the closures. Losses on the Island railways had risen but £90,000 would be saved if the closures were implemented. Figures issued to support the railways' case demonstrated how the burden of servicing old debts had returned to haunt the Island railways.

Income and expenditure year ending 31st December, 1951	Income £	Expenditure £	Interest £	Loss £
all lines	214,630	374,526	159,896	271,173
Whippingham, Wootton & Ashey	2,178	3,101		

The County Council responded by publishing a booklet entitled *The Case for the retention of the Island Railways*. It was pointed out that the closures were not simply a question of profit or loss in an Island heavily dependent for its prosperity on the holiday trade. The railways were an essential component in handling tourist traffic that would otherwise be thrown onto the narrow and winding roads. Quoting figures to show how traffic fluctuated, passenger numbers in week ending 9th August, 1952 were said to be 83 per cent higher than the week of 12th July when the railways made their census. The Bembridge branch might see 2,000 passengers on Saturdays and on 14th July alone 443 passengers arrived at Bembridge by train within one hour. The Newport-Sandown and Freshwater lines each carried about 1,000 passengers a day in each direction during July rising to 1,400 in August; some trains carried 300-400 passengers.

A second booklet *Proposals for reorganisation of services* suggested a range of economies. A summer-only service on the Bembridge branch could be worked by a rail car that would be available for the Freshwater line in winter. Alternatively the Freshwater line could be operated by a push-pull train that was already available. Savings were possible by working the Ryde-Cowes and Newport-Sandown lines together, the introduction of colour light signals would permit the closure of some signal boxes whilst more fast and through trains to Freshwater and Cowes were needed in the summer.

Closure of the Ryde to Ventnor line was also discussed. As an alternative to rebuilding Ryde Pier to take buses, the railway could be retained to a bus station at St Johns Road and a bus-way in place of the railway to Shanklin; the total cost was put at £1,000,000. However, such possibilities were thought to be remote since, as the *County Press* put it, 'it is impracticable to close the major lines under present conditions without seriously impairing the transport system of the Island as to put the clock back many years ...'

The official response to the suggestions made in the booklets was simple. No amount of expenditure on diesel traction, staffing and other economies would make enough impact on the losses.

The size of the opposition clearly surprised BR and the Ministry of Transport. For the first time a County Council was actively opposing a closure aided by local railway staff. During a meeting with staff representatives in April 1953 Mr Hopkins, Chief Regional Officer of Southern Region, complained about the

NATIONALISATION AND THE FIRST CLOSURES

'grape vine' within the Island that anticipated virtually every move the railways were making. The 'strength of the opposition was unprecedented and the tactics such that there was a grave threat, whatever the final outcome, to our maintaining our timetable of closures, more particularly with the Bembridge branch'. An admission that BR intended to close all the Island's railways did nothing for morale; 'the men in London' had nothing to lose because they had interests in road transport. Of 602 staff working in the Island, the jobs of over 20 per cent were already in jeopardy.

Estimated numbers of displaced staff (all departments)	No.
Newport-Sandown	28
Freshwater line	35
Bembridge branch	19
Ventnor West branch	18
and if all the above closed	7
if Whippingham, Wootton and Ashey closed	6
Administrative staff	not stated
Total	113 *

* Later figures quoted 116, not counting redundancies following closure of the locomotive running shed, stores and carriage workshop at Newport.

Two weeks later BR held a strategy meeting with representatives from SVOC and British Road Services (successors to Carter Paterson). They were told of 'concessions' to be announced at the closure hearing, including the reluctant disclosure of certain financial figures, an agreement to keep the Bembridge branch open for the summer and retain Ashey as an unstaffed halt. SVOC was asked to consider providing a bus service along the narrow roads to Alverstone, to avoid retaining a service between Sandown and Alverstone using a push-pull set.

On 11th May, 1953, the Transport Users' Consultative Committee met at Newport to take evidence from the Isle of Wight County Council, Chamber of Commerce and 36 other objectors. The County Council was represented by a barrister, Melford Stevenson, QC (better known for defending Ruth Ellis, the last woman to hang in Britain). Mr Stevenson relied heavily on the contents of the booklets in making a case for the retention of the Island railways as a whole. Mr Hopkins, who presented the case for the railways, duly announced his concessions and tried to divert attention from the financial figures by claiming they were of no consequence:

> ... the analysis of the position in the island was based on a system devised ... to permit the rapid examination of the position of any branch line. It had not been devised for any special line. Its basis was change .... as between the position of the railways with the line open, and with it closed.

The Committee ruled that the figures had to be disclosed and to give objectors time to study them a fourth day's hearing was convened in London a month later. At the resumed hearing, a representative of the County Council read out a list of discrepancies:

ISLE OF WIGHT
BRADING to BEMBRIDGE LINE

The train service on the Brading to Bembridge Line will be revised on and from
MONDAY, 2nd FEBRUARY, 1953
The complete service in operation from the above date will be as follows :

	\multicolumn{11}{c}{WEEK-DAYS}
	a.m.	a.m.	a.m.	a.m.	a.m.	p.m.	p.m.				
Brading	7.25	8.10	9.10	10.10	11.10	12.45	1.45	—	—	—	—
St. Helens	7.32	8.17	9.17	10.17	11.17	12.52	1.52	—	—	—	—
Bembridge	7.37	8.22	9.22	10.22	11.22	12.57	1.59	—	—	—	—
	p.m.	p.m.	p.m.	p.m.	p.m.	p.m.	p.m.	p.m.			
Brading	2.45	4.10	5.10	5.45	6.45	7.45	8.47	10.12	—	—	—
St. Helens	2.52	4.17	5.17	5.52	6.52	7.52	8.54	10.19	—	—	—
Bembridge	2.57	4.22	5.22	5.57	6.57	7.57	8.59	10.24	—	—	—
	a.m.	a.m.	a.m.	a.m.	a.m.	a.m.	p.m.				
Bembridge	6.41	7.49	8.38	9.28	10.53	11.53	1.28	—	—	—	—
St. Helens	6.46	7.54	8.43	9.33	10.58	11.58	1.33	—	—	—	—
Brading	6.53	8.1	8.50	9.40	11.5	12.5	1.40	—	—	—	—
	p.m.	p.m.	p.m.	p.m.	p.m.	p.m.	p.m.				
Bembridge	2.28	3.28	4.28	5.28	6.28	7.28	8.28	9.28	—	—	—
St. Helens	2.33	3.33	4.33	5.33	6.33	7.33	8.33	9.33	—	—	—
Brading	2.40	3.40	4.46	5.40	6.40	7.40	8.40	9.40	—	—	—
	\multicolumn{11}{c}{SUNDAYS}
	a.m.	p.m.	p.m.	p.m.	p.m.	p.m.	p.m.	p.m.	p.m.	p.m.	p.m.
Brading	11.45	12.55	1.45	3.3	3.45	4.55	5.55	6.55	7.45	8.57	9.55
St. Helens	11.52	1.2	1.52	3.10	3.52	5.2	6.2	7.2	7.52	9.4	10.2
Bembridge	11.57	1.7	1.57	3.15	3.57	5.7	6.7	7.7	7.57	9.9	10.9
	p.m.	p.m.	p.m.	p.m.	p.m.	p.m.	p.m.	p.m.	p.m.		
Bembridge	12.38	1.28	2.1	3.28	4.38	5.23	6.28	7.28	8.38	9.28	—
St. Helens	12.43	1.33	2.6	3.33	4.43	5.33	6.33	7.33	8.43	9.33	—
Brading	12.50	1.40	2.13	3.40	4.50	5.40	6.40	7.40	8.50	9.40	—

BRITISH RAILWAYS

The last timetable for the Brading to Bembridge line beginning 2nd February, 1953.

Announcement of the closure of Bembridge, Freshwater lines, etc. (1953).

BRITISH RAILWAYS

ISLE OF WIGHT

On and from **MONDAY SEPTEMBER 21st, 1953,**
the undermentioned will be **CLOSED :**

BRADING — BEMBRIDGE LINE
NEWPORT — FRESHWATER LINE
WHIPPINGHAM STATION
WOOTTON STATION

ALTERNATIVE ROAD SERVICES are provided by the SOUTHERN VECTIS OMNIBUS COMPANY

Passengers' luggage in advance will be collected and delivered as now, also Parcels and Freight Traffic.

Further Information may be obtained from the Assistant for the Isle of Wight, British Railways, Newport Station (Telephone Newport 2429), or from any Station Master.

Inquiries as to Omnibus Services should be made to the Southern Vectis Omnibus Company, Ltd., Nelson Road, Newport (Telephone Newport 2456), or to the undermentioned Inquiry offices :

NEWPORT : 19 St. James's Square (Telephone Newport 2457)
RYDE : Esplanade Station (Telephone Ryde 2264)
SHANKLIN : Carter Avenue (Telephone Shanklin 2224)

NATIONALISATION AND THE FIRST CLOSURES

- no credit had been given for mails carried on the Freshwater line
- no proper credit had been given for holiday runabout tickets
- revenue from season tickets quoted as £5 for the Freshwater line was known to total at least £98 including £52 paid by the County Council in respect of school children (BR admitted that the income from school children had been accidentally omitted)
- season ticket revenue for the Bembridge branch was given as £42 but the County Council alone paid £72
- no credit had been made of the proportion of fares paid by visitors travelling from the mainland
- permanent way maintenance costs at £500 per mile approximated to the national average but the Island was mainly single line and used second-hand material
- rolling stock on the Bembridge branch was estimated to cost £4,245 to maintain. This was £80 a week for one engine, three push-pull coaches (one used in winter, two in summer, and three on Saturdays), and six coal wagons. The high replacement costs of locomotives and rolling stock could only mean new stock and in the case of the rolling stock, twice the quantity needed

Taking these additions into account, the branches covered their direct operating costs including wages, train working and maintenance so were not a drain on the railway system. Mr Stevenson contended that the true losses were approximately £20,000 (rather than BR's figures for all lines of £271,173) and that could be attributed solely to the Freshwater line. The British Transport Commission later admitted that the closure of more than 160 miles of railway in 1953 saved no more than £146,000 a year and the savings for the Isle of Wight would have been about £20,000. Mr Stevenson added:

> ... the figures have now been demonstrated beyond any doubt as quite wrong. If the same form of accountancy as had been applied to the Island were used for the whole of British Railways, their 1951 profit of £34 million would have been turned into a loss of £40 million.

Despite the evidence, the TUCC recommended the withdrawal of services on the Freshwater branch together with Whippingham and Wootton stations. They could not agree about the Bembridge branch but ordered the retention of the Newport-Sandown line for at least two years and an unstaffed halt at Ashey. The Central TUCC gave the *coupe de grâce* to the Bembridge branch and set the date for closure as 21st September, 1953, to 'allow the railways to meet their summer service commitments'. The closures would reduce income on the other lines and, as a Ventnor councillor put it, 'by cutting the branches the tree would eventually die'. The *Isle of Wight Times* said what everyone was thinking:

> The shrill loco whistles in fact sounded the death knell of the Island railway system. For the dissolution of these branch lines is only the first step in the Railway Executive's ultimate aim to close the entire system, as Island residents are only too aware ...

The County Council enlisted the help of the local MP, Sir Peter Macdonald, who joined a delegation in a visit to the Ministry of Transport and raised the matter in the House of Commons:

'O2' class No. 29 *Alverstone* awaits departure from Freshwater with the final service on 20th September, 1953, carrying a simple 'The last train' headboard. Railway staff, from the left, are fireman S. Stone, driver W. Haywood, station master ? and guard R. Fallick.   *IWSR Collection*

Concurrently the Bembridge branch also closed. Mr Occomore, who had ridden on the first train in stands in the doorway preparatory to the final departure from Brading.   *IWSR Collection*

Almost from the beginning of the working of these nationalised industries we have heard profound dissatisfaction expressed at the way in which they render their accounts. We hear from commercial industries that if they rendered their accounts in the same manner as the nationalised industries, they would find themselves in gaol.

The County Council contended that the closure process had not been done thoroughly and asked that the Minister order a delay until the transport problems of the whole Island were considered at an enquiry. The civil servants would have none of this and warned their Minister that it would undermine the TUCC and force the Minister to act as final arbiter in branch closures: 'This would be an unfortunate position'. A later change of law did, indeed, make the Minister the final decision maker!

The Ministry was particularly concerned at the claim that the Island's roads were unsuited for heavy traffic and the railways should remain open indefinitely with, if necessary, a subsidy in lieu of road improvements. Grants were available for road improvements and one closure had been delayed until the completion of road works. Any extension of funding that allowed railways to remain open until such time, if ever, the roads had been improved had to be resisted. However, not all officials were unsupportive of the railways. One civil servant wrote:

> I am left after reading these papers with a good deal of uneasiness ... I wonder very much whether under more alert, efficient and 'commercial' management, coupled perhaps in the Isle of Wight with drastically reduced general standard of maintenance, the need for losing large sums of money, or alternatively drastically restricting facilities, could not be avoided.

Such comments were not, of course, for public consumption and it is unclear who read them, certainly not the Minister! The Island's representatives lacked the political muscle to force a change of policy and, once the steamroller of branch line closures had been set in motion, even the Ministry of Transport could do little to stop it. Meanwhile, the 1953 Transport Act abolished the Railway Executive on 1st October, 1953 and created Regional Area Boards reporting direct to the British Transport Commission.

The close-knit group of staff faced a crisis as the effects of the closures rippled through all departments in the Island. The Isle of Wight could not absorb the redundancies and men were offered jobs that invariably involved a move to the mainland. This was a real dilemma for those who had spent their whole working lives in the Island and had relatives who also worked on the railways. Despite this blow, during a strike of footplate staff held in May and June 1955 'Services in the Isle of Wight ... were least affected by the strike'.

Responding to a recommendation by the TUCC, the Minister agreed to chair the first of a series of meetings in Newport on 19th October, 1953 with representatives from the Ministry, BR, County Council and SVOC. The meetings were set up to discuss the Island's transport problems but were wound up in 1955 after becoming little more than a talking shop. The County Council pressed for greater availability of cheap fares and pupils travelling to the secondary school in Sandown were transferred to the railway amidst

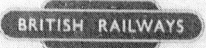

Closure notice for the Newport-Sandown line (1956) displayed at Alverstone.
IWSR Collection/R.C. Riley

NATIONALISATION AND THE FIRST CLOSURES 141

suggestions that SVOC overcharged on its schools contract. In 1954 the Ministry refused a request to reopen the Bembridge and Freshwater lines following claims that the roads were breaking up under the weight of the additional traffic and, after some hesitation, the County Council accepted a grant of £78,000 for road improvements.

In May 1955 the Branch Lines Committee reported that losses on the Newport-Sandown line had grown and recommended that the TUCC be asked to approve the line's closure immediately the figures for the following year were known, as 'there are no grounds for keeping open this unremunerative line'.

Income and expenditure year ending 30th September, 1954	Income £	Expenditure £	Interest £	Loss £
Newport-Sandown	12,743	36,463	8,994	32,714

Immediately closure of the line was formally announced the County Council lodged an objection and a hearing of the TUCC became inevitable. In its evidence, the County Council claimed that closure of the Newport-Sandown line would reduce income on the Newport-Cowes section and the Sandown line should be retained at the expense of that from Ryde to Newport. BR responded by pointing out that Ryde traffic would be inconvenienced if sent via Sandown and making the railways about £8,000 a year worse off if that option were pursued; clearly, the cost of staffing the level crossings was a factor. On 10th January, 1956 the Central TUCC confirmed BR's request to cease services between Newport and Sandown and BR duly implemented the decision with effect from 6th February.

To reassure Islanders who might otherwise have opposed yet another closure, the Chairman of the Southern Area Board sent a letter to the local press:

> Your readers are of course aware of the proposals for closing the Newport-Sandown Line of Railway. Following the recommendation of the Transport Users Consultative Committee in 1953 that the closing of the line then proposed be deferred for two years, the Consultative Committee is shortly to consider the proposal again.
>
> I should like, through you, to repeat quite clearly what has been said publicly and at discussions with representatives of the Island's interests, that the Southern Region of British Railways have no intention of recommending any further closure of the Island's railways, other than the Sandown-Newport line, for a period of at least ten years.

The commitment was refined to pledge seven years' notice to local authorities of any plans to close the Ryde-Ventnor line and five years in respect of the Ryde-Cowes line. There was good reason for such an announcement because the losses were nothing when compared with the income from carrying visitors to the Island on the mainland railways and ferries.

	Working loss £	Contributory value £
Ryde-Ventnor	30,000	638,000
Ryde-Cowes	54,000	108,000
Total	84,000	746,000

SATURDAYS ONLY.

The timings shown on this page will apply from June 5th to September 25th inclusive.

DOWN TRAINS.	a.m.	arr. a.m.	dep. a.m.	arr. a.m.	dep. a.m.	arr. a.m.	dep. a.m.	arr. a.m.	dep. a.m. (Empty)	a.m.	arr. a.m.	dep. a.m.		a.m.	arr. a.m.	dep. a.m.
Portsmouth Hbr. ⎱ Southsea ⎰ Boat (Clarence Pr.)	8 20	...	...	...	...	...	...	...	...	8 50	...	...	...	9 15	...	...
Ryde Pier	8 50	...	...	...	...	...	...	...	...	9 20	...	...	...	9 45	...	...
Ryde Pier Head	...	9 25	...	9 35	...	...	...	...	...	...	9 45	...	...	...	...	10 5
„ Esplanade	...	9 27	9 29	9 37	9 38	...	...	...	...	...	9 47	9 49	...	...	10 7	10 9
„ St. John's Rd.	...	9 32	9 33	9 41	9 42	...	...	...	...	...	9 52	9 53	...	...	10 12	10 13
Smallbrook Jct.	...	9 36	...	9 45	...	...	...	...	...	...	9 56	...	...	...	10 16	...
Brading	...	9 41	9 42	...	...	...	9†54	...	...	...	10 1	10 3	...	...	10 21	10 22
Brading	...	...	9 45	...	...	...	...	...	...	...	10 10	...	...	...	...	...
St. Helens	...	...	9 50	...	...	...	...	...	...	...	10 15	...	...	...	...	...
Bembridge	...	9 53	...	...	...	...	...	...	...	...	10 18	...	...	...	...	...
Sandown	...	9 46	9 50	...	...	9†58	...	...	...	...	10 7	10 9	...	...	10 26	10 28
Shanklin	...	9 55	9X58	...	...	...	...	...	...	...	10 14	...	...	...	10 33	10 36
Wroxall	...	10 6	10X 7	...	...	...	...	...	...	...	...	...	...	...	10 44	10X47
Ventnor	...	10 12	...	...	...	...	...	...	...	...	10 52	...	...	...	...	...
Ashey	...	...	...	...	9 49	...	...	...	...	...	...	...	...	...	...	...
Haven Street	...	...	...	9 53	9 54	...	...	...	...	...	...	...	...	...	...	...
Wootton	...	...	...	...	9 58	...	...	...	...	...	arr. a.m.	dep. a.m.	...	...	...	...
Whippingham	...	...	...	10 1	...	...	...	...	...	...	...	...	...	...	...	...
Ventnor West	...	...	...	...	...	9 40	...	...	...	...	...	...	...	...	...	...
St. Lawrence Halt	...	...	...	...	...	9 44½	...	...	...	...	...	...	...	...	...	...
Whitwell	...	...	...	...	...	9 50	...	...	...	...	...	...	...	...	...	...
Godshill Halt	...	...	...	...	...	9 57	...	...	...	...	...	...	...	...	...	...
Sandown	...	...	...	...	...	...	...	...	...	...	9 49	...	...	...	...	...
Alverstone	...	...	...	...	...	...	...	...	...	...	9 53	...	...	...	...	...
Newchurch	...	...	...	...	...	...	...	...	...	...	9 56	...	...	...	...	...
Horringford	...	...	...	...	...	...	...	...	...	...	9 59	...	...	...	...	...
Merstone	...	...	...	...	...	10 1½	...	...	...	...	10 3½	...	...	...	...	...
Blackwater	...	...	...	...	...	...	...	...	...	...	10 8	...	...	...	...	...
Shide	...	...	...	...	...	...	...	...	...	...	10 12	...	...	...	...	...
Pan Lane Siding	...	...	...	...	...	...	...	...	...	...	...	...	...	...	...	...
Newport	...	...	...	10 6	10 19	...	...	...	...	...	10 16	10 34	...	...	...	...
Cement Mills	...	...	...	...	...	...	...	...	...	...	To Freshwater		...	...	...	...
Medina Wharf	...	...	...	...	...	...	...	...	...	...			...	...	...	...
Gas Works Siding	...	...	...	...	...	...	...	...	...	...			...	...	...	...
Mill Hill	...	...	...	...	10 28	...	...	...	...	...			...	...	...	...
Cowes	...	...	...	10 30	...	...	...	...	...	...			...	...	...	...

DOWN TRAINS.	a.m.	arr. a.m.	dep. a.m.	arr. a.m.	dep. a.m.	arr. a.m.	dep. a.m.	a.m.	arr. a.m.	dep. a.m.	arr. a.m.	dep. a.m. (Eng.)	arr. a.m.	dep. a.m.	a.m.	arr. a.m.	dep. a.m.	a.m.
Portsmouth Hbr. ⎱ Southsea ⎰ Boat (Clarence Pr.)	9 45	...	...	...	...	...	...	10 15	...	...	...	...	...	10 45	...	...	...	11 11
Ryde Pier	10 15	...	...	...	...	...	...	10 45	...	...	...	...	...	11 15	...	...	...	11 41
Ryde Pier Head	...	...	10 25	...	10 35	...	10 45	...	...	11 5	11 15	...	11 25	...	11 35	...	11 45	...
„ Esplanade	...	10 27	10 29	10 37	10 39	10 47	10 49	...	11 7	11 9	11 27	11 29	11 37	11 39	11 47	11 49	...
„ St. John's Rd.	...	10 32	10 33	10 42	10 43	10 52	10 53	...	11 12	11 13	11 20	11 32	11 33	11 42	11 43	11 52	11 53	...
Smallbrook Jct.	...	10 36	...	10 46	...	10 56	...	...	11 16	...	11 36	...	11 46	...	11 56	...	...
Brading	...	10 41	10 42	...	...	11 1	11 3	...	11 21	11 22	11 41	11 42	...	...	12 1	12 3	...
Brading	...	...	10 45	...	...	11 10	...	...	...	...	...	...	...	...	12 10	...	...
St. Helens	...	...	10 50	...	...	11 15	...	...	...	...	...	...	...	...	12 15	...	...
Bembridge	...	10 53	...	...	11 18	...	...	...	...	...	...	...	...	...	12 18	...	...
Sandown	...	10 46	10 50	...	11 7	...	...	11 26	11 28	...	11 46	11 50	...	...	12 7	...	...
Shanklin	...	10 55	10X58	...	...	...	...	11 33	11X36	...	11 55	11X58	...	...	...	...	...
Wroxall	...	11 6	11 7	...	...	...	...	11 44	11X47	...	12X 6	12 7	...	...	...	...	...
Ventnor	...	11 12	...	...	...	...	...	11 52	...	...	12 12	...	...	...	...	...	...
Ashey	...	...	...	10 50	...	...	...	...	...	...	...	...	11 50	...	...	...	...
Haven Street	...	...	...	10X54	Freight.	...	...	...	...	...	...	11X54	Freight.	...	...	...
Wootton	...	...	...	10 58	arr. a.m.	dep. a.m.	...	...	...	...	...	...	11 58	arr. a.m.	dep. a.m.	...
Whippingham	...	...	...	11 1	...	...	...	...	...	...	...	...	12 1	...	...	...
Ventnor West	...	...	...	...	10 40	...	...	...	...	...	...	...	...	...	...	...
St. Lawrence Halt	...	...	...	...	...	...	...	...	...	...	...	...	...	...	...	...
Whitwell	...	...	...	...	...	...	...	...	...	...	...	...	...	...	...	...
Godshill Halt	...	...	...	...	...	...	...	...	...	...	...	...	...	...	...	...
Sandown	...	...	...	...	...	...	...	11 8	...	...	...	...	...	10 48	11 50	...
Alverstone	...	...	...	...	...	...	...	11 12	...	...	...	...	...	...	...	...
Newchurch	...	...	...	...	...	...	...	11 15	...	...	...	...	...	...	...	...
Horringford	...	...	...	...	...	...	...	11 18	...	...	...	...	...	...	...	...
Merstone	...	...	...	11 18½	...	...	...	11X22	11 23½	...	...	...	...	12 5	12 10	...
Blackwater	...	...	...	...	...	...	...	11X22	...	...	...	...	...	...	...	...
Shide	...	...	...	...	...	...	...	11 28	...	...	...	...	...	...	...	...
Pan Lane Siding	...	...	...	...	...	...	...	11 32	...	...	...	...	...	...	...	...
Newport	...	...	...	11 6	11 9	...	...	11 35	...	...	...	12 6	12 9	...	12 22	...
Cement Mills	...	...	...	...	...	...	...	...	...	...	...	...	...	...	...	...
Medina Wharf	...	...	...	...	...	...	...	...	...	...	...	...	...	...	...	...
Gas Works Siding	...	...	...	...	...	...	...	...	...	...	...	...	...	...	...	...
Mill Hill	...	...	...	...	11 18	...	...	...	...	...	...	...	12 18	...	...	...
Cowes	...	...	...	11 20	...	...	...	...	...	...	12 20	...	...	...	...	...

Extract from Saturday Working Timetable (down trains) beginning 5th June, 1948.

Chapter Ten

Traffic and Timetables after Nationalisation

Having looked at the politics that surrounded the Isle of Wight railways after Nationalisation we turn to their operation. The Island was undergoing a boom in the tourist trade as record number of visitors tried to escape from the shortages and restrictions of post-war Britain.

Nos. carried Year	Portsmouth-Ryde Passengers	Portsmouth-Fishbourne			Lymington-Yarmouth Passengers
		Cars	Lorries	Passengers	
1949	3,041,417	22,530	3,904	66,658	483,984
1953	4,461,835	26,677	5,107	88,706	486,723
1957	3,436,097	34,787	4,857	108,828	not known
1961	3,403,563	74,081	6,697	222,625	not known

Nationalisation had been greatly favoured by the staff who hoped for greater job security, better working conditions and improved pay. The Island was suffering a shortage of drivers that had to be covered by the loan of men from the mainland; accommodation was provided in a converted LCDR carriage. Mishaps included one on 30th August, 1948 when the signalman at Shanklin gave the Wroxall-Shanklin staff to the driver of a Sandown train and it had to be returned by road before services could be resumed; the signalman and driver were 'dealt with in accordance with the recognised disciplinary procedure'.

Train services were beginning to recover from the effects of war. The Waterloo-Portsmouth service was increased at the start of the 1948 season from two to three fast trains an hour on Saturdays. They connected with a ferry service to Ryde that was as frequent as the available vessels could manage. The Ryde-Ventnor weekday service of two Ryde-Ventnor trains per hour was supplemented on Saturdays by an hourly Ryde-Sandown working; the Sunday service was hourly with extra trains when required. Services on the other lines were unchanged from previous years. Watchingwell appeared in the public timetable for the first time.

The 1949 timetables were an acknowledgement of a return to normality with a summer service that operated from 23rd May to 24th September. On weekdays, Saturdays excepted, there were three trains per hour from Ryde to Ventnor for much of the day, one of which connected with an hourly train to St Helens and Bembridge. The daily parcels train ran when required but PLA van trains were absent from the timetable. Services on the other lines differed little from previous years, although there were several through trains from Ventnor to Freshwater and Cowes. On summer Saturdays from about 10.00 am there were two trains an hour to and from Ventnor, one of which non-stopped the Ryde stations and Brading, a third to Shanklin and a fourth to Sandown; the Sandown train did not stop at Ryde Esplanade and St Johns Road. The short workings connected with a half-hourly service to Bembridge. The up workings generally matched the pattern of down trains although the up Shanklin and Sandown trains followed each other instead of alternating with the Ventnor

Brading down starting signal is representative of the rail-built post signals that were installed in early BR days. Note also the footpath alongside the down line which had no fence to separate it from the running line. *R.A. Silsbury Collection*

The shortened down platform at Whippingham, rebuilt in 1948. *IWSR Collection*

trains. The service was reduced to hourly at about 6.00 pm although that could be doubled for the next two hours if required. The hourly Ryde-Newport and Newport-Sandown trains ran half-hourly between Newport and Cowes. Freshwater and Ventnor West branch services were less frequent but there were also through trains between Ryde or Sandown and Freshwater. Frequencies on Sundays were roughly half those on weekdays, except for the Ventnor West branch which had no service. This pattern was repeated with only minor adjustments each year until 1966 to take account of the closure of the branch lines.

The increased service in 1949 was fully justified as more passengers were carried at Easter, Whitsun and during the height of the season in August. The use of larger vessels noticeably reduced queues and delays were almost eliminated; extra ferry trips were run on every day of the August Bank Holiday.

The 1950 season began poorly owing to indifferent weather and a drift back to the roads following the abolition of petrol rationing. Traffic to the Isle of Wight was heavy and the August Bank Holiday was a post-war record when the Island railways carried 17,500 more passengers than in 1949. The smooth running of the railway was disrupted at Ryde Pier Head on Monday 19th June when carriages being shunted out of platform 3 collided with a light engine; the signalman and a driver were disciplined. On the morning of 17th August a train from Freshwater overshot a signal at Newport and collided with stop blocks north of the station; there were no injuries but the derailment damaged point rodding and disrupted services for the rest of the day.

Maintenance that had been authorized by the SR continued into 1948, 1949 and 1950 with the completion of permanent way renewals (the Bembridge and Ventnor West branches were not relaid). Rotten signal posts were replaced by rail-built posts carrying upper quadrant arms and fittings, a few of which had made an appearance before the war. A handful of lower quadrant signals survived, including Sandown's platform 3 down starter that had its wooden post heavily strengthened at ground level; others were distant signals with their arms fixed at caution. The concrete works at Exmouth Junction (Devon) supplied loading gauges for Ventnor, St Helens and Medina Wharf along with permanent way huts for relief crossing keepers on the Freshwater line. The Island permanent way men had to make do with their home-made wooden versions, but the huts were much too good to abandon when lines closed and were moved to other parts of the Island. In 1948 Whippingham's down platform was rebuilt in concrete at a cost of £500 but shortened from 242 ft to 100 ft forcing passengers using the station to travel in the train's front carriages. A total of £334 was spent on a similar hut as a public lavatory at Alverstone station and £1,385 on a sectional building for locomotive staff at Newport. Awards for the best kept stations were reintroduced in 1949; Shanklin won the largest station class for two years and Ventnor in 1952.

Early in 1951 a national coal shortage resulted in a reduction of passenger services on the Ventnor West branch and their withdrawal on the Bembridge branch from 11th February to 22nd March; there were strong protests from Bembridge residents who accepted that a Sunday service was not required but wanted their trains during the week. Given that the first line closures were

Crowds queue on Ryde pier waiting to board a ferry, a common sight on summer Saturdays.
IWSR Collection

announced three months later, some cynics later claimed that those in charge had been 'testing the water'. August Bank Holiday traffic was down on the previous year because of bad weather. Trains to Ventnor West were temporarily suspended beyond Whitwell on 8th November following subsidence, the passengers being transported by taxis.

Travel to the Island could be rather fraught during the summer months. Saturday to Saturday bookings remained the norm and during August the sheer number of visitors put the railways and ferries under intense pressure. On peak Saturdays ferries would be met at Ryde by a train to Ventnor, a second to Sandown or Shanklin and once an hour by a third for the Newport line; this worked well if the ferries and railways were running to time. The ferries made extra trips but that caused problems at Ryde where the arrival of two in quick succession would overwhelm the trains. On a typical summer Saturday, 44 trains from Ventnor to Ryde carried an average of 360 passengers and in the reverse direction 46 trains each carried 450 although more than 600 was not unknown! Many travellers were discouraged from repeating their visits. Typical of the comments received were these two, one from a traveller to Ventnor and the other to Bembridge:

> It only took 1½ hours from London to Portsmouth, but it took over 3 hours to get from Portsmouth to Ventnor. At one time there were 4 boatloads waiting at Ryde Pier Head and no sign of a train ...

> First the boat journey. To say it was packed is to put it mildly. We had to stand up all the way across, more like a rush hour ride on a London Tube, than a pleasant sea trip, and were very glad to get off that boat. But the train journey was worse. At Ryde Pier Head we searched the length of the train for a seat - in vain. I asked how long to wait for the next train to Bembridge and was told by the Guard there was room on this train. He took us to the front end of the train and put us in the luggage or Brake van. This too was packed with other people, so we stood to Bembridge. On the way the train suddenly pulled up and several of us finished up in a heap on the floor, it was a wonder that some of the children escaped injury. At Brading we waited for the Bembridge train 30 minutes before it moved off, waiting for the next train I understood from Ryde.

Naturally Islanders did their best to make money when they could. Visitors would face an assortment of trolleys, pram chassis, etc. lined up beside the taxi rank as boys and girls supplemented their pocket money by carrying luggage to the hotels and boarding houses. Many visitors purchased weekly runabout tickets during their stay, the income from which especially benefited the Newport-Sandown and Freshwater lines.

Holiday runabout tickets	Year	Number issued	Receipts £
	1949	167,895	96,341
	1950	164,223	94,642

The return journey was just as difficult. Traffic was so heavy at Sandown and Shanklin that travellers had to queue out of the concourse and down the road; queues would shrink following the departure of a short working only to build up again when passengers were unable to board the full Ventnor trains. The queue to board the ferries at Ryde stretched back along the promenade pier and if the ferries were disrupted would grow as each train added its load. This happened on 9th August, 1952 when a 50 mph gale prevented ferries from entering Portsmouth harbour; the paddle steamer *Whippingham*, which was difficult to handle in bad weather, had to anchor off Ryde Pier, the Fishbourne car ferry was unusable and the Yarmouth service erratic. According to Mr Tuck, an assistant accountant who happened to visit the Island that day, the queue on the promenade pier was about 20 deep and a third of a mile long. The ferry management denied there were more than 4,000 passengers waiting at any one time, so BR ended up making tortuous calculations in an attempt to prove how many could queue in a given length of pier! Queues for the ferries became so common that local boatmen touted for business from those desperate to cross the Solent.

The railways would have had a rosy future if the summer traffic continued throughout the year. In April 1950 the *County Press* published a cartoon entitled 'The First Easter Visitor' to highlight the lack of traffic in the winter months. The winter of 1951-1952 was typical of the post war years:

- The Ventnor West branch served a sparsely populated area although Whitwell people used the line for local and school traffic to Newport. The attractive scenery was no compensation for the walk between the station and town in Ventnor and the change of trains at Merstone.
- The Bembridge branch was used by local residents and school children to connect with the Ryde-Ventnor trains mainly in mornings and evenings.
- The Freshwater line had morning and evening local traffic but little else. The Lymington-Yarmouth ferry generated virtually no traffic for the railway.
- Newport-Sandown was used by some residents for shopping and business from stations that served hamlets without a good bus service.
- Ryde-Cowes was affected by long waits at Ryde Pier Head in each direction. Most traffic was between Newport and Cowes, particularly shipyard workers and Cowes residents who travelled to Newport for shopping and the cinema.
- Ryde-Ventnor was well patronised.

Local traffic was mainly school children to the Island's secondary school. Passenger trains also carried a fair amount of luggage, mail, parcels, milk in churns, fruit and flowers. Goods traffic consisted of locomotive coal, domestic coal and roadstone from Medina Wharf and sugar beet in the reverse direction. St Helens Quay handled only railway stores, the tar traffic having ended in 1950. The Island railways carried approximately 150,000 tons of goods a year prior to the war, but traffic had fallen somewhat by 1949:

Non-passenger traffic handled in 1949	*forwarded*	*received*
Parcels and PLA (conveyed by Carter Paterson) - No. of items	89,096	242,759
Fish and meat - tons	110	2,037
Milk - gallons	604,869	167,080

At Medina Wharf	tons	At St Helens Quay	tons
Coal and coke	105,802	Railway stores	2,856
Other minerals	3,264	Scrap materials	680
Sugar Beet	4,870	Other traffic	1,266
Total	113,936	Total	4,802

Nationalisation of the gas and electricity industries accelerated the decline. Electricity supply had been rationalised in 1928 when a coal-fired electricity generating station at Kingston, East Cowes replaced generating stations at Newport, Ryde, Lake, Ventnor and Yarmouth. A siding to the electricity works at Newport, installed under an agreement with the IWC dated 7th August, 1901, was declared redundant in November 1954. Traffic for the gas industry also vanished during the 1950s when a coal-fuelled gas plant at Kingston replaced four local gas works. In all 60,000 tons of coal traffic a year was lost to the railways; the siding to Shanklin gas works was declared redundant on 3rd November, 1957 and that at Ryde was clipped and padlocked out of use on 23rd May, 1958.

The 1952 summer season was a good one despite high winds and snow that affected ferry services in March. The poor weather may have been a factor when on 17th March a tramcar collided with the stop blocks at Ryde Esplanade.

The unrivalled beauty of a journey along the Ventnor West branch was not enough to prevent its closure. There were eight return passenger workings and a single goods train on weekdays that ran if required; no trains ran on Sundays. A document prepared as justification for closure disclosed that passenger numbers during a 'typical Summer week' and a 'typical Winter week' varied from a high of 122 per train to a low when some ran empty; the average summer loading was 20 and eight in winter. There was some milk traffic but farmers already had to use other stations when the line was closed on Sundays. An average of three wagons of coal arrived at Ventnor West a week and 134 wagons of sugar beet were shipped out during the season.

There were no Sunday trains on the branch, so the last trains ran on Saturday 13th September, 1952. Locomotive No. 27 *Merstone* carried a wreath and white boards bearing the inscription 'British Railways, Farewell to Ventnor West, 1900-1952'; since the locomotive was not push-pull fitted, Ventnor West signal box had to be opened so that it could run round the two-coach push-pull set. During one of the busiest days for years, locals made a last sentimental journey over the railway. Several hundreds of passengers and well wishers began assembling at Ventnor West station an hour before the last arrival from Merstone. The packed train departed from Ventnor at 7.57 pm lit by magnesium flares to assist the television cameraman and to the sounds of 'Auld Lang Syne', a jazz band and a fusillade of fireworks and fog detonators. Every crossing, bridge and station was crowded with people paying their last respects. The journey was hampered by the pulling of the communication cord but the train eventually arrived at Merstone to a further explosion of fog detonators. Any notion that the proceedings could be regarded as a form of celebration was countered by widespread expressions of regret at the closure. One member of staff commented, 'If half the people who are interested in this line today had been as interested in the last two years we should not be closing'. The poet John Betjeman described it as 'bureaucratic vandalism'. On 11th May, 1953 the

Post-nationalisation sets of carriages allocated to Newport had a preponderance of the heavier, SECR vehicles. A down Freshwater services leaves Newport hauled by 'O2' class No. 34 *Newport* and formed of two SECR and one LBSCR coaches during 1953. *IWSR Collection*

Traffic during the winter on the Newport-Sandown line justified only SECR carriages, a brake third with the guard and a composite with some first class accommodation. 'O2' class No. 33 *Bembridge* leaves Shide with an up train. *IWSR Collection*

signalling on the branch was decommissioned and in November contractors began lifting the track using a road crane and lorry; the work was completed after removal of the girder bridges in May 1954.

Elsewhere, it was 'business as usual'. Special railway and ferry services were operated for the Review of the Fleet on 15th June, 1953 and Coronation of Queen Elizabeth when all the ferries not employed on normal services were packed with spectators. That year passenger numbers travelling via Ryde topped 4,000,000 for the first and only time. 'The Tourist' through train ran for its last season and what must have been the last accident on the Freshwater line took place on 24th June when a train collided with a platelayers trolley between Carisbrooke and Watchingwell. Anticipating the next round of closures, several photographs were taken at Newport on 6th August, 1953 for the Ministry of Transport:

- 4.52 pm - the empty bay platform No. 1 is seen prior to the arrival of a train from Freshwater.
- 4.53 pm - platform 3 had about a dozen passengers wait for the Sandown train. A Ryde train in platform 4 was due to go out at 5.10 p.m.
- 4.54 and 4.55 pm - crowds of people were leaving the Freshwater train.
- 4.57 pm taken from the footbridge - 'passengers are not leaving the station but are crossing to platforms 3 and 4 for the Ryde and Sandown trains.' Platform 3 was crowded with passengers waiting for the Sandown train. Of 243 passengers that arrived on the Freshwater train, 115 boarded the Sandown train, 110 the Ryde train, 10 travelled to Cowes and eight left the station. This was, of course, peak season.

On the evening of 20th September, 1953 the last passenger trains ran on the Bembridge and Freshwater lines, much to the chagrin of enthusiasts who wanted to attend both events. There was real regret at the closure of lines whose histories had been so closely bound up in the holiday trade. The Island's charm was typified by 'the funny little trains' on which visitors loved to travel during their stay. The closures were deeply resented by local people who accepted that the lines did not earn their keep during the winter, but justified themselves in summer and kept coal traffic off the narrow winding roads. With attention focused on the Bembridge and Freshwater lines, the closure of Whippingham and Wootton stations passed by almost unnoticed.

On the Bembridge branch a three-coach train hauled by locomotive No. 28 *Ashey* made its last journey from Bembridge at 9.41 pm. Booking clerks issued 189 tickets for the train but many more had purchased their tickets earlier in the day and upwards of 300 packed into the carriages. In what became a regular mixture of solemnity and gaiety at Island railway closures, members of Bembridge parish council attended dressed in black, a trumpeter tried to play the Last Post whilst others cheered the train on its way. Crowds thronged the platforms at St Helens and Bembridge to witness the event. The train ground to a halt each time the communication cord was pulled until the guard tired of the process and was given permission to disconnect the continuous brake. Upon returning to Bembridge passengers lingered to see the locomotive run round the train before departing with its darkened carriages. Many regarded the closure as merely *au revoir*, but hopes that the line would reopen the next season were not fulfilled.

Hundreds gathered at Freshwater station to give a rousing send off to the last train. Hauled by No. 29 *Alverstone,* it carried a placard in green and white surmounted by two small union flags baldly announcing 'Last Train'. There were the same mixtures of emotions in a crowd that thronged the station lit by no more than the porter's lamp - presumably the gas lamps had not been lit! Many did not bother with the formality of a ticket whilst others purchased a return ticket that they would never use. The train was packed but somehow a few managed to join it at Yarmouth for the run to Newport. Groups witnessed the train's passing at level crossings, etc. and waved lamps that were answered by loud blasts on the whistle. Those at Carisbrooke witnessed an explosion of fog detonators even though the train did not stop!

There had been criticism of transfer time between the ferries at Ryde and the Cowes trains - often as much as 35 minutes - so the winter timetable was altered from 1st February, 1954 to reduce journey times by approximately 20 minutes in winter and 5-6 minutes in summer. Winter weekday services were recast so that trains crossed at Newport instead of Haven Street and locomotives inter-worked on both Ventnor and Cowes lines. 1954 was also the last year that trains ran on Christmas Day, when a two-hourly service was operated from Ryde to Ventnor and Cowes; the Sandown line did not open. Today the absence of trains on Christmas Day is taken for granted but before Nationalisation most lines had a service.

Prolonged rain and high winds disrupted the ferry service in November 1954 and on 8th December trains terminated at Ryde St Johns Road after the sea began breaking over the pier; passengers were taken by bus to the Esplanade and by tram to the pier head. On 22nd September a lengthman was killed by a train close to the tunnel and on 26th December, 1955 a passenger and guard were injured when a Cowes train collided with a carriage and van in a platform at Pier Head.

On Sunday 5th February, 1956 the last passenger trains ran between Newport and Sandown. The *Isle of Wight County Press* wrote:

> The white gates swing shut, halting a procession of impatient motorists, while a busy little engine puffs breathlessly into the station. A pause, then, as it chugs happily out, billowing white smoke, the gates clank clear again and the vehicles stream away.
>
> This performance has been repeated daily for 81 years at the seven level crossings on the Newport-Sandown railway line but after tomorrow evening these hold-ups will be a thing of the past, for then the gates will close for good behind the last train and the final chapter in the history of the line will end...
>
> Whether an avid engine spotter or an impatient motorist there will be few who will not regret the final closing of the gates at Pan, Shide, Blackwater, Merstone, Horringford, Newchurch and Alverstone tomorrow. There is a Lilliputian air about these austere but friendly platforms with their few travellers and shining milk churns which captures the imagination and recalls past days. The affectionate pride of the Islanders in this over-criticised and ill-fated railway is shared by many visitors who good-naturedly termed it 'quaint' and although the wheels of the last train will be urgently repeating their final message to the metals 'I'm the last, I'm the last' tomorrow evening, Islanders should be grateful for many years of faithful service.

Whippingham signal box had closed on the same day as the Newport-Sandown line when the single line section became Newport (South)-Haven

TRAFFIC AND TIMETABLES AFTER NATIONALISATION   153

Street. At Ashey the lever frame in the station building was replaced by a two-lever ground frame on 10th April, 1956. There is evidence that trains continued to call at Whippingham and Wootton when officialdom was not in evidence!

The loss of train services to Freshwater and Sandown had a dramatic effect at Newport where the station was host to the Assistant for the Isle of Wight and his staff, a locomotive shed, stores and carriage paint shop. The reduced size of the Island network had already raised questions over the viability of the district office and whether an Assistant for the Isle of Wight was needed. Fortunately for Mr Gardener, management of the Island railways from Woking was thought to be impracticable and the cost of transferring his office to a new building at Ryde was prohibitive. Other departments were not so fortunate; Newport running shed closed in November 1957, the carriage paint shop followed in September 1959 and the stores in January 1961. Staff savings of £10,680 a year were partly offset by higher light engine mileage and the cost of extra accommodation at Ryde; a concrete sectional building at Newport was dismantled and moved to Ryde. The signals to the Freshwater line were disconnected on 16th September, 1956 and the running line severed immediately to the east of Towngate viaduct. The signals to the Sandown line were taken out on 2nd March, 1958. Soon afterwards the South signal box was replaced by a ground frame that locked the drawbridge and an auxiliary single line token instrument on the down platform. The Sandown line points were removed, the nearby scissors crossover replaced by plain points and the up loop was converted to a headshunt serving the up sidings.

Removal of track on the closed lines had been deferred for at least a year as a concession to the County Council. The track on the Bembridge branch was described as largely scrap but that on the Freshwater line was 'generally good' and railway staff had wanted to recover the material; in the event it was sold for use on colliery lines in the North of England. Work began at Sandown in February 1957 with the removal of the south junction, run-round loop and siding next to platform 3. Track in the platform was left as a headshunt to sidings at the north end of the station. The line from Brading to St Helens remained in use as a siding until 17th November, 1957 for movements of condemned stock to the quay; the track was lifted soon afterwards. The contract for removing the track and bridges on the Freshwater line was let to Mayer & Newman, a London firm, who subcontracted the work to H.B. Jolliffe & Co. of Cowes. Some track in Freshwater station was lifted in November 1956 but a complete removal did not begin until May 1957. Track lifting reached Thorley at the end of June and Carisbrooke by August. Dismantling of the viaducts near Newport began on 2nd December and was completed in February 1958. The drawbridge to the Sandown line at Newport was removed in December 1963 ostensibly to pay for repairs to that on the Ryde line.

The track beds of the Sandown and Freshwater lines were sold to the County Council in June 1961. During an auction on 5th October, 1962, which realised a profit to the County Council of £5,535, the houses at Blackwater, Shide, Newchurch, Alverstone, Ningwood, Petticoat crossing and Causeway crossing were sold, after which all became private residences. The railway and harbour at Bembridge were sold to a new Brading Harbour Improvement Company

At Ashey the former down loop had been converted to a siding in the late 1920s; in September 1953 loco coal wagons were stored there because of shortage of space at Ryde St Johns. The instability of the land at the Ryde end of the up platform is evident in the angle of the running-in board.
IWSR Collection

We have been unable to locate a view of the Gas Works siding at Ryde in use. This picture dating from the late 1950s is taken from Rink Road bridge looking south with the Gas Works siding obviously out of use.
Roy Brinton Collection

which had plans to develop the harbour for 'yachting and commercial purposes'; St Helens station building became a private house but that at Bembridge was demolished. The County Council purchased the toll road from Bembridge to St Helens and abolished the toll.

Capital expenditure on the railways had fallen away. In 1954 life-expired Webb & Thompson electric train staffs were replaced by key token instruments along with 'shunt ahead' signals at Sandown and Shanklin and section locks to the home signals. During the next six years the rest of the Ventnor and Cowes lines were provided with key token instruments:

Date introduced	Section of line
7th December, 1954	Sandown to Shanklin
17th December, 1954	Shanklin to Wroxall
18th June, 1957	Wroxall to Ventnor
23rd June, 1957	Ryde St Johns Road (winter) and Smallbrook Junction (summer) to Brading
24th June, 1958	Cowes to Newport in place of Tyer's No. 7 tablet
26th June, 1958	Newport to Havenstreet in place of Tyer's No. 6 tablet
27th November, 1960	Havenstreet to Ryde St Johns Road (winter) and Smallbrook Junction (summer)

A major programme of permanent way renewals on the railway pier at Ryde and through Esplanade station occupied the winter of 1958-1959. Sections of track were renewed whilst keeping in use one running line and two platforms at Pier Head. The arrangements mirrored earlier work in 1906 so evidently the same plans were used. During the course of the work, an area inspector, who was in charge of the single line working, was killed on 28th April, 1959 whilst walking through the tunnel, the second fatal accident in the tunnel within five years. £6,500 was spent at Pier Head on more awnings for passengers awaiting embarkation but other stations on the Ryde-Ventnor line received little more than a coat of paint.

Neglect was far more obvious on the Ryde-Cowes line. North of Newport, Cement Mills was derelict and derailments were commonplace in the weed-covered sidings at Medina Wharf. However, coal traffic was still being handled at Cowes and the gasworks siding near Mill Hill. At Newport the bustle that characterised the station in former years had almost disappeared. The offices were still occupied, as was the goods yard, but the refreshment room closed and the sidings were host to no more than coal wagons and spare carriages. After the closure of Newport shed, the asbestos-clad locomotive running shed became derelict and by 1960 was open to the sky; it was demolished soon afterwards leaving the ornate IWC water tank standing in isolation. The workshop building and adjoining land was rented to the Vectis Stone Company.

At Wootton, the siding became disused after the local coal merchant, Charlie Osborn, retired in August 1959 although it remained *in situ* until the line closed. Haven Street station was renamed Havenstreet from the beginning of the summer train service on 9th June, 1958 'to conform with local usage'. Earth movements resulted in the short-lived removal of part of the platforms at

The derailment of a goods brake van at Shanklin on 27th August, 1962 necessitated the attendance of the Ryde breakdown crane. In the upper illustration some local lads are obviously watching matters with interest, while inspector F. Etheridge, *left*, and Shanklin ganger A. Western discuss what should be done in the lower illustration. The demolished buffer stop can be seen to the right of the van. *(Both) IWSR Collection*

TRAFFIC AND TIMETABLES AFTER NATIONALISATION

Ashey in 1961; a new running line has been built on the alignment of the former down siding and a new short platform to replace the subsiding up platform. Some tidying up work remains to be done as well as recovery of the old up line. *IWSR Collection*

Wootton and Ashey. At the latter the ground frame was abolished on 29th June, 1960 and the siding removed so that the running line could be realigned along the site of the down loop; a new platform and shelter came into use on 18th June, 1961. There were a number of speed restrictions as other earth slips went unattended. Plans to relay a short section of track were abandoned when the closure decision was announced and the 'new' rails were recovered from the lineside where they awaited laying.

At Ryde the driver of the pier tram allegedly failed to 'take care' when on 24th April, 1958 it rammed the luggage trolley. Ryde tunnel was closed on 1st and 9th October, 1960 owing to flooding. On 30th January, 1961 heavy rain and earth slips caused more havoc; services to Cowes were restored the next day but the Ventnor line did not reopen until 3rd February. On Monday 27th August, 1962 a goods brake van toppled onto the running line at Shanklin during shunting of the morning goods train; it was mid-afternoon before the line was cleared. In October 1963 a locomotive derailed at Cowes on points between the signal box and coal siding; trains used the second platform until it was re-railed five hours later.

The winter of 1962-1963 was notable for a four month spell of arctic weather called the 'Big Freeze'. The Island railways were first affected on 28th December, 1962 when the mail train hit a herd of steers sheltering under Truckells bridge. Two days later, on Saturday night 30th December, the Isle of Wight was struck by a severe blizzard. The *Isle of Wight County Press* reported how the 'railway heroes' fought to reopen the railways the next day. On the Ventnor line drifts at Rowborough and beyond Shanklin were cleared by mid-afternoon whilst the Cowes line was cleared of drifting snow near Cement Mills by noon. Road transport was paralysed, towns and villages were cut off and Ventnor could not be reached by bus for 24 days. Locals crowded onto the trains and even took over the guard's vans. The most frequent question was, 'What would we have done without the trains?'

OFFICIAL NOTICES, ETC.

BRITISH RAILWAYS BOARD

PUBLIC NOTICE

Transport Act — 1962

WITHDRAWAL OF RAILWAY PASSENGER SERVICES.

The Southern Region of British Railways, hereby give notice in accordance with Section 56 (7) of the Transport Act, 1962, that they propose to discontinue all existing railway passenger services between Ryde (Pier Head) and Ventnor and between Ryde (Pier Head) and Cowes.

It is proposed to operate a shuttle service on the Railway between Ryde (Pier Head) and a rail/bus interchange point at Ryde to be agreed with the Isle of Wight County Council or, in default of agreement, as determined by the Minister.

The proposal involves withdrawal of passenger facilities from the following stations:—

Ryde (St. John's Road)	if not required for interchange purposes.
Brading	Ashey
Sandown	Havenstreet
Shanklin	Newport
Wroxall	Cement Mills Halt
Ventnor	Medina Halt
	Mill Hill
	Cowes

It appears to the Board that the following alternative services will be available:—

ROAD.

The Southern Vectis Omnibus Company Ltd. operate the under-mentioned services in this area:—

Summer and Winter

Service No.	Route
1/1A	Ryde—Cowes
2	Newport—Cowes
3/6	Newport—Ryde
4/4A	Ryde—East Cowes
5	Newport—East Cowes
8	Ryde—Shanklin
9/10/10B/11	Newport—Ventnor
12/22	Sandown — Freshwater
14	Sandown—Cowes
16	Ryde—Niton
17	Cowes—Ventnor
20	Ryde—Ryde St. John's Rd.
30	St. Helens—Ventnor
31	Cowes—Gurnard
33	Shanklin—East Cowes
43	Newport—Sandown

Summer Only.

Service No.	Route
26	Sandown—Yarmouth
27/28/29	Ryde—Alum Bay
44	Sandown—Shanklin
45	Shanklin—Ventnor
47	Sandown—Ventnor

Summer Saturdays Only.

Express	Ryde—E. Cowes
Express	Newport—Cowes

Summer Sundays Only

Service No.	Route
35	Newport—Cowes
38	East Cowes—Sandown

The Southern Vectis Omnibus Co., Ltd., are prepared, if authorised, to augment their existing services with additional journeys, as necessary, between the interchange point in Ryde and any of the places now served by rail. On peak Summer Saturdays these additional journeys would operate, as appropriate, on a limited stop basis.

Any users of the rail services which it is proposed to discontinue and any body representing such users may lodge an objection in writing within six weeks of 29th February 1964, i.e. not later than 11th April 1964 addressing the objection to:—

The Secretary,

Transport Users' Consultative Committee
for the South Eastern Area,

3/4, Great Marlborough Street,

London, W.1.

If any such objection is lodged the services cannot be discontinued until the Transport Users' Consultative Committee has considered the objections and reported to the Minister of Transport, and the Minister has given his consent to the closure under Section 56 (8) of the Transport Act, 1962.

The Committee may hold a meeting to hear objections. Such a meeting will be held in public and any persons who have lodged an objection in writing may also make oral representations to the Committee.

If no objections are lodged to the proposal the services will be discontinued on 12th October 1964.

D. McKENNA,
General Manager.

Official notice of closure for passenger train services 1964.

Chapter Eleven

The Second Round of Closures

The first hint that further closures were under consideration came in 1961 when it became known that a working party had been set up to look at economies in operating the Island railways (see *Chapter Fifteen*), but this activity was overshadowed by another reorganization.

On 1st January, 1963 the British Railways Board was formed out of the ashes of the British Transport Commission, the consequence of another Transport Act. The Board's Chairman was Dr Richard Beeching who had been Technical Director of Imperial Chemical Industries Limited. Charged with returning the railways to profitability, he instigated a thorough line-by-line analysis of passenger and goods traffic (taken in week ending 23rd April, 1961) used in a paper entitled *The Reshaping of British Railways*, more commonly known as the Beeching Report. It set out a vision for the future of Britain's railways, but also recommended the closure of numerous 'unprofitable' lines including those in the Isle of Wight. Published in March 1963, the Beeching Report caused an uproar that set the scene for one of the most bitter and acrimonious fights the Isle of Wight has ever seen. Notices appeared all over the Island and letters of complaint engulfed the local press, BR and Ministry of Transport.

At Ryde it was proposed 'to strengthen the railway pier and convert it for a greatly increased tramway capacity. The space on the Esplanade released by the railway would provide an effective bus station'. However, the Borough of Ryde objected to the bus station and the County Council warned it would refuse planning permission on traffic grounds. BR then suggested the retention of a rail link to St Johns Road where there would be a bus station on the site of the locomotive running shed and passenger facilities in the station buildings. The close relationship between bus and railway management attracted a great deal of adverse publicity when it became known that BR was willing to help pay for bus terminals and subsidise replacement bus services.

The next round in the fight began on 11th February, 1964 when BR formally announced its intention to withdraw services on the two lines from 12th October. The closures were automatically postponed when the Isle of Wight County Council gave notice to the TUCC of its objections. The Council's case was published in the local press during April: '14 reasons to save I.W. Railways. A memo to Mr Marples' (the Minister of Transport) read the *Isle of Wight Times* and 'Case for the Island Railways' said the *Isle of Wight Chronicle*.

On 11th June, 1964 the TUCC began a three-day hearing at Newport. BR updated its figures of alleged losses.*

	Income £	Expenditure £	Loss £
Ryde-Ventnor	119,000	142,600	23,600
Ryde-Cowes	33,000	121,700	88,700
Total	152,000	264,300	112,300

* The additions for interest were no longer included but neither was there any mention of the contributory income generated by Island visitors on the mainland railways and ferries.

The TUCC Chairman announced that, after reading 149 letters of objection, the committee were satisfied there was hardship but needed to quantify the amount of that hardship. BR claimed that 2,800,000 passengers used the ferries each year of which 2,000,000 patronised the Island railways. This compared with 16,000,000 bus journeys; each holidaymaker 'brings two suitcases'. As far as the committee was concerned, these figures had relevance only to the amount of subsidy SVOC might need in order to operate replacement bus services!

L.H. Baines, Clerk of the County Council, represented about 50 objectors including the Island's MP, the County Council, other local authorities, organizations and individuals. He believed that the number of passengers was underestimated 'there are about 600,000 people for whom hardship was to be caused, who were not referred to by the Board. It would require 12,000 double-deck bus loads to clear them ... What have they done with them? Have they driven them over the cliffs like the Gadarene swine?'

Mr Baines showed a film of the crowds and queues for trains and ferries during July and August 1963. In the year ending September 1963 3,000,000 people used the Ryde to Portsmouth ferries of which 1,477,737 arrived from the mainland and 1,521,342 travelled in the opposite direction; on 10th August alone 54,507 people passed through Ryde Pier Head. On peak Saturdays, for every three passengers carried to Wroxall and Ventnor, roughly six went to Sandown and seven to Shanklin. SVOC would need to operate at least 48 additional buses per hour at peak times, including 45 along the Ryde to Sandown road. There were road safety fears at Ryde and through Brading. Up to £1,000,000 would have to be spent on road improvements and, given that the Island possessed no trunk roads, a quarter of the cost would fall on the ratepayers; at that time a 1d. rate produced just £13,000 a year. As an alternative to closure, it was suggested that BR could charge a supplementary fare for the journey along Ryde Pier.

Members of the Isle of Wight Railway Retention Association had mounted an extensive 'Save our Railways' campaign to raise awareness of the threat to the Island railways. They raised a petition, that its chairman presented to the committee, signed by 58,586 visitors and 23,147 local residents. Evidence was given on behalf of hotel keepers that over 50 per cent of visitors depended on public transport to reach the Island and during their stay. Ferries worked at saturation point during the peak weeks and motorists frequently cancelled their holidays when unable to get a booking on the vehicle ferries. Only in recent years had there been a shift from the traditional Saturday to Saturday holiday in July and August to mid-week bookings or breaks at other times of the year. Local passenger traffic included a large number of school children.

Each year over 25,000 tons of freight traffic was carried, mainly coal from Medina Wharf but also flowers and vegetables from Sandown and Newport to Ryde. Some 20,000 boxes of flowers and 5,000 boxes of cucumbers, lettuce and strawberries were put on the railway at Sandown for London's Covent Garden. Local consumption was equally important and nurserymen warned that 'many of us would immediately go out of business' if the number of visitors fell. Even the brewery in Ventnor relied on the railway for the rapid delivery of yeast from London. Retailers who used the railways included Mac Fisheries, whose boxes of fish packed in ice were carried by passenger train from Ryde Pier Head to those towns where the firm had a retail outlet, and F.W. Woolworth & Co., whose goods were carried in large wooden boxes. Messrs Readers, who had factories at Cowes and Freshwater, regularly dispatched a van load of lampshades from Newport every afternoon; the firm supplied Woolworth's stores throughout the country.

Mr F.P.B. Taylor, line manager of the South Western Division of Southern Region, represented BR. He explained that the shuttle service along the pier could carry 2,000 passengers an hour, equivalent to 40 buses. Since there were already 38 bus departures from the Esplanade that number would double to 80 per hour. He maintained that a perfectly adequate bus station could be created on Quay Road and continued:

> Queuing which arose at the Pier Head on return journeys was very unfortunate. It was difficult to see what could be done about it. Unfortunately, as soon as the holiday was over the homeward urge overtook everyone at the same time and 'like lemmings, they all rushed towards the sea'. If returning holiday makers were more sensible they would linger longer at Ryde until the queue situation had eased, and if they had money to spend it could benefit the commerce of Ryde.

In Mr Taylor's opinion, more than necessary had already been spent on repairs to Ryde Pier and a reprieve for the railways in whole or part would merely add to those costs. He claimed that the 'steeply graded and tortuous railway route' beyond Shanklin would be a disproportionate drain in terms of staff and maintenance since *only* 20 per cent of the holiday traffic was to Wroxall and Ventnor. The location of Ventnor station was a disadvantage as buses could take visitors right into the town (one wonders whether a funicular would have made a difference - probably not). Ventnor was more than 30 minutes by train from Ryde so an hourly service during winter months needed two trains and crews instead of one if the railway terminated at Shanklin. The significance of Mr Taylor's statement only became clear after the closure decision had been announced.

The 1962 Transport Act had simplified the closure procedure by making the Minister of Transport the decision maker. Before the recommendations of the Isle of Wight hearing could be considered a general election was called for October 1964. Whilst Britain's voters elected a Labour Government the Islanders won no friends when they re-elected their Conservative MP, Mr Woodnutt. The election was followed by the appointment of a new Minister of Transport and Chairman for the BR Board, not that there were any obvious changes in policy. The resulting delay merely added to the frustration of local people not helped by press headlines: 'Rail decision wanted' said the *Isle of Wight Mercury*. Meanwhile, every minor problem became headline news. The summer timetable had to be abandoned on 4th July, 1964 because of a shortage of serviceable locomotives. Mark Woodnutt (who had become the Island MP in 1959) complained that highly-placed railway officials were trying to reduce the train service in advance of the Minister's decision and were engaged in 'subterfuge to pervert the true course of justice'! A robust reply from David McKenna, General Manager of the Southern Region, claimed that major overhauls of locomotives in the Island were 'an expensive matter' and not in the interests of the taxpayer. He denied any deceit and suggested the MP got his facts straight before sending his letter to the press. Assured that the service

During the last summer of steam operation 'O2' class No. 24 *Calbourne*, in rundown condition, departs Ryde Pier Head with a Shanklin train, whilst one of the Grafton steam cranes is engaged in dismantling No. 1 road.
IWSR Collection

could be operated with 11 locomotives, Mr Woodnutt countered '... what will happen when the eleventh breaks down?'

It was not until 7th July, 1965 that the Minister of Transport, Tom Fraser, was advised in Ministerial briefing papers that: 'The recommended decision (to keep open only Ryde-Shanklin) is something of a Solomon's judgement. It will not be entirely acceptable to anyone, but equally it would not arouse serious opposition'. The civil servants apologised that the Minister was being asked to make a decision quickly because of the adverse publicity that the delays were generating. Mr Woodnutt met Mr Fraser on 19th July when he was assured that the Minister was aware of the facts and had seen the film shown to the TUCC. There were no concessions since the closure decision had been made over 10 days earlier!

The Minister's decision was made public on 28th July, 1965 in a press release. He accepted that electrification of the railway to Ventnor would add to capital and operational costs that could not be justified. Buses served the town centre more conveniently than Ventnor railway station and could provide an adequate service; the same applied to the Ryde-Cowes line. He refused permission to close the Ryde-Shanklin section on the grounds that closure would cause serious hardship for holiday makers and added that the line must be modernised, for which BR would be allowed to charge higher fares.

News of the decision spread well beyond the shores of the Island. The national press reported the Minister's statement on their front pages: 'Fraser saves a holiday line' said the *Evening Standard*; 'Four stations saved' *The Guardian*; 'Nine stations to Close on Isle of Wight' *The Times*; 'Island Line reprieved by Fraser - holiday fares to rise' *Daily Telegraph*. Mr Woodnutt capitalised on the decision, '... the Labour Party had published advertisements saying "Save the Island's railways from Tory massacre by voting Labour". This is yet another broken pledge. They have killed off the body and left us one limb admittedly the most important one'. The inevitable outcry was followed by a further flood of letters to the Ministry of Transport. Objectors were angry that BR had gone back on promises to give advance notice of closures. The excuse that the 1962 Transport Act overturned such commitments worried the Ministry: 'We must avoid appearing to be in cahoots with BR over dealing with what is alleged to be a breach of faith by them'.

BR announced that it proposed to withdraw services from the Shanklin-Ventnor section on 4th October, 1965, but the County Council lodged objections, saying that the replacement bus services were inadequate, because SVOC had not yet committed itself to run a service connecting with every train. The Traffic Commissioners sided with SVOC but an appeal was lodged with the Minister who eventually ruled in favour of the Commissioners.

Encouraged by a change of Minister and 'confidential' BR figures showing that the whole line could be run at a small profit, Mr Woodnutt and the County Council lobbied the Ministry in the hope that the closure decision could be reversed. The last passenger trains ran on the Cowes line on 20th February, 1966, several days before a Parliamentary debate on 9th March. The Minister doggedly stuck to her statement that the closures were a matter for BR.

Numerous letters to the latest occupant of the Minister's seat, Barbara Castle, included one from a Ventnor hotel owner. As a 'life-long supporter of the Labour

Party' he explained that Ventnor had only one industry - tourism - and any loss of revenue would seriously affect the economy. He asked for a public enquiry but also hinted at the political damage that the closures had done to the party locally. Alone amongst all the letters, telegrams, and Parliamentary Questions this almost brought about a change of heart. Although the Minister was unhappy with her predecessor's decision, an internal memo dated 15th March, 1966 noted:

> You had a short discussion this morning with the Minister about the railway closures on the Isle of Wight ... The Minister decided eventually to let the closure stand, and has asked that a sympathetic reply should be sent in her name...

Although the last trains ran to Ventnor on Sunday 17th April, 1966, the fight continued. Mr S.G. Conbeer, Hon. Secretary of the Isle of Wight Railway Retention Association, summed up the thoughts of many when he wrote to the *Isle of Wight Mercury*:

> This railway carries 300,000 passengers per year and makes about seven per cent profit per annum. Its closure will undoubtedly menace gravely the future of Ventnor and Wroxall as thriving holiday centres.

On 17th May, 1966 a BR official wrote an internal memo warning that a proposed direct bus service between Ryde and Ventnor would suck away traffic from the railway and jeopardise its profitability. His suggestion that the decision to terminate the railway at Shanklin be reversed was rejected as it was felt that an about-face at that late stage would be difficult to justify. That summer, most visitors to Ventnor chose to take the bus from Ryde rather than face another change at Shanklin.

By the Autumn of 1966 the consequences of the closure had become common knowledge. On 25th November members of the Ventnor Hotels Association told how they had suffered a 25 per cent drop in trade during the summer, little casual traffic now came to the town and there had been a shift in the remaining business to car owners.

In December 1966 the Ryde-Shanklin line closed so that work on converting the line to electric traction could be completed. The reopening of the railway in March 1967 was celebrated by a special lunch at Shanklin. Mr McKenna gave a speech to invited guests when he repeated that BR had wanted to close the Shanklin line and, despite modernisation, it would be a drain on the taxpayer. He believed 'it would be up to the Island authorities to make an offer to help pay for the Ventnor extension'. Mr Woodnutt preferred to concentrate on BR's optimistic forecasts for retaining the traffic to Ventnor:

> ... I don't say they have only got ten per cent of the traffic but the figure is far nearer ten per cent than 90 per cent... On the basis of these figures it is a more economic proposition to run the line through to Ventnor and make a profit by holding the whole of the traffic rather than just a run to Shanklin and make a loss...

It was June 1968 before BR admitted that it had lost most of the through traffic and railway passengers booked from the mainland to Ventnor had fallen by more than 80,000 in 1967 compared with 1965.

Behind the scenes there was a considerable amount of correspondence involving the Isle of Wight County Council, BR and the Ministry. BR was not averse to reopening and extending electrification to Ventnor, but was not prepared to bear the capital and operating costs without some financial input from local or central government. The County Council was determined not to burden local ratepayers, a high proportion of whom were pensioners, and concentrated on lobbying the Ministry in the hope that it would order BR to fund the work. Realising that the local authorities would not come up with any money and fearing that a concession would set a precedent, BR abruptly closed the correspondence saying that 'Re-opening of lines is not in accordance with our present policy'. The County Council finally abandoned attempts to get the line reopened on 30th July, 1970 (by which time track lifting was under way) after it became clear that the Ministry of Transport would not intervene; the cost had risen to an estimated £264,000. The decision to close the railway to Ventnor might well have been 'an unfortunate error of judgement' but no-one would publicly admit it.

The end of steam

In September 1963 work began on rebuilding the railway pier at Ryde. The solid concrete decking had been causing problems during poor weather and in 1947 two 40 ft spans were rebuilt in an 'open' type of steel constructed to give less resistance to waves; they were successful and after lengthy delays approval was given to spend £284,000 on rebuilding the remainder of the pier. Occupying the winter months, the wrought iron girders and concrete decking were replace by steel longitudinal and cross-members to which the track was fixed; new timber decking was provided. Cowes line trains terminated at St Johns Road and Ventnor trains worked over the up line to Esplanade under the 'one engine in steam' regulations with a locomotive at each end.

The 1965 summer service was enlivened by an incident at Ryde Pier Head on Saturday 19th June when one bogie wheel on locomotive No. 22 *Brading* left the rails on the crossover; trains along the pier were stopped and passengers had to use the pier tram or walk. During the following winter work recommenced on replacing four spans of the railway pier beyond Pier Head signal box and services terminated at Ryde Esplanade. As an hourly service to Ventnor and a two-hourly frequency to Cowes was in operation the sequence of operation at Esplanade went as follows. A locomotive would arrive from Ryde shed and position itself at the down starting signal to await the arrival of a Cowes train. The Cowes train would deposit its passengers in the up platform before running forward onto the pier clear of the emergency crossover (to make life more bearable for staff a three-lever frame was installed on the up platform in a small hut to operate the crossover and a shunt signal) and shunting back into the down platform where the locomotives would be changed. The locomotive from the Cowes train would take over the next Ventnor line train whose locomotive would run back to Ryde shed.

Anticipating closure, on 3rd October, 1965 some 600 members of the Locomotive Club of Great Britain ran a 'Vectis Farewell Tour' behind No. 24 *Calbourne* double-headed by No. 14 *Fishbourne* on the Ventnor section. Passenger services to Cowes

Weeds are beginning to take over at Newport whilst the station quietly awaits the end. Only one arm remains on the large signal bracket that formerly guarded access to both the Ryde and Sandown lines. The loop line has been cut back to a siding and the footbridge has lost its roofing.
IWSR Collection

After demolition of the locomotive shed at Newport, spare locomotives were often stored at Sandown. No. 14 *Fishbourne*, fresh from a repaint stands with Nos. 18 and 17 which have both had temporary panels attached to the cab sides for winter storage. *A.E. Bennett*

THE SECOND ROUND OF CLOSURES

actually ended on a wet Sunday 20th February, 1966. All day the trains were busy and the three-coach sets had been strengthened by an additional carriage to cope with the numbers. Cowes station, which normally took no more than £5 on a winter Sunday, sold over £100 worth of tickets and takings at Ryde were just as high. Hundreds of people turned out to see and ride on the final departure from Cowes at 8.31 pm hauled by locomotive No. 22 *Brading*; the last mail bags were loaded at Newport before an arrival at Ryde at 9.22. A working in the opposite direction left at 9.38 pm in charge of No. 14 *Fishbourne*. Amongst the passengers were two descendants of Michael Ratsey, the Cowes boat builder, who had cut the first sod of the CNR in 1859 and travelled on the first train between Cowes and Newport. The *Southern Evening Echo* reported:

> It was the end of the line for the Ryde-Newport-Cowes rail link last night and in at the death of the 14-mile stretch were hundreds of Islanders and railway enthusiasts.
> Many of them packed the last trains in either direction, whilst others paid their respects from station platforms, bridges and other vantage points *en route*.
> Fireworks, handbells, and frequent whistles from the locomotives set the mood for the sentimental journeys.

Services between Shanklin and Ventnor ended on Sunday 17th April, 1966, a day that was also marked by cold and wet weather. At 8.30 pm enthusiasts and local people witnessed the departure of No. 14 *Fishbourne* and a full train. The last train in the opposite direction was met by cheers at Shanklin, crowds at Wroxall and a continuous cannonade of fog detonators before arriving in Ventnor station at 10.10 pm. The *County Press* captured the mood:

> Oldest member of the staff at Ventnor Station was Mr A. O. Widger, of Whitwell, who is retiring after nearly 49 years' service. He has been at Ventnor since 1930 and spent 17 years at Ventnor West Station. He saw the last train out from there fourteen years ago, and told a *County Press* reporter 'I never expected to see it happen again at Ventnor Station'.

Mr Widger was one of many railwaymen to retire or take redundancy. Even Mr Gardener, the last Assistant for the Isle of Wight, and his office were not immune; he retired in December 1966.

BR had written to traders in July 1965 warning that it proposed to withdraw freight services from the Island stations within three months. The merchants began to go over to road transport but this took place in a rather piecemeal fashion. Cowes signal box closed in April 1966 when T. Gauge & Sons stopped taking deliveries at the station. The remaining goods and engineers trains were worked under the 'one engine in steam' regulations using a temporary wooden train staff. Goods traffic officially ended in May when Medina Wharf was sold to Corralls, the dominant coal merchant in the Island. However, BR continued to land locomotive coal and other materials at the wharf 'at normal commercial rate' and as part of a *quid quo pro*, hauled coal for Corralls (successors to Fraser & White) to Newport, where the firm had purchased part of the goods yard for a depot, and to Ryde where a similar sale had been delayed because of uncertainty over the future of the site. The last train from Medina Wharf seems to have run on 24th October when Newport signal box closed.

Smallbrook Junction signal box opened for the duration of the 1966 summer timetable so that trains could use the double track to St Johns Road and then

In anticipation of closure of the remaining Island lines, the Locomotive Club of Great Britain ran a 'Vectis Farewell' tour on Sunday 3rd October, 1965. 'O2' class No. 24 *Calbourne*, fresh from overhaul, nameless and in plain black livery, handled the Ryde-Cowes and return leg alone, but for the run to Ventnor and back was joined by 'O2' class No. 14 *Fishbourne*, seen here approaching Smallbrook Junction on the down leg. *IWSR Collection*

The chalked inscription on the back of LBSCR brake third No. 4168 says it all! 31st December, 1966, the final day of steam passenger operation by BR; 'O2' class No. 14 *Fishbourne* has arrived at Shanklin adorned with a 'Farewell to IoW steam' wreath on the smokebox door and a 'Last day of steam' headboard on the buffer beam. *R.A. Silsbury Collection*

closed for the last time on the night of 17th-18th September, 1966. The last steam trains had also run over the railway pier and from the start of the winter timetable on 18th September services reverted to an hourly frequency between Ryde Esplanade and Shanklin, worked by two trains with a 50 minute layover at Shanklin. As the down line between Ryde Esplanade and St Johns Road was out of use, trains between the two stations were topped and tailed by a locomotive.

Plans to create a parcels concentration depot at Ryde St Johns Road were abandoned in favour of a cheaper alternative at Newport where roller doors were installed in the parcels office and most of the ground floor gutted. Beginning on Monday 19th September, 1966, parcels were carried in trailers via the Portsmouth-Fishbourne ferry and then to Newport for sorting and distribution. Similar arrangements were introduced for bulk mail after BR insisted that the 1 ton weight limit on Ryde Pier could not be ignored for mail vans. The morning mail boat to Ryde Pier was replaced by a vehicle ferry to Fishbourne.

The end of steam working on 31st December, 1966 drew people from far and wide. To mark the event 500 members of the Locomotive Club of Great Britain gathered at Ryde Esplanade to board a specially hired five-coach train. It departed at 12.15 in drizzle hauled by locomotives Nos. 24 *Calbourne* and 31 *Chale* with No. 17 *Seaview* at the rear as far as St Johns Road; the return journey from Shanklin was in brilliant sunshine, such is the way with the Island's weather.

The final departure for Shanklin was hauled by No. 14 *Fishbourne* specially steamed for the occasion and carrying a wreath on the smokebox door. Although due to leave at 9.40 pm, the late arrival of the ferry from Portsmouth meant that it was 9.53 before the train left Ryde Esplanade banked by No. 27 *Merstone* at the rear until St Johns Road. By the time it left St Johns Road over 500 people had packed into the compartments and brake vans and as the train called at each station it was met by crowds of onlookers and the sound of

Last Passenger Trains							
Route	Date	Time* pm	Engine No.	Driver	Fireman	Guard	
Ventnor West-Merstone	13.9.1952	7.57	27	J. Sewell	L. Harris	R. Seaman	
Bembridge-Brading	20.9.1953	9.41	28	W. Jefferies	A. Lock	F. Jenvey	
Freshwater-Newport	20.9.1953	9.34	29	W. Haywood	S. Stone	R.J. Fallick	
Sandown-Newport†	5.2.1956	7.50	33	Not known	J. Nicholson	S. Hebbes	
Newport-Sandown†	5.2.1956	7.49	17	W.G. Vallender	P. Harbour	W. Dibden	
Cowes-Ryde Esplanade#	20.2.1966	8.31	22	J. Townson	C. Hackett	R. Childs	
Ryde Esplanade-Cowes	20.2.1966	9.38	14	K. West	J. Farrington	S. Wells	
Ventnor-Shanklin	17.4.1966	8.30	14	J. Townson	C. Hackett	T. Courtney	
Shanklin-Ventnor	17.4.1966	10.10	24	Not known	Not known	Not known	
Ryde Pier Head-Ryde Esplanade	17.9.1966	9.35	Details not recorded				
Ryde Esplanade-Shanklin	31.12.1966	9.40	14	P. Harbour	R. Knapp	R. Yule	
Shanklin-Ryde St Johns Road	31.12.1966	10.12	14	P. Harbour	R. Knapp	R. Yule	
Ryde Pier Tramway	26.1.1969	11.15	Car 2	H. White		A. Bowler (conductor)	

* All times given are departure times except for Shanklin-Ventnor (10.10 was arrival time at Ventnor).
† Sandown line trains crossed at Merstone.
# The 9.38 pm Ryde Esplanade-Cowes would have worked back as empty stock but may have carried passengers.

In May 1967 the last seven 'O2s' await cutting up; from the left are Nos. 20, 25, 28, 17, 33, 14 and 22.
IWSR Archive

fireworks and fog detonators. Arriving at Shanklin at 10.28, the locomotive ran round its train and, 25 minutes after its arrival, began the return journey to Ryde St Johns Road where the train terminated; arrival at Ryde was slightly delayed by the traditional pulling of the communication cord. Having detached itself from the train *Fishbourne* went to the locomotive shed where the fire was dropped for the last time. For the first time in over a century the Isle of Wight was without any steam trains. The *County Press* summed up the situation:

> For more that a century steam trains have made a significant contribution to the life and development of the Island. On New Year's Eve an era which began in 1862 came to a clanking, hissing halt at St Johns Road Station, Ryde, where, just an hour before midnight, one of Britain's oldest locomotives arrived with the last steam passenger train.

Within days the withdrawn locomotives and carriages were hauled to Newport; the last movement north of Newport took place on 4th January when No. 24 *Calbourne* propelled No. 18 *Ningwood* to Cement Mills siding for breaking up. The carriages were broken up in Newport's Freshwater yard and in April No. 27 *Merstone* was steamed to shunt its fellows into position before they too were dismantled. Once the stock movements had ended the junction at Smallbrook was removed. Track lifting between Shanklin and Ventnor began in the summer of 1970 followed by the Cowes-Ryde line in January 1971.

Chapter Twelve

Southern Vectis, Vectrail and Others

The wide-ranging Nationalisation of Britain's transport system in 1948 included the stage carriage services of Southern Vectis Omnibus Company and a number of large hauliers, including firms that had acted as carriers for the railway companies.

Freight carrying operated locally under the name Carter Paterson, soon to be known throughout the country as British Road Services. There was further consolidation in the Island when Pickfords were amalgamated with Shepard Brothers, who operated their own vessels to a wharf at Newport. By 1953 the combined company had reduced the number of road vehicles based in the Island from 40 to 23, although it was said that eight more would be needed when the branch lines closed.

Southern Vectis

SVOC entered Nationalisation under some difficulty. Between 1938 and 1950 revenue had fallen in inverse proportion to operating costs made worse by heavier than average wear and tear on the Island roads, a punitive fuel tax imposed in 1951 and a recession in the Cowes area following the loss of wartime industries. Several bus routes were running at a loss during the winter months and the company was desperate for extra business.

The Road Passenger Executive, of which SVOC was a subsidiary, drew up a number of area schemes at the behest of the British Transport Commission for integration of road and rail services that invariably concluded buses should replace trains. In 1952 SVOC was allowed to purchase West Wight Motor Bus Co. and Enterprise Service (operators of a direct Newport-Sandown service) - both would have benefited from a railway closure. There were other state-sponsored acquisitions ostensibly to provide a comprehensive network but which, in reality, created a monopoly; only the route to Seaview remained in independent hands. SVOC branched out into coach excursions and successfully promoted its round-the-Island coach tours to the detriment of the ferries.

The railway closures were not anticipated to cause the SVOC any problems, quite the reverse. Between 1954 and 1956 the fleet of SVOC buses rose to 200 after the order of 47 'Lodekka' vehicles designed to pass under low bridges. Most rail closures could be replaced by additional buses running on existing routes. To give the Ventnor West branch as an example, its services were replaced by just two additional journeys on route 9 from Newport to Ventnor via Merstone, Godshill and Whitwell.

Only one new bus service was introduced as a direct consequence of the closures in the 1950s. Route 39 from Bembridge to Shanklin via St Helens and Brading was described by one local councillor as '... an apology for a bus service, which would be a serious disability to residents' since it could be

Cartoon published by the *Isle of Wight County Press* in 1953.

withdrawn after three months' operation; the service lasted until June 1958. Most visitors to the Bembridge area preferred to use the tramway down Ryde Pier and an equally uncomfortable No. 8 bus. The journey between Ryde and Bembridge in peak season was fraught with danger because of suitcases and camping gear blocking the passageway and rear platform; this was despite the provision of an extra luggage rack on the lower deck.

SVOC also introduced a through Ryde to Freshwater bus service during the summer. There was no direct transfer between train and bus at Newport station, supposedly because numbers in the winter did not justify a service to the town centre. The company was determined not to water down the benefits gained from the closures and resisted any extension of interchangeable ticketing or equalisation of bus and train fares. Islanders soon had cause to regret the growing monopoly of the bus. In February 1956, the same month that the Newport-Sandown line closed, SVOC applied to the Traffic Commissioners for permission to revise its fare structure for weekly and season ticket holders with increases of between 33 and 40 per cent; local people linked the increases to the railway closures but they were actually because of fuel rationing during the Suez crisis. By the end of the decade many bus fares were dearer than rail.

Following the closure of the Freshwater line in 1953, visitors who had previously travelled across the Island on 'The Tourist' through train were forced to take the bus. Anyone travelling on the top deck was guaranteed an uncomfortable, nauseous journey on the narrow twisting country roads made worse by frequent brushes with overhanging branches. Small wonder that few bothered. SVOC provided the means of seeing the Island's charms from the comfort of a coach, of which it built up a sizeable fleet. Intense competition with several private operators was especially evident along The Esplanade at Ryde, where dozens of coaches were parked as the drivers touted for business from passing pedestrians - just as had happened a century before!

Publication of the Beeching Report was followed in May 1963 by a conference at Newport attended by representatives of local authorities, business and hotel interests, commercial organizations and trades unions. Claims that SVOC could cope with the traffic were dismissed by a local councillor:

> When the other lines closed the bus company said it could do just as well as the railways - and even better... But what happened in the 10 years since then? Services have been reduced all over the island and fares increased. What hope can we expect from the bus company in the future?

The 1960s closures resulted in the creation of route 39 from Shanklin railway station via Wroxall to Ventnor. It attracted little custom as most visitors preferred a new summer only limited-stop bus service route 16A from Ryde to Ventnor. The routes were short-lived as the Island suffered a fall in the number of visitors and more residents switched to cars. Route 16A was abandoned in 1971 but route 39 lingered until April 1983 when it ran only on summer Saturdays before being abandoned at the end of the summer season. The loss of route 39 was keenly felt, but it was not until 4th October, 2004 that Wight Bus reintroduced a service between Shanklin station and Ventnor.

Reversing Nationalisation

The idea that Nationalisation could be reversed took many years to take root. A Conservative Government privatised the road haulage industry in its 1953 Act but kept the railways and buses under tight control. This led, in the eyes of some, to an unholy alliance between the railways and bus companies whilst the haulage industry was free to continue creaming of the most profitable traffic from the railways.

There was no shortage of people who wanted to operate the Isle of Wight railways but they lacked the financial and political muscle to make an impact. There was no provision for the sale of a railway that might become a competitor or be proved by private interests to make a profit. It was many years before BR could be persuaded to sell closed lines to preservation societies. When the first closures were proposed the *Portsmouth Evening News* published the following letter on 23rd August, 1951:

> The threat to close down the whole of the Isle of Wight Railways and throw all traffic on to the road transport system is yet another example of British Railway practice: i.e., to operate orthodox steam railways or nothing. I consider the closure would ignore a useful opportunity to convert the system to a fast light railway network, using, if not electric, diesel railcars. Such units would run as single or multiple units as required and would not need elaborate station and signalling staffs that a full-scale railway demands, and are to be seen in many other countries, notably on the European continent.

The County Council used these suggestions as part of its fight against the closures but ignored calls to take over the Bembridge branch. The Isle of Wight Travel Ltd was formed by a consortium of local businessmen to raise £1,000,000 and take over the existing and closed lines with the exception of the Ventnor

West branch. The company was taken seriously by railway managers who discussed just how much a private concern should be expected to pay for the redundant 'assets'.

George Bennie, inventor and promoter of the Bennie Airspeed monorail, proposed a circular route linking Cowes, Ryde, Ventnor, Freshwater and Newport using trackbeds except between Cowes and Ryde where a shorter route was envisaged. The monorail had a single rail 14 ft above ground level from which aluminium cars were suspended by bogies and guide rails; 12 cars could each accommodate 50 passengers. Using diesel or electric propulsion, there were exotic claims about their ability to travel at speed around the Island. Regarded as a joke by the Ministry of Transport, the project had the tacit agreement of the Isle of Wight County Council but the £4,000,000 price tag meant that it went no further.

When rumours of more closures emerged in March 1963, Mr H.E. Dory, a Director of Austrian Travel Agency Ltd of London, wrote to the Ministry asking for a lease of the railways at a nominal cost. He was no more successful than Mr Stoner who, speaking on behalf of Isle of Wight Travel Ltd, commented 'we should be masters in our own home. Until we are we shall continue to have crisis after crisis'. Privatisation would become the future for Britain's railways but not for another 30 years.

Vectrail

The Vectrail Society, an abbreviation of Vectis Electric Railway, was a commercial undertaking formed in March 1966 by a group of local men. They planned to reopen the Ryde-Cowes line and looked forward to the day they could also manage the Ryde-Ventnor line. Vectrail proposed to install overhead trolley wires at a cost of £150,000 and purchase eight-year-old German electric cars, at approximately £2,500 each, or new bogie cars with a top speed of 65-70 mph costing £37,000 apiece. Electricity was to be drawn from the Southern Electric Board's distribution system at 11 kV or 33 kV and converted to 600 volt d.c.; automatic colour light signals would be interlocked with the points.

Predating the creation of Vectrail, Southampton businessmen Charles and Reginald Ashby formed the Sadler Rail Coach Company and began experiments with a new type of lightweight rail coach on a length of the Meon Valley railway at Droxford. Custom built by Strachan's (Hamble) Ltd, a local firm of coach builders, the 'Pacerailer' was based on the firm's luxury road coach designs and built on an AEC 'Reliance' coach chassis adapted to run on a railway. Painted in a blue-grey livery, the single-ended four-wheel prototype had a wheelbase of 20 ft, an unladen weight of 6 tons powered by a nine litre engine giving a fuel consumption of 11 miles a gallon and a maximum speed of 58 mph. The wheels had metal flanges and solid rubber tyres, air-operated doors and folding steps for use at halts without platforms. Inside it had padded seating for 60 passengers and space for prams and luggage; there was air conditioning, fluorescent lighting, a radio telephone, public address system together with an auto-ticket issuing machine and change-giver. Described as costing between £12,000 and £20,000, it was claimed that production vehicles 'to suit the Island lines' would cost only £7,500. The rail coach was exhibited on a low loader at the Island Industries Fair at Ryde Airport from 21st to 30th June, 1967, but returned immediately to Droxford where it was burnt out by vandals in 1970.

Following discussions with the County Council, Vectrail and the Sadler Rail Coach company decided to pool their resources. Charles Ashby told the local press in September 1966 of plans for an operating company with him as Managing Director. Sadler-Vectrail Ltd would lease the trackbed from the County Council, buy the permanent way from BR and operate Mr Ashby's diesel rail coaches. He hoped to get the project 'going about Christmas...' Vectrail envisaged a service of two trains per hour carrying passengers at fares cheaper than charged by BR and SVOC. There would be car parks at the principal stations and bus-stop type halts at Fairlee on the eastern edge of Newport and Dodnor just north of the town. BR refused to countenance an interchange station at Smallbrook Junction but said it would not object to a third track to Ryde St Johns Road; 'the service will cater for the public - the public will not have to cater for us', Mr Ashby said.

Thoughts of operating Mr Ashby's rail coach between Shanklin and Ventnor led to a site meeting at Shanklin on 10th June, 1966 with representatives from BR and the County Council. The idea was abandoned after BR quoted £15,000 for track alterations to allow running into one platform or to a separate terminus south of Landguard road bridge. BR also rejected a proposal to operate the rail coach on the Ryde tramway saying that it would 'be detrimental to revenue to be earned by our own trains'.

Sadler-Vectrail Ltd was formed on 1st February, 1967 with a share capital of £40,000 but failed to tempt Islanders to invest in the undertaking. The County Council was not convinced that the company had the necessary financial backing and negotiations ceased until some progress had been made in the purchase of the permanent way. Unfortunately, BR would not discuss that until the trackbed had been sold to the County Council nor would it permit Sadler-Vectrail to carry out repairs or maintenance. In July 1970 Mr Ashby withdrew and at a meeting on 9th September, 1970 it was decided to abandon the whole scheme. Although Vectrail passed into oblivion it gave time for railway preservation in the Isle of Wight to become an established fact.

The first two 'O2s' ran in LSWR livery until 1925; No. 206, to become 19, heads a down train at Sandown in 1923.
IWSR Collection

When the IWR locomotives were repainted in SR livery they retained their nameplates on the tank sides, resulting in a cramped lettering layout. When nameplates were adopted for all locomotives in 1928, the first so adorned, ex-FYN No. 2, had a similar style, fortunately not perpetuated. Proud staff show off newly repainted Ex-IWR No. 14 *Shanklin* at Ryde St Johns Road *c.*1925.
IWSR Collection

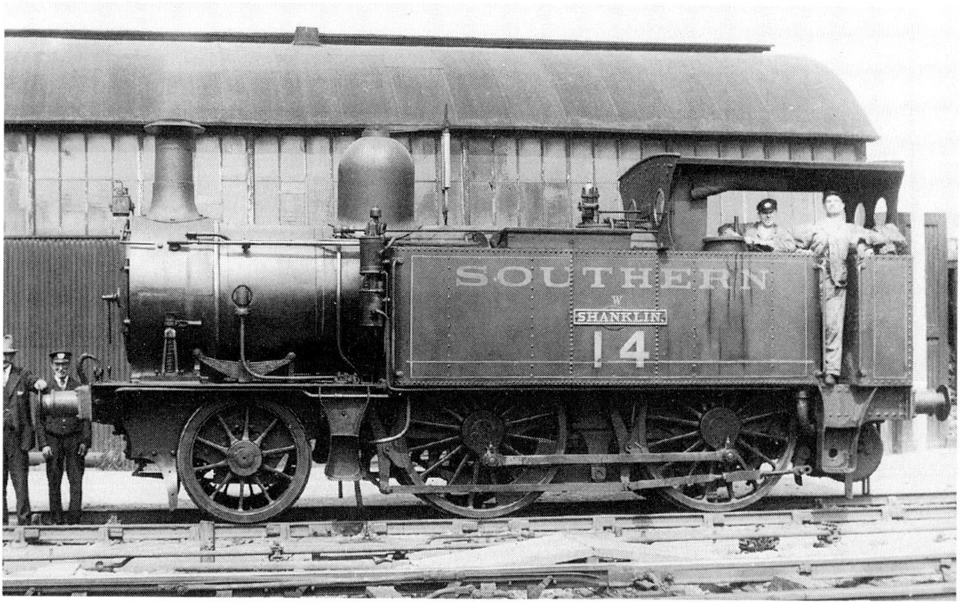

Chapter Thirteen

Steam Locomotives

The Southern Railway inherited 18 steam locomotives and a petrol driven rail motor car from the Island companies. Most were Beyer, Peacock 2-4-0T locomotives or second-hand LBSCR 0-6-0Ts of classes 'A1' and 'A1x'. They were expensive to maintain and it was hardly surprising that the new owners would replace them.*

Discussions about suitable locomotives probably began in 1921 when Sir Herbert Walker inspected the Isle of Wight railways. The Island companies were asked not to incur any heavy expenditure, so in October 1922 a request to the IWR Board for spare parts was passed to the LSWR. Eastleigh works drawing office prepared drawings of the larger *Bonchurch* and the nearest LSWR equivalent, class 'O2', showing how they could fit the IWR loading gauge.

The LSWR had a number of branch lines worked principally by 0-4-4 tank locomotives of class 'O2'. Sixty were built between December 1889 and March 1895 in the LSWR workshops at Nine Elms under the management of William Adams as replacements for elderly 2-4-0Ts on branch lines where heavier locomotives were barred. There were also 34 class 'G6' 0-6-0Ts built from 1894 onwards for shunting and local goods workings. Driving wheels, motion, boilers and cylinders were interchangeable between the classes, although the 'G6' class and the last batch of 'O2s' had cab roofs 6 in. higher than the remainder. After the introduction of electric trains on the LSWR suburban network during World War I there was a surplus of tank locomotives and, by 1923, withdrawals of older 4-4-2Ts were well under way. Fortunately no members of class 'O2' had been withdrawn before the need arose for locomotives in the Isle of Wight.

LSWR Nos. 206 and 211, undergoing routine overhaul at Eastleigh, were fitted with shorter Drummond chimneys to fit the loading gauge of 12 ft 3⁵⁄₁₆ in., about 10 in. less than on the mainland. To work with the existing stock, a Westinghouse brake pump was mounted on the side of the smokebox connected to an air reservoir on the left-hand tank. A repaint in LSWR green with white and black lining completed the work. In May 1923 a posse of tugs towed a hired Admiralty floating crane from Portsmouth to Ryde Pier Head where the pair were lifted onto the rails in platform 3. The 'O2s' were put to work on Ryde-Ventnor line services and proved most satisfactory. They could haul a packed train up to Ventnor with relative ease and only reached their limits after the arrival of heavier bogie carriages in the 1930s.

For the summer service beginning 9th July, 1923 five locomotives were needed to work the IWR section and six the IWC, the latter being an increase of one compared with previous summers; one locomotive was steamed by the FYN for its service. Weight restrictions prevented the heavier locomotives from working on Medina Wharf, the Bembridge branch, Freshwater line and over Newport drawbridge and Cement Mills viaduct.

* A summary, including arrival, departure and withdrawal dates is in *Appendix Five*.

When the class 'A1' and 'A1x' 0-6-0Ts were painted in SR livery, the standard size 'Southern' filled the top of the tank side, making it appear larger than normal. Ex-IWC No. 10 is seen at Newport c.1928.
IWSR Collection

In May 1924 ex-FYN No. 1 was overhauled and allocated as the Medina Wharf shunter, although photographs of her there are rare. As No. W1 *Medina* she is seen marshalling LBSCR opens at Medina Wharf sometime after naming in 1929.
IWSR Collection/A.B. Macleod

During the first inspection of the Island railways by SR management in August 1923 the need for more locomotives was discussed. Richard Maunsell, SR chief mechanical engineer, was asked to arrange the transfer of two of a standard type each year for the next six years, a corresponding number of the existing locomotives to be broken up 'unless it is considered necessary to retain one or two of them for dealing with extra traffic'. Eastleigh had already sent two 'O2s', so the transfer of more from the same class was assured once bridges and track had been strengthened.

By August 1923, the SR had settled upon a livery and numbering system for its locomotives. Locomotives on the mainland retained their pre-Grouping number with a prefix; LSWR locomotives carried 'E' (for Eastleigh works), LBSCR 'B' (Brighton) and SECR 'A' (Ashford). Island locomotives were allocated running numbers in a 'W' series: FYN - 1-2; IWC - 4-12; and IWR - 13-18 (*Sandown* was withdrawn before it could gain a number); the 'O2s' were numbered from 19 onwards.

Prompted by experience with the first pair of 'O2s', in January 1924 Eastleigh prepared more drawings that added lifting links on the side tanks, altered tyre sections and adjusted the brake pull rods, the latter probably due to the fiercer action of the Westinghouse brake. LSWR Nos. 205 and 215 shipped by barge to St Helens were in a partly dismantled state so they could be unloaded by the cranes on the quay. Renumbered 21 and 22, they were painted green but lettered in medium chrome yellow lettering (an imitation of gilt) described by A.B. MacLeod:

> The original Southern locomotive livery was always, for some reason, described as 'Sage Green', which for anyone acquainted with a sage bush, it certainly was not. In fact the colour was a true olive green, exactly the colour of a good green olive.

The lettering was laid out as follows:

SOUTHERN	6½ in. high
w	3 in. high
21	18 in. high

The running numbers, e.g. **No.** (coupling) **22**, were repeated in 5 in. numerals on the front and rear buffer beams; they were also stamped on the motion to assist in reassembly. No. 206 underwent an overhaul at Ryde in April 1925 and left the workshops carrying this livery with the number 19; 211 became No. 20 after August 1925. The livery was applied to other Island locomotives except for Nos. 4, 6, 7 and *Sandown* which were withdrawn carrying their pre-Grouping liveries.

The shipment of locomotives via St Helens was not repeated because the SR had purchased its own floating crane. On Sunday 26th April, 1925 'O2s' Nos. 23 and 24 were lifted onto the crane's deck and towed by tugs from Southampton to Medina Jetty where the crane off loaded them. The advantages of using the crane were obvious and it became the preferred method of shipping locomotives and rolling stock. 'O2s' Nos. 25 and 26 arrived in June carrying a new livery about which Mr MacLeod wrote:

> In 1925 the colour was changed to the coach green, a deeper mid green shade similar to the old Great Central Railway locomotive colour, the lining remaining the same as before, white line with square panel corners bordered by a black band.

A redistribution of the existing locomotives resulted in the appearance of IWR locomotives at Newport shed and some from the IWC at Ryde. By the summer of 1925 there were sufficient 'O2s' to work all Ryde-Ventnor line trains. Their arrival followed enquiries in April 1925 to establish why so many locomotives had to be kept in steam. The report contained some interesting information about working practices at Ryde and Newport:

> The services at present arranged, involve 17 Engines being lighted per diem. The total number of Engines on the island is ... Newport 13 ... Ryde 8 ... Of this number, two are always in shops undergoing a general repair and one is generally stopped for heavy running repairs. It will therefore be realised that the running repairs necessary to maintain these Engines in an efficient order have to be carried out during the night and the washing-out of Engines has also to be done in the very early hours of the morning... this is a practice which should at all costs be prevented, as the Engines go into the Depot, fires dropped, steam blown out, washed out with cold water, and lit up again in the space of a few hours with consequent serious effect and possible damage to the firebox. The Boiler Inspector also is emphatic upon the question of dirt being in those boilers due to the existing methods of washing-out.

Duty No. 10 at Medina Wharf was rather onerous where, because of a shortage of siding space, a locomotive had to be away from shed for 26 hours at a time. Far from achieving a reduction, an increase was recommended so each could have a 'shed day' when the boiler was washed out and minor repairs attended to. The Island allocation was increased to 23.

The workshop at Newport closed in May 1925 after No. 12 received an overhaul and repaint. Henceforth a Newport-based locomotive destined for overhaul would be dispatched via Sandown so that it faced the correct way for admission to Ryde works. It might then spend a week running-in on the Bembridge branch and be turned on the Bembridge turntable before taking the direct route back home.

The 'O2s' carried Adams boilers that in some cases were as old as the locomotives themselves. Since they had a healthy future in Isle of Wight service the SR built two batches of 15 Drummond pattern boilers, six of which were carried by Nos. 27-32 sent between March 1926 and May 1928 and based at Newport. Compared with a handful built during LSWR days, the boilers were stockier in appearance with a curve to the casing at the bottom. They had to be fired differently from the Adams type because, if not carefully handled, could suffer from erratic steaming and priming. Ryde works spent much time in swapping them around in an attempt to cure the problems but to no lasting effect. The Ryde-based locomotives Nos. 19-26 retained their existing Adams boilers until more of that pattern could be built or reconditioned. It became regular practice for Ryde works to replace a boiler due for overhaul with a spare shipped from the mainland, the defective boiler being transported on a converted IWR carriage truck to St Helens where a barge took the boiler to the mainland. Whether Eastleigh works sent the same boiler back to the Island after overhaul was a matter of luck.

Work to upgrade the bridges and track so that the 'O2' class could run throughout the Island did not keep pace with withdrawals and that created a shortage of locomotives to work the branch lines and goods trains. Following a derailment in 1926, the LBSCR 0-6-0Ts had to be taken off the Freshwater line leaving only four 2-4-0Ts to work both the Bembridge and Freshwater lines. Improvements to the track were quickly put in hand and within months the 0-6-0Ts were back in charge of the line. Of the five class 'A1' and 'A1x' 0-6-0Ts inherited from the FYN and IWC, No. 9 was withdrawn but the others received overhauls and class 'A1x' boilers. Three more were transferred between 1927 and 1929; Nos. 3, 4 and a second 9 had been rebuilt by the LBSCR to class 'A1x', but for Isle of Wight service each received an extended coal bunker and a tool box on the left-hand tanks. Nos. 2, 3 and 10-12 carried push-pull equipment for the Ventnor West branch.

The provision of nameplates had been suggested in 1925 but three years elapsed before Eastleigh works cast a batch of brass plates for the Isle of Wight locomotives. No. 2 *Freshwater*, left Ryde works in October 1928 with the **SOUTHERN**, nameplate, running number and prefix crowded on the tank sides (*see* (a) *below*). In subsequent namings the prefix and running number were moved to the bunker sides and the **SOUTHERN** repositioned so that it was one-third from the top of the tank sides, the nameplate being one-third up from the footplate; the **SOUTHERN** lettering was reduced in size on those locomotives that had smaller tanks (*see* (b) *below*). They carried yellow and black lining to tank and bunker sides and ends, along the footplate framing and on the driving and trailing wheels. Locomotives undergoing complete repaints had the borders of the number and name plates lined out and a LSWR style power classification letter was painted on the footplate frame behind the front buffer beam; the **W** prefix, carried on bunker sides, was left off after the abolition of prefixes to mainland running numbers in 1931. The two surviving IWR locomotives, Nos. 13 *Ryde* and 16 *Wroxall*, had their IWR nameplates replaced by the SR pattern. The last locomotive to receive a nameplate was 30 *Shorwell* when overhauled in June 1931.

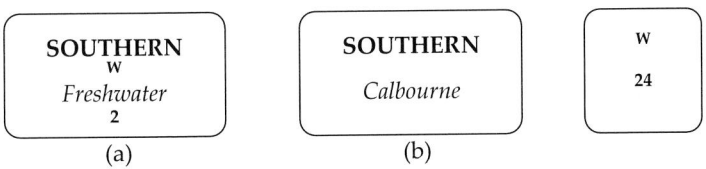

(a)   (b)

So that signalmen at Ryde could differentiate between IWR and IWC trains, IWR locomotives carried lamps or discs on the smokebox or bunker top whilst IWC locomotives carried lamps over each buffer. When Ryde and Newport sheds began exchanging locomotives Ryde works scampered to fit additional lamp irons. 'O2s' Nos. 19-26 arrived carrying lamp irons each side of the

Six class 'O2s' carried Drummond boilers when transferred. In addition, this view of No. 28 shows the three bunker coal rails with sheeting at the sides to prevent coal falling onto platforms. Note also that the six LSWR pattern lamp brackets are still carried.
IWSR Collection

smokebox door painted white to show they were not in use; they were left off when the locomotives received new boilers. In 1930 an Island-wide system of route discs (or lamps at night) and duty numbers came into use; duties 1-12 were carried by Ryde locomotives and 13 onwards were used at Newport.

Soon after Mr MacLeod took charge of the motive power there was a heavy snowfall and 16 *Wroxall* was fitted up with brooms tied to its guard irons. A wooden snow plough was made for fitting to the front buffer beam of an 'O2', but its capabilities were never tested as the snow did not return whilst he was at Ryde!

To avoid steaming a shunting locomotive within Ryde works yard a hand-powered tractor was constructed. To quote its designer, Mr MacLeod,

> A wooden chassis and a platform was made to suit the rail wheels and give enough space for two men to stand and turn handles, which would be connected to a vertical shaft in a column by bevel cog wheels and thence to the gearbox. The gearbox came from the Ford parts. There would be a ratio of 1 to 1 for travelling light, and 4 to 1 for propelling the wagons, etc. The connection to the rail wheels would be made by chains and coupling rods on the wheels to stop slipping.

Given the name *Midget*, two men could move 20 tons of stock without great effort. *Midget* began its shunting duties in January 1930 but fell into disuse after the departure of its inventor to the mainland in 1934 and was broken up in 1938.

A report written on 6th November, 1930 referred only to three non-standard Island companies' locomotives (Nos. 1, 13 and 16); they were 'in sufficient good condition to work to end of 1931' and it was not necessary to send a further LBSCR 'A1x' 0-6-0T that had been offered for the summer of 1931. This, the 27th locomotive, metamorphosed into one of three LBSCR class 'E1' 0-6-0Ts sent in 1932.

The reconstruction of Medina Wharf increased its capacity to handle coal and other minerals but the passenger service during the summer restricted the number of coal trains that could be handled between Medina Wharf, Newport and over the Sandown line. The 'O2s' had been designed to haul 100 ton trains but those in the Isle of Wight were cleared to haul up to 160 tons; that was not enough and Mr MacLeod convinced his superiors that a larger version of the 'A1x' 0-6-0T was needed.

The first three of four LBSCR class 'E1' 0-6-0Ts entered Eastleigh works for overhaul, including the fitting of new boilers with Drummond chimneys to comply with the Island loading gauge and Westinghouse brakes in place of the vacuum system. Since the 'E1s' were expected to work both passenger and goods trains they were painted in lined passenger green. Nos. 1-3 were shipped to the Isle of Wight in July 1932 followed by No. 4 in 1933. Three Island locomotives were renumbered to create separate blocks of running numbers: class 'E1': 1-4, class 'A1x' 8-14 (No. 2 renumbered 8, 3 to 13, 4 to 14), and class 'O2' 19-32. The maximum loads of passenger and goods trains were increased and the power classification letters revised.

By 1932 Ryde shed was turning out eight locomotives with a ninth in reserve on peak Saturdays; apart from two for the Bembridge branch all were 'O2s'. When the 'East and West Through Train' began running in 1932, an 'E1' worked

Route Discs

<u>In use from *circa* 1930</u>

Disc	Route
+ / O + O	Ryde Pier Head and Cowes
+ / + O O	Brading and Bembridge
O / + + +	Ryde Pier Head and Ventnor Newport and Freshwater
+ / + + O	Newport and Sandown Cowes and Ventnor via Merstone
+ / O + +	Newport and Ventnor West
+ / ⊙ + O	Shunting engine

<u>Used following the introduction of non-stop trains</u>

Disc	Route
O / + O +	Ryde and Ventnor not stopping at all stations
+ / + + O	Brading and Bembridge during the early 1930s

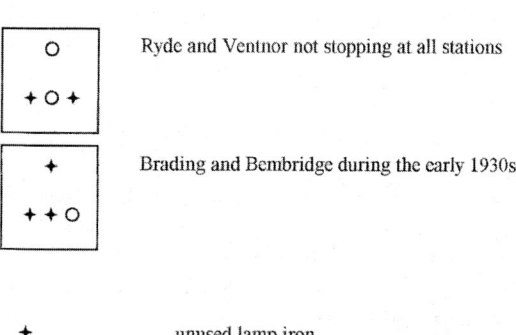

+   unused lamp iron
O   white disc or lamp at night
⊙   red lamp day or night

All are viewed head on.

STEAM LOCOMOTIVES

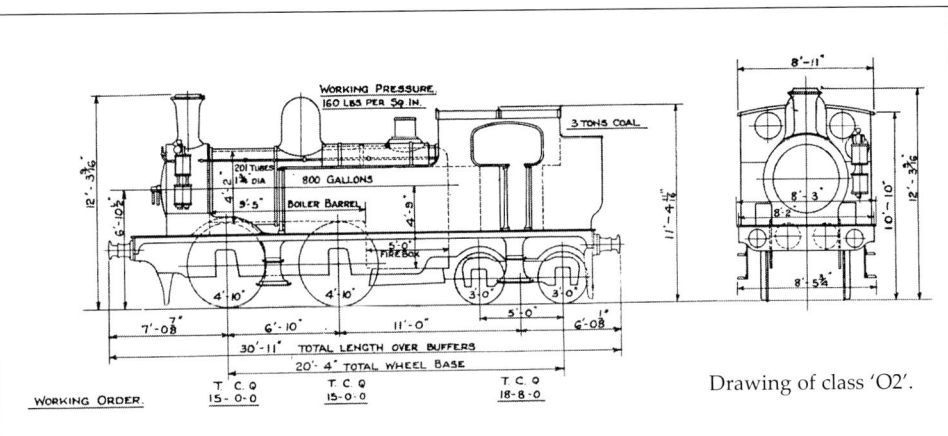

Drawing of class 'O2'.

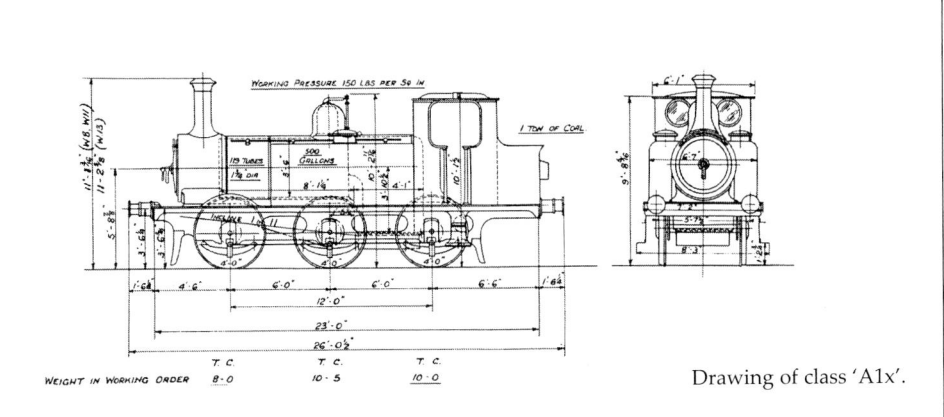

Drawing of class 'A1x'.

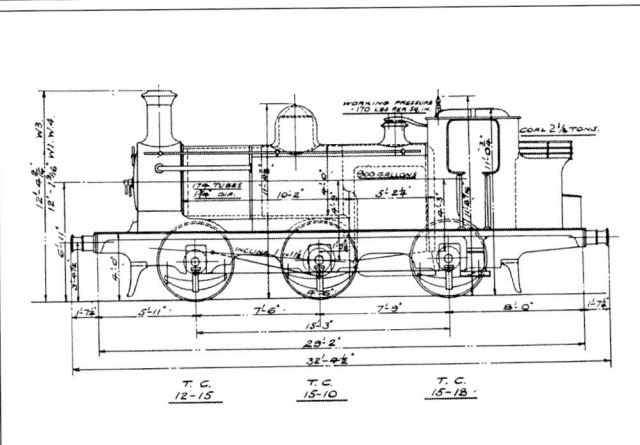

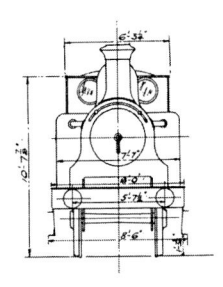

Drawing of class 'E1'.

The wooden snowplough devised by A.B. Macleod and fitted to an 'O2' at Ryde shed, but which was never used in anger!
IWSR Collection/A.B. Macleod

STEAM LOCOMOTIVES

The hand-powered tractor *Midget* in use shunting Ryde works soon after construction.
(Both) R.A. Silsbury Collection

Less than a week after transfer, 'E1' class No. 1 *Medina* stands resplendent in Newport Yard. Note the open coal rails, which were quickly plated in. *IWSR Collection/F.M. Butterfield*

A first attempt at increasing the bunker capacity of the 'O2s' saw Nos. 27 and 31 fitted with a fourth coal rail. No. 27 *Merstone* displays this modification at Newport c.1931.
R.A. Silsbury Collection/A.B. Macleod

the Shanklin to Newport leg with an 'A1x' 0-6-0T to Freshwater. Twelve months later 'The Tourist' was hauled by an 'E1' between Ventnor and Newport and an 'O2' over the Freshwater line. Although an 'E1' was initially kept at Ryde, it was not long before all the class were based at Newport. One worked from Newport to Ventnor with a goods train and after its 'Tourist' duty took a goods train up to Medina Wharf before spending the remainder of the day shunting. Another of the class worked 'The Tourist' in the reverse direction. Designed for goods work, they suffered from poor riding and a surging sensation at speed that had an unpleasant effect on passengers travelling in the first carriage. No. 4 *Wroxall* had its wheels balanced at Ryde works and when this proved satisfactory the other three were similarly treated.

Beginning on summer Saturdays in 1929, turnover locomotives were employed at Ryde Pier Head. The locomotive of an incoming train would wait at the buffer stops until its carriages departed hauled by a different locomotive; it then took charge of the next departure. In 1933 locomotives began to interwork, e.g. a Newport locomotive might work a Ventnor line train between journeys to Cowes or Freshwater. This helped to share out the burden of operating a busy summer service and avoided stationing men and locomotives at Ryde that would be needed only on peak Saturdays.

The 1½ ton coal capacity of the 'O2s' proved to be a handicap at peak times. The 'O2s' carried three coal rails when they arrived, except Nos. 27 and 31 which had four. In August 1932, No. 19 *Osborne* left Ryde works after an overhaul with an upward extension of the bunker in the style of those carried by tank locomotives on the Great Western Railway. Despite increasing capacity to 2¼ tons it blocked the view from the rear cab windows. In September No. 26 *Whitwell*, quickly followed by Nos. 22 *Brading* and 23 *Totland*, emerged with an improved version that extended the bunker back and upwards from the buffer beam to give a capacity of 3¼ tons and a range of 200 miles; the design had much in common with the bunker carried by recently-built class 'Z' heavy shunting locomotives. Starting with Ryde-based locomotives, the bunker was eventually fitted to the Island 'O2s' and subsequent arrivals when prepared at Eastleigh works. During 1932 and 1933 locomotives were fitted with cab doors. 'E1' No. 2 *Yarmouth* was fitted with a weather side screen on its right-hand side that could be folded back into the cab when not required, but it took up too much space and was soon removed.

There was a fatal accident on 22nd April, 1933 in Ryde shed when a fireman was crushed between the buffers of No. 19 *Osborne* and 13 *Carisbrooke* whilst the latter was being pushed back to make room for No. 18 *Ningwood*. On Sunday 21st May, 'O2s' Nos. 26 *Whitwell* and 27 *Merstone* had run to St Helens to be weighed on the 50 ton weighbridge; upon their return to Brading the coupled wheels of 26, which was hauling 27, derailed on worn points blocking the branch and the down main lines. Until No. 26 could be recovered, Ventnor trains used the up line; Bembridge branch passengers were carried by Southern Vectis buses. No. 31 *Chale* was working on the Freshwater line when it was derailed at Freshwater on 23rd June whilst running round its train; the cause was attributed to the stiffness of the locomotive after its recent overhaul combined with the super-elevation of a sharp curve at the point of derailment.

Locomotive restrictions 1923 to 1932

	From 9.7.23	From 1.10.23	From 14.7.24	From 22.9.24	From 12.7.25	From 21.9.25	From 11.7.26	From 10.7.27	From 17.6.28	From 7.7.29	From 6.7.30	From 5.7.31	From 18.6.32
Only to run Ryde-Ventnor			6 21 22 206 211	6 21 22	6								
Only Ryde-Ventnor Newport-Sandown				21-22 206 211									
Only Ryde-Ventnor Newport-Sandown Ryde-Cowes					206, 211, 21-4 *	19-26 *	19-30 *	19-31		19-32			
Newport drawbridge and Cement Mills viaduct		Not Nos. 206 211											
Bembridge branch	No locomotives weighing 35 tons or more	Only *Ryde Shanklin Wroxall*	Only 4 5 8 *Ryde Shanklin Wroxall*			Only 4 5 8 13-16	Only 8 13-16	Only 1-2 8 10-14 16	Only 1-3 8 10-13 16		Only 1-4 9-13 16		
Freshwater line		Not 6 or 7	No locomotives weighing 35 tons or more. Not No. 7					Only 1-2 10-12	Only 1-3 10-12		Only 1-4 9-12		Only 1-4 9-13 16
Medina Wharf	Only 9-12		Only 1-2 9-12										
Ventnor West branch									Only 1-3 10-12$				Only 1-4 9-12

A summary of restrictions taken from SR Working Timetables. Sometimes the official records lagged behind actual events.
* Speed limited to 10 mph over Cement Mills viaduct. $ "and 8 one day a week for relief purposes

Maximum loads of trains and classification of locomotives

Classification of locomotives	Prior to 1932	From 1932
A.	w17-32 (class O2)	Class E1
B.	w1 4 9 10 12 16	Class O2
C.	w2 3 11 13	Class A1x

Maximum loads of trains Passenger between	Prior to 1932 A.	B. Tons.	C.	From 1932 A.	B. Tons.	C.
Cowes and Newport	187	125	100	195	187	125
Newport and Ryde	131	85	70	190	155❶	90
Newport and Merstone	187	150	140	195	187	150
Merstone and Sandown	150	100	80	195	155	100
Ryde and Ventnor	150	100	80	170	155❶	100
Merstone to Ventnor West	131	85	65	150	135	90
Ventnor West to Merstone	125 *	80	60	150	135	90
Brading and Bembridge	-	100	80	-	155	100
Newport and Freshwater	-	85	65	170	140	90

❶ in good weather conditions the loads may be increased to 160 tons.

Goods between	A.	B. Numbers of loaded goods	C.	A.	B. Numbers of loaded goods	C.
Newport to Cowes	38	25	20	30	25	20
Cowes to Medina Wharf	38	25	20	40	26	20
Medina Wharf to Newport	38	40①	33②	61⑥	40	30
Newport to Ryde	25③	16	12	40	30	16
Ryde to Newport	25③	16	12	40	40	30
Newport and Merstone	40	35	26	61	36	30
Merstone to Sandown	28	20	15	53	30	20
Sandown to Merstone	28	20	15	40	30	20
Ryde to Ventnor	28	20	15	45	30	23
Ventnor to Ryde	28	20	15	45	30	20
Merstone to Ventnor West	25 *	16	12	25	18	16
Ventnor West to Merstone	20 *	14	10	30	20	14
Brading and Bembridge	-	25④	20⑤	-	40	30
Newport to Freshwater	-	16	12	30	18	16
Freshwater to Newport	-	16	12	20	18	16

① or 25 minerals, ② or 20 minerals.
③ from 1 May to 30 September, 20 wagons of coal of 30 or goods may be hauled between Newport and Ryde.
④ or 15 minerals, ⑤ or 12 minerals, ⑥ limited to 25 minerals when stopping at Cement Mills to attach wagons.

Two loaded wagons of minerals (coal, chalk, ballast, etc.) equalled three wagons of other goods.
Three empties equalled two loaded goods wagons.

* after the track was relaid on the branch in 1930.

'O2' class No. 19 *Osborne* displays the experimental larger bunker at Ryde St Johns in August 1932. The weld lines of the new platework can just be made out.
R.A. Silsbury Collection/A.B. Macleod

The final design of enlarged bunker fitted to the 'O2s' can be seen in the view of No. 28 *Ashey* at Newport coaling stage; the livery is believed to be unlined malachite green with pre-war style lettering.
R.A. Silsbury Collection

STEAM LOCOMOTIVES

Four 'O2s' arrived in May 1936 in exchange for four class 'A1x' 0-6-0Ts sent back to the mainland. No. 12 *Ventnor* was already out of use and neither it nor No. 10 *Cowes* ran again. Three class 'A1x' 0-6-0Ts remained at Newport shed for the Medina cement trains and Ventnor West branch. One of the new arrivals, No. 15 *Cowes*, lacked brass beading to the wheel splashers (as did some of the 'G6' 0-6-0Ts). That year No. 31 *Chale* was the last of the existing Island 'O2s' to receive a 3 ton bunker when it underwent heavy repairs. At the same time an Adams boiler was substituted for the Drummond pattern and, between 1936 and 1938, all the 27-32 series of 'O2s' were similarly treated.

The retirement of Richard Maunsell in 1937 was followed by the appointment of Oliver Bulleid as chief mechanical engineer and a change in locomotive livery. Ryde works kept to the existing livery until October 1939 when lining was abandoned as a wartime economy measure; Nos. 4 *Wroxall* and 24 *Calbourne* were the first to emerge in this style. Commencing with No. 29 *Alverstone* in April 1941, unlined black was applied with yellow-shaded green 'Bulleid' style lettering. The 'E1s' were did a fair amount of work and received reconditioned boilers, but overhauls of the remaining locomotives were scaled down and surplus locomotives were stored in sidings around the Island. There were several mishaps that caused damage, but no locomotives had to be written off.

Towards the end of the war, Ryde works, began painting locomotives in malachite green 'as bright a mid-green as there is' with scarlet buffer beams and backgrounds to nameplates; yellow and black lining was applied in the same style as that carried pre-war. The **SOUTHERN** lettering was 9 in. high except for the 'A1x' class that were 6 in.; to the right of the coupling on the buffer beam were 3 in. high numerals. Peter Allen visited the Island in April 1946 when he noted a mixture of liveries:

- pre-war lined green   'A1x' No. 11
- pre-war green but unlined   'E1' No. 4, 'O2' No. 24
- unlined black   'E1s' Nos. 2-3, 'A1x' No. 8, 'O2s' Nos. 14-16, 19-20, 23, 25, 30, 32-33
- unlined malachite green   'O2s' Nos. 18, 22, 28-29
- lined malachite green   'E1' No. 1, 'A1x' No. 13, 'O2s' Nos. 17, 26, 31
- undergoing repair   'O2s' Nos. 21, 27

Ryde works had difficulty in catching up on arrears of maintenance and at one time it was thought that two 'O2s' would return to the mainland for overhaul. However, by the time the floating crane returned from war service in 1947 the position had eased and only No. 29 *Alverstone* was sent to Eastleigh for overhaul. No. 29 was accompanied on its return journey by 'O2' No. 34 *Newport* in exchange for 'A1x' No. 11 *Newport*. No. 34 was in LSWR Drummond green with white and black lining using paint said to have been left over from a restoration job. The number was applied on the rear of the bunker using 4½ in. size shaded numerals; the same size numerals were used on the front buffer beams of both locomotives with a gilt **W** to the left of the coupling; Ryde Works had long-since stopped applying the prefix to its locomotives.

It had been evident before the war that the 'O2s' were beginning to struggle with the heavy trains on the Ryde-Ventnor line. Intended as a possible

Post-war finery, lined malachite green and 'Sunshine' lettering on No. 31 *Chale* waiting to work a Sandown train at Newport in August 1947.
IWSR collection/R.C. Riley

'O2' class No. 34 *Newport* in Eastleigh shed prior to transfer to the Island in 1947. The lighter green livery is very evident whilst the bunker back number numerals were to be unique on the Island.
IWSR Collection

replacement, LBSCR class 'E4' 0-6-2T No. 2510 was selected for transfer to the Island and entered Ashford works on 29th October, 1946 for repairs, the fitting of a shorter chimney and modifications to the footsteps. No. 2510 was run in locally before dispatch to Eastleigh works for weighing and inspection; it was ready for shipping to the Isle of Wight at the end of the year, but gales and heavy snow delayed its arrival until 22nd February, 1947. By the time No. 2510 entered service in April it had been banned from entering Ventnor station so could not be used as intended. Elsewhere, heavier coal and water consumption outweighed any advantages it may have had over the 'O2s'. No. 2510 was relegated to spare locomotive at Newport until returned to the mainland in 1949.

The Island's railwaymen had great hopes for Nationalisation and during 1948 Ryde works, with almost indecent haste, began turning out locomotives bearing the title **BRITISH RAILWAYS** in unique hand-painted shaded lettering. Green locomotives might appear in traffic with small grey patches covering the **SOUTHERN** lettering and then painted green before the application of new lettering; the patches could still be made out in photographs. 'O2s' Nos. 15 *Cowes*, 33 *Bembridge* and 'A1x' No. 13 *Carisbrooke* carried smaller 6 in. numerals on the bunker sides. The first locomotive noted carrying BR lettering was No. 15 *Cowes* working the Ryde-Ventnor line on 8th April, it was joined by No. 17 *Seaview* on 24th April when the first Newport locomotive was seen, No. 33 *Bembridge*. The black locomotives were 'nationalised' by the application of lettering in the same yellow-shaded green style used during the war. Ignoring No. 2510 which remained in **SOUTHERN** lettering, the last two Island locomotives to be altered were 'O2s' Nos. 25 and 34 in August 1948. No. 34 retained its LSWR green boiler, etc. but the tank sides and bunker were repainted in lined malachite green; it lasted in this peculiar state until painted black after May 1952. By September the position was:

- unlined black   'E1s' Nos. 2-3, 'A1x' No. 8, 'O2s' Nos. 14, 16, 23, 'E4' No. 2510
- lined green   'E1s' Nos. 1, 4, 'A1x' No. 13, 'O2s' Nos. 15, 17-22, 24-34

In January 1949 Ryde works began painting locomotives in a black with grey, cream and red lining. At first the lining was similar to an arrangement used on the London & North Western Railway with lining on the bunker side that extended no higher than on the tank sides, straight lining to the footplate framing and none to the splashers and sandboxes. No. 14 *Fishbourne* was lettered by hand **BRITISH RAILWAYS** in unique plain cream lettering but Nos. 16 *Ventnor* and 17 *Seaview* ran with blank sides until about August when they received the BR totem, described as 'an emaciated lion balancing on a bicycle wheel'. The nameplates had to be lowered to accommodate the totem and the power classification letter was repositioned to the bunker side below the running number. Push-pull fitted 'O2s' Nos. 35 and 36 were transferred for use on the Ventnor West branch in place of 'A1x' Nos. 8 and 13. Nos. 35 *Freshwater* and 36 *Carisbrooke* were painted lined black carrying nameplates but no number plates; the running numbers were in cream numerals on the front buffer beams.

Of the existing locomotives two 'E1s' received additional sandboxes below the front buffer beam and several 'O2s' were fitted with roof ventilators in an

'E4' class No. 2510 heads a trial working from Ryde St Johns to Wroxall on 8th June, 1947, having already been banned from Ventnor because it fouled the platforms. The post-war malachite green livery applied to the coaching stock is carried on LBSCR brake third No. 4161.

IWSR Collection/K. Nichols

Nationalisation saw a rapid application of a new identity; 'O2' class No. 23 *Totland*, in unlined wartime black, displays the hand written 'British Railways' on an obvious new black patch. The bunker number plate has also lost its 'Southern Railway' lettering. Note also the pristine SECR brake third No. S4142 with grey waist chalk panel and destination board.

R.A. Silsbury Collection

attempt to reduce temperatures in the cabs (including Nos. 14-18, 20-22, 24-32 and 34). Island locomotives never carried smokebox door number plates but the painted numbers on the buffer beam were retained; those that carried bunker number plates had the **SOUTHERN RAILWAY** chipped off them. Small shed plates made an appearance on smokebox fronts: '71F' for Ryde and '71F' for Newport (from 1st July, 1954 '70II' and '70G' respectively). The last locomotive in malachite green, No. 32 *Bonchurch*, was repainted black when overhauled in 1953. Only No. 3 *Ryde* still carried the full **BRITISH RAILWAYS** lettering; the 'E1s' and No. 36 *Carisbrooke* were unlined black.

Early BR papers gave an insight into the system for keeping locomotives in repair. It had been the practice since IWR days to avoid carrying out heavy overhauls during the summer season and, towards the end of each summer, the Assistant for the Isle of Wight would meet with the locomotive foremen to agree a programme of repairs for the ensuing months. All locomotives were needed during the summer months when, even as late as 1953, Newport shed turned out nine 'O2s' and three 'E1s' on weekdays or ten 'O2s' and one 'E1' on Saturdays. BR classified the 'E1s' as goods locomotives but the Island quartet were still regularly rostered for 'The Tourist'.

The SR ceased to manufacture major components for classes 'O2' and 'G6' in 1936 and withdrawals began on the mainland just before the onset of war. This resulted in the reappearance of Drummond boilers on Island locomotives after overhaul, including one of the three LSWR-built boilers, and many withdrawn locomotives were cannibalised for spare parts. Between July 1954 and April 1957 four of the Isle of Wight 'O2s' (Nos. 15, 19, 23 and 34) were withdrawn with a combination of cracked main frames, worn out cylinders and boilers that needed heavy repairs; at least eight others had their frames repaired by welding. Detail differences became more pronounced with flush or visible riveting around the smokebox and on the front of the buffer beam, fluted instead of flush coupling rods and patches on the tank sides.

The 'E1s' were in an even more parlous state. The boilers were nearing the end of their lives, spares were hard to come by and most of the class on the mainland had already been broken up. They spent increasing periods in store until withdrawn between 1956 and 1960. After No. 4 *Wroxall* went in 1960 the Isle of Wight was finally operated by a single class of locomotive.

After the barge service to St Helens Quay came to an end, boilers, wheels and other spares were transported via Thetis Wharf, Cowes and by road to Newport for onward delivery by rail to Ryde (one boiler still bore marks left by a mainland number plate on the smokebox door). As the closure of the Newport-Sandown line would remove the last means of turning locomotives, an effort was made to ensure that they faced the same direction. No. 15 *Cowes* was towed around 'the triangle' as it was touch and go whether it or No. 28 *Ashey* would be scrapped.

The closure of Newport motive power depot in November 1957 coincided with the introduction of a new totem on the tank sides that Mr MacLeod described as 'a half lion emerging from the crown holding a crumpet'. The BR power classification letter ('0P' for the 'O2s' and '2F' for the 'E1s') was applied on the bunker sides immediately above the running number and until 1960 locomotives kept the SR classification letter below the running number.

The first 'O2' 'nationalised', No. 15 *Cowes* with 'British Railways' lettering but retaining lined malachite livery is seen at Ryde Esplanade in August 1949. The bunker sides were later repainted and lettered with 6 in. high numerals.   *IWSR Collection/H. Wheeler*

When lined black was decided upon as the new BR livery, initial repaints kept the bunker lining at the same height as that on the tanks. 'O2' class No. 16 *Ventnor* displays this style at Ryde St Johns in April 1949, prior to the BR totem becoming available.   *IWSR Collection/R.R. Bowler*

The absence of any modern SR tank locomotives that could be sent to the Island prolonged the lives of the 'O2s'. Several classes of locomotive throughout the BR system were considered as replacements, including GWR class '57XX' 0-6-0Ts that were rejected because of their poor condition. In 1960 serious thought was given to the transfer of BR Standard class '2' mixed traffic 2-6-2Ts, of which 30 had been built in 1953 and 1957. In order to bring them within the Island loading gauge the chimney had to be reduced by 6½ in., the dome by 2¹⁄₁₆ in., the cab roof by 1 in., the side cab windows removed and the vacuum brake replaced by the Westinghouse air brake. Eastleigh works prepared the necessary drawings but after No. 84022 arrived at Eastleigh it was realised that the class needed expensive overhauls so the 'O2s' were left to soldier on. The idea was resurrected in 1965 when more design work was done; No. 84014 was sent to Eastleigh but was again in such poor condition that the project was abandoned.

Withdrawals began again with No. 25 *Godshill* at the end of 1962. It had derailed on trap points south of St Johns Road station on 22nd August, 1957 causing cracks in the driving wheels that ultimately led to its demise. In 1964, during the ultrasonic testing of components, No. 36 *Carisbrooke* failed its 'fitness test' as the *Isle of Wight County Press* called it. When the cylinders of the other 'O2s' were examined the motive power department reached crisis point after four locomotives were condemned. The summer Saturday service on 4th July, 1964 (which required 14 locomotives) could not be operated and problems escalated when No. 26 *Whitwell* broke a crank pin at Havenstreet. Locomotive diagrams were hurriedly rearranged to cut out light running to Ryde shed for coal and water by substituting coaling at Ventnor using a mechanical grab crane hired for the purpose. Two sets of cylinders found at Eastleigh and Exmouth Junction were rushed to the Island but mishaps continued unabated. When No. 22 *Brading* broke a crank pin near Mill Hill in October the flailing coupling rod pierced a side tank; No. 31 *Chale* failed at Ashey on 26th January, 1965 when a broken piston wrecked a pair of new cylinders.

Nos. 14, 18, 21, 26 and 30 were laid aside for withdrawal in anticipation of the line closures in October 1964 but when they were delayed, No. 14 underwent a wheel change and with Nos. 21 and 26 was returned to service; Nos. 18 (which had lost a set of wheels to No. 14) and 30 never ran again. The CME warned that the remaining 14 locomotives would have to be returned to the mainland for heavy boiler repairs costing £10,000 each if they were to remain in traffic beyond the end of 1966.

'O2' No. 24 *Calbourne* received a general repair and a reconditioned boiler ready for the summer 1965 service; it was painted in unlined black carrying just its running number and the BR totem. No. 27 *Merstone* left works at the end of July 1966 and thereafter the survivors received attention in the running shed to keep them in service. The brass name and number plates had to be removed to prevent theft but, as a final gesture, those still in service were fitted with smaller metal replacements bearing the name painted in cream on a black background.

For the last day of steam working on 31st December, 1966, Nos. 14, 17, 22, 24, 27, 28 and 31 were in steam. The oldest of the 'O2s', No. 14 *Fishbourne*, hauled the last return journey to Shanklin, just as it had taken the last passenger trains to Cowes and Ventnor.

Locomotive shed allocations

Year end	Ryde shed	Newport shed(s)	Locomotives arrived	Locomotives withdrawn	Locomotives to mainland	Total in service at end of year
1922	seven IWR 2-4-0Ts					18
1923	13-18 206 211	1-2 4-12	206 211			19
1924	5 6 16 18 19-22	1-2 4-12	21-22			21
1925	5 16 19-24	1-2 4 7-15 17	23-26			22
1926	13 16 19-24	1-2 7-14 17-18 25-26	27-30	4 6 15		22
1927	13 16 19-24	1-2 8 10-12 14 18 25-30	3 31	5 7 9 17		23
1928	13 16 19-24	1-2 3 8 10-12 25-31	32	14		23
1929	13 16 19-24	1-2 3 8 10-12 25-32	4	18		23
1930	13 16 17-24	1-2 3-4 10-12 25-32	9 17-18	8		26
1931	3 17-24	1-2 3-4 9 10-12 25-32				26
1932	3 9 13$ 17-26	1-2 4 9 10-12 13 16 25-32	1-3	1* 13*		27
1933	3 9 13 17-26	1-2 8$ 10-12 14$ 16 27-32	4	16*		27
1934	3 9 13 17-26	1-2 4 8 10-12 14 27-32				27
1935	3 9 13 17-26	1-2 4 8 10-12 14 27-32				27
1936	14-24	1-2 4 8 10-12 14 27-32				27
		1-4 8 11 13 25-33	14-16 33			27
	unchanged 1937-1946					27
1947	14-24	1-4 8 13 25-34 2510	29 34 2510			28
1948	14-24	1-4 8 13 25-34 2510			11 29	28
1949	14-24	1-4 25-36	35-36			27
	unchanged 1950-1954					27
1955	14 16-18 20-22 24	1-4 25-33 35-36		15 19 23 34		23
1956	14 16-18 20-22 24 26 27 29 30 35 36	1 3-4 25 28 31-33		2		22
1957	3-4 14 16-18 20-22 24-33 35 36	Newport shed closed November 1957		1		21
1959	4 14 16-18 20-22 24-33 35 36			3		20
1960	14 16-18 20-22 24-33 35 36			4		19
1962	14 16-18 20-22 24 26-33 35 36			25		18
1964	14 16-18 20-22 24 26-31 33 35			32 36	9 10 12 14	18
1965	14 16-17 20-22 24 26-29 31 33 35			18 30	8 13 2510	16
1966	14 16-17 20 22 24 27 28 31 33 D2554		D2554	21 26 29 35		14
						11

Former Island company locomotives are shown underlined.

* returned to the mainland after withdrawal. *Sandown*, 9 and 10 were withdrawn after return.

$ Class A1x locomotives 2, 3 &. 4 were renumbered 8, 13 & 14 in 1932 after the arrival of class E1 1-3.

When the BR totem was applied, it necessitated the lowering of the nameplates. On 'O2' class No. 17 *Seaview* the undercoat shows where the nameplate used to be. The low bunker lining was kept at the same height as the tanks. Ryde shed June 1950.
IWSR Collection

Even in their final years the Island 'O2s' retained their dignity; No. 14 *Fishbourne* in final BR livery stands at Shanklin with an up train in June 1966 bearing a replacement tin nameplate.
IWSR Collection/H.C. Casserley

Prior to 1966, withdrawn locomotives had been dismantled at Ryde. No. 18 was an exception as it was sold to H. B. Jolliffe Ltd; on 22nd December No. 14 towed it to Newport and on 4th January, 1967 No. 24 propelled it to Cement Mills siding for breaking up. Nos. 14, 16, 17, 20, 22, 27, 28, 33 and 35 were hauled to Newport where they were left standing in the up platform to await a buyer. On 18th April No. 27 was steamed to shunt the other eight into the Freshwater yard so that Jolliffe could begin breaking up No. 27; the task was completed in August when No. 33 succumbed to the breaker's torch.

Nos. 24 *Calbourne* and 31 *Chale* were kept at Ryde to assist in the electrification of the Shanklin line and were withdrawn in March 1967. Although *Calbourne* was saved for preservation, *Chale* was cut up at Ryde St Johns Road yard in September by A. King & Sons of Norwich.

The last locomotive to be repaired at Ryde works was 'O2' class No. 27 *Merstone*. On 26th July, 1966 the works' staff pose in front of the locomotive before it left. *J. Mackett*

Chapter Fourteen

Passenger and Goods Rolling Stock

Over 100 carriages and 500 goods vehicles passed from the Island companies into the ownership of the SR:

Numbers of Island companies' vehicles taken over by the SR

Passenger stock	IWR	IWC	FYN	Total	Goods stock	IWR	IWC	FYN	Total
Thirds	20	17	5	42	Open wagons	189	251	21	461
Brake thirds	-	6	2	8	Covered vans	12	45	4	61
Composites	18	13	4	35	Cattle trucks	3	8	5	16
Brake composites	-	3	1	4	Rail and timber wagons	13	9	-	22
Saloon first	-	1	-	1	Brake vans	2	3	1	6
Passenger guard's and luggage vans	11	2	-	13	Tar tank wagons	2	1	-	3
					Horse boxes	1	1	-	2
Total	49	42	12	103	Total	222	318	31	571

To this list must be added a Drewry rail motor car from the FYN, four tram cars and a flat truck on the Ryde Pier tramway and some mobile steam cranes at Medina Wharf and St Helens Quay. Less than 10 were classed as engineer's stock, including three hand cranes and four ballast wagons.

The SR decided to replace the existing stock with vehicles from its constituent companies that would be cheaper to maintain. As with the locomotives, the age of the replacement stock was of less importance than their ease of maintenance.*

Passenger Carriages and Vans

The SR numbering scheme was based on the LSWR system with blocks of numbers separated by wheel type, class and company of origin. Stock for the minor companies were allocated numbers following on from the constituent companies, but the first transfers to the Island carried numbers in the LSWR or LBSCR blocks. From 1925 arrivals carried numbers immediately preceding, in place of, or following, the Island companies' stock and most of the previous arrivals were given new numbers at Ryde in 1929 and 1930. The first set numbers for Isle of Wight carriages were allocated in 1926 and initially occupied numbers between 481 and 499.

Whilst the numbers of carriages running in the Island were of interest from a maintenance point of view, the operating department was more concerned about seating capacity. The following summary lists the number of seats inherited from the Island companies, after second class compartments in the IWR stock had been downgraded, and the eventual allocation for the Island during SR days (the exact number of seats fluctuated when there were transfers and withdrawals).

---

* A list is in *Appendix Six*. More information can be found in *Isle of Wight Passenger Rolling Stock*, by R.J. Maycock and M.J.E. Reed, Oakwood Press, 1997.

An LBSCR 6-compartment brake third S4155 stands at Ventnor.
IWSR Collection

Post-war passenger carriages were either SECR or LBSCR bogie stock. SECR 8½-compartment third No. 2440 is seen at Ventnor shortly before the end of steam working.
IWSR Collection

Carriage seating capacity	IWR	IWC	FYN	Total	Island allocation
First class	258	184	72	514	580
Third class	1,660	1,326	410	3,396	3,800

To meet immediate needs, Eastleigh works prepared nine LSWR bogie coaches formed into three-coach sets. The carriages were taken from the company's spare stock of non-corridor, arc-roofed bogie carriages and needed only an overhaul, repaint and replacement of the vacuum brake by the Westinghouse air system. They carried LSWR lined green livery but were lettered **SR** at cantrail height apparently using LSWR transfers. In July 1923 an Admiralty floating crane carried one set at a time to Ryde Pier Head where they were lifted onto the track in platform 3 on the eastern side of the station.

During the course of the August 1923 inspection it was noted that '... A large proportion of the carriages are out of date. Some are lighted by Electricity, some by Coal Gas and others by Oil. None are steam heated. The Westinghouse Brake is the one generally adopted but five of the Carriages are fitted only with the Vacuum Automatic Brake'. Mr Maunsell was asked to arrange to transfer 10 or 12 vehicles from the mainland each year for the next six years to replace existing stock. They would be painted in SR livery and equipped with electric light, steam heating and the Westinghouse brake, a convenient use for fittings taken from mainland stock after conversion to the vacuum system.

Although there were upwards of 60 spare LSWR carriages lying at Micheldever, no more went to the Isle of Wight because of a decision to send them to the Eastern Section in place of SECR carriages undergoing rebuilding as electric stock. Lancing works provided five sets of LBSCR Stroudley and Billinton four-wheel carriages that had been laid aside for breaking up. After they were fitted with the electric light and steam heating the first two sets were shipped by barge to St Helens Quay in August 1924. They were accompanied by a LBSCR Stroudley horse box and a six-wheel saloon that had the centre wheels replaced with truss rods to ease its passage over tight curves in the Island. They were followed by three LSWR six-wheel passenger guard's vans that Eastleigh works had converted to four-wheel stock.

Meanwhile, Ashford works formed the carriage portions from eight withdrawn SECR railmotors into two-coach sets, two pairs for the Sheppey branch and two for the Freshwater line. Four LCDR six-wheel carriages that had previously worked the Sheppey branch were converted to four-wheel two-coach push-pull sets for the Ventnor West branch. The four-wheel carriages could be sent immediately, but the bogie carriages had to wait until April 1925 when the floating crane made its first visit to the Island. The SECR bogie carriages could not be used as intended, as they fouled the bridges on the Freshwater line, and when moved to the Bembridge branch a van had to be attached to supplement their limited luggage accommodation; they were returned to the mainland in 1927.

By then a mid-green carriage livery had been adopted. Mouldings were picked out in pale cream lining and even the steel-panelled SECR carriages were lined out as if the wood mouldings existed. **SOUTHERN RAILWAY** lettering with matching running numbers were placed along the upper mouldings and **First** and **Third** on doors at waist level.

The three LBSCR bogie carriages purchased for preservation in 1967 included composite No. 6349, seen here restored at Havenstreet to SR malachite green livery. *R.T. Relf*

Labelling of trains. Extract from SR Appendix to Working Timetable 1930.

LABELLING OF TRAINS.

The standard method of labelling Trains is by means of side destination boards showing the names of the destination Stations and certain of the intermediate Stations.

The various types of boards are worded as under, and a board appropriately lettered should be fixed on each side of each Brake Coach.

Lettering on Boards.

OBVERSE.	REVERSE.
BRADING. ST. HELENS. BEMBRIDGE.	*BLANK.*
NEWPORT. CARISBROOKE. YARMOUTH. FRESHWATER.	*BLANK.*
RYDE. SANDOWN. SHANKLIN. VENTNOR.	*BLANK.*
RYDE. HAVEN STREET. NEWPORT. COWES.	SANDOWN. MERSTONE. NEWPORT. COWES.
MERSTONE. ST. LAWRENCE. VENTNOR WEST.	NEWPORT. MERSTONE. VENTNOR WEST.

The boards must be maintained in a clean condition and should they require to be repainted they must be sent to the Chief Mechanical Engineer at Ryde, St. John's Works, accompanied by a letter stating that a Stores Requisition will follow.

The Station Masters at Newport, Bembridge and Ryde Pier Head will be responsible for seeing that the boards are withdrawn for renovation and when such are despatched for renewal particulars must be sent to the Divisional Operating Superintendent's Office at Newport, who, in turn, will make a Stores Requisition in the usual way.

Having transferred carriages that could best be described as stopgaps, the SR identified a standard design that could be spared. Many six-wheel carriages built by the LCDR in the 1880s had been converted by the SECR to four-wheel and formed in close-coupled sets. The first of over 90 carriages and vans arrived in 1926 and by the summer of 1929 they had complete charge of the Ryde-Ventnor line and Bembridge branch. Running in two- and four-coach close-coupled sets, they were used on the Ventnor line with loose carriages in trains of up to 10 carriages. The LSWR bogie carriages, LBSCR four-wheel carriages and IWC and FYN carriages operated the Newport based services. Such was the growth in traffic that in 1929 the General Manager authorized an increase in the Island's allocation of third class seats by 600; this was met by the transfer of additional LCDR carriages. At the end of 1930 the total number of carriages peaked at 140; there were 19 passenger luggage and guard's vans. The last IWR carriages had been withdrawn in April 1929 and most IWC, FYN and LBSCR four-wheel stock followed in February 1931.

The availability of surplus bogie carriages on the mainland sparked off a second phase in the modernisation of the Island stock. In 1930 the IWC and LSWR bogie carriages were placed on the Ryde-Ventnor services with two newly-arrived LCDR bogie carriages, the first of 40. For their new duties, Ryde works altered three of the LSWR brake thirds to increase their seating capacity and overhauled the IWC carriages. By the summer of 1932 there were five 6-coach trains of bogie stock and two 10-coach trains of four-wheel stock working on the Ventnor line. That year, LCDR bogie carriages were used for a new daily through train between the east coast resorts and Freshwater. Twelve months later the train was running with an IWC bogie saloon carriage and in 1934 was joined by a LBSCR bogie saloon that had replaced the LBSCR four-wheel saloon; the two Brighton saloons were unique in possessing lavatories, but the through train lacked corridors so only a few passengers could avail themselves of this facility!

Mr MacLeod introduced carriage destination boards in a style used on mainland suburban services. They were carried on the sides of carriages and vans painted and lettered to match the carriage livery. The boards came into use in 1930 and lasted into the 1950s. Although the paint shop at Newport continued to turn out fully-lined carriages during the 1930s, the lining was simplified by omitting the lining below waist level. Some carriages had been partially or wholly clad in steel sheeting before their transfer and Ryde works began 'tin-sheeting' the existing carriages to give them a more modern appearance.

Between 1936 and 1939 LBSCR steel underframe bogie carriages and some LSWR bogie passenger guard's vans arrived as replacements for the four-wheel stock, three IWC bogie carriages and the LSWR bogie carriages. Such was the pace of change that some LCDR four-wheel carriages lasted in Isle of Wight service for barely six or seven years. Three LBSCR bogie push-pull carriages arrived for the Ventnor West branch in 1938 and a two-coach set for the Bembridge branch in 1947, although only the former was push-pull operated. By the end of 1938 the Isle of Wight possessed 100 carriages and 15 vans running in 20 set trains.

Carriage workings and station platform programme
Ryde Pier Head - Saturdays - Summer service 1934

Arrivals					Departures				
Engine Duty	From	Time due	Platform No.	Notes	Time	To	From platform	Engine duty	Notes
R1	St Johns Road	3.17	3						
N8	St Johns Road	3.55		light engine	4.0	Ventnor	3	R1	
R2	St Johns Road	6.35		light engine	4.5	Cowes		N8	
N1	Cowes	6.48	2		6.58	Ventnor	1	R2	
R4	St Johns Road	6.55		light engine	7.5	Cowes	2	R4	
R1	Ventnor	7.7	3		7.25	Ventnor	4	N1	fish & parcels
N2	Cowes	7.42	2		7.50	Ventnor	3	R1	
R6	St Johns Road	8.0		light engine	8.15	Shanklin	4	R6	parcels
R5	St Johns Road	8.5	3		8.25	Cowes	4	N2	
N12	Newport	8.14	2		8.55	Ventnor	1	R5	
R2	Ventnor	8.40	3		9.0	Cowes	2	R7	
R4	Cowes	8.46	4		9.18	Ventnor	3	R2	
R7	St Johns Road	8.50		light engine	9.23	Freshwater	4	N12	
N1	Ventnor	9.31	1		9.55	Ventnor	1	R4	
N3	Newport	9.41	3		10.3	Cowes	2	N3	
R1	Ventnor	10.3	4		10.18	Sandown	4	N1	
N6	Newport	10.8	3		10.30	Ventnor	1	R1	
R8	Ventnor	10.12	1	fast Shanklin	10.47	Freshwater	3	N6	
R6	Sandown	10.34	2		10.54	Ventnor	2	R8	fast Sandown
R7	Cowes	10.42	4		11.13	Ventnor	1	R6	fast Shanklin
R5	Ventnor	10.46	1	fast Shanklin	11.23	Ventnor	2	R5	
N1	Sandown	11.4	2		11.48	Ventnor	3	R7	fast Sandown
R2	Ventnor	11.8	3	fast Sandown	11.53	Sandown	2	R2	
R3	Ventnor	11.30	2		12.0	Freshwater	4	N1	
R4	Ventnor	11.39	1	fast Shanklin	12.13	Ventnor	1	R3	fast Shanklin
N5	Sandown	11.57	2		12.20	Ventnor	2	R4	
R1	Ventnor	12.2	3	fast Sandown	12.48	Ventnor	3	N5	fast Sandown
N4	Newport	12.9	4		12.53	Sandown	2	R1	
R8	Ventnor	12.30	2		1.5	Cowes	4	N4	
R6	Ventnor	12.39	1	fast Shanklin	1.13	Ventnor	1	R8	fast Shanklin
R2	Sandown	12.57	2		1.20	Ventnor	2	R6	
R5	Ventnor	1.2	3	fast Sandown	1.48	Ventnor	3	R2	fast Sandown
N6	Cowes	1.9	4		1.53	Sandown	2	R5	
R7	Ventnor	1.30	2		2.5	Cowes	4	N6	
R3	Ventnor	1.39	1	fast Shanklin	2.13	Ventnor	1	R7	fast Shanklin
R1	Sandown	1.57	2		2.20	Ventnor	2	R3	
R4	Ventnor	2.2	3	fast Sandown	2.40	Freshwater	4	N3	
N3	Cowes	2.12	4		2.48	Ventnor	3	R1	fast Sandown
N5	Ventnor	2.30	2		2.53	Sandown	2	R3	
R8	Ventnor	2.39	1	fast Shanklin	3.13	Ventnor	1	N5	fast Shanklin
N7	Freshwater	2.44	4		3.20	Ventnor	2	R8	
R5	Sandown	2.57	2		3.48	Ventnor	3	R5	fast Sandown
R6	Ventnor	3.2	3	fast Sandown	3.53	Sandown	2	R6	
R2	Ventnor	3.30	2		4.3	Cowes	4	N7	
R7	Ventnor	3.39	1	fast Shanklin	4.13	Ventnor	1	R2	fast Shanklin
R4	Sandown	3.57	2		4.20	Ventnor	2	R7	
R3	Ventnor	4.2	3	fast Sandown	4.48	Ventnor	3	R4	fast Sandown
N6	Cowes	4.9	4		4.38	Cowes	4	N6	
R1	Ventnor	4.30	2		4.53	Sandown	2	R6	
N5	Ventnor	4.39	1	fast Shanklin	5.13	Ventnor	1	R1	fast Shanklin
N3	Freshwater	4.46	4		5.35	Cowes	4	N3	
R6	Sandown	4.57	3		5.20	Ventnor	3	N5	
R8	Ventnor	5.2	2	fast Sandown	5.47	Ventnor	2	R6	fast Sandown
R5	Ventnor	5.30	1		5.51	Sandown	1	R8	
R2	Ventnor	5.39	3	fast Shanklin	6.15	Ventnor	3	R5	fast Brading
N7	Cowes	5.46	4		6.40	Cowes	4	N7	
R3	Sandown	5.53	2		6.22	Sandown	2	R2	
R7	Ventnor	6.3	1		6.47	Ventnor	1	R3	fast Shanklin
R4	Ventnor	6.19	3	fast Sandown	6.55	Ventnor	3	R7	
R1	Ventnor	6.44	2		7.10	St Johns Road		N5	light engine
N1	Cowes	6.53	4		7.18	Shanklin	2	R4	fast Sandown
N5	Ventnor	6.57	1		7.30	Newport	4	N1	
R6	Ventnor	7.34	3	berth in platform 1	7.23	Ventnor	1	R1	
N6	Cowes	7.46	2		8.20	Cowes	2	N6	
R5	Ventnor	7.57	4	empty	8.25	Ventnor	4	R6	
R3	Ventnor	8.24	3		8.30	St Johns Road		R5	light engine
N4	Freshwater	8.40	2		9.5	Ventnor	3	R3	
R4	St Johns Road	8.50	4	PLA vans	9.10	Cowes	2	N4	
R1	Ventnor	9.22	3		9.15	St Johns Road		R4	light engine
N3	Cowes	9.28	2		9.40	Ventnor	3	R1	
					9.45	Newport	2	N3	

R - Ryde engine, N - Newport engine

PASSENGER AND GOODS ROLLING STOCK 209

Following the outbreak of war, surplus carriages were given a coat of grey paint and stored in sidings throughout the Island. Those in regular use received an unlined malachite green livery bearing **SOUTHERN** in yellow-shaded black lettering at waist level, matching numerals for the running numbers and the class **1** or **3** applied below the waist moulding; early repaints carried a round topped **3** rather than the official flat topped style.

Two LCDR bogie carriages, a LSWR passenger guard's van and a couple of open wagons had been broken up after a derailment at Watchingwell in January 1939 and to make good the shortfall two LSWR carriages were kept in use. One LBSCR brake third succumbed following an accident at St Johns Road on 7th April, 1940 and the two LSWR carriages were withdrawn in 1942.

By the end of the war the wood underframes and running gear of the LCDR carriages was in a bad way and each was taken into Ryde works for repairs and a repaint in malachite green livery; even so, there was a distinct shortage of serviceable stock. The SR rarely wasted its money, but a failure to enlarge the loading gauge to mainland standards restricted the choice of replacement stock. The condition of the LCDR stock dictated that replacements would be needed and in August 1944 a template carriage was run over the Island system. The Chief Civil Engineer refused permission to use various LSWR carriages but the operation of SECR carriages might be possible.

On 22nd February, 1947 the floating crane delivered a SECR 60 ft carriage, No. 1060. Few clearance problems were encountered, but there was an excessive gap between the foot boards and curved platforms. Meanwhile, with the assistance of a carpenter loaned from Eastleigh, Ryde works fitted LBSCR third No. 2416 with templates so that the loading gauge could be checked before the arrival of more stock. No. 1060 was returned to the mainland in May, when the floating crane delivered a LBSCR push-pull set for the Bembridge branch and three SECR composites.

The SECR composites were to the same length as the LBSCR carriages, i.e. 57 ft. Previously running in three-coach non-corridor sets each with a lavatory brake third, lavatory composite and brake composite, for IW service the carriages were rebuilt as thirds, composites and brake thirds with half the carriage given over to luggage, mail and parcels. The 'birdcage' guard's lookouts and roof vents had to be removed to fit the loading gauge but even so there were only inches to spare when passing through Mill Hill tunnel, Cowes. Ryde works renumbered the composites, removed the lavatories and fitted the Westinghouse brake. The remaining 49 were rebuilt at Lancing works. The arrival of the SECR carriages was matched by the withdrawal of the last IWC bogie carriage and the LCDR carriages; some were returned to the mainland on the floating crane but the bodies of others were sold off locally. The replacements were more comfortable to ride in but had a lower seating capacity, so the total number of carriages increased. This third phase in the replacement of passenger stock ended in October 1950 with the return of seven LSWR passenger guard's vans in exchange for SR luggage vans. By the end of 1950 there were 58 LBSCR and 52 SECR carriages and 15 vans on the Island.

The heavier SECR carriages were concentrated in Newport-based sets, freeing LBSCR carriages for the Ventnor line. LBSCR brake thirds were formed at the 'country' end of sets so the SECR brake thirds with their large luggage compartments would be near the landing stages at Ryde Pier Head. Ventnor sets generally ran with three or four carriages in winter and six in summer, three of the six being lighter LBSCR vehicles. Newport sets had two or three carriages in winter, but might run with four or five at other times depending on availability.

In February 1948 carriages began appearing in malachite green livery without the **SOUTHERN** lettering and third class marking on the carriage doors but with a **S** prefix to the running number; SECR carriages transferred in 1948 also carried this style. Island repaints in 1949 carried Gill Sans yellow lettering applied by hand and the SECR carriages sent that year were similarly treated. It was not until July 1950 that the first carriage appeared from Newport paint shop in the official livery for local passenger stock. Painted crimson with yellow lettering, lining in black and gold was applied above and below the droplights; later repaints omitted the lining. By 1953 most Island carriages carried the crimson livery.

Set formations changed whenever a carriage was removed for overhaul or at the start and end of the summer season. Once the disruptions of the war years had been made good, an Island carriage might last up to four years between heavy repairs with more frequent checks on brakes, etc. The first SECR bogie carriage entered Ryde works for overhaul in 1951.

Closure of the Ventnor West, Bembridge and Freshwater lines was followed by the withdrawal of 17 carriages and vans, including the push-pull carriages and horse box. The moratorium on lifting the permanent way for 12 months also applied to the disposal of the rolling stock. Staff were refused permission to strip out seating material before the carriages were sent to St Helens Quay for storage so the vandals did the task for them. Between February 1956 and March 1959 a further 16 carriages and vans were condemned. The first withdrawals were broken up at St Helens; after the rail link was taken out in 1957 condemned stock was dumped in temporary sidings at the Cement Mills sidings north of Newport for scrapping by scrap merchants H.B. Jolliffe & Co. As on previous occasions, a few carriage bodies were sold off to local residents. Four SECR brake thirds were rebuilt as passenger brake vans to replace the remaining LSWR and LCDR bogie vans.

Special trains were run prior to the closure of the Newport-Sandown line to make sure that SECR brake thirds would be at the Pier Head end of trains and LBSCR brake carriages at the opposite end. The crimson livery was abandoned in 1957 when an unlined green livery was adopted. Some carriages were still crimson when withdrawn in 1959 and green did not became the norm until 1960.

The need to retain stock for only a few days a year became more obvious after the branch lines closed. Carriages for Ventnor line services had been stored during the winter months in sidings at Brading Quay on the Bembridge branch, in a long siding south of Brading station and at Ventnor. A replacement for Brading Quay was found at Sandown where the closure of the Newport-Sandown line freed the Newport line platform for one set. On summer Saturday mornings the train was timetabled to depart in passenger service from the platform, but had to be flagged away by the signalman as the starting signal had been removed. Locomotives would regularly double-head down trains from Ryde to collect their trains.

By July 1964 there were 56 carriages and 11 vans running in seven sets for the Ventnor line (sets Nos. 490-494, 497, 500) and four for the Cowes line (sets Nos. 485-488). They were described as 'working antiques' but that won them no special privileges and withdrawals began again after the Cowes line closed in February 1966. After first class was abandoned in January 1966, composites were either withdrawn or had their markings painted over (the green appearing markedly fresher than the rest of the paintwork). The last carriage to receive attention was No. 2442, a SECR bogie third, which left Ryde works in July.

After the summer season ended in September 1966 most of the carriages were dumped at Newport and broken up. Eleven carriages, running in a five-coach and two three-coach sets, and a few vans, were kept back until steam services ended. They were towed to Newport in January 1967 and although six carriages and a few vans were saved for preservation, the remainder were broken up later that year.

Ryde Pier Tramway Stock

On 1st January, 1924 the SR inherited from the Ryde Pier Company:

- a motor car rebuilt in 1911 by Pollard & Sons, a local firm, with a new body on an underframe salvaged from a four-wheel tramcar supplied by George Starbuck & Co. in 1871 or 1872. It worked on the east track.
- the 'Grapes' trailer car built by the company in about 1871. It worked with the Pollard car on the east track.
- a four-wheel motor car and trailer rebuilt in 1907 from a six-wheel car supplied in 1892 by Lancaster Carriage & Wagon Co. They worked on the west track.
- a four-wheel mail and luggage trolley that could be attached at the south end of a motor car when required.

When electric working on the tramway ended in November 1927, the two electric motor cars were replaced by petrol-engined motor cars Nos. 1 and 2 supplied by the Drewry Car Company of Birmingham. The motor cars worked with the existing trailers (Nos. 3 and 4) until 1936 when the 'Grapes' car was badly damaged in a collision with the buffers at the Pier Head. The remains were purchased privately and after restoration presented to Hull museum. Eastleigh works constructed replacement trailers Nos. 7 and 8 which matched the motor cars in style and capacity, whilst in 1939 Ryde works built a new luggage trolley No. 9. The cars and trolley went through various changes in livery and diesel engines were fitted to the motor cars in 1959 and 1960. After the tramway closed in 1969 car No. 2 was purchased for preservation but had to be dismantled before it could be removed from the tramway; the derelict chassis still exists. The remaining stock was broken up at Ryde Esplanade.

Although predominantly a passenger railway, freight traffic was still carried, especially coal from Medina Wharf. The maximum load for an 'E1' class between Medina Wharf and Newport was 45 minerals and No. 4 *Wroxall* has a very lengthy train waiting to leave the Wharf sidings. Of interest is the fourth wagon, the unique LBSCR open rebuilt as a 7-plank mineral; also the rake of six LBSCR vans probably berthed between duties on PLA traffic.

IWSR Collection/A.B. Macleod

No. 28391, one of over 450 LBSCR-pattern coal wagons, is seen at its usual 'home', Medina Wharf.
IWSR Collection

Goods and Engineer's Stock

The Island companies' goods vehicles were allocated running numbers by the SR in blocks divided by type and origin. New arrivals were given numbers in adjoining blocks, except for some early arrivals and those in engineer's use.
The majority were coal wagons with capacities ranging from 5 tons to 15 tons. At first it was proposed to send standard 12 ton open wagons in parts for assembly in the Isle of Wight. However, Lancing works had outstanding orders for LBSCR 10 ton wood underframe wagons and the SR placed more to keep the works in full employment pending a reorganization of the workshops. The wheel sets were not to a standard RCH pattern and by sending some to the Isle of Wight their maintenance would be better managed. The same thinking led to the transfer of LBSCR covered vans, cattle trucks, bolster and road vehicle trucks, the newest available examples being selected. In 1924 there was a batch of new wagons with raised round ends for tarpaulin bars that were never fitted; they were cut down when next undergoing repairs. By 1925 the SR had estimated how many goods vehicles would be needed and two years later a start was made on a wholesale replacement of the Island companies' stock.

Nos. of goods vehicles	Open wagons	Covered vans	Cattle wagons	Brake vans	Flat wagons	Bolster wagons	Tar tanks	Service stock	Total
IWR, IWC & FYN	462	61	15	6	11	11	3	11	580
Estimated 1925	470	40	10	10	*	10	3	27	570
Actual at 31.12.32	459	48	7	13	23	20	2	46	618

* not mentioned.

In 1924 18 dropside wagons arrived from Ashford for permanent way use. They were followed In 1927 by 18 LBSCR dumb-buffered ballast wagons to assist with permanent way renewals, but they were withdrawn when the work ended in 1932. On 18th May, 1927 three flat trucks, fitted with temporary wooden bolsters and carrying a consignment of 45 ft-long rails, were being shunted at Newport from the up main to the Sandown line when the centre wagon twice derailed. The bolsters were blamed for holding the rails too rigidly, despite having been Island practice for many years, and instructions were given for the transfer of some LBSCR single bolster wagons. Before they arrived an identical derailment took place at Newport on 17th July, 1928.

A handful of LSWR vehicles were sent at the request of J.C. Urie, who managed Ryde works for a time. They included four LSWR road vehicle trucks and two underframes from LSWR covered vans to replace those under IWR tar tank wagons. The need for 10 ton brake vans with side doors capable of carrying stores and other 'smalls' between Newport and Ryde was met by the transfer of LSWR road vans, there being no suitable LBSCR examples.

Isle of Wight goods vehicles were painted in the mainland livery of brown lettered **SR** in large white letters and matching small lettering at the bottom left and right ends. The ends of brake vans were vermilion and engineer's wagons red oxide. Most of the Island companies' wagons were scrapped before they could be repainted, but those surviving beyond 1927 generally carried SR livery

A batch of LBSCR steel ballast wagons sent to the Island in 1947 had short lives. Several can be seen in the siding at Blackwater in 1949 or 1950. Not only do they carry the final SR lettering but the earlier large SR lettering is also visible.
BR/OPC Collection

Four LSWR road vans were rebuilt with second balconies. No. 56047 forms the rear of a goods train in early BR days.
M. Reed

and running numbers. Each batch of arrivals was followed by the withdrawal of a like number of old wagons, those with smaller capacities being the first to go. Twelve redundant IWR and IWC 10 ton and 12 ton open wagons became locomotive coal and ash wagons lettered in a style specially drawn by Mr MacLeod. Two covered vans were lettered for fish traffic after complaints that the smell was permeating into passengers' luggage.

The end of horse racing at Ashey in 1930 was followed by the withdrawal of a GER horse box that had been owned by the IWC; a LBSCR vehicle (sent as a replacement for the IWR horse box in 1925) sufficed for the Island's needs. Mr MacLeod's departure from the Island in January 1934 was quickly followed by the withdrawal of one IWC cattle wagon and four open wagons (two each from the IWR and IWC). This left only a handful of revenue earning vehicles of Island company origin, two IWR tar tank wagons and an IWC (former MR) brake van rebuilt with end balconies for the Shide-Cement Mills cement trains. Four LSWR road vans were rebuilt with balconies at both ends and sanding gear for the Medina Wharf coal trains. Livestock traffic fell away so in 1935 three of the six cattle wagons were rebuilt as covered vans. However, the Chaplin traffic ended in 1937 and St Helens Quay became a dumping ground for surplus vans and machinery wagons; several of the latter were later broken up. Engineer's stock included three IWR and IWC hand cranes, some steam cranes at St Helens, two IWC tank wagons converted to weed killer wagons, locomotive coal wagons and a handful of breakdown and stores vans. At the end of 1936 the total number of goods vehicles stood at 563, not counting engineer's stock.

The Island was unusual in having very few private owner wagons. Associated Portland Cement Manufacturers, owners of the cement mills, possessed 35 chalk wagons painted yellow and originally lettered **VECTIS** in shaded lettering; later repaints bore a Blue Circle roundel. Of two sizes, they had a single end door at the Cowes end and no side doors. A few chalk wagons were shipped back to the mainland after the cement works closed in July 1943 and the MR brake van was withdrawn in 1946. The only other private owner wagons in SR days were two 'Royal Daylight' tank wagons.

In 1936 changes were made to the lettering of goods stock. The large **SR** was replaced by smaller initials above the running number at the left end and, unlike the mainland, the majority of the Island fleet received the new style by the time war broke out. During the war, the size of lettering was further reduced and the wooden bodies of wagons were left unpainted, apart from small black panels on which the lettering was applied.

Maintenance of the goods stock fell away during the war. One van was burnt out during an air raid at Medina Wharf in May 1942 and many wagons were roughly patched with tinplate to keep them in traffic. Six replacements of LBSCR origin transferred in 1947 were in poor condition so, in 1948 and 1949, 88 SR 13 ton open wagons were sent and an equivalent tonnage of wagons broken up. The 13 ton wagons were preferred for locomotive coal, leaving the smaller wagons for the merchants. Some covered vans were used as stores vans and others returned to the mainland where they re-entered service for a short time. As replacements for the IWR tar tank wagons, two tenders from withdrawn LSWR locomotives were sent in 1947 but they returned to the

The solitary LSWR large road van, No. 56058 at Medina Wharf. *IWSR Collection*

Two of the best known Island departmental vehicles were the two weed killer wagons, latterly Nos. DS428 and DS443 seen in the sidings at Newport, both showing signs of recent repair. The wagon on the right, DS3138, is the match truck for the MR six-wheel hand crane No. 429s.

IWSR Collection

A few LSWR machinery trucks were sent to the Island. No. 60562 was the last survivor.
M. Reed

mainland in 1950 after the traffic ended. Ten LBSCR steel dropside ballast wagons also arrived in 1947, but they suffered badly from corrosion and were soon discarded in favour of the existing dropside wagons; over the years they and the locomotive coal and ash wagons received LBSCR oil axleboxes and other fittings during repairs.

Ryde works retained the capability to repair wood-bodied stock and it was common to see part-dismantled wagons standing in the open whilst undergoing repairs. The neatly painted liveries of the pre-war years had gone and the goods fleet displayed a hotchpotch of brown, grey and black; some with the ironwork picked out in black, others not. It was a long time before the grey BR goods livery became established in the Isle of Wight and even then many wagons were never fully repainted.

The first line closures resulted in the scrapping of the cattle wagons in 1956, along with most of the covered vans and a quarter of the brake vans, bolster and flat wagons. Those wagons that remained in traffic were mainly employed in carrying coal from Medina Wharf and, after a clear out in 1960, only 150 LBSCR and 80 SR open wagons remained. The majority were broken up at Newport or Ryde in 1966 and 1967.

A similar fate awaited the engineer's stock. The LBSCR bogie saloon was converted to a breakdown van in 1959 but it was broken up at Ryde in 1967 with the weed killer tank wagons and other surplus stock. A few wagons were kept back for permanent way maintenance.

A typical LBSCR single bolster wagon No. 59052. IWSR Collection

Motor coach No. S22S being loaded onto MV *Camber Queen* at Portsmouth. Note the auxiliary ramp used to relieve stress on the ferry's loading ramp. Although officially recorded as being transferred to the Island on 22nd February, 1967, this photograph is dated 21st December, 1966!
IWSR Collection/BR(S)

The first electric car transferred to the Island was involved in various trials, being hauled by 'O2' class No. 24 *Calbourne* with a LBSCR covered van adapted as a match wagon. The cavalcade is seen south of Ryde St John on 4th September, 1966. *J. Mackett*

Chapter Fifteen

'Modernisation'

The question of how to modernise the railways in the Isle of Wight had exercised the minds of managers for years. The locomotives and rolling stock were life-expired and maintenance costs were growing. The restricted loading gauge meant that only certain stock could be used.

On 18th June, 1960 the *Isle of Wight County Press* reported that a thorough inquiry was under way to establish the most economic way of operating the Island railways. Diesel locomotives were regarded as a heavy investment, but modern steam locomotives could be adapted for use with the existing rolling stock. There was also a suggestion that the existing carriages could be replaced by 65 London Transport tube cars (*see Chapter Seventeen*). The ideas were not pursued, partly because it was hoped that closures would take the problem away.

Planning

In 1961 a working party was set up to consider how passenger traffic could be transferred to road, report on terminal facilities at Ryde Pier Head and give an estimate of the costs involved. In a report dated 25th September, the lowest estimate for adapting the pier for buses was quoted as £500,000 but that did not include the provision of a bus turning circle. A travolator similar to one at Bank station on the Waterloo & City underground line could be purchased for £1,050,000 but needed protection from the weather. Having rejected these options, the working party recommended the retention of a tramway along the railway pier and a new bus station at The Esplanade at a total cost of £162,000.

The recommendation was not to the liking of senior management, who wanted to rid themselves of all responsibilities in the Isle of Wight, and asked the working party to report again on the cost of adapting the pier for buses. A second report, dated 22nd June, 1962, pointed out that the sea level was within four feet of the pier decking at spring high tides so it would be necessary to raise the level of the pier, enlarge the pier head to create a bus turning circle and demolish the existing buildings at a likely cost of £1,250,000. The bus company was worried about the effects of side winds as there were no crash barriers strong enough to stop a bus from toppling into the sea. Estimates for the tramway and Esplanade bus station had risen to £250,000 but still compared favourably with the other option. Details were given of suitable rolling stock:

- two three-car trains of LT 1931-1934 tube stock would each cost £200-500 to purchase and £1,000 to overhaul. Powered by Gardner bus engines (maintained by SVOC) costing £7,000 each, the total bill was £23,000.
- the same number of SR 1940s 'augmentation' trailers from four-car electric units could be overhauled at £2,000 each or £9,000 for the two conversions to motor cars, a total of £35,000. Being heavier, they needed more powerful engines and a spare engine.
- new cars would cost £9,000 each and two power units £7,000, a total of £68,000.

When it became apparent that trains might have to work to St Johns Road, the SR trailers fell out of favour because they could not pass round the 8½ chain curve at Esplanade station and through Ryde tunnel. Specially built motorised luggage vans or LT cars could be used if fitted with Ruston & Hornsby 275 hp diesel generators, a type interchangeable with those in the Southampton docks locomotives (later known as class '07').

Although BR hoped for permission to close the Ventnor and Cowes lines, ways of reducing existing operating costs were considered. Several recommendations in a report dated 7th August, 1964 were later implemented:

1. Operate one train per hour on both lines except on summer Saturdays when there would be two to Ventnor, one to Shanklin and one to Sandown. That would require eight locomotives, 14 on summer Saturdays and 51 carriages. Their replacement by tube or other stock was not thought worthwhile.
2. Operate a 'bus stop' system by converting 10 carriages to saloons (two in each Ventnor train and one in Cowes trains), abolish first class and employ guards and five travelling ticket collectors to issue tickets.
3. Withdraw booking staff from Brading, Sandown, Shanklin, Wroxall and Ventnor except on summer Saturdays and Sundays. Newport, Mill Hill and Cowes to be unstaffed throughout the year saving 25 permanent and 19 casual staff.
4. Close the signal boxes at Brading, Sandown, Shanklin, Wroxall, Ventnor, Havenstreet, Newport and Cowes, saving 22 jobs after the installation of 'Rye' type automatic crossing loops operated by 'no signalmen key tokens'.
5. Transfer collection and delivery of parcels and unaccompanied luggage to British Road Services.
6. Purchase five 10 ton lorries for the freight traffic saving 285 wagons and six brake vans.
7. Make management and permanent way staff savings. In the long term, closure of the Cowes-Newport section would be pressed.

Towards the end of 1964 it became apparent that the Ryde-Shanklin line would remain open. A project team was set up and, following a meeting with Ministry of Transport officials on 5th February, 1965, rough estimates were prepared for operating a service by steam, diesel or electric power:

Estimated operating costs	Likely period of operation	Income p.a. £	Expenditure p.a. £	Capital cost £	Additional cost every 15 years £
Pier shuttle using diesel-powered tube stock	perpetuity (60 years)	87,500	57,200	326,500	47,500
Shuttle to St Johns Rd using diesel-powered tube stock	perpetuity (60 years)	100,000	73,800	310,000	95,000
Ryde to Shanklin steam service then a pier shuttle service	3 years 12 years	176,000	162,500	244,300	-
Ryde to Shanklin using electric-powered tube stock	10 years	176,000	122,000	526,500	-

'MODERNISATION'

The Minister's decision in July 1965 to order the retention *and* modernisation of the Ryde-Shanklin line forced the project team to reconsider the various options. Imaginative but time-consuming proposals for atmospheric or Neverstop (Lausanne type) railways were discarded, despite being advocated by at least one member of the BR Board. Conversion to a light railway and removal of most signalling was precluded by a need to operate five trains per hour at peak times. The rebuilding of Ryde tunnel and the curved platforms at Ryde Esplanade to take restriction C1 rolling stock was also rejected as it would cost over £1,000,000. Possible motive power included:

1. BR type 2 2-6-2T locomotives with the existing carriages. Each needed alterations costing £725 to suit the Island loading gauge, plus £6,000 in heavy repairs and £18,000 a year to maintain for an expected life of just seven years. Separate locomotives so increased operating costs that the line would lose £68,000 a year. The carriages cost £20,000 to maintain in 1964 rising at 5%-7% a year and had a remaining life of 10 years.
2. Diesel locomotives. Nine new locomotives would cost at least £65,000 each, i.e. £585,000. Re-geared 350 hp diesel shunters could not achieve the desired speed of 40 mph and lacked train heating. Swindon-built 650 hp diesel hydraulics (later known as class '14') exceeded the 15 ton axle load and needed expensive and time-consuming alterations to fit the loading gauge.
3. LT had considered using diesel engines mounted on match trucks to power trains over non-electrified lines but design and control problems required time to resolve and had not been costed.
4. Diesel multiple units rebuilt to the Island loading gauge were likely to cost the same as 46 new diesel-electric carriages at £900,000, including £15,000 for transportation to the Island.
5. Motor luggage vans powered by 600 hp diesel generators, each able to haul six vehicles, cost over £30,000, but £3,000 could be saved if the generators were used to power the motors in LT stock. Their performance would be inferior to multiple unit stock.
6. LT stock powered by diesel engines. The purchase and conversion of 46 cars would cost £400,000, including transport to Isle of Wight, but the motor cars exceeded the 15 ton axle load.
7. LT stock powered by batteries costing £513,000. A battery weighed an unacceptable 36 tons plus 18 tons in alkaline occupying at least 20 ft of a motor coach. Lead acid batteries at £361,000 were cheaper but even heavier.
8. Electric third rail operation was estimated at £203,000 plus £25,000 for signalling and telecommunications and £37,000 for fencing. Purchase and conversion of the LT tube stock added a further £87,600. An idea that overhead trolley wires might be cheaper than the third rail was quickly scotched!

The availability of tube stock at attractive, i.e. scrap prices, was an opportunity not to be missed. The most favoured option was to fit diesel engines as there was a reluctance to spend capital on transformers, conductor rail and other fixed works that might only be needed for a short time. This attitude changed after the project team proved that the most cost effective solution was electrification using LT stock operating on the Southern Region third rail system. Diesels might have been a viable alternative if all the lines remained open. Steam traction had not yet been ruled out because when first approached in February 1965 the local electricity board said it could not install an adequate electricity supply until the Autumn of 1967.

BR sent a paper to the Ministry of Transport in November 1965 quoting an estimate of £454,800 for electrification from Ryde to Shanklin and another £76,000 to Ventnor. The work had not been properly costed because staff were preoccupied with the Bournemouth electrification. It was envisaged that the peak service on summer Saturdays and bank holidays would be five trains per hour to Shanklin with two continuing to Ventnor. At other times there would be two per hour, one all stations to Ventnor and the other terminating at Shanklin after running non-stop to Sandown. An hourly service would operate in winter.

Details of the estimated revenue were disclosed during a meeting with the Isle of Wight County Council. To discourage discussion, BR warned that the Ventnor extension was 'quite uneconomic' and the railway to Shanklin was itself only being retained 'on Ministerial directive' so BR was effectively acting as agents for the Ministry of Transport. The Ministry would not have seen it quite that way!

Estimated annual revenue (as disclosed to the County Council in November 1965)		Ryde-Shanklin	Shanklin-Ventnor	Ryde-Ventnor
Income		£	£	£
1963 passenger revenue - adjusted to February 1965 level		132,000	15,700	
add for new fare structure		45,000	500	
	Total	177,000	16,200	193,200
Expenditure				
train movement		63,400	10,000	
terminal		24,100	1,300	
track and signalling		41,500	5,000	
other expenses		4,000	-	
agency charges - deducted if Ventnor extension operated		-	-1,300	
	Total	* 133,000	15,000	148,000
Profit or loss				
train working		44,000	1,200	45,200
less interest at 7%		32,000	6,000	39,000
	Total	12,000	-5,800	6,200

* Income would be reduced by £23,000 if the rail unions failed to agree to dual purpose staff (depot staff who would drive trains at busy times). Staffing numbers would be reduced from 395 permanent and 47 casual staff to 119 permanent and 7 casuals, plus another eight if the Ventnor section remained open.

Implementation

Having obtained the agreement of the Ministry of Transport, in July 1966 BR formally announced plans to modernise the railway between Ryde and Shanklin at a cost of £500,000. Some work could be carried out whilst the steam trains were running but the line had to close between December 1966 and March 1967 so that it would be completed before the summer season. During the 10 week closure, passengers would be carried by the pier tramway from Ryde Pier Head to the Esplanade where they transferred to buses running to the railway timetable.

The electrification was based on the Kent coast and Bournemouth line schemes but modified to suit the Island; i.e. the switch gear was non-standard and designed for smaller loadings such as on tram systems. The Island electricity supply to the local grid was only 11 kV and South Eastern Electricity Board had to install a 33 kV supply from its Wootton Common Grid Station direct to new brick substations built by BR at Ryde St Johns Road, Rowborough (about one mile north of Brading) and Sandown. 1,000 kW silicon diode rectifiers fed current to the trains at 700-750V dc. Trains could still run if Rowborough substation was out of commission, but the voltage drop and ability of the substation to detect faults over long distances meant that 'series only' working had to be introduced if Ryde or Sandown were switched out. An electrical control room at the Ryde substation was managed by Outdoor Machinery Department staff (until they were made redundant) and then by depot train maintenance staff, who also carried out routine maintenance and repairs to the substations. Supervision of the electricity supply was transferred in about 1975 to Havant control room (and later to Eastleigh) but depot staff continued to act as Controllers in the event of the loss of control from the mainland. The section on the pier could be isolated at Ryde Esplanade by the operation of hook switches (manually operated, conductor rail-mounted switching links); a gap in the conductor rail allowed trains to run into Esplanade station when the pier section was switched off.

Materials for the project began arriving in August 1966. Fifty-five foot lengths of 106 lb. conductor rails were selected to fit the barges, shipped to Medina Wharf and taken by train to a temporary dump at Sandown. Construction began of the substations and during October track relaying was under way on the double line from Brading to Sandown; by the middle of December the conductor rail was on site and the first three miles from Shanklin had been installed. Redundant signals at Smallbrook were cut down and two signals were salvaged from Havenstreet, one to replace the down starting bracket at Ryde St Johns Road and the other at Shanklin.

Reconstruction of the railway pier had reached Ryde Pier Head station. Platform 1 was taken out of use early in 1966 and work began after steam trains ceased using the station in September. BR cut the rebuilding cost from £100,000 to £70,000 by reducing the number of platforms but much of that saving was lost after a decision to create a double sided platform so that passengers could board a train on its west side and detrain on the east; it reduced stock requirements by one train. A second platform with a single face was retained

The taste of things to come; a train of conductor rail loaded onto LBSCR single bolsters heads through a closed Newport station in the late summer 1966. The wagons in the sidings appear to be loaded with ash and clinker.
IWSR Collection/T.R. Genower

The first underground car shipped to the Island was No. S38S on 1st September, 1966 and it ran trials behind 'O2' class No. 24 *Calbourne* and a LBSCR covered van converted to an adaptor wagon; it is seen here in the up platform at Ryde St Johns Road. The date must be after 18th September as only one arm remains on the down starting gantry, indicating that Smallbrook box had closed for the last time and that only the up line was in use to Brading.
IWSR Collection

for use whenever a second train had to be at the station. During the replacement of decking, etc., the trackbed was raised to suit the low floors of the tube cars. Redundant signalling was removed and the locomotive water tower demolished.

At Ryde Esplanade, where the platforms were built partially over the shore, they had to be reconstructed at a lower level to suit the height of the car floors and could not begin until steam traction ended in December 1966. In September 1966 the down line through Ryde tunnel was taken out of use and two months later the track was lifted ready for new drains and a deeper layer of ballast to reduce flooding. These reduced the loading gauge from 13 ft 6 in. to 12 ft 3½ in. Early in the new year the up line received the same treatment. To save money staff refuges were not provided.

At St Johns Road double track working to Smallbrook was made permanent. The down starting bracket signal was removed along with a facing crossover and the down loop was converted to a siding. The permanent way was completely relaid and the number of sidings in the works yard reduced. The carriage shed was intended to become a maintenance depot and provided with one 2-car inspection pit and an existing short pit was retained in road No. 1. The adjoining turnery kept its short pit but one external pit under the hoist was boarded over. The roof of the Smith shop, with its distinctive IWR water tank, was removed as was the corrugated iron workshop in the yard. On the west side of the station the two goods sidings were cut back and one raised on old sleepers to create an unloading ramp. After use as a temporary workshop, the locomotive running shed stood empty until demolished at the end of 1969. The connection to the up sidings and unloading ramp were taken out on 2nd February, 1975, after which the site was cleared.

In January 1967 the signal box at Smallbrook Junction was demolished and the line to Cowes severed, leaving a point and catch point protected by two aspect colour light signals worked remotely from St Johns Road (ignoring those in Ventnor tunnel, they were the first colour lights in the Island). Plans for an expensive 40 mph junction were abandoned but a sand drag was added so that trains could approach the down signal whilst another was on the single line; the up signal was repositioned so that trains would clear the single line section. Sidings at Brading, Sandown and Shanklin were removed, except at Sandown where the track into platform 3 was kept to serve two engineer's sidings. At Shanklin a 400 ft headshunt was retained at the Ventnor end and a scotch block fitted in the up loop so that a spare train could be stored in the platform. A long waiting shelter was provided in the station yard for travellers queuing to board buses to Ventnor during the summer.

After several tests, the distance between distant and stop signals was reduced to take account of the improved braking of the tube trains. Most home signals were removed and distant arms fixed at caution; the only working distant signals were some colour lights at Smallbrook. The signal boxes at Ryde Pier Head, St Johns Road, Brading and Sandown remained in use. Shanklin box opened on peak Saturdays when two trains had to be in the station at the same time; an arriving train would continue into the headshunt before reversing into the up platform. On other occasions trains reversed in the down platform where an up starting signal (salvaged from Havenstreet) was worked remotely from Sandown. The electric key token instruments were replaced with unique 3-position 'tokenless block' instruments, one in each direction of running in each box, interlocked with track circuits and treadles guarding the entrance and exit to each section; no longer would signalmen have to leave their box in all weathers to exchange tokens with the train crew. The existing bell signals between boxes was retained but when Shanklin box was closed the signalman at Sandown had to exchange bell signals with himself using a special block instrument. New fencing was erected along the line to discourage trespass.

Meanwhile, a crisis had developed as by July 1966 costs had spiralled to £623,000, not counting the rebuilding of Ryde Pier. This prompted hurried discussions amid fears that the project would be cancelled. One official wrote 'After all we are only building a railway for a few holiday makers and they should not be given too much fancy treatment'. BR admitted that the tube stock would have limited seating accommodation and the 'degree of comfort' would not be high. By November 1966 the figures had been massaged down to a more acceptable £546,300 after the Ministry agreed to dispense with ground level lighting along the platforms at Ryde Esplanade, allow a 9 in. difference in height between platforms and car floors, and omit sand drags at each end of the double line section between Brading and Sandown; instead the Ministry insisted that trains stop at every station. Bridge works at Lake were also deferred as was any rationalisation of the stations. A planning manager who visited the Island in February 1966 described Ryde Esplanade station as a shambles, at St Johns Road the footbridge was in a bad state, he wanted to get rid of most facilities at Brading, Sandown was a vast place and Shanklin a miserable station; the only demolition was at Ryde works for a cleaning siding.

Estimated capital expenditure All figures are approximate	Nov. 1965 Ryde - Shanklin	Jul. 1966 Shanklin- Ventnor	Nov. 1966 Ryde- Shanklin	Ryde- Shanklin
Costs -	£	£	£	£
conductor rail, substations, etc.	203,000	56,000	232,000	232,000
rolling stock	87,600	12,000	124,000	129,500
depot for rolling stock	20,000	-	24,200	24,200
signals and telecommunications	25,000	3,000	35,500	35,500
alterations to Ryde railway pier	70,000	-	83,000	60,900
track work to raise speed limit to 40 mph	15,500	-	28,000	5,500
high speed turnout at Smallbrook	2,700	-	9,000	4,700
fencing	37,000	5,000	28,300	28,300
alterations and raising of track at stations	-	-	50,000	34,100
berthing facilities at Ryde St Johns Road	-	-	12,500	2,600
temporary accommodation at Ryde	-	-	625	1,000
drainage and track lift in Ryde tunnel	-	-	8,272	incl. in above
supervisory control cable from the mainland	-	-	2,500	-
miscellaneous equipment	-	-	2,500	incl. in above
Less -				
residual value of displaced assets	-6,000	-	-12,000	-12,000
Total	454,800	76,000	623,000	546,300

The first tube car was transported to Ryde on 1st September, 1966 for gauging trials. Three days later it ran to Shanklin with a match truck converted from a LBSCR covered van and locomotive No. 24 *Calbourne*. A covered van was equipped with high voltage test equipment and, after the Ryde substation was energised, tests were carried out in the down siding. Before current was switched on a locomotive and motor car made trips to check the conductor rail position and ensure that no structure fouled the shoe gear. Between St Johns Road and Pier Head the test train was hauled by a recently-arrived diesel shunter as clearances were too tight for a steam locomotive through the tunnel.

In January 1967 some crossings and a hundred yards of track at Wroxall were removed for use at Shanklin in contravention of an order by the Minister of Transport that it be left in place between Shanklin and Ventnor for at least 12 months. Such was the sensitivity to the line closures that the incident attracted headlines in the local press: 'Isle of Wight line ripped up "in error"' as the *Portsmouth Evening News* put it. There were accusations of dirty tricks made worse by an inept statement from BR headquarters that it was policy to reuse assets.

Had the authorization been given for electrification of the line between Shanklin and Ventnor, the envisaged service of two trains per hour beyond Shanklin would have necessitated crossing loops at Shanklin and Wroxall plus a single platform at Ventnor. The cost of upgrading the electricity supply to a substation near Wroxall had not been included in the estimates and was a

A seven-car train of pre-1938 tube stock is seen arriving at Sandown from Shanklin on 31st July, 1969. *R. Maycock*

significant factor in the decision not to proceed with the work.

On Wednesday 1st March, 1967 the track between St Johns Road and Shanklin was energised and three days later a trial timetable with four return trips a day commenced; trains began running to Pier Head on 15th March and the public service began on 20th March. Despite the talk about modernisation there was little to show for the expenditure. Most points and signals were still mechanically worked albeit with simplifications to take account of multiple unit operation and the cessation of goods traffic. The stations retained their grimy green and stone colours, the new British Rail corporate image being indicated by station signs in black on white at Pier Head and St Johns Road. But elsewhere the Southern Region target name boards on the lighting standards were lowered so that they could be seen from the 'new' trains.

The Ferries

At the same time, but separately financed, were improvements to the Portsmouth-Ryde ferry service. The working party had concluded in 1961 that the use of hovercraft or hydrofoils would show no great advantage over the existing ferries because of the seasonal traffic, nor was it feasible to divert the service to Fishbourne. Of the three diesel vessels and three coal-fired paddle steamers, the latter had become uneconomic owing to rising coal prices, a decline in excursion traffic and cessation of the service to Southsea. After being used on only three occasions in 1961 the paddle steamer *Whippingham* was withdrawn the next year; *Sandown* followed in 1965 and *Ryde* was destined to

The first of the new generation of larger ferries was MV *Cuthred*, seen entering Portsmouth Harbour in 1969. *R.A. Silsbury Collection*

go in 1969.

During the Autumn of 1966 mechanically-operated gangways were brought into use at Portsmouth and Ryde Pier Head. The diesel vessels *Shanklin, Brading* and *Southsea* were refitted to give more circulation space at loading points. A veranda covering the main deck was rebuilt and lengthened to create an upper deck aft of the funnel for seating displaced from the main deck; lacking a covering for bad weather, it could also be unpleasant when downwind of the funnel! On the lower deck, the former first class saloon and bar were rebuilt with new seating and a replacement bar was built in part of the hold, for which there was little need after the transfer of most mail and parcels traffic to road. These alterations made it possible to reduce turn-round times to 15 instead of 30 minutes, maintain the peak capacity of 3,400 passengers per hour and reduce the number of vessels in service.

By then the ferries had a competitor, as in July 1965 Hovertravel Ltd began operating a hovercraft service between Southsea and George Street slipway, Ryde. Sufficient travellers were prepared to pay a first class fare for a 10 minute journey so the hovercraft has become an established part of the Island transport scene.

Investment in the Portsmouth-Ryde route paled into insignificance when compared with expenditure on vehicle ferries. Visitors who wished to take their cars to the Island had to regard the exercise as a military operation because it was necessary to reserve a space on the vehicle ferry months in advance of the journey. In 1959 an additional vessel, *Freshwater*, was delivered for the Lymington-Yarmouth route. Two years later £1,000,000 was spent on constructing a new terminal at Portsmouth and a wider slipway at Fishbourne. New vehicle ferries *Fishbourne* and *Camber Queen* entered service in July and August 1961 replacing the three old vessels; by reducing the crossing time to 45 minutes carrying 34 cars at a time they doubled capacity. Demand was so pent-up that the new ferries made little impact despite the introduction of 24 hour working on both routes 12 months later. Those who secured a night-time crossing often had the dubious pleasure of losing a night's sleep.

It was only after they were replaced by larger vessels in the 1980s that demand peaked. By then the Island had been transformed as locals, visitors and businesses came to depend increasingly on road transport.

Numbers carried Portsmouth-Fishbourne

Year	Cars	Lorries	Passengers
1962	100,870	8,711	310,322
1966	153,543	14,796	435,763
1970	228,433	23,455	660,249
1975	278,836	42,453	869,433
1980	320,912	53,022	1,016,117
1985	470,069	71,752	1,581,169
1987	524,811	88,906	1,839,177

1967 Ryde and Shanklin service

All departures were from Ryde Pier Head. Trains called at all stations and took 22 minutes between Ryde and Shanklin. All connected with Southern Vectis buses running to Ventnor at Shanklin station.

20th March to 19th May and from 11th September, 1967

Week days - 07.18 and hourly to 20.18, 21.28.

Sundays - 08.23 and hourly to 20.23, 21.28.
12.23 and 16.23 ran from 7th to 21st May and 17 to 24th September only.

20th May to 10th September, 1967

Monday to Friday - 07.18, 08.18, 09.18 and 09.48, then at 18 (to Sandown only), 25 and 48 minutes past the hour to 12.48, 18 and 48 minutes past the hour to 18.18, 19.18, 20.28, 21.28.

Saturdays - 06.48, 07.21, 07.33, 08.09 and every 12 minutes to 18.45, 19.21, 19.33, 20.21, 21.28, 22.20.

Sundays - 07.18, 08.28, 09.18 and 10.18 (to Sandown only), 10.25, 11.18 (to Sandown only), 11.25, 11.48, 12.48, 13.18, 14.18 (to Sandown only), 14.25, 15.18 and hourly to 20.18, 21.28.

The first day of public electric services, 20th March, 1967. The 11.59 Shanklin-Ryde Pier Head service arrives at Ryde St Johns Road formed of unit No. 041, whilst units 031 and 042 stand in the down loop and works sidings. *IWSR Collection/A. McIntyre*

Chapter Sixteen

The Ryde to Shanklin Line

The railway reopened to passengers on Monday 20th March, 1967 with a basic service of one train per hour. On weekdays from 20th May to 9th September the service increased to three trains per hour, one of which terminated at Sandown; the maximum 12 minute frequency operated on summer Saturdays. The trains carried no goods, parcels, mail or unaccompanied luggage. Some fares were increased to offset expected operating losses, although the Minister of Transport refused a request for increases of 50 per cent! The reopening was marked by a special train from Ryde Pier Head, leaving at 12.18 pm, carrying BR managers and invited guests to Shanklin where lunch was taken in a local hotel.

The closures in 1966 had shortened the railway to 8½ miles with stations at Ryde Pier Head, Esplanade, St Johns Road, Brading, Sandown and Shanklin. The maintenance depot was at St Johns Road but there were also engineer's sidings at Sandown. Double track existed from Pier Head to Smallbrook Junction and Brading to Sandown. The loop and headshunt at Shanklin were used at busy times when two trains needed to be at the station at the same time.

Apart from faulty signals, there were few technical problems. However, the increased service frequency, speed and unsprung weight of the trains began to cause damage to the permanent way, especially at rail ends where they were poorly supported by the shingle ballast. This led to a policy of welding alternative rail joints to reduce maintenance and later to lay granite ballast sent from the mainland.

The absence of de-icing and snow clearing equipment led to the closure of the line on 8th December, 1967 and a power failure at Fawley stopped services for almost an hour on 5th August, 1968. A start was made on painting the railway and tramway stations at Ryde St Johns Road and Ryde Pier Head (a waste of money for the tramway as it soon closed) in black and off-white with white window frames, yellow steelwork under canopies and vermilion doors. Signs in the latest style completed the 'modern image'.

A change of Government policy was marked in 1968 by a Transport Act that wrote off most of BR's debts and introduced the payment of grants from central funds for passenger services where there was a social need. The Ryde-Shanklin line never delivered the expected profits and in 1972 BR received a two year grant of £204,000 for the Shanklin line, the first of many subsidies. Politics bedevilled events as Government attempted to off-load responsibility for local transport to councils, who were equally anxious to avoid a burden that ratepayers would have to pay for! A 1974 Transport Act gave County Councils supplementary grants for investment but that merely encouraged BR, the MP and local politicians to argue over the need to keep the Shanklin line open, the amount of any financial support and how the money was spent.

When the electrification of the Shanklin line was discussed it was agreed (but never made public) that the Ryde Pier tramway would close once the electric

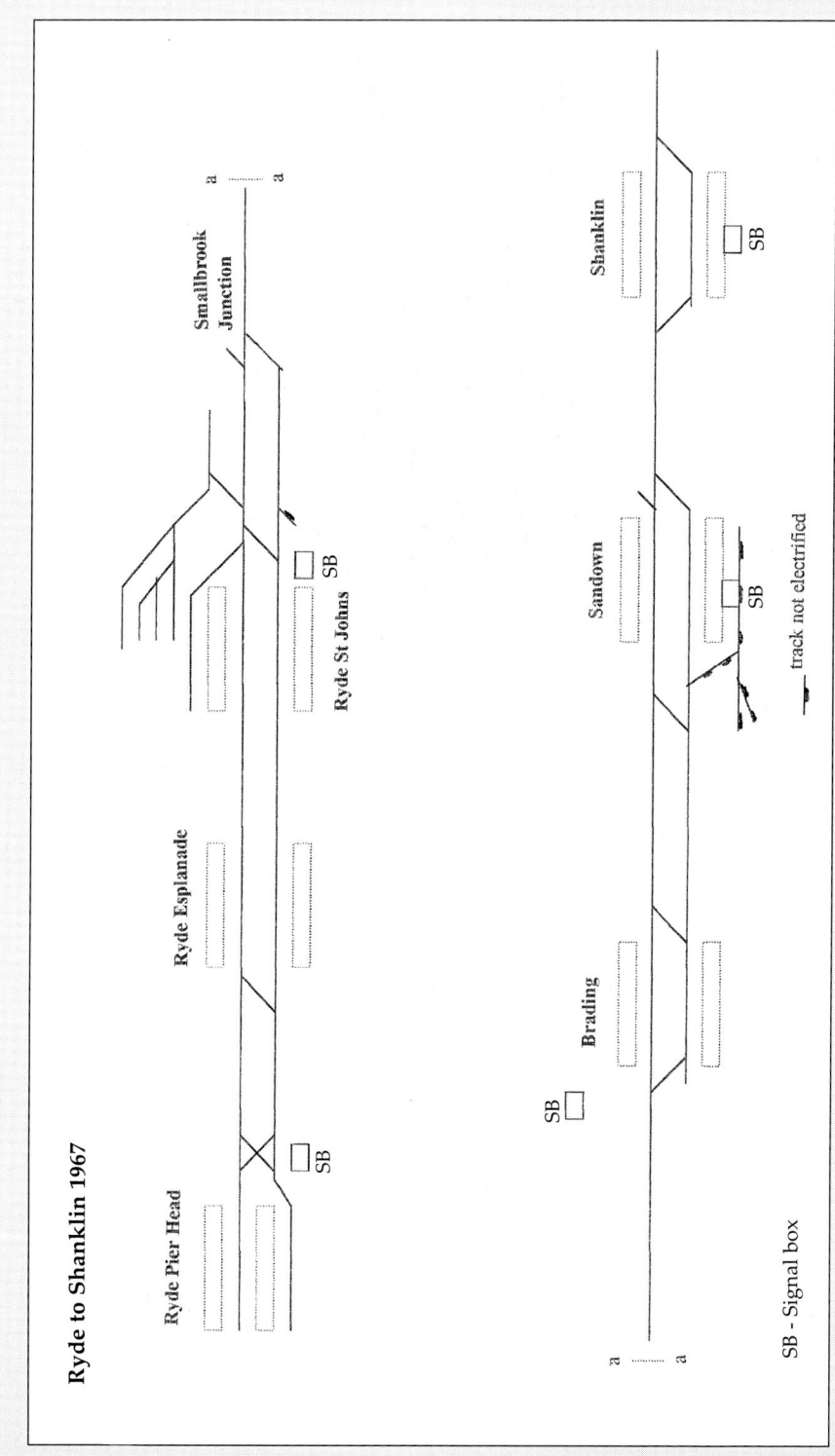

service had bedded in. BR pointedly omitted to make any statement about its future until March 1968 when closure proposals were put forward. The tramcars and permanent way were life-expired so the TUCC hearing into the closure became a formality. After all, who would use the tramway in preference to tube cars with upholstered seats and heating? In their favour, the tram cars ran when required whereas the electric trains had a set timetable that took no account of delays to the ferries. There were also problems during bad weather; in December 1968 high seas shorted out the conductor rail and resulted in the substitution of taxis, one of many such occasions.

On 26th January, 1969 the tramcars ran for the last time, embellished with a wreath and BR flags. Beginning the next day, the Shanklin service was supplemented at busy times by a shuttle service between Ryde Pier Head and Esplanade, the train continuing empty to St Johns Road to reverse. Colour light signals were installed between Esplanade and St Johns Road stations to permit the departure of a train from St Johns Road before the preceding train had left Esplanade and allowing eight trains an hour to run on that section. To cope with crowds on the down platform at Ryde Esplanade, an exit was opened close to a footbridge across the running lines that had been lifted into position during the night of 14th-15th July, 1969. The tramcars were broken up in April 1970 and after the rails were removed in October 1971, the decking, pier head tramway station and pavilion were demolished; an office for Trinity House was erected on the site of the tramway station but today even that has gone.

Closure of the tramway helped to reduce staff and maintenance costs. The introduction of conductor-guard working on 30th November, 1969 resulted in the closure of booking offices at Ryde St Johns Road, Sandown and Shanklin during the winter months and of Brading permanently; passengers had to board the last car and pay the guard. Passenger numbers did not justify the 10 minute peak service to Shanklin so it was reduced to a 15 minute frequency.

The greater speeds of trains and a need for adequate sighting distances for drivers prompted the replacement of several foot crossings by bridges. In the Autumn of 1969 a footbridge was erected principally for schoolchildren attending Gatten and Lake Primary School in place of Alresford Crossing, Lake. Twelve months later, the line south of Sandown closed from 17th to 19th November, 1970 whilst the railway bridge at Lake Hill, known for its faded inscription 'Too Low For High Bridge Buses', was replaced by a longer steel span; the road was widened and lowered during the following winter.

Ferry services were cancelled for several hours during a severe storm in November 1972. A 6 ft hole appeared under the up line near Ryde Esplanade, apparently caused by subsidence into an old cellar, and resulting in single line working between Pier Head and St Johns Road for several weeks (the cellar had to be filled in when it again gave trouble some years later). During gales on 11th February, 1973 a train hit a tree near Brading.

The railway had advantages over the bus. The journey time had dropped to 19 minutes from Ryde to Shanklin (by steam it was 28 minutes down and 26 minutes up), the trains were reliable and had room for bicycles, prams and luggage. The bus was timed to take 35 minutes but often took longer; it might be full, had little extra room and was a 'tedious and uncomfortable' journey that

234 THE ISLE OF WIGHT RAILWAYS FROM 1923 ONWARDS

Ryde Esplanade viewed from the newly installed footbridge with unit No. 036 heading a Shanklin train in 1969. The new exit from the down platform is visible behind the down starting signal, whilst the buildings on the up side have yet to be altered. Note also the up home colour light signal.
R.A. Silsbury Collection

1978 and the buildings at the south end of Ryde Esplanade had been demolished for a bus interchange. The down platform has lost its covering and is occupied by unit No. 043 working the pier shuttle. Unit No. 031 heads a Shanklin train away from the former up platform, regaining the up line by means of a crossover under the photographer. The down starting signal has been replaced by a colour light, whilst that on the up line has been altered to act as a down starting signal.
R.A. Silsbury Collection

stopped short at Ryde Esplanade. Local fares in 1973 were 30p by train whether single or return compared with a single bus fare of 16p. The majority of rail passengers were tourists who crowded the trains on summer Saturdays but some locals were attracted by the convenient service.

'Improvements' to the railway during the 1970s should really be regarded as retrenchment. The stations had a neglected air with faded paint and grass growing on the platforms. In thick fog on 9th March, 1973 the vessel *Shanklin* sliced into Ryde Pier, severed the promenade pier and almost demolished Pier Head signal box. Reprieve for the signal box was short lived as it was already in poor condition, it closed temporarily in October when single line working was introduced on Ryde Pier and was abolished permanently on 5th May, 1974. The box was later removed along with the signals and points at Pier Head and Esplanade; a plan to renew the scissors crossover at Pier Head was abandoned and a replacement that had already been assembled was sold to the Bluebell Railway. Henceforth, Shanklin trains used the up line along the pier and regained double track by means of a new crossover at the landward end of Esplanade station controlled by colour light signals worked remotely from St. Johns Road. To supplement the Shanklin service during the summer months a single train operated a shuttle service on the down line.

In February 1973 at Ryde Esplanade construction began of a new booking office and parcels office at the north side of the concourse in place of inadequate facilities at the opposite end of the station. During May and June 1976 the station was repainted in white, black and orange but the down platform covering and building remained untouched until demolished in early 1978, a new wall and waiting shelter being erected before the summer season.

After the local authority compulsorily purchased Newport station, a replacement Parcels Concentration Depot opened at Ryde St Johns Road on 1st May, 1972 but closed after cartage and delivery was abolished by BR in 1981. During 1975 the barrow crossings at Brading and Sandown were removed for safety reasons along with a foot crossing south of Sandown which was replaced by a subway at a cost of approximately £14,500. In January 1976 demolition commenced of the buildings and covering on the Sandown up platform leaving the signal box standing in isolation; it was said to sway in high winds!

By the summer of 1975 the peak service had fallen to three trains per hour; a half-hourly service operated during the following winter. The local press voiced closure rumours, made worse in 1976 when BR warned that this might happen if central Government did not pay for new rolling stock. Stephen Ross, the Island MP, later entered the fray by calling the stations 'a positive disgrace' and criticised the condition of the rolling stock. In November 1979 the *Isle of Wight County Press* wrote that:

> The Isle of Wight is the 'Cinderella' of the country's rail system and the first impressions gained by many visitors are coloured by the sight of 'Cinderella's coaches', discarded London Underground coaches travelling to and from Ryde Pier.

Adverse weather continued to affect the service: there were gales in January 1976, a heatwave caused fires along the trackside on 6th June and 29th June, ice

Motor car No. S5 heading a down working at Ryde St Johns Road has had the end cab doors plated over and 'Ryde Rail' lettering and emblems applied. *R.A. Silsbury*

Unit No. 485045 in 'Ryde Rail' NSE livery heads a down working at Ryde St Johns on 15th August, 1987. *R. Silsbury*

on 11th January, 1977 and fog on 2nd July. A cow that strayed on the line was electrocuted on 22nd August, gales brought down a tree near Smallbrook in November 1978, a blizzard on 30th-31st December with drifting snow at Rowborough stopped trains and heavy seas repeatedly shorted out the conductor rail on Ryde Pier.

The headshunt at Shanklin had not been used regularly since the abandonment of the 12 minute interval service. In 1977 the up platform was taken out of use and the signal box closed on 28th July, 1979, when the signals and permanent way in the headshunt and up platform were removed. Landguard Manor road bridge was demolished in October 1979 after the erection of substantial buffer stops and a northern extension to the down platform; the signal box was demolished in January 1980 and after the up platform was cleared of buildings it became a flower bed.

In 1981 passenger numbers on summer Saturdays were down by about 2,000 on previous years, the Portsmouth-Ryde route carried approximately 2,400,000 and 1,016,117 travelled via Fishbourne. The last of the diesel vessels were withdrawn after the delivery of two catamarans in April 1986, but within days there were complaints about their limited carrying capacity and poor handling in anything other than calm conditions. Nevertheless, maintenance and staffing costs were reduced (a catamaran had a crew of five and a diesel vessel 14) so a £600,000 operating loss in 1985 was transformed into a profit two years later.

In 1985 local staff devised the name *Ryde Rail* as a brand name and began applying it to stock undergoing overhaul. The name was short-lived as on 10th June, 1986 Network SouthEast was launched, a new division whose responsibilities covered local BR services surrounding London. Work began on a £250,000 two year programme to renovate and repaint the stations in a different livery of black, white and red. The platform covering on the eastern platform at the Pier Head was demolished in November and December 1986 and Sandown down goods yard was sold for housing.

Plans were announced to replace the buildings at Brading with a 'bus stop', a fair indication of the level of traffic, but after protests there was a change of heart and the buildings, signal box and footbridge were awarded grade II listed status by the Department of Environment. When the station's gas lamps were converted to electricity they marked the end of the last gas-lit station on the BR system.

Meanwhile, the County Council contributed £30,000 towards the £80,000 cost of constructing a halt at Lake. It came as something of a surprise to some local residents who had not been consulted and, fearing an influx of road traffic, objected to the Council's contribution. The 110 metre wooden platform and waiting shelter were completed by Dyer & Butler of Southampton ready for the start of the summer timetable on 11th May, 1987; a formal opening took place on 9th July. Convenient for the nearby beach and cliff path, on one Saturday 220 people used the halt in 2½ hours.

During the summer of 1987 a 20 minute service operated on weekdays and Sundays but hourly in the evenings (during the previous year only an uneven half-hourly service operated). The pier shuttle ran on Saturdays when passengers might exceed the capacity of the Shanklin train. A 20 minute service operated during the following winter despite the poor condition of the rolling stock.

Above: No. 03079 heads an up engineer's train in connection with the singling of the Brading to Sandown line in October 1988.
IWSR Collection/BR(S)

Right: Looking north from Sandown signal box on 4th November, 1988. Unit No. 485043 awaits a down working to clear the newly singled line to Brading; the light ballast marks the position of the new point. Class '03' No. 03079 and various stock are stabled in Brickfields sidings and the former Newport bay.
R.A. Silsbury

THE RYDE TO SHANKLIN LINE

In February 1986 there was heavy snow but by running a train through the night and using a de-icer car the line remained open at a time when road transport was badly disrupted. Services along Ryde Pier had to be suspended on 9th October, 1987 owing to severe gales, passengers being taken to the Pier Head in minibuses hired from SVOC. The hurricane that battered Southern England and destroyed Shanklin Pier brought down trees that blocked the line for several hours on 16th October; services recommenced at 10 am, well before many lines on the mainland. Worse was to follow on 5th January, 1988 when Monkton Mead Brook overflowed, flooding St Johns Road station and Ryde tunnel.

To save £50,000 a year in staff and maintenance costs, double line working between Brading and Sandown ended on Friday 28th October, 1988. The signal boxes at the two stations officially closed the following day but a cable fault led to the reopening of Sandown box until a new cable was laid. Sandown box finally closed on 25th February, 1989.

The points to the crossing loop at Sandown were set for running into the left-hand road and effectively became 'sprung points' when trailed through. Hydraulic springs reset the points about 10 seconds after the last vehicle had passed through. Colour light indicators showed a yellow light when the points were correctly set for a facing movement. The points to the engineer's sidings were clipped and locked out of use.

Ryde St Johns Road signal box became the sole signalling 'centre' for the line. The mechanical frame continued to control points and signals at Esplanade, Smallbrook Junction and in the station, backed up by point and signal indicators on the block shelf; the track circuit status appeared on the signal box diagram. A small 'micro' panel was added to the block shelf to control the signals and monitor the points and track circuits at Sandown. At a separate panel the signalman could shut down all three electricity substations in an emergency when control from the mainland was lost. In February 1990 the signal box at Sandown was demolished, followed a month later by the removal of the second track between Brading and Sandown. After years of disuse the station building at Brading was leased to the town council and the station flat at Sandown was let out as council meeting rooms, after refurbishment and furnishing at a cost of £100,000.

By then closure of the line had become 'politically unacceptable' and a decision was made to introduce newer tube cars. In preparation for their arrival £250,000 was spent on alterations to the depot at Ryde St Johns Road. The work included a new machine shop, stores building, a raised track in No. 1 road and a cleaning platform on No. 4 road which came into use on 17th July, 1990 replacing cleaning facilities next to the down platform. The facilities were formally opened by Sir Robert Reid, Chairman of the British Railway Board, on 21st March, 1990. Transformed by the delivery of 'new' rolling stock, the railway looked forward to a new lease of life. Just one incident marred the new arrangements when, on 21st January, 1991, a train ran away from Shanklin without its driver; the station was promptly closed so that the trackbed could be levelled and the platform rebuilt to eliminate the falling gradient.

Although the journey time between Ryde Pier Head and Shanklin had lengthened to 24 minutes after the opening of an interchange station with the

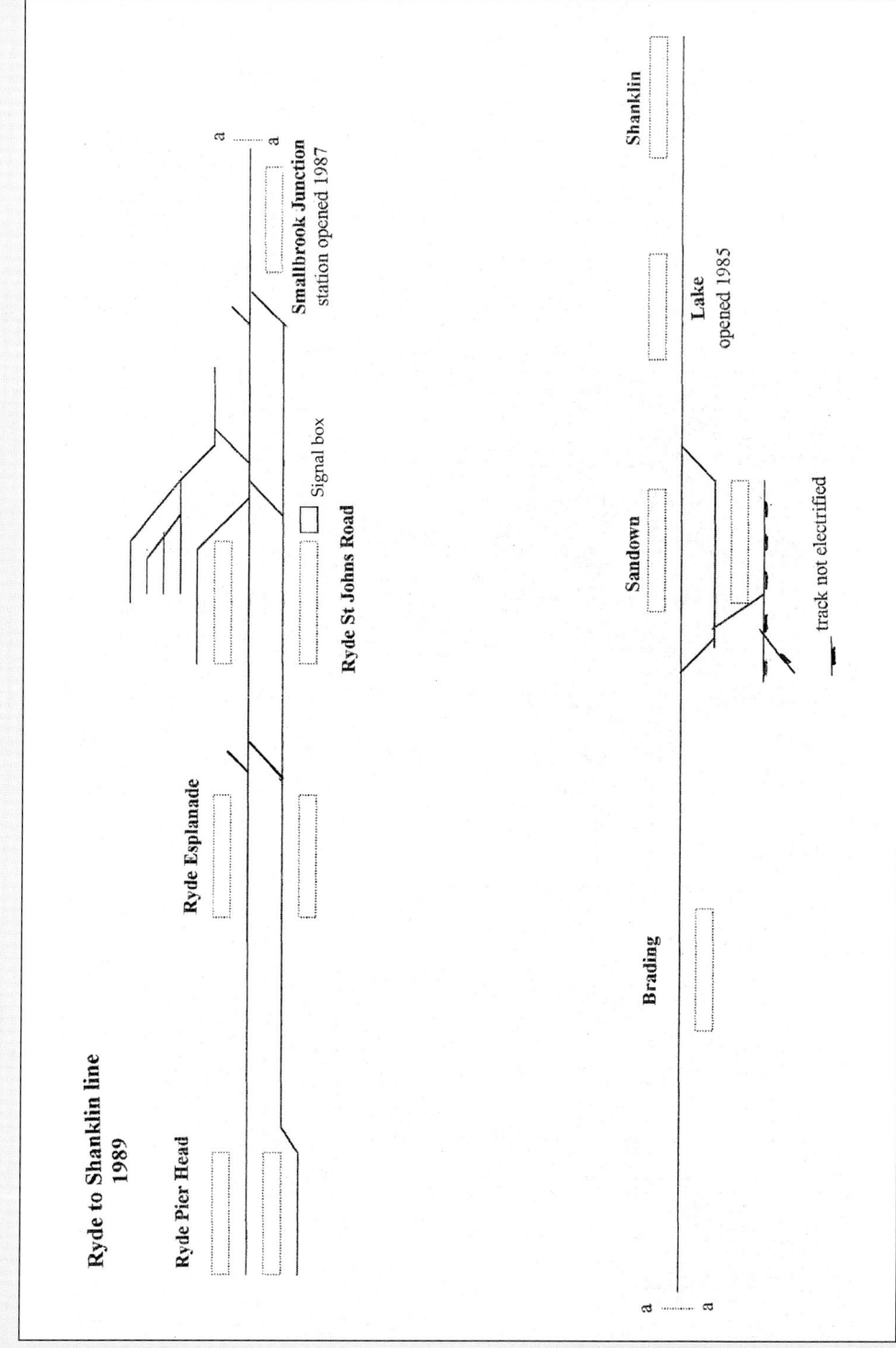

Left: Following demolition of the up side canopy and buildings, Sandown signal box towers over the replacement 'bus shelter'
 IWSR Collection/BR(S)

Below: The up direction point indicator at Sandown, lit when the point is correctly set.
R.A. Silsbury

Isle of Wight Steam Railway (IWSR) at Smallbrook on 21st July, 1991, it and the halt at Lake brought some useful business that helped offset a decline in the holiday traffic. There had been a marked shift from visitors travelling at weekends to weekday journeys; this reflected a more flexible attitude by hoteliers, a wish to avoid crowded trains and dearer mainland railway tickets on Fridays and Saturdays. Privatisation of BR's non-railway assets had begun in 1980 with the sale of its hotels. They were followed by the shipping division, renamed Sealink on 1st January, 1979, sold to Sea Containers in 1983 to become a new subsidiary, Sealink British Ferries. The Treasury, high on the drug of privatisation, then concentrated on other targets.

In November 1984 James Sherwood, the Chairman of Sea Containers, mentioned that his company was prepared to take over the Shanklin line. BR rejected the idea claiming that privatisation was not possible until it had closed! Five years later SVOC proposed that it, the Isle of Wight County Council, Sealink, Hovertravel and others each take a 10 per cent share in the line. Chris Green, Director of Network SouthEast, emphasised that it was definitely not for sale. The brand name *Island Line* was adopted with effect from 15th May, 1989.

The approaches were made at a time when railway privatisation was again on the agenda. BR had been unable to eradicate its losses in running Britain's railways and privatisation was seen as a solution. By the Autumn of 1992 the debate was gathering momentum. John MacGregor, the Transport Secretary, announced that the Shanklin line might be capable of being franchised or sold off to a private operator. Within months a consortium made up of SVOC, Wightlink (the new name for Sealink's Isle of Wight ferries), Hovertravel and Red Funnel ferries again expressed interest in taking over the line. There were high hopes that the railway might reopen to Ventnor and members of the Ventnor Railway Association lobbied for a commitment from the Government and prospective franchisees. A delay then ensued whilst the Government passed the necessary legislation.

There isn't a great deal to Lake Halt, merely a wooden platform, some fencing, lighting and a bus stop-type shelter. Unit No. 008, carrying the dinosaur livery, leads a second two-car unit on an up working to Ryde Pier Head, 10th June, 2006. *R.J. Maycock*

A change of ownership for Wightlink in 1995 was followed four years later by the introduction of a new 'FastCat' yellow and white striped livery on the Portsmouth-Ryde catamarans; in 2000 two more catamarans and an additional large car ferry were delivered. Journey times had been reduced to:

Portsmouth-Ryde	15 minutes by catamaran
Portsmouth-Fishbourne	40 minutes by vehicle ferry
Southsea-Ryde	8 minutes by hovercraft

In preparation for privatisation, the Ryde-Shanklin line was one of several parts of BR that became shadow franchises on 1st April, 1994. Retaining the name *Island Line*, the Isle of Wight Train Operating Unit was created with a Franchise Director, Production, Commercial and Finance managers based in offices on the upper floor of Sandown station building; the town council had fortuitously vacated the premises at the end of February.

Of 10 applicants for the franchise, the successful bid was the one that demanded the least subsidy and at 2 pm on 13th October, 1996 Stagecoach Holdings Plc, the bus operator, assumed management of the 8½ mile railway. Ownership of the track and structures passed to Railtrack Plc and the rolling stock to Eversholt Leasing. Of the 25 franchises formed out of the BR network, the line was unique in being vertically-integrated (track and trains operated in a single ownership). This allowed *Island Line* to set its own maintenance standards and priorities, albeit overseen by Railtrack (since replaced by Network Rail) as landlord, and keep responsibility for maintenance of the track and some structures through the appointment of contractors.

The short periods of the franchises were a handicap as, echoing what was said in 1935, a commercial undertaking such as Stagecoach had to get a return for its investment. Stations were repainted in yet another livery of Oxford blue and magnolia; Ryde Esplanade was the first to be done in May 1995. Ryde St Johns Road station was tidied up in May 1998 when the concrete fence separating the up platform from the locomotive yard was removed, along with a wooden building that had latterly been used by the train crews; in March 2000 the IWR footbridge was replaced by a new structure at the opposite end of the platforms. The railway suffered badly from flooding on Christmas Eve 1999 when the formation was washed out near Smallbrook Junction and the depot inundated. In March 2006 the line was closed whilst the tunnel roof under Ryde Esplanade was replaced by concrete beams at considerable expense so that heavier vehicles could use the road.

Stagecoach did its best to market Island Line. Through tickets were issued encompassing the company's buses on the mainland, the catamarans, Island Line, SVOC and IWSR; a residents railcard gave a 40 per cent reduction on journeys after 10 am on weekdays and all day at weekends for £5. Single fares were reduced to match those charged on buses and discounted day returns introduced. In an attempt to boost the sale of railway tickets to other parts of Britain, on which the company received commission, the booking office at Shanklin was reopened. Revenue rose to £729,000 in the year ending 31st March, 1996 but this made little impact on the subsidy. The 47 employees in January 1995 fell to 36 by early 1998:

Nos. of staff	Managers	3	Drivers	8	Ticket office	4
	Administration	1	Conductors	9	Barrier staff	2
	Depot staff	6	Signalmen	3		

The reduced numbers of staff ended any hopes of operating a pier shuttle. Between Ryde and Shanklin a 20 minute frequency was the exception and on most days an uneven 20 and 40 minute service operated. Stagecoach hoped to introduce a 30 minute interval matching the catamaran service but found this was impossible without a crossing loop at Brading.

In a report for the Strategic Rail Authority in 2002 it was estimated that structures would last for at least 30 years and the rolling stock for ten. A more flexible service with driver-only trains and an additional crossing loop depended on one thing, money. The Isle of Wight Council avoided any commitment that raised local taxes, but commissioned a second report that recommended extensions to Ventnor and Newport funded by central government.

Privatisation has done the Ryde-Shanklin line few favours. The separation of operation from the ownership of rolling stock and maintenance through various contractors seems only to have increased costs. The railway is burdened with payments to Network Rail that bear no relation to the cost of work carried out and rent to HSBC bank, the latest owners of the rolling stock, out of all proportion to their worth. On 2nd November, 2004 the Strategic Rail Authority launched 'community railways' in the hope that subsidies could be reduced as an alternative to closures. This helped focus minds because, despite carrying over 1,000,000 passengers, the railway is the most heavily subsidised line on the Network Rail system. On 20th June, 2005 a Community Rail partnership met for the first time at Sandown with representatives from a number of local organizations including Wightlink and the Isle of Wight Council.

Some tangible results are beginning to make themselves apparent. Park and ride car parks have been established at Ryde St Johns Road, Brading, Sandown and Shanklin stations and the construction of a modern interchange at Ryde Esplanade is planned. Another positive sign is the inclusion of the railway in the South Western franchise and its award to Stagecoach for a further 10 years. What changes will that lead to?

A Journey Over the Line

Trains deposit travellers at the harbour station at Portsmouth, a 1930s terminus that fails to display its assets to the full. The fragmented nature of Britain's transport system is reflected in the existence of separate booking office and refreshment areas for the railways and Wightlink, operator of the Portsmouth-Ryde route. An inevitable queue is followed by the boarding of one of four catamarans that operate to Ryde.

The view of Ryde Pier from the sea has changed little in recent years. The neat 1920s station building is complemented by a preserved crane, slightly marred by a covered way to keep travellers dry in poor weather. The Ryde Pier Company's pier head has lost its Victorian buildings and presents a sad sight amongst a clutter of parked cars. Having walked to the railway station and past its 'Victorian' style refreshment area we reach the platforms, only one of which remains in regular use. The platform bordering the track on the east side is devoid of all covering and the rails are rusty with disuse.

Standing on the west of the station, the squat tube train is somewhat off-putting but once on board there is the reassurance of travelling in something that LT consigned to a museum. During the summer a four-car train might be sampled but often just two cars suffice. The train runs to Ryde Esplanade along what used to be the up running line; the down line is used only when the up line is undergoing repairs. Last rebuilt in the 1960s bridge 1,* as the railway pier is known to the engineers, is as expensive to maintain as ever it was. Between the railway and promenade piers are the rusting remains of the tramway pier; visitors to the town must either wait for the train or walk the ½ mile length of the promenade pier in all weathers.

Visitors who prefer to use the hovercraft service from Clarence Pier, Southsea are landed at a slipway adjoining Quay Road close to Ryde Esplanade station. The station badly needs some money spent on it. The down platform and station subway (bridge 2) are rarely used whilst a section of up platform extending over the pier has been closed off - the remainder suffices for the present stock. Whilst the booking office is quite new, the uninviting prospect of the concourse discourages any loitering. Leaving the station, the train passes under a footbridge (bridge 2A) to the hovercraft terminal before gaining double track over a crossover guarded by colour light signals worked remotely from St Johns Road signal box. The train passes the pump house on the up side as it dives down to Ryde tunnel (bridge 3), the entrance to which proclaims the date of completion wrongly as 1881. After a journey that hints of the tube cars' previous life on London Underground, the train emerges from the tunnel and curves past recently-built housing on a section of the RPC tramway extension. Then follows a run to the back of the town passing under Rink Road (bridge 4), past the abandoned gasworks, under Park Road (bridge 5) and a bus garage before reaching St Johns Road (bridge 6).

Ryde St Johns Road station, the operational base for the line, is also the largest station on the railway. The road approach leads to the IWR building and canopy on the up side, a survivor of many alterations over the years. Two platforms are in use; the up platform has lost its well known concrete fencing whilst on the down platform is a shortened awning with an IWR monogram on the supporting brackets. A replacement for the footbridge (bridge 8) stands at the south end of the platforms. The signal box at the end of the up platform is now the only working box on the line. There are a few mechanically worked points and upper quadrant signals in the station area but most are remotely controlled colour lights. The goods yard and locomotive shed on the west side of the station have long since been removed. On the east side is a siding on the site of the down loop, two tracks run into the maintenance depot (the former carriage and wagon workshop), one into the 1864 IWR locomotive shed and a fourth siding used for train washing. This siding used to continue into the Smith Shop, now a shell with walls but no roof, which is used for storage.

Double track ends just beyond Smallbrook bridge (No. 12) at a point where colour light signals and a sand drag protect the single line. A few yards beyond is Smallbrook Junction station with its wooden platform on the up side of the line; trains stop whenever the steam railway is operating.

* As listed in the SR Bridge List.

One of the 'dinosaur' trains approach the terminus at Ryde Pier Head on 10th June, 2006. The track on the left is used only when the 'main' line is undergoing repair. Pedestrians who walk the length of the promenade pier must, today, run the gauntlet of motor cars travelling to and from the pier head car park. *R.J. Maycock*

Unit No. 006 leads a down train into Shanklin station. The platform in the foreground is an extension that was built when Landguard Manor bridge was demolished. New buildings have occupied part of the goods yard, 10th June, 2006. *R.J. Maycock*

THE RYDE TO SHANKLIN LINE 247

Leaving Smallbrook the railway parts company with Monkton Mead brook, a source of much flooding even today, and begins to climb through woods. This section seems to accentuate the low height of the tube stock and gives the unique impression of an animal scurrying to its lair. Reaching the summit near Truckells (bridge 18) where much work to stabilise the cutting has been necessary, the line falls towards Brading passing under Rowborough bridge (No. 20) and Wall Lane (bridge 23). A footpath along the trackbed of the Bembridge branch curves in on the left immediately before the train stops in the former up platform at Brading station. Brading is an unexpected survivor. The station master's house is privately owned and the other IWR buildings stand in as good a condition as nature allows. The station building has been restored and acts as a community centre also offering refreshments and bicycle hire! The footbridge (bridge 25), disused down platform and signal box wait for a day when the remainder of the station regains its former glory.

The dash along the banks of the Eastern Yar and the mainly level section towards Sandown emulates the non-stop run between Acton Town and Hammersmith on the Piccadilly line, on which the stock used to run. Passing over the river (bridge 31) and main road (bridge 32) the track enters a cutting that hides the railway from the town of Sandown.

Sandown station is the only crossing point south of Smallbrook but is a shadow of its past. The trains look lost in the long platforms that would easily accommodate the whole of the fleet! The station building on the down platform has had new windows and internal alterations that have done little to enhance its appearance. However, it has a reasonably comfortable enclosed waiting area and a small snack bar. The subway leads to an up platform populated by ugly modern waiting shelters. A fence along the back of the up platform hides a headshunt to two overgrown sidings at the north end of the station; on 14th May, 2005 a new entrance to the up platform was opened principally for children attending the nearby schools. The down goods yard has long since vanished under a housing estate and if plans to move the crossing loop to Brading are implemented, more of this rambling site will eventually be sold off.

An ascent of the gradient past Los Altos park and over Lake Girder bridge (No. 36) is followed by a stop at Lake Halt close to a subway (bridge 37) under the line; the wooden platform on the down side of the line is bare except for a modern waiting shelter that has had to be renewed because of vandalism. Despite this, many people find it a more convenient stopping place than Sandown or Shanklin stations.

For the first time since leaving Ryde, a view of the sea opens up as the railway passes under Skew footbridge (No. 37A) before curving under the main road at Lake Skew bridge (No. 38) followed by Alresford Road footbridge (bridge 38A) just before the railway terminates at Shanklin. The former down platform and buildings are all that remain; gone is the crossing loop, up platform and goods yard. Inside, the passenger accommodation mirrors Sandown. The railway ends in substantial buffer stops guarding a void left by the demolition of Landguard Manor bridge (No. 40). The trackbed towards Ventnor has become a footpath.

Motor car No. S22 stands in Ryde Works yard carrying blue/grey livery, grey doors and 'Isle of Wight' branding. *R.A. Silsbury*

Trailer No. S43 in blue/grey and specially lettered for its 60th anniversary. *R.A. Silsbury*

Chapter Seventeen

Rolling Stock after 1966

A suggestion that London Transport tube stock might be suitable for the Isle of Wight was first put forward by BR's Line Manager on 18th October, 1961. In a letter to LT it was written that 65 trailer cars might be needed as replacements for the existing carriages worked as block sets in push-pull fashion by separate power cars. Although nothing came of the enquiry it set the scene for subsequent events.

In 1963 BR approached LT with a request to purchase some tube cars for use on Ryde Pier. Two driving motor cars and four trailers were set aside to await the outcome of the closure hearings. The cars were amongst the last of 1,466 built between 1923 and 1934 that were coming to the end of their lives on LT. Although described as 'standard' stock, the cars had been built by a number of manufacturers and were standard only in having compatible equipment, steel underframes, timber body framing and steel panelling. The cars were slower and carried fewer passengers than newer stock, but the bodies were in reasonable condition and they could be expected to give a few years' service on less demanding duties.

In May 1964 BR warned that trains might have to run to St Johns Road and the number of cars required had increased to 12. Six driving motor and six trailer cars were subsequently purchased for £3,300 and transferred to Micheldever (between Basingstoke and Winchester) for storage. The release of a press notice announcing their purchase in August, just after the TUCC closure hearing, inflamed public opinion in the Island despite the assurance that it was 'not an attempt to pre-judge Mr Marple's decision'.

By October 1964 requirements had risen to 39 cars for Ryde-Shanklin (five seven-car trains and a spare four-car unit), an additional seven-car train for Ryde-Ventnor and more if the Cowes line remained open. LT had a sizeable number of withdrawn cars but was anxious to dispose of them without further delay. Consequently, on 2nd January, 1965 the BR Works and Equipment Committee agreed to pay £14,860 for a further 61 cars, the purchase to be kept 'absolutely quiet'. Thirty-two cars joined the previous 12 in store at Micheldever whilst the remainder were kept by LT at its Ruislip depot.

Plans for the Ryde-Shanklin electrification envisaged a peak service of five trains per hour operated by 46 cars running in seven-coach trains of units that in BR parlance were designated '4-VEC' and '3-TIS' (a parody on Vectis, the Roman name for the Isle of Wight) seating 238 second class passengers. The four-car units had two driving motor cars flanking two trailers; coupled to the Shanklin 'D' end of four-car units, the three-car units had a control trailer, trailer and a driving motor car. BR also wanted a spare driving motor car and three-car unit. The cars were allocated running numbers in the series S1S to S49S and S92S to S96S (Nos. 51 to 62 and 71-86 were occupied by the Waterloo & City line underground stock).

249

250 THE ISLE OF WIGHT RAILWAYS FROM 1923 ONWARDS

Unit formations as proposed 1966

Unit	'A' DM	T	T	'D' DM	Unit	CT	T	'D' DM
041	S10S	S27S*	S41S	S1S	031	S26S	S91S	S7S
042	S2S	S29S*	S42S	S21S	032	S28S	S92S	S9S
043	S12S	S31S*	S43S	S3S	033	S30S	S93S	S11S
044	S4S	S33S*	S44S	S23S	034	S32S	S94S	S13S
045	S14S	S48S	S45S	S5S	035	S34S	S95S	S15S
046	S6S	S49S	S46S	S25S	036	S36S	S96S	S17S
spare car	S8S				037	S38S	S47S	S19S

* Control trailer used as trailer. 'A' cars faced Ryde, 'D' cars and the 3TIS units were at the Shanklin end.

The best examples from the cars stored at Micheldever and Ruislip were selected for Isle of Wight service. In March 1966, the first were transferred to the LT workshops at Acton for a mechanical and electrical overhaul to give them 10 years' life. This included attention to electro-pneumatic brakes and traction motors, new power and lighting wiring and changes to suit the SR earth return system; the centre collection gear and tripcocks were removed and the return circuit connected to the traction motor frames. During the course of the work a number of motor cars became available from the Northern City line and as their electric cabling had been renewed they were substituted for a like number of older cars. Trailers with end passenger doors were rejected in favour of older cars without end doors because of the sharply curved platforms at Ryde Esplanade; for the same reason passengers were not allowed to use the end doors on other cars. BR had asked if the cars could be equipped for one-man-operation, but had second thoughts when quoted £1,000 per motor car.

There was another short-lived proposal to carry parcels using two gutted control trailers, but the idea was abandoned after it was found that the luggage cages would not fit in the cars.

Although LT had quoted an estimate of roughly £90,000 for rehabilitating the cars BR discovered this did not include their purchase and, to make matters worse, by July 1966 purchase and rehabilitation costs had grown to £124,000. Possible economies included saving £8,000 by reducing the number of cars in each train from seven to six, and £9,000 by dispensing with the four spare cars. After a review of requirements, in September BR decided to send just one spare car. The 43 cars sent to the Isle of Wight consisted of:

19 driving motor cars mainly built
   in 1931 and 1934   S1S-S11S, S13S, S15S, S19S-S23S, S25S
10 control trailers dating mainly from 1925   S26S-S34S, S36S
14 trailers built in 1923   S41S-S49S, S92S-S96S

After leaving Acton works the cars were towed to Wimbledon, from where they ran under their own power to the BR depot at Stewarts Lane (three-car units were hauled by a previously transferred four-car unit). At Stewarts Lane a bay of seats was replaced by a luggage rack and the adjoining window panelled over; Acton works had already reupholstered seats in a nondescript LT moquette. Cars were painted in a livery of plain rail blue with yellow cab ends and brown underframes (a brown roof was proposed in the project files); the running number was applied on body sides at waist level at the right-hand end and a white BR double-arrow symbol next to the driver's door on motor cars. The unit number was in black on the cab end above the driver's door. Interior ceilings and the sides above waist level were painted white whilst the lower panels, partitions, ends and doors were mushroom. They were the first complete trains to appear in the new BR corporate blue livery. One minor addition to motor cars was a whistle taken from SR electric locomotives that were being fitted with horns.

A cost-conscious BR had to consider alternatives to the traditional method of transferring stock to the Island using the floating crane (see *Appendix Eight*). When the transfer of six cars was first mooted a barge carrying six vehicles was quoted as costing £1,600 compared with the use of a low loader and car ferry at £150 a trip.

Once Stewarts Lane had finished work on them, units underwent trials on the Waterloo main line before running under their own power to Fratton goods yard, Portsmouth, to await shipment to the Island. Fratton was also the base for Island drivers undergoing familiarisation training on the 'new' stock and one train could often be spotted running between Fratton and Haslemere.

The first car was craned onto a Pickfords road transporter but the remainder were run up a temporary loading ramp. Hauled by a road tractor unit, trailers were taken straight onto the car ferry at Broad Street, Portsmouth, off at Fishbourne and to St Johns Road where the transporter backed down the approach road and goods yard to an unloading ramp. The first car was hauled off by a steam locomotive and match truck but on subsequent occasions a winch was used.

Two tractor units were needed to manoeuvre a transporter carrying one of the heavier motor cars but the weight caused some problems. A temporary bridging ramp was provided to span the gap between the ferry and slipway so that no part of the vessel's ramp bore an excessive weight. The transporter and one tractor would be loaded first, the bridging ramp removed, the ferry loaded with other vehicles and the second tractor unit and bridging ramp last. Only certain sailings could be used because unloading at Fishbourne had to be carried out on a rising tide to avoid the risk of grounding. The vessel reversed into position to allow the bridging ramp to be unloaded and then turned round before unloading continued. After the bridging ramp had been placed in position the transporter and tractor units were brought off.

A single control trailer No. S38S (subsequently renumbered S26S) was taken to the Island on 1st September, 1966 for gauging trials. Several followed during December and the rest went over in 1967. Trailer cars could be carried by the ferries on their booked service sailings but the motor cars with their extra tractor unit had to travel on special sailings. A significant number of the planned sailings were missed because of bad weather and the schedule of deliveries had to be constantly changed.* This meant that not all cars had arrived at Ryde when services commenced on 20th March, 1967 but they were ready for the peak summer service. Car No. S22S was damaged at Fratton by some mainland stock and No. S46S collided with No. S48S when being unloaded at Ryde; all three were repaired by fitters sent from Acton works.

* The summary of cars In *Appendix Seven* lists arrival dates based on the best available information.

Unit formations in 1967

Unit	'A' DM	T	T	'D' DM	Unit	CT	T	'D' DM
041	S20S	S27S*	S41S	S13S	031	S26S	S47S	S1S
042	S22S	S29S*	S42S	S15S	032	S28S	S92S	S3S
043	S2S	S31S*	S43S	S19S	033	S30S	S93S	S5S
044	S4S	S33S*	S44S	S21S	034	S32S	S94S	S7S
045	S6S	S48S	S45S	S23S	035	S34S	S95S	S9S
046	S8S	S49S	S46S	S25S	036	S36S	S96S	S11S
spare car	S10S							

* Control trailer used as a trailer.

The stock proved surprisingly reliable once teething troubles with damp in the electrics and sticking doors had been overcome. Unfortunately, within weeks it was discovered that the stock had wider flanges, that on LT were accommodated by locating every check rail ⅛ in. further from the running rail than on BR. The speed limit, which had just been raised to 45 mph from the 40 mph in steam days, was reduced to 40 mph and 10 mph across points. Meantime, in addition to their normal maintenance work, staff began turning down wheel flanges of the whole fleet on the works' wheel lathe (in those days it took staff two days to change two pairs of motor wheels and one day to change a bogie of trailer wheels). In January 1968 the line speed reverted to 45 mph for most of the line south of St Johns Road, 20 mph north to Pier Head and 10 mph across points and crossings.

BR sent an enquiry to LT in August 1967 asking about eight additional cars (a seven-car train and a spare driving motor) but most of the rejected cars had been sent for scrap and those that remained did not fit in with BR's needs. Instead, it was proposed to form two Ryde 'A' end three-car units plus a four-car unit using the spare 'A' end driving motor car S10S and a 'D' end three-car unit. Three driving motor cars and four control trailers were sold by LT to BR and transferred to Micheldever during 1968. The cars were never used, either for the Ventnor extension or as replacements for the Ryde tramway, and were sold for scrap in 1970; by then the cost of making them serviceable stood at £21,800. Far from needing additional trains to cover for the closure of the Ryde Tramway in January 1969, a reduction in the peak Shanklin service reduced requirements to five trains, including the pier shuttle.

At the end of 1967 driving motor car No. S15S was damaged in a shunting accident in Ryde workshop. A replacement was sought from LT but a strike intervened and it was October 1970 before it entered Acton works for an overhaul and repaint in the BR rail blue livery. The new S15S cost BR £4,300, higher than the £3,600 estimate for repairing its predecessor, and did not go to the Island until 21st March, 1971.

The blue livery faded badly in the sea air so the stock had to be repainted during the winter of 1971-1972; car interiors were done 12 months later. Three cars (Nos. S23S, S45S and S48S) were withdrawn after a shunting accident on 10th September, 1973, another (S25S) followed after vandalism and a fire on 8th September, 1975 and two more (S19S and S30S) in 1982. Nos. S19S and S30S became grounded stores vans at Sandown and Ryde respectively. In a repeat of past practice, withdrawn cars were stripped of useful spares before breaking up.

On one occasion when icy weather stopped the electric trains, 15 passengers crammed into the cab of the engineer's diesel locomotive and were taken from Sandown to Ryde Pier Head. Ryde Works asked for de-icing equipment but BR headquarters estimated it would cost several thousand pounds and refused the request. Staff took the matter into their own hands and in 1974 fitted a tank in the cab of control trailer No. S31S linked to rail level using domestic plastic tubing. Lights connected to the pickup shoes showed a man riding in the cab on which side was the conductor rail so he could turn on the appropriate tap! 'It works perfectly ... and cost about £70'.

The cars were steadily deteriorating and one, sometimes two cars would be under repair at a time. More work could be done during the winter when the reduced operating mileage eased pressure on stock availability and routine maintenance. The ability to uncouple cars from units made it possible to prioritise work and carry out interior and exterior overhauls at different times.

A variation in the livery appeared in 1976 when the passenger doors and shoe gear were painted light grey, useful for showing which doors were in use! The **'S'** suffix to car numbers was omitted. Interiors began appearing painted in lime green and later apple green with eau de Nil window frames. A start was made on replacing the maple wood lagged floors with plywood and lino where the condition demanded; the first car to receive a completely new floor returned to service in December 1980. Upholstery was being renewed using a BR blue moquette.

In January 1982 a unit appeared in Inter-City blue and grey with yellow and black ends, **Isle of Wight** lettering in white along the sides of motor cars and black painted surrounds to cab windows. It was not unknown for Ryde to apply grey window panels to a car previously in all blue livery, if the condition permitted, so that a unit would have a uniform appearance. Black panels covering the LT destination panels bore the BR class '485' (four car) and '486' (three car) and set number in white lettering. Although the stock were class numbers '452' (four car) and '451' (three car) between 1969 and 1973, painted class numbers did not appear until 1982. In 1983 the cars were made non-smoking, more floors were replaced and the seating material renewed. Funded partly by the Isle of Wight County Council, the work was done at Acton and Ryde using a standard LT District Line design of orange and brown moquette.

Rumours that the stock would be replaced appeared repeatedly in the local newspapers. In 1977 it was reported that the Government would not find £4,000,000 for purpose-built stock. A year later rail buses, using components made for Leyland National buses, were rejected after the estimated cost rose to £5,000,000. During 1983, redundant 1956-built Merseyrail electric carriages were considered. An Island unit was fitted with a hardboard template and given a trial between Ryde St Johns Road and Pier Head. The template was damaged when it hit Park Road bridge and had to be adjusted to get under Rink Road before the trial was abandoned.

Despite the embarrassment of operating such stock, BR celebrated the 60th anniversary of the entry into LT service on 28th January, 1924 of the oldest car, 1923 Cammell Laird trailer S43, by giving it a repaint and the lettering **1924** [BR arrow] **1984**. Ryde Works held an open day and the car operated in a special train for visiting enthusiasts.

In January 1985 it was decided to form five-car units with two driving motor cars and three trailers seating 174 passengers. Following the running of two-car units that winter, two 52-seat units were created.

Unit formations in 1985

Unit	'A' DM	T	T	T	'D' DM	Unit	'A' DM	'D' DM
041	S2	S26*	S92	S27*	S1	031	S20	S11
042	S4	S28*	S42	S29*	S3	032	S22	S15
043	S6	S32*	S43	S31*	S5			
044	S8	S19	S44	S33*	S7			
045	S10	S34*	S94	S93	S9			

* Control trailer used as a trailer. Spare trailers S41, S46, S47, S95.

The reformations took time to achieve because they coincided with a programme to renew the lighting and carry out body repairs. Work also began on panelling over the end cab doors of motor cars to reduce draughts and make them more weatherproof. The use of unit numbers was temporarily abandoned and anything from two to seven cars might be seen depending on the season. To identify trains for maintenance purposes, a temporary white number (1-5) was applied to the bottom left-hand corner of the cab front on motor cars. The letters **Ryde Rail** and a white outline of the Island were painted on each body side, repeated in black on driving ends; the class and set number were repositioned between the top of the driver's windows.

Before the programme could be finished Network SouthEast was created. Three cars re-entered traffic in May 1987 carrying the striking and colourful Network SouthEast livery. Grey lower panels were separated from the blue window surrounds by a broad white band on which was a narrow red band; a narrow white line ran along the gutter strip. The Network SouthEast insignia was applied on the white waistline panel with the BR double arrow symbol and **Ryde Rail** in white on the blue panel behind the driver's door. The cab ends were still yellow but with a wide black band at window height, in the centre of which was a small version of the insignia above a white outline of the Isle of Wight and the letters **Ryde Rail** underneath; with this repaint the S prefix to the running number was abolished.

By 1987 only 27 cars were fit for service. To replace a withdrawn driving motor car Ryde works recreated a fully working control trailer (No. 28) to run with a motor car in a two- or three-car unit. The shortage of stock was not helped by flooding in January 1988 when a number of traction motors were damaged.

BR had taken an option on the purchase of the next generation of tube car, the 1938 stock. They were the first to have electrical equipment below the floor instead of in cabinets behind the driver's cab; this increased passenger accommodation whilst avoiding the expense of lengthening platforms. Over 1,000 cars were built as replacements for obsolete stock and for an ambitious expansion of the LT network, not all of which was completed. Although attractive to look at, this revolutionary design was difficult to maintain and the cars gained a reputation for unreliability. The first withdrawals of 1938 stock in the 1980s had been rejected by BR because of their poor condition and a programme of rewiring the old stock was authorized to keep them in service until better tube stock became available.

It had been hoped to buy some Central Line 1962 tube stock as it was newer and slightly better designed. Unfortunately, it too was rejected after an inspection of some sample cars at Ruislip. The 1959 stock was in a better condition but was unlikely to become available before the early to mid-1990s. However, the need to replace the existing stock was so urgent that the last remaining 1938 cars were inspected at Golders Green. Although considered by LT to be in poor condition, they were accepted and all 43 available cars were bought.

The operational need was for a four-car unit of new stock. However, the 1938 cars were semi-permanently coupled and could not be split for maintenance. It was impracticable to double the length of the workshop at Ryde and a compromise using three cars was rejected because three cars would be overcrowded in summer and the power supply would not support the use of six-car trains south of Sandown. Eventually a scheme was devised to create two-car units that, although seating only 84, when run in pairs gave a capacity comparable to the trains they replaced; the workshop still had to be extended by about three metres to accommodate the two cars units.

The first four cars arrived at British Rail Engineering Ltd, Eastleigh on 11th November, 1988 ready for a start on extensive alterations. Each pair of cars was stripped to the bare shells, asbestos removed and all the equipment overhauled. The cars were rewired so that they would operate as pairs, Shanklin 'D' end cars had their motor generators replaced by a compressor and both cars had the pickup shoe gear removed from the trailing ends. Splash guards were fitted underneath the traction resistances to guard against damage from a rough wave on Ryde Pier. Work on the bodies included new beech wood window surrounds, aluminium ceiling panels sprayed off-white and grey speckled linoleum on the floors, except in doorways which had a ridged rubber finish. Luggage racks were not thought necessary but the seating was completely new, the frames being stainless steel, the seating material described as Network Blue Blade moquette and blue painted armrests. Additional wiring was installed to operate a more powerful heating system, fluorescent lighting, inter-crew communication, a public address system together with passenger open and close door push-buttons. The cars were transformed into brightly lit and well-heated accommodation even on the coldest days. A guard's control panel was left in Ryde 'A' end cars. In the cabs were new seats for the driver and BR speedometers, taken from various SR electric stock, calibrated to an optimistic 90 mph; the cars regularly operated at their official maximum speed of 60 mph on the mainland but were restricted to 45 mph in Island service. Modifications were made to the acceleration and braking rates to take account of the absence of a trailer car and the brake blocks were changed to improve performance in wet weather. New whistles were made when insufficient could be obtained from the old stock. The exteriors were finished in a revised Network SouthEast livery with light grey lower panels and a darker shade of blue than hitherto. The grey and red colours swept up diagonally at the driving ends and over the driving cab doors. Car sides carried the Network SouthEast insignia at one end,

The first unit of 1938 stock was launched on 13th July, 1989 and car No. 221 of unit 001 stands at Ryde Esplanade with the pier shuttle after running an inaugural special to Brading. *R.A. Silsbury*

the running number at the opposite end and in between the *Island Line* name and logo; the inner trailing ends of cars were painted grey. At the driving ends, window surrounds were black and the rest of the cab below cantrail height was yellow; the unit number appeared in white under the driver's window whilst a ventilator grill above the cantrail was picked out in black. The interiors were painted blue, light grey and white with dark grey doors. The work, which created virtually new trains, cost in the region of £900,000.

The first unit 001 reached the Island in early July 1989 but in the absence of loading ramps was craned onto a low loader at Fratton and off at Sandown; this became the pattern for subsequent arrivals and departures. The introduction of larger ferries had removed the weight distribution problems that existed in 1966 but height was still an issue. The bogies were removed and transported on a separate lorry so that the bodies could be carried on a modified flatbed lorry trailer. Even so, only the newer ferries on the Fishbourne route could be used, each unit making up three lorry loads, two with the bodies and one with the four bogies.

An inaugural run of unit 001 between Ryde Pier Head and Brading took place on 13th July, 1989 but it was then withdrawn for testing and crew training. Units transferred at the end of September entered service a month later and had taken sole charge by February 1990; the last arrived on 21st June, 1990. Three four-car trains were needed for the 20 minute peak service plus a train for the pier shuttle. Two further cars were renovated and dispatched to the Island in April 1992 along with two spare body shells (known as unit 010, cars 130 and 230, they never carried these numbers). The remaining cars were stripped of spare parts before being sent for scrap.

THE ISLE OF WIGHT RAILWAYS FROM 1923 ONWARDS 257

Unit formations in 1992

Unit	'A' DM	'D' DM	Unit	'A' DM	'D' DM
001	121	221	006	126	226
002	122	222	007	127	227
003	123	223	008	128	228
004	124	224	009	129	229
005	125	225			

Each delivery was usually matched by the return of old stock. Five of the old cars were sold to LT for use in a vintage train and two (27 and 44) were repainted in LT red and cream livery at Ryde before they returned to the mainland. The five cars ran under their own power from Fratton to Wimbledon on 18th October, 1990 and then onto the LT system. Other cars were taken by road to Ruislip where they were stripped for spares. Three cars (control trailer 28, de-icer control trailer 31 and driving motor car 5), kept for the pier shuttle and de-icing duties, last ran in passenger service on 12th January, 1991, ran their last de-icing trip on 17th February and were withdrawn on 31st May, 1991. They were broken up at Sandown in May 1994 with another control trailer 26 that had been kept for possible preservation.

The cessation of the pier shuttle in 1991 and a reduction in the operating frequency to Shanklin created a surplus of stock. On 28th January, 1994 unit 005 collided violently with the buffer stops at Ryde Pier Head and car 125 never ran again; car 223 had previously failed so their partners were joined and returned to traffic. Several cars, including the damaged cars and stores cars, were withdrawn and later scrapped leaving only six two-car units in service.

The remaining cars received mechanical overhauls during which key components, including traction motors, were sent for refurbishment to REW, the engineering section of LT based at Acton. One or two units are dealt with each year, on a roughly three year cycle. Lockers for guards' equipment were installed in 'A' cars in 1994 and 1995 reducing the number of seats in the car from 42 to 40 and tripcocks for an automatic train stop device were fitted in 2002-2003.

On 21st March, 2000 two units entered traffic painted blue with decals based on a dinosaur theme; by the end of the year five units had received the dinosaur livery. A sixth unit 007 was painted in London Transport red with cream window pillars, a grey roof, black underframes, yellow warning panels on the driving ends and, at first, carried LT lettering and numerals. Flooding of the depot ruined months of work and it did not enter service until 27th January, 2003; unit 009 was repainted to match, but lacking the LT lettering, and entered service on 1st October.

Cars extant in 2004

Set	'A' DM	'D' DM	Livery	Name	Notes
001	123	221	Network SouthEast		Stored 'off lease' (since scrapped).
002	122	225	Dinosaur	Raptor	
004	124	224	Dinosaur	T-Rex	
006	126	226	Dinosaur	Terry	
007	127	227	LT red		
008	128	228	Dinosaur	Iggi	
009	129	229	LT red	ex-Bronti	

Despite their age, there are no plans to replace the cars with more modern vehicles.

London Transport-liveried unit No. 007 stands at Ryde St Johns Road with the 10.49 Ryde Pier Head-Shanklin service on 23rd October, 2006. The 'IWR' monograms in the brackets of the shortened canopy show up well; unit No. 008 stands in the down siding in the shadow of Ryde works.
R.A.Silsbury

ROLLING STOCK AFTER 1966

Engineers' Stock

To assist in rebuilding the railway pier the contractors brought two self-propelled steam cranes from the mainland but they were returned when the work was completed. On 12th July, 1966 twelve low-sided wagons were dispatched to Redbridge for shipment to the Island as no single bolster wagons were to be had on the mainland. They arrived at Medina Wharf in a partly dismantled state and were taken to Ryde for rebuilding as bolster wagons using new steel bolsters fabricated on the mainland, timber for the low sides and ends being made up locally. On 7th October, 1966 a Pickfords low loader brought over a class '05' diesel shunter No. D2554 and later that month a ballast tamping machine No. DS72. A BR 'Flatrol' well wagon No. DB900032 spent several months on the railway carrying transformers from Ryde to the substations; it returned to the mainland in March 1967.

After electric services began, most of the steam stock was withdrawn and broken up. Ryde locomotive shed was used as an improvised workshop to rebuild some LBSCR open wagons to dropside ballast wagons, two bolster wagons were fitted with dumb buffers at one end for use as match trucks and several SR passenger luggage vans became stores vans. Two SR goods brake vans sent to the Island in May 1967 were followed by an assortment of vehicles including open wagons, ballast hopper wagons, flat wagons and a Wickham rail car.

As the class '05' was suffering from gearbox problems, a replacement Drewry diesel locomotive No. 03079 was sent to the Island on 8th April, 1984. At first the cab was not altered (the up platform canopy valance at St Johns Road was trimmed and the up line under Smallbrook bridge lowered) but after a winter's use and an encounter with Park Road bridge it had to be reduced in height. No. 03179 arrived on 30th June, 1988, unique amongst its class to carry Network SouthEast livery, and had its cab altered at Ryde. The class '05' and some of the wagons were sold to the IWSR. The last arrivals from the mainland were a pair of match wagons that had been used with the 1938 cars; they were off-loaded at Sandown in April 1992.

The engineers' stock fell into disuse after maintenance was put out to contract. In June 1998 No. 03079 was sold to the Derwent Valley Light Railway near York. No. 03179 left at the same time to become depot shunter at the WAGN depot, Hornsey, London. Most of the wagons went to the IWSR or for scrap in 2000 leaving only a 'Dogfish' ballast hopper wagon and two match wagons. Maintenance was taken over by road/rail vehicles that have visited the line when required.

Left: The engineers' stock spent almost all of its time lurking in the sidings at Sandown, with infrequent forays usually at night. The singling of the Brading-Sandown section gave an opportunity to see it in action in daylight and all the active vehicles are in use at the north end of Brading on 29th October, 1988. *IWSR Collection/BR(S)*

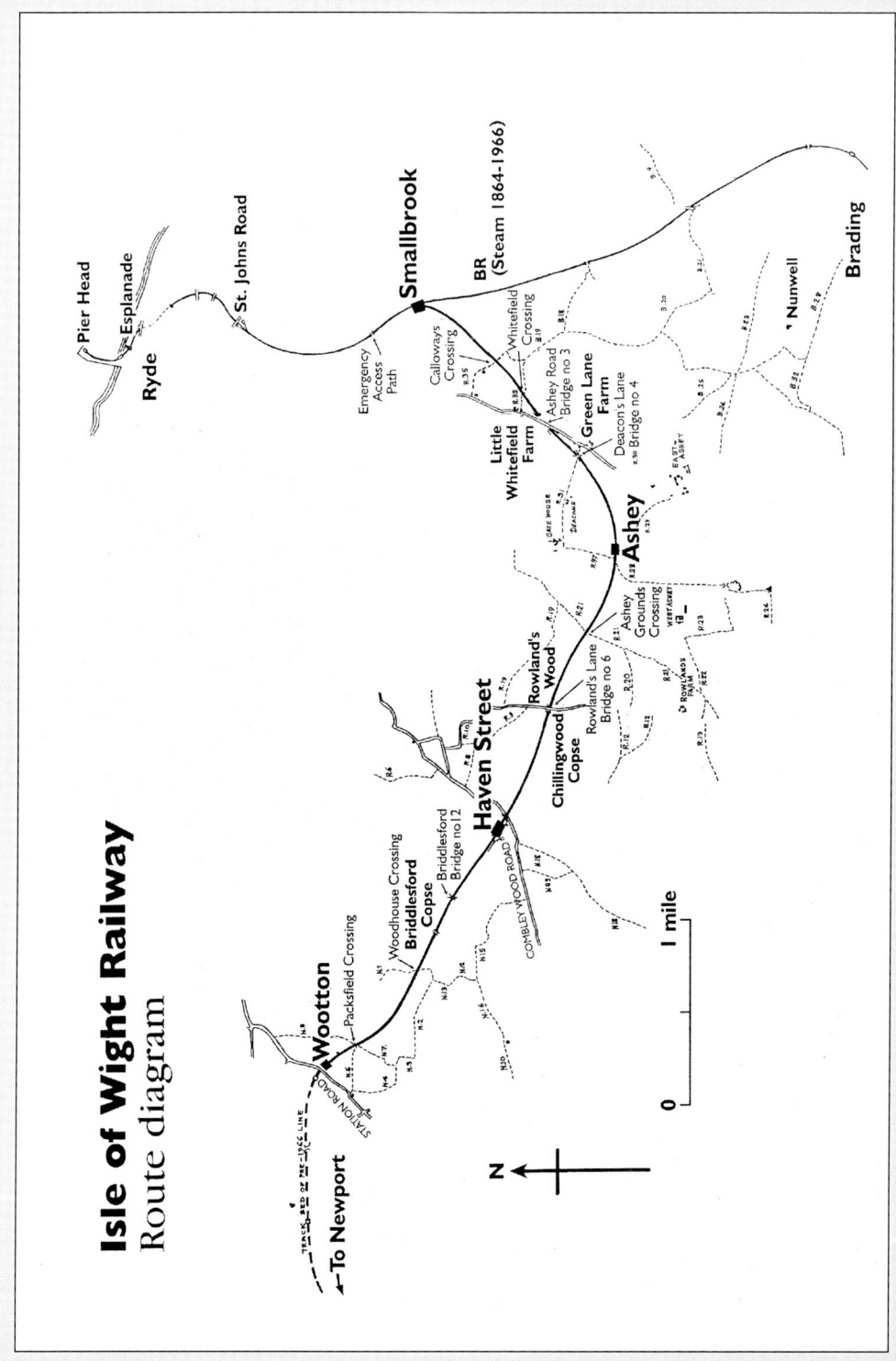

Chapter Eighteen

Railway Preservation in the Isle of Wight

During SR days the preservation of Isle of Wight railway artefacts was considered. A.B. MacLeod had 2-4-0T *Ryde* restored to IWR condition before it joined other historical locomotives stored in the paint shop at Eastleigh works. They were scrapped in 1940 during the wartime drive for scrap metal. Most of the Isle of Wight locomotive name and maker's plates were preserved and several are on display at the National Railway Museum in York and at Havenstreet.

In 1960 the Bluebell Railway considered purchasing 'E1' 0-6-0T No. 4 *Wroxall* but its poor condition meant that there were better candidates to be had on the mainland. In 1966 several preservation groups attempted to purchase Isle of Wight locomotives and carriages for use on the mainland but they were defeated by high transportation costs. A small IWR hand crane was purchased by its makers Kirkstall Forge Co. and BR shipped back four goods wagons where they eventually joined the National Railway Museum collection. A collection of narrow gauge stock accumulated following the closure of a brickworks at Rookley has also since gone to the mainland.

An Isle of Wight Steam Railway

The Wight Locomotive Society was formed in April 1966 to purchase a class 'O2' 0-4-4T locomotive for static display. The impetus for the Society began in London and what its members lacked in age and experience they made up for in enthusiasm. The Society did not plan to own a railway but wanted to establish a base at Havenstreet in the expectation that Vectrail would permit the running of steam trains on the Ryde-Cowes line.

By the time the Society approached BR, locomotives Nos. 24 *Calbourne* and 31 *Chale* had been reserved so this narrowed the choice to Nos. 22 *Brading* or 33 *Bembridge*. *Calbourne* and *Chale* were kept at Ryde to assist with the electrification works but the remainder, along with most carriages and wagons, were dumped at Newport until sold for scrap.

Prospects for the Society were not good. By October 1966 it had raised only £36, not even enough to buy a nameplate, and seemed doomed to failure. Nevertheless, members did not give up and collected enough cash on the last day of steam working to purchase five carriages. After other purchasers for the locomotives fell by the wayside the Society was given the opportunity to buy *Calbourne* where it stood at Ryde. *Calbourne* was the obvious choice as it had had a major overhaul 18 months before withdrawal and an Adams pattern boiler. The £900 purchase price was achieved only with difficulty and by then the junction with the Cowes line at Smallbrook had been removed. *Calbourne* was transported to Newport by low-loader on 15th August, 1969 to join the carriages. Also at Newport was a sixth carriage purchased privately, a crane

When 'A1x' class No. 11 *Newport* first arrived at Havenstreet for preservation it was cosmetically restored to full IWC lined black livery. August 1975. *R.T. Relf*

Preservation begins and ends with 'O2' class No. 24 *Calbourne*. Currently undergoing an extensive overhaul, Calbourne is pictured in August 1978 when in full health, carrying full SR malachite green livery. *P.J. Relf*

and some wagons reserved by Vectrail and the chassis from Ryde pier tram No. 2; all later passed into the Society's ownership.

After Vectrail abandoned its attempts to reopen the Ryde-Cowes line, the Society rented 1¾ miles of trackbed between Havenstreet and Wootton from the County Council and purchased the track from BR. Even so, the Society was given just five day's notice to vacate Newport station before contractors began lifting the track. On Sunday 24th January, 1971 *Calbourne* ran between Newport and Havenstreet hauling the carriages and wagons to their new home. Members were then faced with the task of restoring the derelict station and railway. To make matters worse visitors wanted to see the Island's latest tourist attraction and ride on a steam train.

The railway began operating a seasonal service in May 1971 although, in the absence of a run-round loop at Wootton, trains had to be propelled in one direction. To assist *Calbourne*, members obtained on loan, and later purchased, an 0-4-0T *Invincible* that had worked at the Royal Aircraft Establishment at Farnborough. Visitors would have been surprised to see two Pullman carriages that had been on display at Beaulieu; one was to be a refreshment room but they were too large and out of keeping with the railway and were eventually sold back to the mainland. Instead, members concentrated on rescuing carriage bodies that had been used as holiday homes, poultry houses, sheds etc. A limited company was formed in 1972* and the railway gained its Light Railway Order in 1978.

At Havenstreet the station building was restored to its former glory and signals, a water tower (from Newport) and coal stage erected but the station had no other covered accommodation or sidings. This was a difficult time as the overhaul of *Calbourne* and other maintenance had to be carried out in the open air. A level site was created for sidings and a start made on the construction of a workshop; its completion in January 1980 proved to be a turning point. An attractive refreshment building was built using bricks salvaged during the demolition of Totland Bay Hotel, roof tiles from a local barn and a serving counter from a London post office; it opened in July 1982. A nearby gas retort house was purchased in May 1983 for use as a museum, office and stores; two years later an extension was added for a shop.

At Wootton there had been numerous earth slips on the site of the station in the cutting west of the road overbridge. After fruitless attempts to stabilise the clay a level site was created approximately 100 yards east of the bridge on a section of line previously on a steep gradient. A run-round loop came into use on 21st August, 1977 but difficulties with the site, and other demands on resources, meant that a platform did not open until August 1986.

Three years later planning began for a 3¼ mile extension towards Smallbrook Junction where the railway met the Ryde-Shanklin line. The trackbed was purchased from the County Council and work began on laying the permanent way. At Smallbrook an interchange station was built in association with BR; it is unusual in lacking road or pedestrian access. The extension opened for traffic on 20th July, 1991 and the halt at Ashey on 2nd May, 1993. Given political and practical goodwill, it is possible to extend the railway to St Johns Road but an

---

* The company was registered as the Isle of Wight Railway (1972) Ltd but to avoid confusion with its predecessors we have referred to the preserved railway as the Isle of Wight Steam Railway, IWSR for short.

On 31st August, 1981 'A1x' class No. W8 *Freshwater* departs Havenstreet for Wootton, some two months after being restored to service. *Iain Whitlam/IWSR Archive*

A new station was constructed at Wootton to the east of, and lower, than the original. 'A1x' class No. 11 *Newport*, in IWCR black livery, is uncoupled from its train ready to run round, August 1991. *IWSR Archive*

attempt to take it beyond Wootton in the direction of Newport would be an expensive task that is beyond the railway's resources.

The railway has actively sought locomotives and carriages that used to run in the Isle of Wight. LBSCR 'A1x' No. 8 *Freshwater* returned to the Island on 25th June, 1979 after years as a static pub sign on Hayling Island and, after complete restoration at Havenstreet, entered service in 1981. More protracted was the restoration of No. 11 *Newport* after its display at Butlins holiday camp in Pwllheli; the locomotive arrived on 17th January, 1975 but took until 1989 to restore. A new boiler for the class was purchased in 1997. Two other surviving Island 0-6-0Ts, Nos. 9 *Fishbourne* and 14 *Bembridge*, are preserved on the mainland.

The steam locomotives have been joined by a class '05' 0-6-0 diesel shunter that arrived at Ryde in 1966 for use on engineering trains. A class '03' diesel has also been purchased for use in emergencies. The chassis from Ryde tram car No. 2 survives in a derelict state. The railway cannot rely solely on its historic locomotives so other steam and diesel locomotives of non-Isle of Wight origin have been acquired on loan.

The IWSR was an early pioneer in the restoration of four-wheel carriage bodies using underframes from SR luggage vans. The pride of the fleet is a carriage built for the North London Railway in the 1860s that was sold to the IWR in 1897. Unlike other preserved railways that run their historic carriages on 'high days and holidays', the carriages have to earn their keep in normal service:

	Thirds SR Nos.	Brake thirds SR Nos.	Composites SR Nos.	Luggage vans SR Nos.
IWR ex-NLR four-wheel carriage			(IWR 46) 6339	
LBSCR four-wheel carriage	2343			
LCDR four-wheel carriages	2515	4112	6369	
LBSCR bogie carriages	2416	4168	6348	
SECR bogie carriages		4145, 4149	6375	
SR four-wheel vans				1046, 1052

Many more carriage bodies have been acquired for preservation and, at the time of writing, LCD composite No. 6369 is undergoing restoration. The railway has a representative collection of goods stock, including LBSCR open wagons, single bolster wagons and a machinery wagon, a LSWR road van and two hand cranes. A converted cattle wagon is on loan from the National Railway Museum. Other vehicles have been purchased for permanent way maintenance.

The new century has been marked by more improvements at Havenstreet. Extensions have been made to the refreshment room and, during 2002, land was purchased for sidings at the west end of the station. On 21st May, 2004, HM Queen Elizabeth II opened a carriage and wagon workshop, the first stage in a 10 year project partly funded by the Heritage Lottery Fund that includes the restoration of five carriages and four wagons. Since the railway possesses one of the most historic collections in Britain, it is only fitting that the next projects include the construction of covered accommodation to house all the railway's operational rolling stock.

The sylvan setting of the IWSR station at Smallbrook is obvious in this view looking towards Havenstreet. The signal box can just be glimpsed in the background, 10th June, 2006.
R.J. Maycock

Smallbrook IWSR station seen looking towards the buffer stops, 10th June, 2006. Will the railway ever be extended to Ryde? *R.J. Maycock*

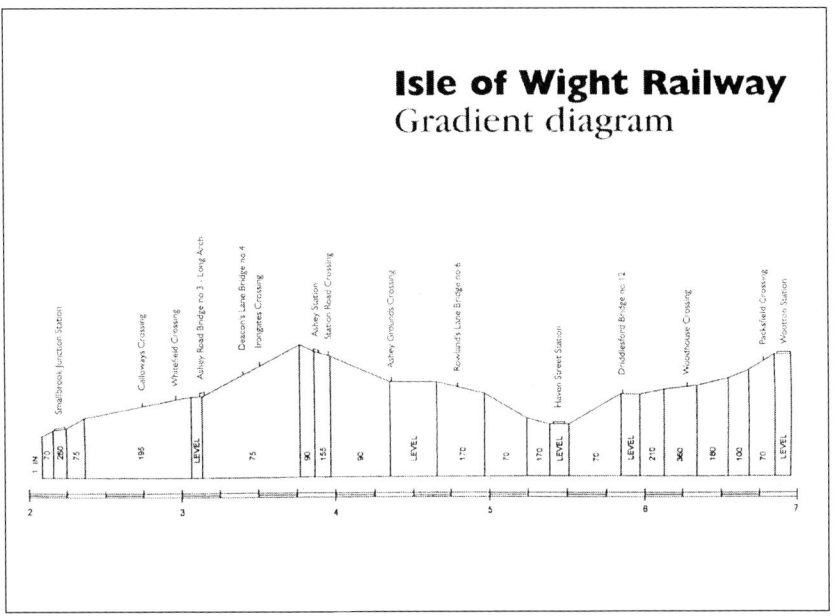

A Journey Over the Railway

A visit to the railway is perfectly possible during a day trip from the mainland. The electric train calls at the interchange station at Smallbrook Junction whenever the steam railway operates and is met by a train of elderly wooden-bodied carriages, none of which is less than 80 years old, pulled by one of the railway's steam locomotives.

Smallbrook Junction station consists of two quite separate timber platforms for the electric and steam railways constructed at the point where the former Ventnor and Cowes lines diverged; the concrete foundations of the old signal box can be glimpsed in the undergrowth between the platforms. As was the case in steam days, there is no road access apart from an emergency footpath. On the steam railway side of the station is a run-round loop with spring operated points at the Ryde end and points at the opposite end worked from a two-lever ground frame locked by the single line token. The ground frame is located in a wooden signal box rebuilt from the box that once stood at Whitwell and, as at Wootton, is operated when required by the train crew.

Leaving the station on a tight curve the train begins its journey to Ashey, Havenstreet and Wootton. Glimpses of the rolling countryside have become more common in recent years as the accumulation of trees and shrubs have been cleared away. The uphill gradient eases somewhat as the railway passes through Swanpond Copse, a stretch of dense woodland, before emerging into farmland and passing Calloways Crossing, one of several occupation crossings on the line. The Ryde-Arreton road crosses the railway at a very shallow angle at Whitefield bridge, also called Ashey Road bridge or Long Arch (bridge 3); it has been widened in recent years to create the nearest thing to a tunnel on the railway. The line climbs as it passes under Green Lane or Deacon's bridge (bridge 4) before emerging in open countryside with views of Ashey and Brading Downs. Curing to the right, the climb from Smallbrook comes to an end shortly before reaching Ashey Halt.

Ashey station originally had two platforms and a crossing loop, but the 1876 station building and up platform have long since passed into private ownership. They stand surrounded by the mature trees that have been a feature of the station for virtually all its life. A platform and brick shelter constructed in 1961 on the site of the former down platform serves the steam railway. As the train passes over the station crossing, a low embankment can be glimpsed curving to the left as it heads towards a chalk scar high on the downs; this is the long abandoned quarry branch.

Curving towards the north-west, the railway descends as it passes through open fields, across Ashey Grounds foot crossing, and levels shortly before entering Rowlands Wood. The line passes under Rowlands Lane bridge (bridge 6) followed soon afterwards by Black bridge (No. 7) over a private road. Emerging from the wood on a steep falling gradient open fields presage a crossing of Havenstreet bridge (No. 9) and the entry into Havenstreet station.

Havenstreet is the headquarters of the IWSR. The 1926 station buildings, with the built-in signal box, keep the character of the Southern Railway and the crossing loop performs its intended function on busy days. There is a shop and museum housed in the impressive gas retort house which was built in 1886 to supply gas to the village and a modern refreshment room on the other side of the line. The station is also host to all the paraphernalia of a working railway, including locomotive and carriage workshops and numerous sidings. The station's attractions have been joined by a picnic area, adventure park and woodland walk.

Leaving Havenstreet, the railway climbs steeply as it heads north-west towards Wootton. This heavily wooded section through Briddlesford Copse passes below a cart track at Briddlesford bridge (No. 12) before the line levels for a short distance. The climb recommences before passing over cattle creeps at Woodhouse Farm bridge (No. 13) and Parkfield bridge (No. 15). Wootton station is on a left-hand curve on a site levelled from the original 1 in 70 gradient, the ruling gradient for the line. The terminus created by the railway lacks the facilities at Havenstreet but the setting cannot be bettered. The simple run-round loop mirrors that at Smallbrook Junction with its ground frame housed in a signal box that was once at Freshwater. There is public access to the station and some parking space but visitors may find it more convenient to use the larger car park at Havenstreet.

The site of the old station at Wootton disappeared many years ago when the trackbed of the railway through the cutting immediately beyond the road bridge was filled in. More recently, a cycle track has been created along the trackbed of the railway to Whippingham.

Appendix One

Isle of Wight Chief Officers from 1923 to 1966

Acting district superintendent	George R. Newcombe	1923
Assistant divisional operating superintendent	Charles N. Anderson Charles A. de Pury	1923-1925 1925-1930
Acting district civil engineer and locomotive, carriage & wagon superintendent, later assistant to the chief mechanical engineer and locomotive running superintendent	Horace. D. Tahourdin John C. Urie Alistair. B. MacLeod	1923-1926 1927-1928 1928-1930
Assistant for the Isle of Wight	Alistair. B. MacLeod J.E. Bell George H. R. Gardener * Gordon L. Nicholson * George H. R. Gardener	1930-1934 1934-1940 1940-1943 1943-1946 1946-1966

* In an acting capacity.

Appendix Two

A Chronology of Relevant Isle of Wight Acts of Parliament

This summary contains the name of the Act, a brief description of its main effects and the Parliamentary reference.

The Railways Act 1921
Reorganization and further regulation of railways. Schedule 1 contained a list of constituent and subsidiary companies forming part of the Southern Group.
11-12 Geo. 5 Ch. 55. Date of incorporation 19th August, 1921.

The Southern Railway Act 1924
Included the transfer of ownership of the Ryde Pier Company to the Southern Railway.
14-15 Geo. 5 Ch. 66. Date of incorporation 1st August, 1924.

The Southern Railway Act 1925
Included powers to build a railway in Ventnor and widen the Ryde to Ventnor line between Sandown and Shanklin.
15-16 Geo. 5 Ch. 50. Date of incorporation 31st July, 1925.

270 THE ISLE OF WIGHT RAILWAYS FROM 1923 ONWARDS

The Southern Railway Act 1926
Included powers to widen the Ryde to Ventnor line between Sandown and Brading.
16-17 Geo. 5 Ch. 92. Date of incorporation 4th August, 1926.

The Southern Railway Act 1927
Included powers to build a quay at Medina, dredge and reclaim land.
17-18 Geo. 5 Ch. 23. Date of incorporation 29th June, 1927.

The Southern Railway (Road Transport) Act 1928
Powers to provide road transport.
18-19 Geo. 5 Ch. 104. Date of incorporation 3rd August, 1928.

The Southern Railway Act 1929
Included powers that sanctioned the purchase of property at Newport and Cowes.
19-20 Geo. 5 Ch. 48. Date of incorporation 10th May, 1929.

The Southern Railway (Air Transport) Act 1929
Powers to provide air transport and construct aerodromes.
19-20 Geo. 5 Ch. 57. Date of incorporation 5th May, 1929.

The Transport Act 1947
Powers to establish the British Transport Commission and nationalise the regional railway companies.
10-11 Geo. 6 Ch. 49 Sch. 3 Pt. 1. Date of incorporation 6th August, 1947.

The Transport Act 1953
Powers to denationalise long distance road transport and replace the Railway Executive by area boards.
1-2 Eliz. 2 Ch. 13. Date of incorporation 6th May, 1953.

The Transport Act 1962
Powers to abolish the British Transport Commission, create a British Railways Board, substitute regional boards for area boards and simplify line closure procedures.
10-11 Eliz. 2 Ch. 46. Date of incorporation 1st August, 1962.

The Transport Act 1968
Powers to restructure BR finances, remove regional boards, introduce grants for removal of surplus facilities and subsidies for individual lines kept open because of social need.
1968 Ch. 73. Date of incorporation 25th October, 1968.

The Railways Act 1974
Powers to replace subsidies with a block Public Service Obligation grant and Transport Supplementary Grants administered by County Councils.
1974 Ch. 48. Date of incorporation 31st July, 1974.

The Railways Act 1993
Powers to divide the railway network into franchises.
1993 Ch. 43. Date of incorporation 5th November, 1993.

Appendix Three

Signal Diagrams

During SR days a handful of new signal boxes were brought into use:

Signal box	Brought into use	No. of levers	Notes
Ryde St Johns Road	4.12.1928	40	Replaced North and South boxes.
Smallbrook Junction	18.7.1926	20	New junction.
Wroxall	8.7.1924	12	New crossing loop.
Haven Street	18.7.1926	16	New crossing loop replacing that at Ashey.
Freshwater	18.5.1927	10	Replacement box on a new site.

Other work that resulted in changes to signalling included:

- the construction of an additional platform at Ryde Pier Head,
- a second track between Brading and Sandown, and
- a remodelled junction with the Freshwater line at Newport North

The number of single line sections was reduced following the closure of signal boxes at Carisbrooke, Whitwell and Whippingham. Blackwater ceased to be a block post on 7th June, 1934 but a block post remained at Newchurch until the Sandown line closed in 1956. The cessation of services on the Ventnor West, Bembridge, Freshwater and Sandown-Newport, Ryde-Newport-Cowes and Shanklin-Ventnor lines resulted in the closure of many signal boxes. The remaining boxes between Ryde and Shanklin closed after the line was electrified leaving one box at Ryde St Johns Road to control the whole line. The IWSR has restored the original lever frame at Havenstreet and added ground frames at Smallbrook Junction and Wootton.

Ryde Pier Head 1933

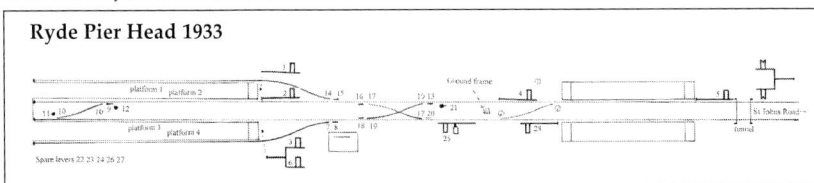

Ryde St Johns May 1931

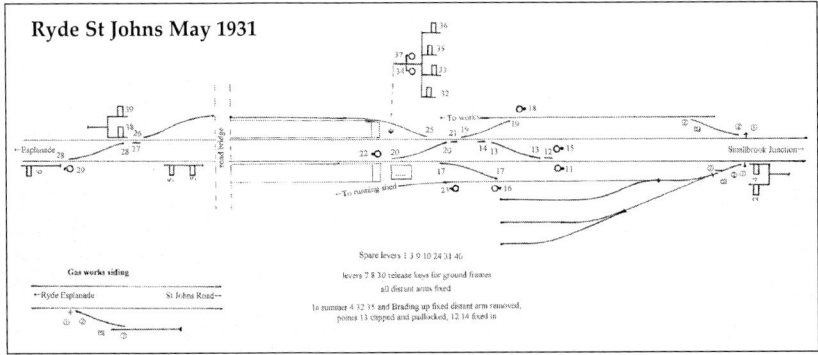

272 THE ISLE OF WIGHT RAILWAYS FROM 1923 ONWARDS

Smallbrook Junction 1926

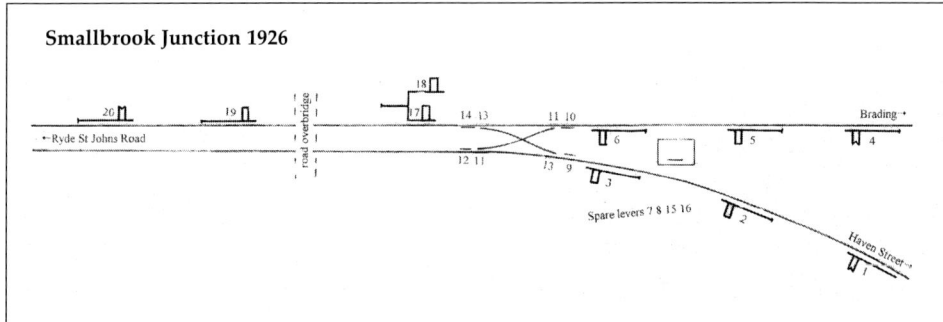

Brading 1931

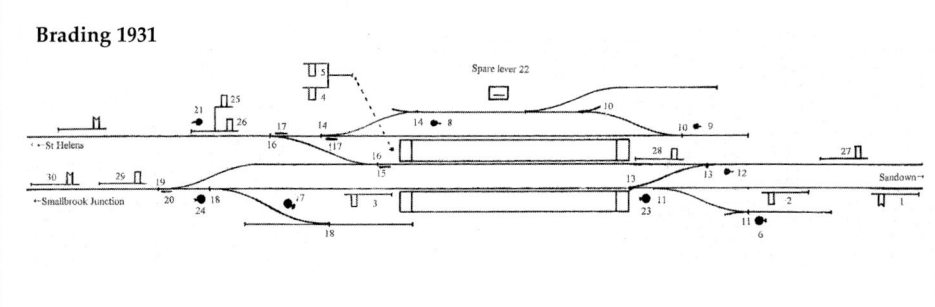

Sandown 1930 onwards

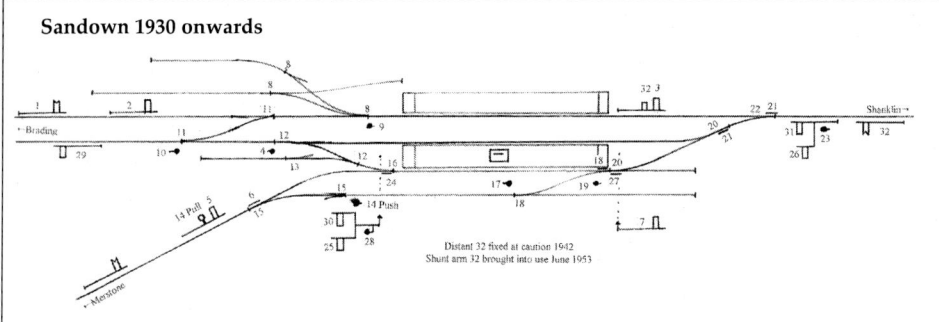

Shanklin

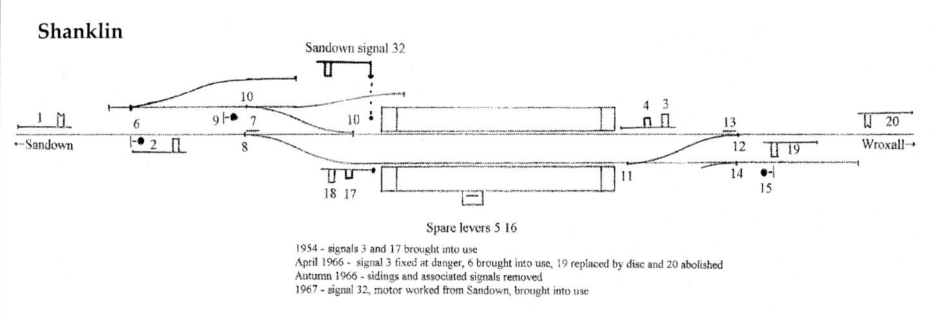

1954 - signals 3 and 17 brought into use
April 1966 - signal 3 fixed at danger, 6 brought into use, 19 replaced by disc and 20 abolished
Autumn 1966 - sidings and associated signals removed
1967 - signal 32, motor worked from Sandown, brought into use

APPENDIX 273

Wroxall 1924

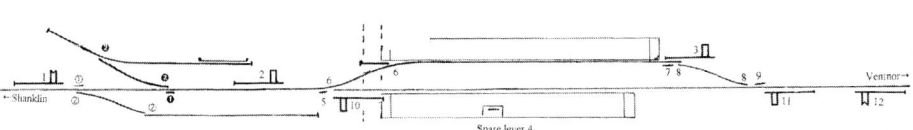

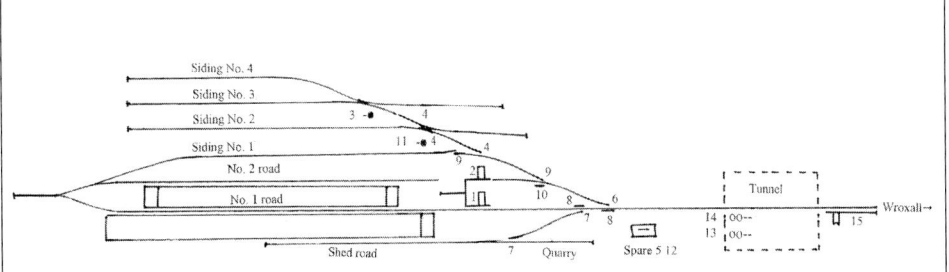

Ventnor 1933

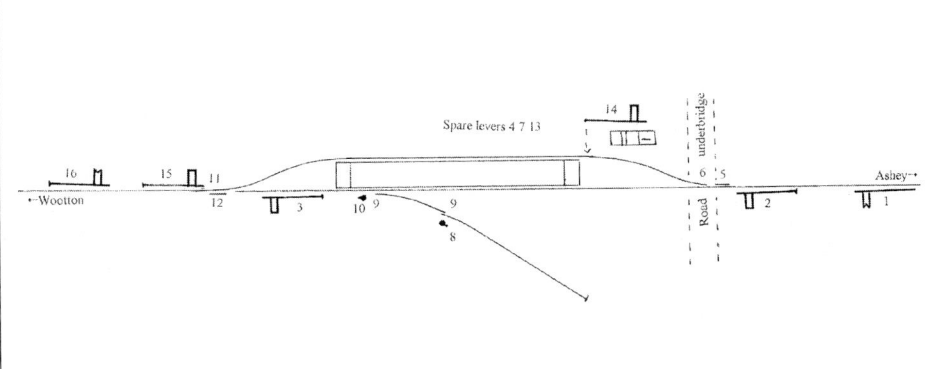

Haven Street 1926

274 THE ISLE OF WIGHT RAILWAYS FROM 1923 ONWARDS

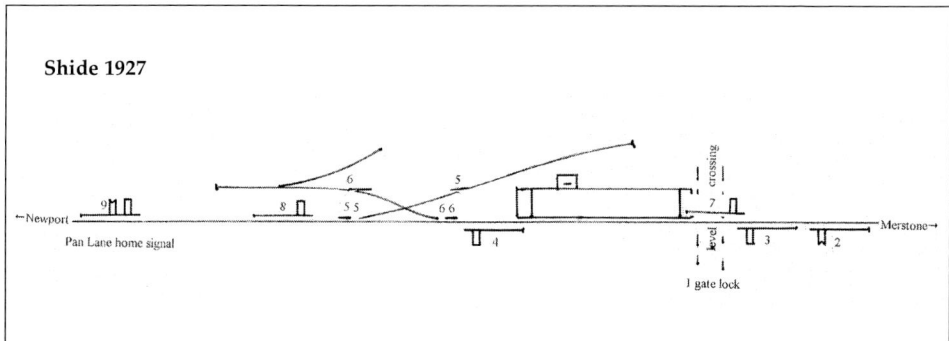

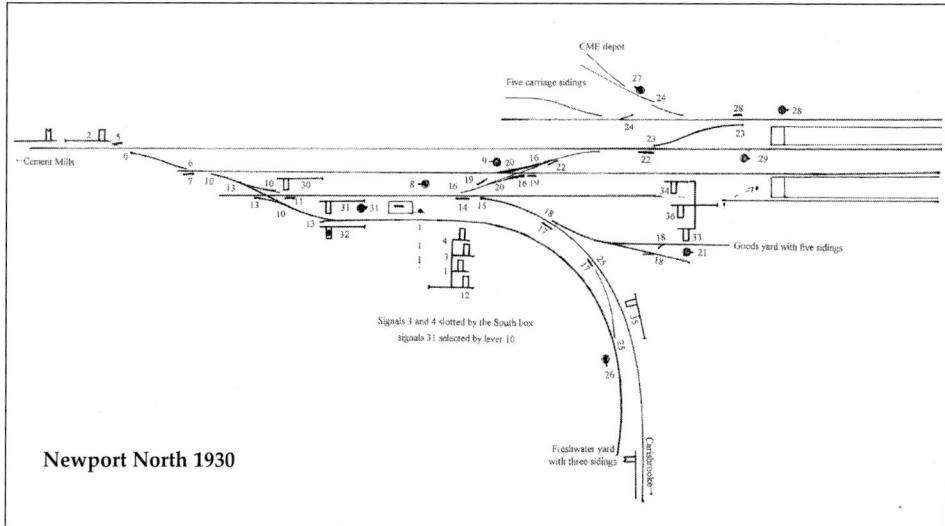

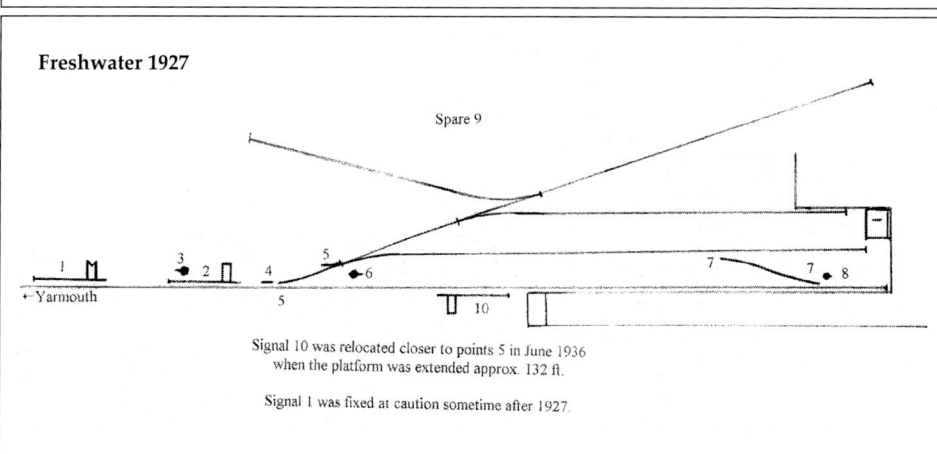

APPENDIX 275

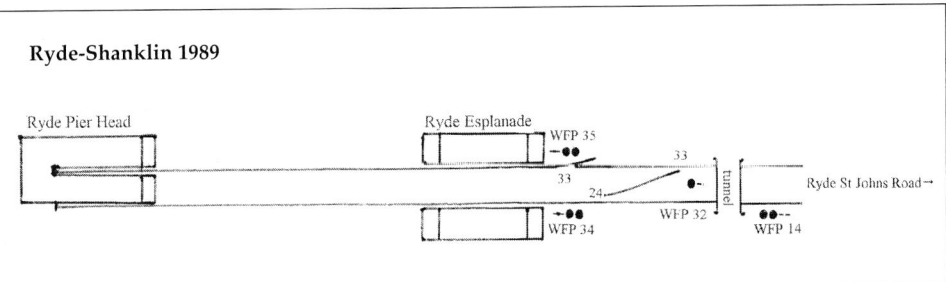

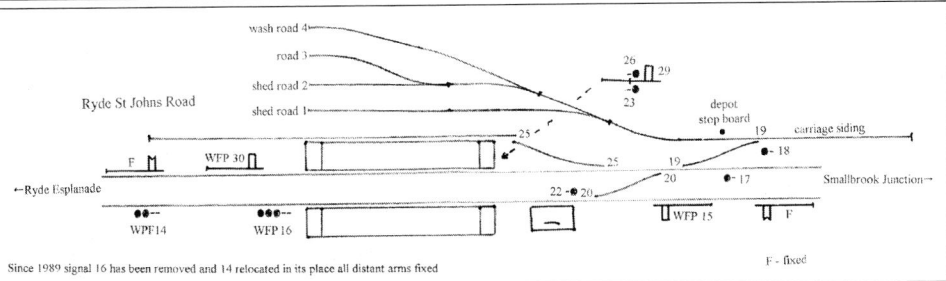

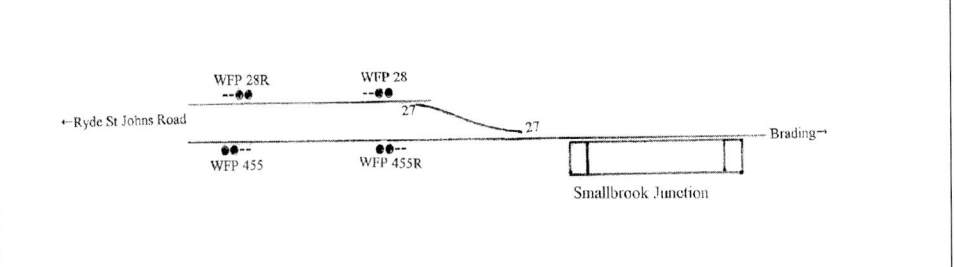

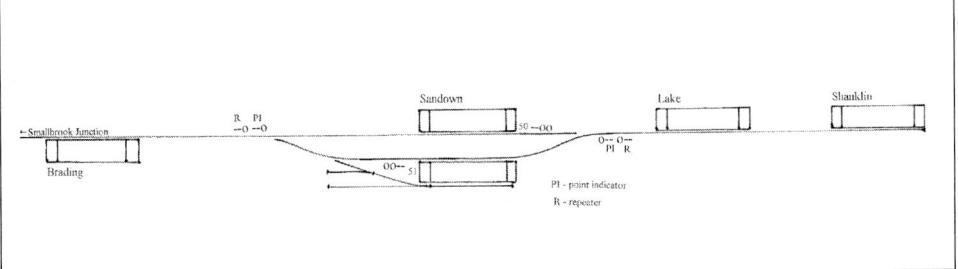

Excluding those made redundant through line closures, the following signal boxes were closed.

Newport FYN station	23.7.1924	Newport South	23.5.1958
Carisbrooke	1924	Smallbrook Junction	17.9.1966
Yarmouth	1924	Ryde Pier Head	5.7.1974
Whitwell	15.9.1932	Shanklin	28.7.1979
Whippingham	6.2.1956	Brading	29.10.1988
Ashey	10.4.1956	Sandown	25.2.1989

Appendix Four

Dates of Opening and Closure of Stations

	Open to passengers	Open to goods	Closed to passengers	Closed to goods
Ryde Pier Head	12.7.1880			
Ryde Esplanade	5.4.1880			
Ryde St Johns Road	23.8.1864	12.1864		1966
Smallbrook Junction	20.7.1991			
Brading	23.8.1864	12.1864		1966
Sandown	23.8.1864	12.1864		15.11.1965
Shanklin				6.12.1965
Lake Halt (first)	1889		by 1923	
Lake Halt (second)	11.5.87			
Wroxall	12.1866	1871	18.4.1966	4.10.1965
Ventnor	10.9.1866	8.1866	18.4.1966	4.10.1965
St Helens	27.5.1882	1.8.1878	21.9.1953	21.9.1953
Bembridge	27.5.1882	(?)1882	21.9.1953	21.9.1953
Ashey	20.12.1875	1876	21.2.1966	21.9.1953
Havenstreet	3.1876	1886	21.2.1966	(?)21.9.1953
Wootton	3.1876	1898	21.9.1953	21.9.1953
Whippingham	20.12.1875	1876	21.9.1953	21.9.1953
Newport (CNR)	16.6.1862		20.12.1875	
Newport	20.12.1875	1876	21.2.1966	1966
Medina Wharf		12.1878		1966
Mill Hill	5.1871	by 1877	21.2.1966	circa 1913
Cowes	16.6.1862	1877	21.2.1966	16.5.1966
Alverstone	1.2.1875	10.1878	6.2.1956	6.2.1956
Newchurch	1.2.1875	1886	6.2.1956	6.2.1956
Horringford	1.2.1875	1883	6.2.1956	6.2.1956
Merstone	1.2.1875	by 1878	6.2.1956	6.2.1956
Blackwater	1.2.1875	1883	6.2.1956	6.2.1956
Shide	1.2.1875	1875	6.2.1956	6.2.1956
Godshill Halt	20.7.1897	20.7.1897	15.9.1952	15.9.1952
Whitwell Halt	20.7.1897	20.7.1897	15.9.1952	1.7.1941
St Lawrence Halt	20.7.1897	20.7.1897	15.9.1952	30.9.1930
Ventnor West	1.6.1900	1.6.1900	15.9.1952	15.9.1952
Newport	1.7.1913	1.7.1913	1.9.1923	1923
Carisbrooke	20.7.1889	1888	21.9.1953	21.9.1953
Watchingwell Halt	8.5.1897	24.11.1897	21.9.1953	1944
Calbourne	20.7.1889	1888	21.9.1953	21.9.1953
Ningwood	20.7.1889	1888	21.9.1953	21.9.1953
Yarmouth	20.7.1889	1888	21.9.1953	21.9.1953
Freshwater	20.7.1889	1888	21.9.1953	21.9.1953

St Lawrence opened as Ventnor (St Lawrence) and was renamed in July 1900, Ventnor Town was renamed Ventnor West on 9th July, 1923, Blackwater became Blackwater (Isle of Wight) on 9th July, 1923 and Haven Street was renamed Havenstreet on 9th June, 1958.

Ashey, Godshill, St Lawrence and Watchingwell all became unstaffed halts in SR days. Whitwell became a partly unstaffed halt from 16th March, 1928 and was unstaffed from 1st July, 1941. Brading became an unstaffed halt from 30th November, 1969.

Goods traffic was officially withdrawn from the remaining stations on 16th May, 1966 but some coal was still carried until Autumn 1966. These are official dates of closure and in the case of goods traffic cannot be relied on as reflecting actual events. There were also stock movements after closure as often a train was run to recover useful assets and any remaining rolling stock on the line.

Appendix Five

Summary of Steam Locomotives

Date built	Builder	Class	Type	Orig. No.	LBSCR Name	SR IW No.	SR IW Name	To IW	Returned to mainland	Wdn
12.1876	LBSCR	A1	0-6-0T	46	Newington*	2	Freshwater	6.13	4.5.49	#11.63
7.1880	LBSCR	A1x	0-6-0T	77	Wonersh	3	Carisbrooke	5.27	4.5.49	9.59
7.1880	LBSCR	A1x	0-6-0T	78	Knowle	4	Bembridge	9.6.29	19.5.36	$10.63
12.1872	LBSCR	A1	0-6-0T	75	Blackwall*	9		3.1899		1926
12.1876	LBSCR	A1x	0-6-0T	50	Whitechapel	9	Fishbourne	28.5.30	19.5.36	$11.63
7.1874	LBSCR	A1	0-6-0T	69	Peckham*	10	Cowes	4.00	19.5.36	12.36
3.1878	LBSCR	A1x	0-6-0T	40	Brighton*	11	Newport	1.02	22.2.47	#9.63
9.1880	LBSCR	A1x	0-6-0T	84	Crowborough*	12	Ventnor	11.03	5.5.36	12.36
12.1889	LSWR	O2	0-4-4T	178		14	Fishbourne	5.5.36	-	1.1.67
12.1890	LSWR	O2	0-4-4T	195		15	Cowes	19.5.36	-	13.5.56
6.1892	LSWR	O2	0-4-4T	217		16	Ventnor	5.5.36	-	1.1.67
12.1891	LSWR	O2	0-4-4T	208		17	Seaview	28.5.30	-	1.1.67
9.1892	LSWR	O2	0-4-4T	220		18	Ningwood	28.5.30	-	5.12.65
9.1891	LSWR	O2	0-4-4T	206		19	Osborne	4.5.23	-	5.11.55
3.1892	LSWR	O2	0-4-4T	211		20	Shanklin	4.5.23	-	1.1.67
9.1891	LSWR	O2	0-4-4T	205		21	Sandown	7.24	-	1.5.66
6.1892	LSWR	O2	0-4-4T	215		22	Brading	7.24	-	1.1.67
10.1890	LSWR	O2	0-4-4T	188		23	Totland	26.4.25	-	19.9.55
12.1891	LSWR	O2	0-4-4T	209		24	Calbourne	26.4.25	-	#14.3.67
11.1890	LSWR	O2	0-4-4T	190		25	Godshill	25.6.25	-	30.12.62
12.1891	LSWR	O2	0-4-4T	210		26	Whitwell	25.6.25	-	1.5.66
6.1890	LSWR	O2	0-4-4T	184		27	Merstone	17.3.26	-	1.1.67
7.1890	LSWR	O2	0-4-4T	186		28	Ashey	17.3.26	-	1.1.67
7.1891	LSWR	O2	0-4-4T	202		29	Alverstone	20.4.26	-	1.5.66
9.1892	LSWR	O2	0-4-4T	219		30	Shorwell	20.4.26	-	12.9.65
4.1890	LSWR	O2	0-4-4T	180		31	Chale	5.27	-	14.3.67
11.1892	LSWR	O2	0-4-4T	226		32	Bonchurch	24.5.28	-	25.10.64
8.1892	LSWR	O2	0-4-4T	218		33	Bembridge	19.5.36	-	1.1.67
7.1891	LSWR	O2	0-4-4T	201		34	Newport	20.5.47	-	19.9.55
5.1890	LSWR	O2	0-4-4T	181		35	Freshwater	13.4.49	-	2.10.66
6.1891	LSWR	O2	0-4-4T	198		36	Carisbrooke	13.4.49	-	14.6.64
1.1879	LBSCR	E1	0-6-0T	136	Brindisi	1	Medina	4.7.32	-	17.6.57
10.1880	LBSCR	E1	0-6-0T	152	Hungary	2	Yarmouth	4.7.32	-	15.9.56
3.1881	LBSCR	E1	0-6-0T	154	Madrid	3	Ryde	4.7.32	-	13.6.59
11.1878	LBSCR	E1	0-6-0T	131	Gournay	4	Wroxall	23.6.33	-	20.10.60
12.1900	LBSCR	E4	0-6-2T	510	Twineham	2510		22.2.47	5.4.49	9.62

* Inherited from the FYN and IWC.
# Preserved at Havenstreet. $ Preserved on the mainland.
'A1x' Nos. 2, 3 and 4 were renumbered 8, 13 and 14 in 1932.
'O2' No. 29 was sent to the mainland for an overhaul on 22nd February, 1947 and returned on 20th May, 1947.

278 THE ISLE OF WIGHT RAILWAYS FROM 1923 ONWARDS

Class:	A1x	O2	E1	E4
Wheel type	0-6-0T	0-4-4T	0-6-0T	0-6-2T
Length overall	26 ft 0½ in.	30 ft 10¾ in.	32 ft 4½ in.	35 ft 3 in.
Cylinders (inside)	12-14* in. x 20 in.	17½ in. x 24 in.	17 in. x 24 in.	17½ in. x 26 in.
Coupled wheels	4 ft	4 ft 10 in.	4 ft 6 in.	5 ft
Trailing wheels	-	3 ft	-	4 ft
Wheelbase	12 ft	20 ft 4 in.	15 ft 3 in.	21 ft 6 in.
Boiler diameter	3 ft 5⅛ in.	4 ft 3 in.	4 ft	4 ft 3 in.
Boiler length	7 ft 10 in.	9 ft 5 in.	10 ft 2 in.	10 ft 10¾ in.
Firebox length	4 ft 1 in.	5 ft	4 ft 7 in.	5 ft 8¼ in.
Type of boiler	A1x	Adams	Drummond	Marsh	R.J. Billington
Heating surface - boiler	463 sq. ft	898 sq. ft	785 sq. ft	952 sq. ft	947½ sq. ft
firebox	55 sq. ft	87 sq. ft	87 sq. ft	87 sq. ft	93¼ sq. ft
total	518 sq. ft	987 sq. ft	872 sq. ft	1,039 sq. ft	1,040¾ sq. ft
Grate area	10 sq. ft	13.83 sq. ft	14.9 sq. ft	15½ sq. ft	17.43 sq. ft
Working pressure (psi)	140 lb.	160 lb.	150 lb.	170 lb.
Tank capacity	500 galls	800 galls	900 galls	1,409 galls
Bunker capacity	10 cwt	1½ t.	15 cwt	2¼ t.
Weight in working order	28 t. 5 c.	46 t. 18 c.	44 t. 3 c.	57 t. 10 c.
Tractive effort	7,600 lb.	17,245 lb.	18,600 lb.	19,180 lb.

* In December 1928 they carried: 12 in. diameter cylinders - No. 3, 13 in. diameter cylinders - Nos. 2, 11, 14 in. diameter cylinders - Nos. 4, 10, 12.

The LBSCR class 'A1' 0-6-0Ts were rebuilt with new boilers to class 'A1x' and received larger 1½ ton coal bunkers:

IW No.	rebuilt to A1x	in	larger bunker fitted	in
FYN 2 later 8	by SR	3.32	by SR	4.24
IWC 9	not	-	by IWC	circa 3.17
IWC 10	by SR	4.30	by IWC	circa 6.15
IWC 11	by IWC	7.18	by IWC	7.18
IWC 12	by IWC	7.16	by IWC	7.16
3 later 13	by LBSCR	11.11	by SR	upon transfer
4 later 14	by LBSCR	11.11	by SR	upon transfer
9 (2nd)	by LBSCR	5.20	by SR	upon transfer

The following 'O2s' carried Drummond pattern boilers:

Locomotive No.	From
18	5.58 to 3.62.
22	3.63 to withdrawal.
25	1.48 to 11.51.
27	2.26 to 6.38 and 3.56 to 7.61.
28	3.26 to 6.36.
29	3.26 to 4.37 and 2.50 to 9.52.
30	4.26 to 9.38 and 5.54 to 1.57.
31	4.27 to 12.35 and 1.63 to withdrawal.
32	3.28 to 9.37.
33	4.48 to 12.50.

Between 1932 and 1935 the 'MacLeod' bunker was fitted to 'O2s' at Ryde Works, the Ryde-based locomotives being dealt with first. New arrivals received the larger bunker at Eastleigh before transfer. It had a coal capacity of 3 tons increasing the weight in working order to 48 t. 8 c. Nos. 35-36 carried push-pull equipment and weighed slightly more.

Appendix Six

Summary of Passenger and Goods Stock

Carriages

LSWR bogie carriages   Nos. 4106-7, 3150-3, 5100-2
  9 to IW 2-4.7.23. 3150-3 and 5100-2 renumbered 4138-41 and 6384-6 in 1930-1.
  Withdrawn 26.4.39 except 4141 and 6385 on 23.9.42.
LBSCR four-wheel Stroudley stock   Nos. 1793-1794, 3665/70/74/86, 5799-5800
  8 to IW 2.8.24. 3665/70/74/86 and 5799-5800 renumbered 4142-5 and 6387-8 in 1930.
  Withdrawn 1931.
LBSCR four-wheel Billinton carriages   Nos. 2343-2345, 4113-8, 6370-2, 7996
  13 to IW 1924 and 1925. Withdrawn 1931 except for 7996 25.8.34.
SECR bogie rail motor carriages   Nos. 4109-4110, 6366-6367
  4 to IW 26.4.25. Returned to the mainland in 5.27.
LCDR four-wheel push-pull carriages   Nos. 4111-4112, 6368-6369
  4 to IW 31.8.24. Withdrawn 6.38.
LCDR four-wheel carriages   Nos. 2476-2520, 4099-4102, 4119-50, 6373-6393
  89 to IW 1926-30. Withdrawn 1932-1938 except 4124/33/50 in 4.49.
LCDR bogie carriages   Nos. 2418-2437, 4109/10/13-7, 6358-61/88/94-6400
  39 to IW 1930-1934. Two withdrawn 1939, remainder 1948-1949.
LBSCR bogie carriages   Nos. 2404-2417, 4118/21-3/51-75, 6344-56, 6362-3, 6986
  54 to IW 1934-1939. Withdrawn 1954-1966, except 4167 in 4.40.
LBSCR bogie push-pull carriages   Nos. 4167/9, 6366-6367, 6987
  4169, 6367, 6987 arrived 31.5.38. 4167 and 6366 arrived 20.5.47. Withdrawn on 8.5.54.
SECR bogie carriages   Nos. 2438-2458, 4134-4149, 6364-5, 6368-80
  52 to IW 1947-1949. Withdrawn 1956-1966.

Passenger vans

LSWR passenger guard's & luggage vans   Nos. 7, 35, 57, 995-1003, 1007, 1254/75/83
  16 to IW 1924-1930. 7/35/57 and 1254/75/83 renumbered 1004-6 and 2232-4 1927-29.
  2234 renumbered 1016 on 22.9.33. Withdrawn 1933-1939 except 1003 on 8.5.54.
LSWR bogie passenger guard's vans   Nos. 1014-5, 1017-23
  9 to IW 1936-8. Withdrawn 10.10.50 except 1021-2 on 6.10.56.
LBSCR horse box   No. 3113
  To IW 26.4.25. Renumbered 3370 6.4.29. Withdrawn 8.5.54.
LCDR passenger guard's & luggage vans   No. 1008/9/13, 2235, 4381
  1008/9/13 and 2235 to IW 1930-1933. 2235 renumbered 1010 by 3.32. Open carriage
  truck 4381 converted from LCD brake third 4135 in 12.36. Withdrawn 1936-7 except
  1008 2.9.50 and 4381 25.2.56.
LCDR bogie passenger guard's vans   Nos. 1011-2
  To IW 4.7.32 and 23.6.33. Withdrawn 1957.
SECR bogie passenger guard's vans   Nos. 1013-1016
  4 rebuilt from SECR brake thirds 4138-41 in 1956-1957. Withdrawn 19.11.66.
SR four-wheel luggage vans   Nos. 1046-1052
  7 to IW 10.10.50. Withdrawn 1966-1967.

Ryde Tramway Stock

Petrol motor cars   Nos. 1 and 2
     To IW 1927. Withdrawn 1969
Trailer cars   Nos. 7 and 8
     To IW 1936 and 1937. Withdrawn 1969.
Luggage trolley   No. 9
     Built at Ryde Works 1939. Withdrawn 1969.

Goods stock

LBSCR 10 ton open wagons

457 to IW	1924	26119-26123, 26131-26145	1930	27721-27795
1925		18988-18990	1931	27796-27881
1926		18980-18987, 18991-19017/33-34/60-75	1937	27545
1927		28321-28388	1937	64392
1928		28389-28458	1947	27882-27887
1929		28253-28300, 28459-28485		

     Withdrawn 1948-1966 except for six rebuilt as dropside ballast wagons.
SR 13 ton open wagons   27888-27975
     88 to IW 1948-1949. Withdrawn 1960-1966.
LBSCR 8 & 10 ton covered vans   46924-46974 and 437S
     48 to IW 1927-1931 except 46924-6 rebuilt 1935 from LBSCR cattle wagons and 437S arrived 1937.
     46932 withdrawn 30.7.41, the remainder 1948-1960.
LBSCR cattle wagons   53371-53376
     6 to IW 1927-1929. 53374-6 rebuilt as covered vans 1935. 53371-3 withdrawn 1956.
LSWR goods brake vans   56044-56055 (10 ton), 56056-7 (15 ton),
                                                   56058 (18 ton)
       15 to IW. 56044-56055 arrived 1925-1932. 56044/7-9 rebuilt 1933 with a second balcony and sanding gear. 56045/50 withdrawn 1.6.38 upon arrival of 56056-7, 56054 in 1948 upon arrival of 56058 and the remainder 1955-1967.
LBSCR single bolster wagons   59033-59052
       20 to IW 1928-1930. Withdrawn 1960-1967, except for two retained as converted wagons.
Road vehicle trucks   60561-4 (LSWR) 60565-60583 (LBSCR)
       23 to IW 1927-1930. 60561/3-5/9/73/76-7 withdrawn 1937-8, 60570 in 1945, the remainder 1956-68.
LSWR tar tank wagons   61384-5
     To IW 20.5.47. Returned to mainland 10.10.50.

Engineers' Stock

SECR dropside ballast wagons   62885-62904
     20 to IW 1924 and 1931. Two withdrawn 1931-2 but most of the remainder lasted until 1968.
LBSCR 4 ton dropside ballast wagons   62905-22
     18 to IW 1927. 62908/16 withdrawn 1928, the remainder in 1931.
LBSCR 21 dropside ballast wagons   62792/8/62801/4/5/10/1/6/7/20
     10 to IW 1947. Withdrawn 1955.

       Three IWR and IWC hand cranes, match trucks, a water tank and tool van were given numbers 425S-429S. Subsequent conversions to tool vans, etc. carried numbers scattered throughout the departmental series. Most were existing stock that had been withdrawn from traffic.

Appendix Seven

Summary of Stock after 1966

Pre-1938 Tube Cars

IW No.	Built	Maker	LT No.	Type/end	To IW	Entered service	First Withdrawn IW unit	To mainland	Disposal	Scrapped
1	1934	MCW	3703	DM D	5.12.66	20.3.67	031	6.6.90	20.6.90	6	7.1.93
2	1934	MCW	3706	DM A	27.4.67	20.5.67	043	7.9.90	2.10.90	5	
3	1931	MCW	3251	DM D	2.3.67	20.3.67	032	1989	28.9.89	3	4.10.90
4	1934	MCW	3702	DM A	15.12.66	20.3.67	044	25.9.89	28.9.89	3	4.10.90
5	1931	MCW	3185	DM D	29.4.67	20.5.67	033	13.5.91		2	23.4.94
6	1931	MCW	3084	DM A	14.4.67	15.5.67	045	1.2.90	14.3.90	4	23.8.91
7	1931	MCW	3209	DM D	17.4.67	26.4.67	034	7.9.90	4.10.90	5	
8	1931	MCW	3074	DM A	19.12.66	22.3.67	046	6.6.90	20.6.90	6	8.1.93
9	1931	MCW	3223	DM D	13.4.67	26.4.67	035	3.1.89	13.3.90	4	23.8.91
10	1934	MCW	3696	DM A	3.3.67	20.3.67	spare	6.6.90	20.6.90	6	5.1.93
11	1934	MCW	3705	DM D	17.2.67	22.3.67	036	8.1.90	16.3.90	6	15.1.93
13	1931	MCW	3141	DM D	17.12.66	20.3.67	041	3.85		1	6.87
15 (I)	1931	MCW	3253	DM D	28.2.67	20.3.67	042	7.10.67		1	10.5.69
15 (II)	1931	MCW	3273	DM D	21.3.71	17.7.71	042	11.4.88		2	8.5.89
19	1928	UCC	3045	DM D	28.4.67	20.5.67	043	12.82		2	21.4.89
20	1928	UCC	3308	DM A	6.12.66	20.3.67	041	11.4.88		2	8.5.89
21	1928	UCC	3041	DM D	16.12.66	20.3.67	044	3.85		1	6.87
22	1929	UCC	3010	DM A	22.2.67	20.3.67	042	14.11.86		2	16.5.89
23	1927	MCW	3315	DM D	15.4.67	15.5.67	045	10.9.73		1	4.5.74
25	1927	MCW	3313	DM D	20.12.66	22.3.67	046	8.9.75		1	10.82
26	1925	MCW	5294	CT A	1.9.66	20.3.67	031	7.9.90		2	18.4.90
27	1925	MCW	5279	CT *	7.12.66	22.3.67	041	18.1.90	3.10.90	5	
28	1925	MCW	5304	CT A	18.2.67	20.3.67	032	13.5.91		2	14.4.94
29	1925	MCW	5293	CT *	11.2.67	22.3.67	042	25.9.89	28.9.89	3	16.10.90
30	1925	MCW	5312	CT A	21.4.67	20.5.67	033	12.82		1	7.87
31	1925	MCW	5283	CT *	25.4.67	20.5.67	043	13.5.91		2	16.4.94
32	1925	MCW	5290	CT A	19.4.67	26.4.67	034	4.9.89	28.9.89	3	15.10.90
33	1925	MCW	5291	CT *	9.12.66	20.3.67	044	20.9.89	26.9.89	3	13.10.90
34	1925	MCW	5302	CT A	10.4.67	26.4.67	035	6.6.90	22.6.90	3	20.10.90
36	1927	MCW	5350	CT A	13.2.67	22.3.67	036	3.85		1	6.87
41	1923	CL	7286	T	6.12.66	20.3.67	041	12.9.86		2	8.5.89
42	1923	CL	7280	T	12.2.67	20.3.67	042	27.11.86		2	16.5.89
43	1923	CL	7275	T	26.4.67	20.5.67	043	30.9.88	5.7.89	3	25.10.90
44	1923	CL	7281	T	10.12.66	20.3.67	044	3.2.90	3.10.90	5	
45	1923	CL	7293	T	18.4.67	15.5.67	045	10.9.73		1	4.5.74
46	1923	CL	7283	T	12.12.66	22.3.67	046	14.2.86		2	16.5.89
47	1923	CL	7279	T	29.11.66	20.3.67	031	11.87	5.7.89	3	30.10.90
48	1923	CL	7298	T	12.4.67	15.5.67	045	10.9.73		1	4.5.74
49	1923	CL	7296	T	13.12.66	22.3.67	046	7.10.90	2.10.90	5	
92	1923	CL	7285	T	27.2.67	20.3.67	032	4.10.88	26.9.89	3	14.10.90
93	1923	CL	7282	T	24.4.67	20.5.67	033	18.1.90	16.3.90	3	20.10.90
94	1923	CL	7287	T	20.4.67	26.4.67	034	3.10.89	13.3.90	3	17.10.90
95	1923	CL	7292	T	11.4.67	26.4.67	035	5.3.90	14.3.90	3	23.10.90
96	1923	CL	7290	T	26.2.67	22.3.67	036	3.85		1	6.87

Makers: MCW - Metropolitan Carriage & Wagon Co., Saltley, Birmingham.
UCC - Union Construction & Finance Co., Feltham, London.
CL - Cammell Laird & Co., Nottingham.
Type: DM = driving motor, CT = control trailer, T = trailer, * = 'D' end control trailer used as trailer
End = A cars formed at the Ryde end of units, D formed at Shanklin end.

Car 26 arrived numbered 38. 19 and 30 were given departmental numbers 083569 and 083570 for use as grounded stores vans at Sandown and Ryde St Johns Road.
Disposal details -
1 - scrapped at Ryde.
2 - scrapped at Sandown.
3 - taken from Fratton to V. Berry for scrapping.
4 - moved to Ruislip 9-10.10.90, to Old Watney's Brewery Stepney on 1.7.91 for filming, then to Birds Long Marston 23.8.91 for scrap.
5 - to Ruislip 18.10.90 for LT vintage train.
6 - to Ruislip 11.10.90, cannibalised by LT and then to V. Berry for scrap.

Dimensions in LT ownership were:
49½ ft and 51½ ft (1931/4 motor cars) long, 8 ft 8½ in. wide, 9 ft 6 in. high.
Motor cars seated 30, reduced to 26 for the Isle of Wight and weighed approx. 30 tons. The motor bogie was powered by two GEC 240 hp traction motors. The equipment cabinet occupied over 15 ft of the car's length.
Control trailers seated 44 reduced to 41 and weighed approx. 19¾ tons.
Trailer cars had seats for 48 reduced to 45 and weighed approx. 17¾ tons.
Each Isle of Wight four-car unit was formed with one 49½ ft and one 51½ ft motor car. When reformed as five car units in 1987 both motor cars were 51½ ft.

1938 Tube Stock

IW No.	LT No.	End	To IW	Entered service	First IW unit	Withdrawn	Scrapped
121	10184	A	5.7.89	13.7.89	001	28.6.96	24.4.2000
122	10221	A	26.9.89	7.10.89	002	16.5.95	? 6.2005
123	10116	A	27.9.89	7.10.89	003		
124	10205	A	14.3.90	1.5.90	004		
125	10142	A	15.3.90	11.5.90	005	16.12.94	24.4.2000
126	10297	A	20.6.90	13.7.90	006		
127	10291	A	12.3.90	18.5.90	007		
128	10255	A	21.6.90	29.6.90	008		
129	10229	A	9.4.92	18.6.90	009		
(130)	10139	A	8.4.92			1.3.98	6.2005
221	11184	A	5.7.89	13.7.89	001	16.5.95	? 6.2005
222	11221	D	26.9.89	7.10.89	002	20.6.96	24.4.2000
223	11116	D	27.9.89	7.10.89	003	16.12.94	24.4.2000
224	11205	D	14.3.90	1.5.90	004		
225	11142	D	15.3.90	11.5.90	005		
226	11297	D	20.6.90	13.7.90	006		
227	11291	D	12.3.90	18.5.90	007		
228	11255	D	20.6.90	29.6.90	008		
229	11229	D	9.4.92	18.6.90	009		
(230)	11172	D	8.4.92			1.3.98	6.2005

End = A cars formed at the Ryde end of units, D formed at Shanklin end.
Made by Metropolitan Carriage & Wagon Co. and although described as 1938 stock they were actually delivered 1939-1942.
All those sent to the IW were driving motors. The spare body shells were used as stores vehicles; the unofficial Nos. 130 and 230 were not carried. All the scrapped cars were cut up at Ryde.

Dimensions in LT ownership were: 52 ft 3¾ in. long, 8 ft 6¼ in. wide over body, 9 ft 5½ in. height above rail. Each car had two 168 hp traction motors and weighed 27.4 tons.

APPENDIX 283

Diesel locomotives classes '03' and '05'

Date built	Builder	BR TOPS class	First BR No.	IW No.	To IW	Wdn	Left island	For
5.1956	Hunslet, Leeds	05	11140	D2554*	7.10.66	4.84	23.8.84	IWSR
1.1.60	BR Doncaster	03	D2079	03079	8.4.84	10.93	5.6.98	Derwent Valley Rly
1962	BR Swindon	03	D2179	03179	30.6.88	6.6.96	5.6.98	West Anglia Gt Northern

All were 0-6-0 diesel mechanical shunting locomotives.
* subsequently renumbered 05 001 and 97 803 (not carried)

Class:	05	03
Wheel type	0-6-0DM	0-6-0DM
Length	25 ft 4 in.	26 ft
Width	8 ft 3 in.	8 ft 6 in.
Original height	11 ft 0½ in.	* 12 ft 2⁷⁄₁₆ in.
Wheelbase	4 ft 6 in. + 4 ft 6 in.	4 ft 6 in. + 4 ft 6 in.
Diameter driving wheels	3 ft 4 in.	3 ft 7 in.
Power unit	Gardner 8L3 204 hp	Gardner 8L3 204 hp
Maximum speed	18.25 mph	29 mph
Weight in working order	30 t. 18 c.	30 t. 4 c.

* height reduced after arrival.

Engineers' Stock

Single bolster wagons DB450157/665/957, DB451289/341/924, DB452018/715, DB453084/126/343/374
    12 to IW 1.8.66. Converted from low sided wagons after arrival. Scrapped or sold to the IWSR.
Matisa tamping machine   DS72
    To IW Autumn of 1966. Declared redundant in 5.75, sold to the IWSR but later scrapped.
15 t. ballast goods brake vans   DS55710, DS55724
    To IW 6.5.67. 55710 sold to the IWSR 1985 and 55724 in 2000.
13 t. 'Hyfit' engineering wagons   DB483700/01/25/33
    To IW 1971-3. Sold to the IWSR.
Wickham Railcar   DS3320
    To IW 1973-4. Sold to the IWSR 1976.
Plasser & Theuer power trolley   DB965202
    To IW 1975? Scrapped before 1979.
21 t. private owner hopper wagon   DP101453
    To IW 1978. Scrapped 10.94.
20 t. 'Herring' ballast hopper wagons   DB992419/444/461
    To IW 1979. Scrapped circa 1994.
25½ t. LNER lowmacs   DE263276, DE263289
    To IW 17.8.82. Sold 6.2000 DE263276 to IWSR.
Rail carrier   DS70000, runner wagons DB452219, DB453255
    To IW 17.8.82. Sold to the IWSR 6.2000.
13 t. 'Medfit' open wagons   DB460219, DB461225
    To IW 9.7.86. Sold 2000.
18½ t. GWR sleeper wagon   DW100715
    To IW 9.7.86. Sold 6.2000.
24 t. 'Dogfish' ballast hopper wagons   DB983247, DB992730, DB993598
    To IW 26 & 28.9.89. DB983247 and DB992730 sold 6.2000 (992730 to IWSR).
Match trucks   ADB452604, ADB453641
    Converted 1978 originally for use with Waterloo & City stock. To IW 8.4.92.
Permaquip personnel carriers   68809 and 68810
    68809 to IW 1997, 68810 to IW 11.95. Sold to IWSR in 2005.

Appendix Eight

The SR Floating Crane

On 17th January, 1923 Messrs Cowans Sheldon & Co. Ltd presented a specification to the SR for the supply of a floating crane. This was probably in response to an enquiry made by the LSWR. An order was placed on 3rd March for delivery by 1st January, 1924. Although Cowans built the crane itself, construction of the remainder was subcontracted to Furness Shipbuilding of Haverton Hill, the home of a former IWC locomotive. With a deck area measuring 170 ft by 80 ft and a depth of 12 ft, the crane had no form of propulsion but was fitted with capstans for manoeuvring. Power for the crane's operation was supplied by a steam generating plant, later replaced by a diesel generating set. The total height from waterline to the top of the jib was 230 ft and depending on the angle it could lift up to 150 tons. SR floating crane No. 1 cost £79,277. A schedule of charges existed for the hire of the crane and its crew to any firm needing heavy lifting within Southampton docks.

Prior to 1923 it was usual to transport locomotives and rolling stock to the Island by barge to St Helens Quay or Medina Jetty. In 1916 and 1917 three locomotives left the Island via Ryde Pier Head and Portsmouth using an Admiralty floating crane. The same method was used in 1923 when two LSWR locomotives and nine carriages were landed at Ryde Pier Head. A reversion to barges occurred in 1924 for the transfer of two locomotives and some four-wheel carriages and goods wagons to St Helens Quay; the locomotives were partially dismantled to bring them within the 10 ton weight limit at the quay. Four bogie carriages had to wait until alternative arrangements could be made.

The floating crane arrived at Southampton on 14th September, 1923 but it was the end of 1924 before it was fully operational. The crane made its first journey to the Island on Sunday 26th April, 1925 with two locomotives, a four-wheel saloon carriage, a horse box and four bogie carriages (upwards of a dozen bogie carriages could be accommodated on the crane's deck). The crane would be towed by up to three tugs from Southampton to Medina Jetty where, owing to the risk of grounding, unloading had to be carried out near to high tide; on the first occasion it was reported that unloading commenced at 12.20 pm and was completed in 1 hour 50 minutes.

The floating crane became the preferred method for transporting locomotives and rolling stock to and from the Island, although much of the goods stock sent to the Island in the 1920s continued to be shipped by barge to St Helens Quay. Between 1925 and 1939 the crane made a total of 23 journeys to the Island; the last journey prior to the outbreak of war taking place on 19th April, 1939.

The crane was hired by the Admiralty for use in Portsmouth Dockyard from 7th to 18th April, 1941 along with its five man crew (foreman, crane driver, electrician, fireman and engine driver) and two additional attendants. The Admiralty was responsible for towage to and from Portsmouth, it being returned on 21st April. Later that year the crane was requisitioned by the Ministry of War Transport, the 'hire' beginning 26th September. It ceased to be used commercially on 5th October and left Portsmouth on 19th November destined for No. 1 Military Port on the Clyde estuary.

Once war ended there was a pressing need to send additional locomotives and stock to the Island. In the absence of the crane, there was correspondence concerning the use of a Mark 3 LCT (Landing Craft Tank) to carry three carriages per trip and a large barge conveying either two LBSCR class 'E4' or one 'E3' and one 'E4' locomotive. The SR had a 60 ton floating crane (Ministry of War Transport No. 11) at Southampton but it lacked enough deck area. The combined cost of hiring the crane and other craft was considered excessive.

The 150 ton crane remained on the Clyde until mid-1946 to assist in the fitting out of HMS *Vanguard*. Bad weather delayed the planned departure on 17th June and it did not arrive at Southampton for overhaul until 9th July. On 26th November it was towed to Portsmouth for re-erection of the jib and testing, this being completed on 13th January, 1947; consideration was given to using its return journey to Southampton to take two locomotives from Portsmouth to Ryde Pier Head but more bad weather delayed the first trip to the Island. Amidst snow showers on 22nd February it took a class 'E4' locomotive, a SECR 60 ft long bogie carriage, six LBSCR 10 ton open wagons and a spare class 'O2' boiler; two locomotives were brought back to the mainland. The last of 12 post-war journeys took place on 10th October, 1950 when seven SR vans were sent in exchange for a like number of LSWR vehicles. The floating crane remained at Southampton until May-June 1985 when it was broken up on the site of dry-dock No. 4 following the purchase of a second-hand replacement from Rotterdam.

During the 1950s there were discussions about the closure of the Ryde-Cowes line and some thought was given to alternative ways of transporting stock. Ryde Pier was rejected as a landing point because of the shallow sea bed but assurances were given that a road low-loader could use the Lymington-Yarmouth ferry. After the introduction of larger vessels, the Portsmouth-Fishbourne route, became the preferred route for the transfer of tube and other stock to the Island

Southampton Docks
Charges for use of Floating Crane

	£	s.	d.
For lifts of 15 tons and under			
First hour or part thereof	10	0	0
Second hour or part thereof	5	0	0
Third hour or part thereof and each subsequent hour	2	10	0

	£	s.	d.
With additional charge for each lift			
Over 15 tons and not exceeding 20 tons	5	0	0
Over 20 tons and not exceeding 30 tons	7	10	0
Over 30 tons and not exceeding 40 tons	15	0	0
Over 40 tons and not exceeding 50 tons	25	0	0
Over 50 tons and not exceeding 60 tons	35	0	0
Over 60 tons and not exceeding 70 tons	45	0	0
Over 70 tons and not exceeding 80 tons	55	0	0
Over 80 tons and not exceeding 90 tons	65	0	0
Over 90 tons and not exceeding 100 tons	75	0	0
Over 100 tons and for every additional 10 tons or part thereof	10	0	0

The above charges are exclusive of towage, provision of slings or other plant and labour, and are for ordinary day working only, and for operating within the Dock area.

14th July, 1930

Appendix Nine

Isle of Wight Vessels Operated by the SR and its successors

Vessel	Type of hull/propulsion	Maker	Owners	In service	Withdrawn
Portsmouth-Ryde passenger vessels					
Duchess of Albany	s/ps	Scott & Co., Greenock	1 3	26.12.1889	sold 6.1928
Princess Margaret	s/ps	Scott & Co., Greenock	1 3	23.5.1893	sold 6.1928
Duchess of Kent	s/ps	Day Summers, Southampton	1 3	15.11.1897	sold 6.1933
Duchess of Fife	s/ps	Clydebank Engineering & Shipbuilding	1 3	22.5.1899	sold 11.1929
Duchess of Norfolk	s/ps	D. & W. Henderson, Glasgow	1 3	16.9.1911	sold 1937
Shanklin	s/ps	J. I. Thornycroft, Southampton	3 4	10.1924	sold 1951
Merstone	s/ps	Caledon & Co., Dundee	3 4	4.1928	9.1952
Portsdown	s/ps	Caledon & Co., Dundee	3	6. 1928	sunk 1941
Southsea	s/ps	Fairfield Shipbuilding, Govan	3	13.5.1930	* sunk 1941
Whippingham	s/ps	Fairfield Shipbuilding, Govan	3 4	6.1930	1962
Sandown	s/ps	W. Denny & Bros, Dumbarton	3 4	26.6.1934	1965
Ryde	s/ps	W. Denny & Bros, Dumbarton	3 4	1.7.1937	9.1969
Southsea	s/ds	W. Denny & Bros, Dumbarton	4	1.11.1948	9.1988
Brading	s/ds	W. Denny & Bros, Dumbarton	4	2.12.1948	2.1986
Shanklin	s/ds	W. Denny & Bros, Dumbarton	4	18.6.1951	3.1980
Our Lady Patricia	s/ca	Int. Catamarans, Hobart, Tasmania	5	29.3.1986	
Our Lady Pamela	s/ca	Int. Catamarans, Hobart, Tasmania	5	9.8.1986	
Fast Cat Shanklin	s/ca	Kvaerner Fjellstrand, Singapore	5	16.8.2000	
Fast Cat Ryde	s/ca	Kvaerner Fjellstrand, Singapore	5	9.10.2000	
Portsmouth-Ryde/Fishbourne vehicle ferries					
Adur (II)	tug	South Shields, ex James Dredging	1 3	1919	sold 10.1928
Fishbourne	s/dt	W. Denny & Bros, Dumbarton	3 4	23.8.1927	7.1961
Wootton	s/dt	W. Denny & Bros, Dumbarton	3 4	6.1928	9.1961
Hilsea	s/dt	W. Denny & Bros, Dumbarton	3 4	6.1930	10.1961
Fishbourne	s/vs	Philip, Dartmouth	4	7.7.1961	1983
Camber Queen	s/vs	Philip, Dartmouth	4	29.8.1961	1983
Cuthred	s/vs	Richards, Lowestoft	4 5	28.6.1969	1987
St Catherine	s/vs	Henry Robb & Co., Leith	4 5	3.7.1983	
St Helen	s/vs	Henry Robb & Co. ,Leith	4 5	28.11.1983	
St Cecilia	s/vs	Cochranes Shipbuilders, Selby	4 5	27.3.1984	
St Faith	s/vs	Cochranes Shipbuilders, Selby	5	16.7.1990	
St Clare	s/vs	Remontowa Shipyard, Gdánsk, Poland	5	20.7.2001	
Lymington-Yarmouth passenger vessels					
Lymington	i/ps	Day Summers, Southampton	2 3	9.5.1893	sold 3.1929
Solent	s/ps	Mordey, Carney, Southampton	2 3	3.1902	sold 1948
Carrier	tug	in Holland	2 3	6.2.1906	to barge 1931
Jumsey	tug	hired when required	2 3	1910	1938
Freshwater	s/ps	J. S. White, Cowes	3 4	2.6.1927	sold 1960
Lymington-Yarmouth vehicle ferries					
Lymington	s/vs	W. Denny Bros. Dumbarton	3 4	1.5.1938	18.10.1973
Farringford	s/dp	W. Denny Bros. Dumbarton	3 4	4.3.1948	1.1973
Freshwater	s/vs	Ailsa Shipbuilding Co. Troon	4	21.9.1959	1983
Caedmon †	s/vs	Robb Caledon, Dundee	4 5	7.1973	
Cenwulf	s/vs	Robb Caledon, Dundee	4 5	18.10.1973	
Cenred	s/vs	Robb Caledon, Dundee	4 5	1.1974	

* Lost on war service. † Used Portsmouth-Ryde until 1983. The list excludes miscellaneous craft including launches, coal hulks and tow boats.
Type: i - iron hull, ps - paddle steamer, ds - diesel screw vessel, s - steel hull, dt - double twin screw, dp - diesel paddle vessel, ca - catamaran, vs - Voith Schneider propulsion
*Owners:*1 - The LSWR and LBSCR companies, 2 - LSWR, 3 - Southern Railway, 4 - British Railways, 5 - Wightlink Plc.

Bibliography

Over 50 books relating to the Isle of Wight railways have been published over the years.

General

Rails in the Isle of Wight. P.C. Allen and A.B. MacLeod, George Allen & Unwin Ltd, 1967.
Once Upon a Line (4 volumes). A. Britton, Oxford Publishing Co., 1983, 1984, 1990 and 1994.
The Signalling of the Isle of Wight Railways, Signalling Record Society, 1993.
Southern Vectis, The first 60 years, R. Newman, Ensign Publications, 1989.
The Vectis Connection. Pioneering Isle of Wight Air Services, P. Newberry, Kingfisher Publications, 2000.
Wight Report and *Island Rail News*, magazines of the Isle of Wight Railway.
Isle of Wight Here We Come, The Story of the Southern Railway's Isle of Wight Ships during the War 1939-1945. Hugh J. Compton, Oakwood Press, 1997.

Locomotives and Rolling Stock

A Locomotive History of Railways on the Isle of Wight. D.L. Bradley, Railway Correspondence & Travel Society, 1982.
An Illustrated History of Southern Wagons (four volumes). G. Bixley & others, Oxford Publishing Company, 1984, 1985, 2000 and 2002.
The Island Terriers. M.J.E. Reed, Kingfisher Railway Publications, 1989.
The Isle of Wight Railway Stock Book. R. Silsbury, Isle of Wight Railway Co. Ltd, 1994.
Isle of Wight Steam Passenger Rolling Stock. R.J. Maycock & M.J.E. Reed, The Oakwood Press, 1997.
Tube Trains on the Isle of Wight. B. Hardy, Capital Transport Publications, 2003.

Addendum

Since the publication of this book in 2006 additional research has uncovered some new information. That material is presented here as an addendum.

Dates of opening and closure
A seasonal service from Havenstreet towards Wootton commenced on 12th April, 1971. A new terminus at Wootton opened on 7th August, 1986, the line to a second new station at Smallbrook Junction opened on 20th July, 1991 and the halt at Ashey on 2nd May, 1993.

Chapter 2. Ryde to Ventnor and the Bembridge branch
The alterations at Sandown in 1938-1939 included the diversion of a footpath crossing the line at the south end of the station through the newly constructed Cox's subway.

The Bembridge branch was pull-push operated only during the rebuilding of Bembridge turntable in 1936 when a service was maintained using two A1X 0-6-0Ts with LCDR pull-push set 484. A post-war proposal to install a water supply at the Ryde end of Brading station was abandoned and the LBSCR pull-push carriages on the branch ran as ordinary stock. The luggage accommodation was inadequate during the summer as SECR and LBSCR four and five compartment brake thirds were used on occasions.

Chapter 3. The Isle of Wight Central's lines
In addition to the crossing loop at Merstone on the Sandown to Newport line there was a block post at Newchurch. The crossing loop at Whitwell had been switched out during the Great War. Long Arch bridge was rebuilt in 1929 with brick arches flanking a concrete box. [*IW County Press* 21st December, 1929] In later years Cement Mills viaduct had a frequently ignored 15 mph speed restriction.

Haven Street was unique in receiving a replacement brick built booking office and signal box. The other small stations had wooden buildings, that at Newchurch being erected in about 1930. The concrete toilet block at Alverstone (page 42) was not erected until 1948. At Ashey, the house was let out during the 1920s but the station was staffed until 1953. Unlike Whippingham and Wootton, a halt at Ashey remained open until 1966 owing to the lack of a suitable replacement bus service. At Cowes, the station was modernised *circa* 1930 when LSWR pattern lattice post signals were erected. Cowes line sets were normally four carriages, strengthened by the addition of a "swinger" during high season. A six coach train could be run round at Cowes from platform 1 and four from platform 2. On the Friday in Cowes Week a six coach Ventnor line set was diagrammed to go to Cowes for one of the post-firework specials. Ryde sets were also used on some through trains and ran to Newport for cleaning. A limited amount of maintenance continued at Newport until the running shed closed in 1957. The IWC wheel lathe in the workshop was useable as was the hoist. [Driver Dale, courtesy J. Mackett] Newport Power Station ceased generating in 1928, the building thereafter being used as a store; the siding remained in situ until the line closed.

The photograph on page 36 was taken after construction of the Council houses in the background in 1951. The large bracket signal (not a gantry) in front of the signal box (page 49 lower photo) was erected in about 1920. The plan on page 59 omits the various temporary narrow-gauge tracks in the quarry. The photograph on page 62 (lower) shows an up signal that probably protected Dean Crossing, north of Whitwell.

Chapter 4. Newport to Freshwater
The signalling at Carisbrooke was removed on Tuesday 2nd December 1924. [*Southern Rails on the IW* vol. 1] The class A1/A1X engines were not banned from the Freshwater line but they struggled with the heavier trains, hence the employment of IWR 2-4-0s *Ryde* and *Wroxall*. In addition to the viaducts, about a dozen bridges on the line had to be repaired or strengthened by the SR. The photograph on page 70 (upper) predates the introduction of *The Tourist* through train. The IWC carriage had no set duties during 1927 so was probably a "swinger" for use at

busy times; a year later it was on the Bembridge branch. Lengthening of the platforms at Freshwater and the crossing loop at Ningwood permitted the running of six coach trains but they were needed only on the through workings.

Chapter 5. Developments at Ryde
Several drawings and photographs appear on the wrong pages:
Page 72. Drawing of Ryde Pier Head — Related text on pages 83 and 87
Page 74. Arrangement of track Ryde St Johns to Smallbrook — Related text on pages 77 and 81
Page 78. Drawing of Ryde carriage workshops — Related text on page 88
Page 79. Photographs of Ryde Works — Related text on page 77
Page 80. Drawing of alterations at St Johns — Road Related text on page 83
Page 84. Drawing of Ryde locomotive shed — Related text on page 83
Page 85. Drawings of proposed Ryde shed layout — Related text on pages 77 and 83
The photograph on page 76 (lower) predated the closure of the Sandown-Newport line. The set is a winter formation with just three carriages.

Chapter 6. Traffic and timetables 1923 to 1939
The table on page 90 showing timekeeping of passenger trains was mentioned on page 104. The photographs on page 92 (upper) and 98 (upper) were taken by H. Gordon Tidey.

Chapter 7. Hopes, War and Recovery
John Edward Bell (1904-1962) was a pupil of Maunsell at Ashford Works and prior to 1934 had been an assistant locomotive testing engineer. During the war he served with the Royal Engineers in Africa and India rising to the honorary rank of Lt. Colonel. He was appointed assistant works manager Brighton in 1945, works manager Ashford in 1946 and locomotive works manager Eastleigh 1962.

There were six pylons on St Boniface Down, not eight. The "bomb shelter" on Cowes platform 2 was not built until 1942, by which time the town had suffered several air raids; it was demolished with the station in 1971. Sandown, Shanklin and Ventnor piers were severed but not those within the confines of the Solent, e.g. Yarmouth and Ryde. The cement mills closed to business on 30th June 1944. PLUTO crossed the Solent to Thorness Bay, then across the Island to Shanklin (Driver Dale recalled seeing soldiers digging a trench shortly before D-day alongside the river between Horringford and Newchurch) and through the Chine to Shanklin Pier. A reserve pipeline ran from Horse Boat Slip at Ryde Esplanade, through the railway tunnel, along Monkton Mead Brook, through Whitefield Woods to Brown's ice cream factory, Sandown. [T. Cooper, J. Mackett, R. Brinton and Driver Dale] Following the invasion, four pipelines were laid across the Channel from Sandown Bay to Urville-Nacqueville just west of Cherbourg but they operated for only a matter of days. [*PLUTO Pipe-Line Under The Ocean* by A. Searle] While Mill Hill tunnel was being repaired in 1946 trains ran from Newport to Mill Hill station with an engine at each end. [*IW County Press and Island Rail News* issue 45]

The photographs on page 116 should be credited to Southern Railway, G. L. Nicholson. The officers in the upper photograph were: Vernon A. M. Robertson, Chief Civil Engineer 1944-1951; Leslie Harrington (part hidden), Assistant to the General Manager; Gordon L. Nicholson, Acting Assistant for the Isle of Wight; E. J. Missenden (back to camera), General Manager; Bob Sweetman, Loco Shop Foreman, Ryde; Eric Gore-Brown (back to camera), Chairman; Albert Brading, C&W Shop Foreman, Ryde; Alan Cobb, Loco Engineer Superintendent; R. M. T. Richards, Traffic Manager. Those in the lower one were: Gordon L. Nicholson, Eric Gore-Brown, the Ningwood porter/signalman, E. J. Missenden.

Chapter 8. Omnibuses, Ferries and Aircraft in SR days.
The Vectis bus garage that burned down was at Somerton, not Newport. Frank Aman already had experience of vehicle ferries by the time he obtained SR agreement to take over the Lymington-Yarmouth service. In 1923, with his sons Gerard, an Engineer, and Arthur, a

stockbroker, he obtained an Act to create the Bournemouth-Swanage Motor Road and Ferry Co. The family remained the principal shareholders of the ferry business until 1961. The paddle steamer *Southsea* was mined off the Tyne on 16th February, 1941. The *Solent* was tried on the Portsmouth-Ryde service after the loss of *Portsdown* but could not cope with the south-westerly winds. On one occasion it was unable to berth at Ryde and had to return its passengers to Portsmouth.

The photograph on page 119 is of a Dennis Lance in St James Square, Newport when new in 1936 and should be credited to the late C. G. Woodnutt as should the one on page 126 (upper).

Chapter 9. Nationalisation and the first closures

There were two reports that sealed the fate of the Island railways. In one, SVOC claimed that they could carry all the passengers carried by the railways with the exception of the Ryde-Ventnor line. The other noted that the Island railways employed over 600 staff. The BTC and RE assumed branch lines had no future and put pressure on regional management to expedite closures. The Branch Lines Committee rushed out a report into the Island railways to justify closure of the Freshwater, Bembridge and Sandown-Newport lines. [BR policy files in the National Archives, Kew]

Fraser & White would have been tempted to compete directly with the BTC if could rent and secure road access to Medina Wharf. The track on the Bembridge branch was in a dire state as it had not been relayed since 1931-1932 when second hand sleepers had been used. A LBSCR Terrier 0-6-0 was offered on the off-chance that it would have lessened wear but was refused by the Civil Engineer. He suggested that the branch could be relaid using materials lifted from the Freshwater line for £2,700 but even then it is doubtful if closure could have been long delayed. [BR policy files]

Chapter 10. Traffic and timetables after Nationalisation

The complaints against journey times were identical to those made by Capt. Huish in 1860. Watchingwell did not appear in all timetables although it was in public use. The half-hourly service between Cowes and Newport was reduced to hourly following closure of the Sandown to Newport line. Train stops at Whippingham or Wootton after closure are likely to have been for permanent way staff or shift changes at the Whippingham signal box. Bembridge station building was demolished in 1964. Newport locomotive shed and the coal stage roofing were demolished in 1963 when the Sandown line drawbridge was removed.

The photograph on page 150 (upper) was taken by J. H. Aston and those on page 156 by A. E. Bennett. The view of Ashey on page 157 was taken later than 1961 judging by the weeds on the platform and the absence of the up line.

Chapter 11. The Second Round of Closures

The Ryde-Newport-Cowes line was kept open primarily for the domestic and locomotive coal traffic from Medina Wharf. In 1959 BR planned to close it in 1965 when they expected the Ryde-Ventnor line would also close or be converted to diesel traction. By 1962 BR Southern Region was reluctant to close Ryde-Ventnor but the cost of diesel traction was estimated at nearly £1,000,000. This dilemma was removed by Beeching. A decision to close both lines was taken on 1st January, 1963. In March 1962 the Chief Civil Engineer stated Ryde railway pier would close to trains in September 1963 if nothing was done; a contract for reconstruction was let on 24 October. [BR policy files]

In a memo dated 16th June, 1964 reporting on the TUCC hearing Mr Taylor, South Western line manager, wrote: "We shall be lucky if we succeed in getting the Cowes line closed and extremely fortunate if for the future we can confine our railway activities in the Isle of Wight between Ryde Pier Head and Shanklin only. I do not believe the Ryde St Johns Road proposition was ever seriously 'on' so far as the IW authorities are concerned - they are past masters at trailing red herrings of this kind". [BR Policy files] David McKenna OBE was the son of a former Chancellor of the Exchequer, had a distinguished war record and was BR(S) General Manager 1963-1968. He had previously worked for London Transport. [*Railways South East* 1993]

The service during the 1965-1966 winter was half-hourly to Ventnor and hourly to Cowes (two hourly on both lines on Sundays). The coal merchant at Cowes was called "Gange", not "Gauge". The other coal merchant (Isle of Wight Cooperative Society) ceased using rail in the autumn of 1965. Gasworks siding had previously closed after Corrall's took over Wood & Jolliffe and concentrated local deliveries on Medina Wharf.

The table *Last Passenger Trains* summarised the last official workings. Normally the carriages would have berthed at Cowes overnight ready for the first departure at 6.39am, but on that night the train returned to Ryde carrying passengers and driven by Ken West. Passengers who arrived on the last service to Ventnor hoping for a return trip were less fortunate as that train left as empty stock as did the last train from Bembridge. The caption to the photograph on page 170 is wrong as Nos. 24 and 31 were still in existence at Ryde. The locomotive numbers were "20, 35 ..."

Chapter 12. Southern Vectis, Vectrail and others
Only the stage carriage part of SVOC was nationalised, its coaching arm remained in Tilling ownership. SVOC also took over the stage carriage work belonging to the West Wight Motor Bus Co. (SVOC wanted their Freshwater-Yarmouth route) and again that firm remained coach operators. SVOC began operating coaches in 1938 but greatly expanded its operations after the war. At least one Portsmouth-Ryde vessel was withdrawn because the weekday roundthe-Island excursions could no longer compete with the coach tours.

Circa 1954 buses did meet trains at Newport and may have ran to Freshwater. Bus fares in the early 1950s were much cheaper than rail but that was reversed after large price rises in the late 1950s and early 1960s. The first bus route 39 between Bembridge and Shanklin lasted as an infrequent route 30 until the 1960s. The second route 39 to Ventnor town centre ran from Shanklin railway station (not the bus station) but from January to March 1967 operated as a through Ryde Esplanade to Ventnor service. The short-lived Shanklin-Ventnor "Wight Bus" was not a rail replacement service and did not operate via Wroxall. Mr H. E. Dory was a Director of Austria Travel Agency, one of several firms that wanted to lease the Island railways.

Chapter 13. Steam Locomotives
IWC No. 9 was sold for scrap and broken up at St Helens Quay in 1927. Several reasons have been given for its withdrawal. The photograph on page 182 was taken at Newport; note the light flat bottom rail in the yard.

In 1933 a half-hourly passenger service was introduced between Cowes and Newport, alternate trains continuing to Ryde and Sandown. Goods trains to and from Medina Wharf had to be slotted in, especially along the Sandown line with its solitary crossing loop at Merstone. The withdrawal of FYN 1 *Medina* was inevitable once Medina Wharf had been rebuilt but the arrival of the E1s also spelt the end for IWR 2-4-0Ts *Ryde* and *Wroxall*. They would otherwise have been replaced by more O2s within a couple of years. [SR Working Timetables] There was an additional head code for Cowes to Newport with a disc at the base of the chimney.

The class E1 0-6-0s were not officially barred from the Freshwater line but the Civil Engineer disliked their use because of the many curves. Postwar, after arrival at Ventnor, the E1 worked a train to Ryde Pier Head and back, probably hauling the same set used on *The Tourist*. [T. Cooper and Driver Dale, courtesy J. Mackett]

The unlined wartime malachite green, as shown in the photograph on page 192 (lower), actually preceded the unlined black livery. Starting with A1X 13 ex works in November 1945, those undergoing overhaul were painted in lined malachite green. O2 34 arrived painted in a light green colour (not the LSWR green), one of a handful painted by Eastleigh in experimental liveries. During 1948 all Island locomotives (except No. 2510) had their "SOUTHERN" lettering replaced by BRITISH RAILWAYS.

The use of diesel power was first suggested in 1951 as a way of reducing Island workshop costs but nothing was done because of the policy of closures. In response to an enquiry from a member of the public in 1958, Southern Region management suggested the transfer of BR class 2 2-6-2Ts that were due to be redundant following the Kent Coast electrification in 1959. The necessary funding was not forthcoming. [BR policy files]

Nine O2s were towed to Newport for scrapping on 28 January 1967 in three trains and broken up in the following order: 27 in April 1967, 16 in May 1967, 20 in May-June 1967, 28 in June 1967, 17 in June-July 1967, 33 in July 1967, 14 in July 1967, 22 in July-August 1967.

Chapter 14. Passenger and Goods Rolling Stock
The purpose of the table on page 208 was not explained but on page 189 we mentioned the introduction of turnover engines in 1929 and the inter working of Ryde and Newport based locomotives that began in 1933. First class was abolished on 3 October 1965. The last eleven carriages were hauled in two trains to Newport by 24 *Calbourne* on 3 January 1967. [*Island Rail News* issue 33 - Ryde St Johns signal box train register]

As livestock traffic was on the decline, a 1929 order for the transfer of three LBSCR cattle wagons was cancelled in favour of three covered vans. Three existing wagons were later rebuilt at Ryde as goods vans. Two PDSWJ brake vans were to have accompanied the first LSWR road van 56044 but the order for their transfer was cancelled and they remained on the mainland. [*Southern Wagons Pictorial* by M. King]

The photographs on page 204 were taken by T. Cooper. That on page 206 was of LBSCR composite 6348 at Havenstreet after preservation. The caption on page 212 (upper) refers to the unique wagon that was rebuilt with an additional two planks and transferred in February 1934; it prompted the arrival of SR 13 ton wagons in 1948 and 1949.

The photographs on pages 212 (lower), 216 and 217 (lower) were taken at Medina Wharf in 1965 and 1966 by T. Cooper. That on page 214 (lower) was at Brading and page 218 (lower) was taken from Foxes Bridge Sandown, looking north.

Chapter 15. 'Modernisation'
A 1960 report envisaged that diesel electric motor luggage vans (MLV) would work with five open type coaches and a non-powered driving coach in a seven coach multiple unit seating 600 passengers. For most of the year the formation would be a four set. They would be suitable for freight and departmental use. The stock requirement was to have been:

	Ventnor line	Cowes line	Total
600 hp. MLVs	8	3	11
passenger trailers	35	6	41
driving trailers	9	3	12
vans	4	3	7
Total	56	15	71

An estimate for their construction and transfer to the Island was given as £998,500 although that could be reduced by the abolition of freight traffic and closure of the Cowes line. The option to create a terminus and bus station at Ryde Esplanade envisaged a 175 ft. island platform linked by a ramp to a bus station with 16 bus stands for limited stops services, 12 for stage carriage services and parking nearby for 13 coaches. Buildings were needed for staff, etc. At Pier Head, platform 3 would disappear while platform 1 was reserved for luggage and provided with overhead alphabetical signs indicating where passengers could recover their possessions. If the tramway was to terminate at Ryde St Johns, the locomotive shed, signal box, footbridge and down platform would be replaced by a wider platform, 27 bus stands, space for another 20 buses, lighting and staff accommodation, all for a terminus to be used only from 1 April to 30 October. Six three car trains were needed and double the number of crews. SVOC also wanted more than £10,000 in subsidy. [BR Policy files]

The 1965 plans to employ BR 2-6-2Ts were to be implemented only if electrification was delayed or abandoned. The Swindon built diesel locomotives are thought to have been the "Teddy Bear" class 14 although there is at least one other contender. Virtually every type of railbus or diesel car was considered but rejected. Waterloo & City underground stock were unavailable and LT District Line stock fouled the loading gauge. On 20 August 1964 it became known in BR that Ryde-Shanklin was a "live" possibility and on 31 August third rail electrification was being seriously considered, it being "far simpler than diesel". [BR Policy files] The proper sequence of the electrification work was:

- Prior to 31st December, 1966 the siding connections at Shanklin and Sandown were removed and conductor rail laid for three miles north of Shanklin.
- In January 1967 the siding connections at Brading were removed and laying of the conductor rail continued towards Ryde.
- Until 20th January, 1967 withdrawn rolling stock was being moved to Newport so the junction at Smallbrook was probably severed 21-22 February when the signals, signal box and crossover were removed.
- Track alterations at Ryde St Johns Road were made prior to switching on the power on 1 March 1967 although the signalling was not completed until 10–12 March.
- The first tube train under its own power reached Ryde Pier Head on 14th March, 1967.
  [*Island Rail News* issue 33 - Ryde St Johns signal box train register]

The single sided platform at Ryde Pier Head became platform No. 1 reversing the previous numbering. The largest step down into cars (9 in.) was at Brading. The signalling still allowed trains to enter the single line at Sandown to reverse. [*Island Rail News* issue 34] Plans to replace the three paddle steamers with two diesel vessels were first downgraded to one when *Whippingham* was withdrawn and none when the three existing diesel vessels were refitted in 1966. The use of freight vessels or barges for peak services was also discussed. [BR Policy files]

Chapter 16. The Ryde to Shanklin line
A footbridge at Ryde Esplanade had been considered during the 1950s. Ryde Borough Council bought a span recovered from Towngate Viaduct, Newport when the Freshwater line was being demolished but the proposal was not proceeded with. [The late C. G. Woodnutt]

Chapter 17. Rolling Stock after 1966
The book *Tube Trains on the Isle of Wight* by B. Hardy utilised information from A. J. Barter (LT's IW Project Manager):

- If the Ryde-Shanklin line was to be locomotive hauled the stock requirement was 23 trailers and 23 control trailers, some being converted motor cars with added luggage accommodation. If Ryde-Cowes remained open the need was for 27 motor cars and 34 trailers, in addition to the original 12 cars.
- Caledonian hooters from O2s were fitted to 'A' end cars and main line whistles to 'D' end cars.
- By August 1967 LT had only eight 'A' end motor cars (including two damaged), six control trailers and 38 trailers to choose from when BR enquired about additional cars for a possible Ventnor section reopening. The seven chosen cars were moved to Micheldever on 9th July, 1968 and went for scrap on 11th August, 1970.

294 THE ISLE OF WIGHT RAILWAYS FROM 1923 ONWARDS

- LT sent their remaining "rejected" cars for scrap between 5th June, 1967 and 14th September, 1968.

The first list of tube stock in 1966 included three car unit 037. One of the first units to be completed, on 14th July it was photographed with four car unit 043 on a test run at Raynes Park. [*Railway Magazine* November 2008] In September BR decided to send only a single motor car but motor car S38S had already been transferred to the Island (on 1st September); it was later renumbered S26S and placed in unit 031. The other cars from unit 037 and those in unit 043 were reformed before transfer. Cars S12S (unit 043) and S17S (unit 036) were renumbered S22S (unit 042) and S21S (unit 044); S23S went from unit 044 to 045. [*Tube trains in the Isle of Wight* by B. Hardy] Beginning in 1970, one car was withdrawn at a time for an external repaint, then internally before a second external repaint in the grey doors livery. By 1984 staff had renewed lighting in 11 trailers, heating circuits in five trailers, re-panelled five motor cars and renewed roofs. Upholstery had been replaced twice. [*Island Rail News* issue 34]

After adverse publicity about the profit from renting out old trains, on 23rd March, 2007 ownership of the tube cars was transferred for £1 from HSBC to Stagecoach South West Trains. HSBC also made a partial refund of rent that was used for anticorrosion work and a repaint in LT maroon and cream livery. (Only unit 007 carried "London Transport" lettering with matching gilt shaded numerals; the other units had plain black running numbers.):

Unit	'A' DM	'D' DM	Livery	Painted	Name	Livery	Painted
002	122	225	Dinosaur	14 April 2004	Raptor	LT red	August 2008
004	124	224	Dinosaur	21 March 2000	T-rex	LT red	January 2008
006	126	226	Dinosaur	20 March 2000	Terry	LT red	2009
007	127	227	LT red	24 January 2003*			
008	128	228	Dinosaur	26 July 2000	Iggi	LT red	August 2008
009	129	229	Dinosaur	17 May 2000	Bronti	LT red	2003

* date returned traffic, other dates refer to completion.
[*IW County Press* and *Underground News*, magazine of the London Underground Railway Society]

In 2017 the franchise was transferred to First MTR South Western Trains who had plans to replace the 80 year old stock; the Island is still waiting for that to happen.

It is thought the contractors' steam cranes were scrapped after the pier reconstruction was completed in 1967. Orders were given on 7th April, 1967 to convert six LBSCR open wagons Nos. 27730, 27744, 27766, 27778, 27799 and 28345 to dropside ballast wagons using parts recovered from withdrawn departmental wagons. A second order was made on 18th April for the conversion of 27725 and 27796. The work was carried out in December 1967. Most lasted until 1978 and a few were purchased for preservation. [*Southern Wagons Pictorial* by M. King]

By 1923 there were four self-propelled steam cranes at Medina Jetty (Nos. 1, 12-14) and six at St Helens Quay including one in a dredger (Nos. 2, 4, 5, 8, 10, 16); disposal details are unknown. One crane remained at St Helens after the coal screens were moved to the mainland in 1936. In September 1953 the Civil Engineer wrote that the remaining a 5 ton steam crane No. 5 would be transferred from St Helens to New Cross PW depot. [SR register of fixed boilers and National Archives ref. AN177/86]

Chapter 18. Railway preservation in the Isle of Wight
Several additions have been made to the fleet of locomotives, carriages and wagons at Havenstreet, details of which can be found on the website (iwsteamrailway.co.uk).

Appendix 2. Relevant Isle of Wight Acts of Parliament
The Southern Railway Act, 1925, the powers should read "an inclined railway in Ventnor".
Appendix 4. Dates of opening and closure of stations Cement Mills siding opened between 1878

and the 1890s. After the cement works closed in 1944 the sidings were removed, but not the connection with the main line. The sidings were relaid temporarily for the scrapping of rolling stock in the 1950s. The halt probably opened at the same time as the siding; it was reconstructed in 1905 and closed on 21 February 1966.

Medina Jetty/Wharf opened to goods traffic in November 1878 and closed on 16th May, 1966. The halt may have opened at the same time; certainly a staff halt was there by June 1882. It closed on 21st February, 1966. Dodnor Halt was in use by 1896 as a loading bank for agricultural produce from the Prison Market Gardens and in August 1914 the *IW County Press* mentioned inmates of HM Prison Camp Hill detraining there. A disused concrete platform was in situ when the line closed in 1966. There was also a temporary halt near Ashey for a military camp in 1899. [T Cooper and *Yesterdays Papers* by A. Stroud]

Appendix 7. Summary of Stock after 1966
D2554 did not leave the Island; it was moved to Havenstreet on the date

Appendix 9. Isle of Wight Vessels
The following is an update of Wightlink vessels:

Portsmouth - Ryde passenger vessels:
Shanklin	Withdrawn 30th November, 1950 and sold.
Merstone	Withdrawn December 1950 and sold for scrap September 1952.
Our Lady Pamela	Withdrawn 31st May, 2009. Sold to Danish Shipbreakers and broken up.
Our Lady Patricia	Withdrawn 2006, sold and broken up at Marchwood.
Fastcat Shanklin	Withdrawn 30th January, 2010. Sold in January 2010 to Severn Link for use between Swansea and Ilfracombe. Sold May 2011 to Allen Shipping for service in the Black Sea.
Fastcat Ryde	
Wight Ryder I	High speed catamaran built by FBMA, Philippines, entered service 29th January, 2009.
Wight Ryder II	

Portsmouth - FishbourneVehicle Ferries:
Hilsea	was still in service during 1962. Withdrawn not known.
St Catherine	Withdrawn 15th June, 2009. Sold to Italian buyers Delcomar January 2010.
St Helen	Withdrawn and sold to Italian buyers Delcomar March 2015
Victoria of Wight	Built by Camre shipyard, Yalova, Turkey 2018.

Lymington - Yarmouth Vehicle Ferries:
Freshwater	ran as *Freshwater II* from April 1959. Last sailed 12th September, 1959. Sold 1960.
Caedmon	Withdrawn 21st January, 2009. Sold to Danish shipbreakers and broken up in May 2010.
Cenwulf	Withdrawn 24th January, 2009. Sold to Danish shipbreakers and broken up in May 2010.
Cenred	Withdrawn 26th January, 2009. Sold to Danish shipbreakers and broken up in May 2010.
Wight Light	Built by Kralijevica, Croatia, entered service 25th February, 2009
Wight Sky	Built by Kralijevica, Croatia, entered service 25th February, 2009
Wight Sun	Built by Kralijevica, Croatia, entered service 25th May, 2009

Index

Accidents and mishaps, 21, 23, 25, 29, 33, 39, 44 57, 63, 67, 71, 75, 83, 91, 109, 113, 115, 143, 152, 155, 157, 237
Acts of Parliament, 269, 270
Aircraft, 127, 128
Alverstone, 135, 145
Anderson, Charles N., 11, 269
Ashey, 39, 44, 134, 135, 153, 155, 157, 263, 268
Assistant for the Isle of Wight, 17, 133, 153
Bell, J.E., 17, 107, 269
Bembridge branch, 31, 33, 35, 133
Bembridge turntable, 33
Brading, 233, 235, 237, 247
Bridge works, 14, 37
Carnivals and regattas, 89
Carriages and vans,
  Island companies, 203 *et seq.*, 265
  LBSCR, 205 *et seq.*, 265
  LCDR, 205 *et seq.*, 265, 279
  LSWR, 205, 207, 279
  SECR, 205, 209 *et seq.*, 265, 279
  SR, 209, 265, 279
Chalk trains, 57, 97
Closures, 129 *et seq.*, 149 *et seq.*, 159 *et seq.*, 233
Dates of opening and closure of railways, 5
Dates of opening and closure of signal boxes, 271, 275
Dates of opening and closure of stations, 276
Day, Henry, 11, 13
de Pury, Charles A., 11, 269
Diesel locomotives, 220, 221, 259, 260, 265, 283
Dredging, 31, 35, 57, 113, 120, 121
Electrification, 223 *et seq.*
Engineers' stock, 213 *et seq.*, 259, 260, 280, 283
Evacuation, 109, 123
Fares, 89, 115, 130, 231, 235
Ferries, 65, 115, 120, 121, 123, 125, 228, 229, 235, 286
Formation of the Southern Railway, 9 *et seq.*,
Franchise, 243, 244
Fraser & White, 35, 95, 133
Freshwater, 67, 69
Freshwater, Yarmouth & Newport Railway, 10, 65
Gardener, George H.R., 107, 133, 153, 269
General Strike, 95, 101
Goods traffic, 130, 148, 149, 160, 167, 171, 276
Goods vehicles,
  Island companies, 203, 213, 261
  LBSCR, 213 *et seq.*, 280
  LSWR, 213 *et seq.*, 280
  SR, 215, 217, 280

Haven Street/Havenstreet, 39, 44, 155, 263, 268
Isle of Wight Central Railway, 10, 37
Isle of Wight Railway, 10, 19
Isle of Wight Steam Railway - *see preservation*
Journey times, 104
Lake, 237, 242
Last trains 149-153 163-170276
Locomotives,
  Island companies 177 *et seq.*, 261
  'A1' and 'A1x' class, 181 *et seq.*, 265, 277, 278
  'E1' class, 183-197, 261, 277 278
  'E4' class, 117, 193, 195, 277, 278
  'O2' class, 177 *et seq.*, 261, 277, 278
Luggage, 25, 87, 95, 97, 104, 143, 148, 169, 209, 231
MacLeod, Alistair B., 17, 269
Mails, 91, 95, 101, 109, 123, 169, 231
Maunsell, Richard E.L., 10, 11, 77, 179, 193
Medina Wharf, 53, 57, 167
Midget, 183
Nationalisation, 117, 129
Network SouthEast, 237, 242, 254, 255
Newcombe, George R., 11, 269
Newport, 45, 53, 167, 169, 235
Nicholson, Gordon L., 117, 269
Ningwood, 69, 71
Omnibuses, 33, 118, 130, 171 *et seq.*, 233
Operating practices, 37, 65
Owens, Sir Charles, 9
Parcels, 31, 35, 95, 143, 148, 169
Passenger numbers, 89, 105, 115, 121, 123, 125, 130, 134, 143, 147, 149, 160, 229, 237, 242, 244
Permanent way renewals, 14, 15, 19, 33, 64, 69, 115, 145, 155, 223
Preservation, 261 *et seq.*, 271
Private owner wagons, 215
Private sidings, 29, 35, 57, 63, 71, 88
Privatisation, 173, 242 *et seq.*
Proposed locomotives and stock, 199, 219 *et seq.*
Removal of permanent way and sale of property, 153, 155, 170
Ryde Esplanade, 75, 225, 233, 235, 245
Ryde Joint railway (LSWR & LBSCR), 75
Ryde Pier Company, 10, 73
Ryde Pier Head, 75, 83, 87, 223, 225, 235, 244, 245

Ryde promenade pier, 73, 115, 169
Ryde St Johns Road, 77, 81, 83, 225, 233, 235, 239, 245
Ryde tramway, 73, 233
Ryde tramway stock, 211, 263, 280
St Helens Quay, 31, 133
Sandown, 21, 25, 27, 225, 233, 235, 239, 247
Sandown-Shanklin double track, 23, 239
Sawkins, William J., 13
Seating capacity, 205
Services, 91, 95, 97, 105, 107, 115, 143, 145, 147, 152, 231, 235, 237
Shanklin, 21, 25, 27, 225, 233, 237, 247
Shide, 57
Signal boxes, 44, 45, 63, 64, 67, 75, 81, 85, 134, 152, 167, 225, 235, 239, 271, 275
Signals, 15, 33, 37, 85, 145, 223, 225, 235, 237
Single line sections, 39, 44, 63, 69, 81, 153, 155, 225, 235, 239, 271
Smallbrook Junction, 77, 81, 167, 169, 225, 239, 242, 245, 263, 267
Southern Vectis Omnibus Co. - *see Omnibuses*
Staff, 11, 13, 135, 143
Station improvements, 21, 25, 27, 39, 45, 53, 57, 145, 157
Subsidies, 231, 237, 244
Tahourdin, Horace D., 11, 21, 269
Through trains, 69, 101, 103
Timetables - *see services*
'The Tourist', 101, 103
Transport of stock to the Island 251, 284, 285,
Transport Users' Consultative Committee - *see closures*
Tube stock
  Pre-1938 cars, 219, 221, 227, 231, 235, 249 *et seq.*, 257, 282, 282
  1938 cars, 239, 244, 254 *et seq.*, 282
Urie, John C., 11, 269
Vectrail, 174, 175
Ventnor, 21, 25, 27
Ventnor West branch, 63, 131
Walker, Sir Herbert, 9, 10, 13, 17, 19, 35
Wartime, 107, 109, 113, 115, 119, 123, 125
Whippingham, 44, 134, 145, 153
Whitwell, 63, 64
Wootton, 44, 134, 153, 155, 157, 263, 265, 268
Workshops, 45, 53, 77, 88, 145, 153, 155, 180, 225, 239, 245
Wroxall, 19, 21